Impostors

Temptation

Impostors

Literary Hoaxes and Cultural Authenticity

CHRISTOPHER L. MILLER

The University of Chicago Press
Chicago and London

The University of Chicago Press, Chicago 60637
The University of Chicago Press, Ltd., London
© 2018 by The University of Chicago.
Published 2018
Printed and bound by CPI Group (UK) Ltd, Croydon, CR0 4YY

27 26 25 24 23 22 21 20 19 18   1 2 3 4 5

ISBN-13: 978-0-226-59095-0 (cloth)
ISBN-13: 978-0-226-59100-1 (paper)
ISBN-13: 978-0-226-59114-8 (e-book)
DOI: https://doi.org/10.7208/chicago/9780226591148.001.0001

Published with the assistance of the Frederick W. Hilles Publication Fund of
Yale University.

Library of Congress Cataloging-in-Publication Data

Names: Miller, Christopher L., 1953– author.
Title: Impostors : literary hoaxes and cultural authenticity / Christopher L. Miller.
Description: Chicago : The University of Chicago Press, 2018. |
    Includes bibliographical references and index.
Identifiers: LCCN 2018014121 | ISBN 9780226590950 (cloth : alk. paper) |
    ISBN 9780226591001 (pbk. : alk. paper) | ISBN 9780226591148 (e-book)
Subjects: LCSH: Literary forgeries and mystifications. | Hoaxes. |
    French literature—History and criticism. | African literature (French)—
    History and criticism. | American literature—History and criticism.
Classification: LCC PN71.F6 M55 2018 | DDC 098/.3—dc23
LC record available at https://lccn.loc.gov/2018014121

For Christopher Rivers

Contents

**PART 3 I Can't Believe It's Not Beur: Jack-Alain Léger,
Paul Smaïl, and *Vivre me tue***

Preface

This book attempts to bring French and Francophone identity hoaxes into dialogue with some well-known American ones. *Impostors* has a slightly unconventional structure, fitted to its subject matter and to the approach that I think the material requires. I have not written traditional chapters. The book is divided into three parts: the first about American hoaxes, the second a survey of selected French and Francophone cases, and the third an in-depth study of one French hoax, that of Jack-Alain Léger or "Paul Smaïl." The first two parts comprise analytical narratives of varying lengths, which in many cases must initially revive the fact of the hoax, often forgotten and overwritten after it has been unveiled. One of my goals here is therefore to re-create the spell or illusion of the hoax and to inhabit the virtual reality in which Danny Santiago, JT LeRoy, Vernon Sullivan, Emile Ajar, and Paul Smaïl were all real. The danger of this approach is that the text itself can get buried under a mountain of necessary anecdotal facts: who knew what and when, and so on. So my other goal is, in each case, to go back to the text, reading it first under the spell of the hoax (as best I can reproduce it), and second in light of the real, unmasked authorship. But the process will not always be so neatly delineated, because the line between hoax and truth is not always clear—far from it. And that itself is one of the most interesting "facts" about this.

I would not normally bring up politics in a context like this. But it may be of interest to the reader to know that I began working on the project during the Obama years, and then wrote much of what you will read in the early months of the administration that came next. The presence in the White House of an inveterate, documented liar (with an average of five falsehoods per day, by some estimations) may well have made somewhat "judgy" what otherwise might have been more lenient and carefree interpretations of false-hood here.[1] It is harder to see the fun in deception when the fate of the world seems to depend on resisting lies, "alternative facts," and "fake news." Ironically, one of the president's favorite accusations is "hoax!" So perhaps this is the right moment to look more closely at the workings of falseness.

Acknowledgments

"Another hoax?" my husband would ask wryly, as the UPS truck pulled away, not for the first time that week. For a while, they were coming thick and fast. Without Christopher Rivers, I would have not enjoyed this work nearly as much, nor understood its implications as well. I am grateful for his support and love every day (and for insisting on *La Religieuse* and *Alice*). I am thankful to colleagues who have offered aid and support of various kinds: Emily Bakemeier, David Bellos, Agnès Bolton, Ned Duval, Julia Elsky, Margaret Homans, Shanna Jean-Baptiste, Jill Jarvis, Alice Kaplan, Andrew Kirwin, Marina Kundu and Yves Citton, Michael Printy, Martine Reid, Maurie Samuels, Christelle Taraud, Dominic Thomas, and Richard Watts. The students in my hoaxes seminar of Spring 2018 deserve recognition: Travis Brady, Katie Coyne, Zulfiqar Mannan, and Opelo Matome. A special salute to Ora Avni, whose work on Mérimée it was my pleasure to dialogue with here. I am grateful to Emmanuel Pierrat for authorizing my access to the papers of Jack-Alain Léger housed at the IMEC archive in Normandy, and to the staff of IMEC, especially Marjorie Delabarre. Two anonymous readers for the University of Chicago Press provided numerous suggestions for improvement of the manuscript. Thanks to indexer Siobhan Drummond. At the Press, thanks to Michael Koplow, Randy Petilos, and Alan Thomas.

Introduction

Impostors. The authors studied in this book pose as people they are not, in order to (mis)represent a foreign, ethnic, or *other* culture or class. These writers are literary impersonators, usurpers, and appropriators. All of them *transgress* in some way, by crossing a border of difference, going beyond what is properly "their own" identity and culture and daring to represent—by means of deception, not just fiction—something that is not theirs.

I have not limited the scope of this study to one type of difference—for example race, which nonetheless remains of great importance. I will also look at cases in which a hoax manipulates differences of socioeconomic class, or region, or gender, within the same nation and perhaps race. Any type of difference among humans can be hoaxed, and likely has been. For the purposes of this study, I will use the term "intercultural" to encompass all manner of hoaxable differences, including the "cultures" of race, ethnicity, gender, class, nationality, religion, and more. My main purpose is to show that the intercultural hoax, historically so often associated with the United States and its ethnic multiculturalism, has a long, rich, and comparable history in France, where the state ideology of universalism and the general abhorrence of *communautarisme* makes it an even more surprising mode of expression. While specific cases have attracted attention at various times, this French and Francophone tradition has never received the study it deserves.

*

A hoax is a metafiction, a fiction about a fiction. It is designed not merely to tell a story, but to weave a lie around that story: a lie about the status of the story, its origins, its authenticity, and mostly, its authorship. It is the lie that constitutes the hoax. A story of someone else's culture, honestly told, by an author identified as him- or herself, is not a hoax.

To be truly a hoax, a literary ruse must fool its readers, and in the best cases fool every one of them, at least for a time. A hoax that fools no one is merely a game; a hoax that tricks everyone is potentially very scandalous— and very instructive. When successful, an intercultural hoax reveals preconceived notions about culture and disrupts the concepts of authenticity and genuineness that readers so often seek in representations of "minority" cultures. Each of the case studies that interests me here reflects a *deliberate* attempt to deceive—to lie about the authorship of a text. These authors want their texts, and the persona of the author, to pass as something they are not. This often involves a tremendous amount of planning and subterfuge, sometimes even danger and legal jeopardy. Why do they bother?

Intercultural literary hoaxes are almost always premised on *inequality*, and most of them, in their creative pretense, cross a boundary from a realm of greater privilege to one of lesser privilege. Why does hoaxing almost always follow that trajectory rather than its opposite? Minority literatures and cultures (broadly defined) occupy a special place in the world of hoaxes; they are particularly susceptible to impostures. Cultures deemed less able to represent themselves are often the targets of hoaxes, perpetrated by writers who come from the literate, majority, or Western side. The "essence" of the minority is tapped and extracted, synthesized and faked. The majority's perception is that minority and foreign cultures "need" to be explained to the reading, book-buying majority—and this dynamic has far-reaching cultural and economic ripple effects. The inquiring majority mind wants to know about the minority, which is construed as different, distant, peculiar, inscrutable, mysterious, and perhaps in need of help. This is true whether the minority is an American youth subculture right next door (as in *Go Ask Alice*), a nun cloistered against her will (as in *La Religieuse*), urban ethnic minorities in the United States (as in *Famous All Over Town* and *Love and Consequences*) or in France (as in *Lila dit ça* and *Vivre me tue*), or distant rural Africans (as in *L'Enfant noir*).

Majority/dominant culture, in so doing, establishes itself as the norm, the baseline against which other groups are to be judged. Its literature is literature itself: plentiful, well disseminated, institutionalized, and universal. Majority culture is, so to speak, an open book. Not so for minority or colonized cultures: literacy was largely banned among American slaves in the nineteenth century; there was no Sub-Saharan African fiction in French until 1921, no Beur literature in France until the 1980s. Minorities start from scratch in "acrolect" literatures (written in the language of the masters and the colonizers), and the shortfall must be overcome. So there is a demand for intercultural information, initially procured by dominant hands from nondominant sources and then processed as literature; that demand is both intellectual and commercial. The proferred information is expected to be accurate and authentic. But the strong preference is to eliminate the middle man, the intermediary author, and find nondominant voices that can speak and write for themselves. Given that such sources are typically in short supply, impostors and fakes arise: dominant writers passing themselves off as authentically nondominant. The very unfamiliarity of the foreign, ethnic, or minority culture makes faking possible and, indeed, seems to invite it. What did eighteenth-century Europe know about Formosa? What did the bourgeois French reader of the 1950s know about life in rural West Africa? Could the reading public in Brooklyn really judge the verisimilitude of a West Virginia truck stop sex worker? The divide between dominant and nondominant (often literate and nonliterate) cultures is a fact and a challenge in both intercultural and intracultural contexts, whether a European like Joseph Conrad is writing about Africa or an upper-class Haitian like Jacques Roumain is writing about Haitian peasants. Representations across the "great divide" between more-literate and less-literate sectors respond to a need or desire for information, and such texts are often thought to convey "unheard voices," perhaps "subaltern speech." The perceived information deficit is by its very nature an open invitation to fraud: demand exceeds supply, creating a market for fakes.

Why are minority literatures more sinned against than sinning? Why are their identity positions appropriated more than they appropriate? I will attempt to answer these questions. Neither a blanket condemnation of "cultural appropriation" nor a defense of its rights and prerogatives, this book will attempt to understand some of the long history and ethics of this literary tradition, both inside its homeland, the United States, and beyond, in French and Francophone spaces. Why look across the Atlantic? I will argue that a significant current in French literature has been underestimated: a certain tradition of intercultural hoaxing. It therefore makes sense to look first at the United States and then to move to a different space with different literary, political, and cultural dimensions.

*

Deception is fundamental to literature. Written words are not things themselves, but they make us think they are, or, at least, they disappear as objects, allowing us to "see" an artificial world. The words "Ceci est une pipe" would be no more a pipe than is the picture of a pipe in Magritte's painting. The treason of words goes along with the "treason of images."[1] But we forget the treason. Reading Proust, we picture a real child named Marcel who for a long time used to go to bed early, not a specter nor a pure abstraction. We inhabit the fiction, bracketing all that Plato would remind us about the gap between mimesis and "true reality."

Imitation (in tragic poetry) is "three stages away from nature . . . and the truth,"[2] and stands against "human nature," Plato wrote in *The Republic*. The same man "will hardly practice any of those pursuits worth mentioning at the same time as also making many imitations and being an imitator."[3] Taken at face value, this statement would make the entire enterprise of literary hoaxing undesirable if not impossible for worthy individuals.[4] Plato's further restrictions on imitation, in book 3 of *The Republic*, read like an encoded ban on literary impostures, and more specifically on the very kind examined in this study: "If [our guardians] do imitate, then they must imitate those things which are appropriate for these people from earliest childhood: brave, temperate men, pious, free, and all such things, but they must not do anything contrary to liberty, nor be good at imitating it, nor anything else which is classed as shameful, in order that they may gain no enjoyment of the reality from their imitation of it."[5] The older translation of Plato by Benjamin Jowett makes the danger of impostures even clearer: "lest from imitation they should *come to be what they imitate*."[6] The guardians (for our purposes, writers) are supposed to become, in Ramona A. Naddaff's phrase, "more and more themselves," not others and certainly not others of a lower order. The "dangerous confusion of separate identities" must be avoided; the mimetic artist himself is, for Plato, "the lowest form of human being."[7]

"Impersonating" base people—for Plato, a woman who "abuses her husband," slaves "doing what slaves do," "bad men," "blacksmiths or any other kind of artisan"—[8]will not be allowed. In his State, "we don't have people with double, or even multiple interests, since each man does one job . . . A shoemaker is a shoemaker and not a ship's captain."[9] Plato then makes his feelings about imitation and imposture into an actual ban (in Jowett's more colorful translation): "There is no place" in the Republic for "pantomimic" or "clever multiform gentlemen," deft at imitation and imposture; "the law will not allow them."[10] Such gentlemen and ladies, are, of course the subject of this book. Extrapolating from Plato's view, we could say that a literary imposture (a thing he did not envision) would be *four* times removed from truth: it is neither the Idea that exists in nature, nor the thing that is made or done, nor an authentic imitation of that thing; it is instead a *faked imitation*.[11] But as Stanley Rosen pointedly asks, "What of Plato, who narrates all the *Republic* by disguising himself as Socrates?"[12] Is that not an imposture?

Mary Karr is a much more contemporary, and much more amusing, spokesperson for truth than Plato. She believes in a "truth contract twixt writer and reader" and is wholly opposed to "making stuff up." "It niggles the hell out of me never to know exactly what parts the fabricators have fudged," she writes, going on to compare a memoir laced with "deceits" to a "catshit sandwich."[13] Having consumed two such sandwiches—a fake Holocaust memoir and the spectacular JT LeRoy hoax of the early 2000s—Karr resorted to absolutism about truth.

In our times, we don't much care about Plato's scruples (and many writers and readers don't care about Mary Karr's, either). We live surrounded by screens, fakes, avatars, simulacra, and all manner of imitation, and we don't want to "banish the poets."[14] We wallow in representations and imitations. We are, for the most part, followers of Aristotle, not Plato. "Mimetic activity comes naturally to us," said Aristotle, in complete contradiction to Plato; poetry is rooted in that "propensity" and in the "pleasure which all men take in mimetic objects."[15] Aristotle further blesses the fictional and the virtual (and perhaps even the imposture) when he asserts that "the poet's task is to speak not of events which have occurred, but of the kind of events which *could* occur."[16] Aristotle brought in "a powerful new idea," says Andrea Nightingale: "Literature inhabits an aesthetic sphere that has its own rules and standards."[17] A literary work can be "good" aesthetically without being good politically or even morally (although that, as we shall see, is certainly complicated).[18] Fiction has its own standards and practices and deserves a certain amount of autonomy, what Stephen Halliwell calls "a generous independence from preconceived norms."[19] Literature is capable of so much more than truth-bearing; it is not only what Plato calls an "unmixed imitator of the decent."[20] If the deception of fiction is well executed—"if the book's any good," as one literary hoaxer puts it, if it is *un livre juste*, as another says—then the enterprise is worthwhile. A Francophone literary impostor pleaded, "Where's the crime? Judge me by what I write!"[21] (Rivka Galchen comments, "It's awkward to recognize that *Madame Bovary* couldn't be better written by a French housewife").[22] In a good hoax, as critic Melissa Katsoulis says, "reality itself becomes a problem," and we must ask questions about "literature as the gatekeeper of truth."[23] Boundaries between the literal and the figurative wobble and fall; a good hoax puts us in a hall of mirrors and gives us vertigo.

The literary hoax pits two incommensurable sets of values against each other. On the one hand, the way of truth: representations should be as faithful and transparent as possible, especially concerning the identity of the author; hoaxes are a violation of trust. On the other hand, the way of play: literature—rooted in our natural "propensity" to imitate and take pleasure in doing so—is free to create and distort reality, to manufacture its own realities, beginning with the identity of the author. This can shed light, but it can also disrupt the order of things.[24] Hoaxes serve a purpose. The word "play" is useful here because it suggests both the ludic (fun) and the theatrical (masking, role-playing, impersonating); in other words, both the frequently cited motivation for hoaxing and the method. Plato himself denounced imitation in these very terms: "Imitation is only a kind of *play* [*paidia*, sometimes translated as "game"] or sport."[25]

Kenyan novelist Ngugi wa Thiong'o created a hoax without even trying, merely through the power of fiction, in his novel *Matigari*. Its theme threatened the Kenyan government; its subversive hero has superhuman powers. In his preface to the English translation, Ngugi explains what happened after publication, a scenario that could have been written by Borges or Perec:

> By January 1987, intelligence reports had it that peasants in Central Kenya were whispering and talking about a man called Matigari who was roaming the whole country making demands about truth and justice. There were orders for his immediate arrest, but the police discovered the Matigari was only a fictional character in a book of the same name. In February 1987, the police raided all the bookshops and seized every copy of the novel.[26]

As a result of this involuntary hoax, the hapless police, for a time, did what we all do: they fell into the fiction. When they realized their mistake, they went after the source of the illusion, literature itself.

✶

Aristotelian tolerance for creativity and for the value of mimetic representations—what I am calling the way of play—got a new lease on life in Roland Barthes' famous essay "The Death of the Author." Barthes asks: When Balzac is giving voice to a male castrato who is passing as a woman, Who is speaking? His answer: literature (*écriture*) itself. "All writing is itself this special voice." "The voice loses its origin, the author enters his own death, writing begins." Writing (literature) is a special place in black and white where "identity is lost." If this is so, if the identity of the author is obsolete (a remnant of empiricism, rationalism, and capitalism), then hoaxing is both totally permissible and utterly inconsequential. There is no identity, no origin to steal, so . . . what? Have fun. "Language itself" reigns. Barthes's postauthorial scriptor would have no reason *not* to perform a hoax, would have the means to do it (that "voice"), and a philosophical rationale ready to be deployed after he or she is unmasked: Hey, man, no one is an author anymore![27] Pierre Bayard performed a post-Barthesian thought experiment, rearranging authors, to see what effects it would have on reading and meaning, in a book called *What If Books Changed Authors?*: *The Stranger* by Kafka and *Gone with the Wind* by

Tolstoy. He was thus doing in make-believe what hoaxes actually do: change the perceived author of a work.[28]

But on the other hand, even if we are more Aristotelian than Platonist, even if we usually accept fiction on its own terms and appreciate its own qualities, even if we respect postmodern *écriture*, we all have our limits. Hoaxes test those limits and, I would argue, help us think about them. Where do we draw the line? Beyond what boundaries is fiction not supposed to wander? When does fiction become a lie? At what point does our internal Plato rise up and cry: No, this is a violation of the truth! (Example: Oprah, outraged by James Frey's deceptions in *A Million Little Pieces*.) I will use this simplified opposition between Plato and Aristotle—in a working opposition between truth and play—from time to time in the course of this study as shorthand for, on the one hand, an insistence on truth and exclusive self-representation, and on the other, a more tolerant view that appreciates the value, beauty, and perhaps even "truthiness" of a good hoax. (Truthiness "indicates both distance from the truth and reliance on the appearance of it," writes Kevin Young.)[29] We will see that hoaxes operate in a constant crossfire between play and truth.

To write is to other yourself, even when writing about yourself. Writers are constantly producing their own doubles. Romain Gary was far from unique in his desire "to recommence, to relive, to be an other." By hoaxing, he explained, he was scratching a primal human itch: "the oldest protean temptation of man, that of multiplicity."[30]

Writers are expected to represent and speak for (or as) things they are not, even in nonfiction: a child (even themselves in their own childhoods), a dog, a provincial French housewife. "Like it or not, all writers are 'cultural impersonators,'" writes Henry Louis Gates, Jr.[31] Ventriloquism is, for all intents and purposes, required of all novelists. Many famous works of literature invent the voice of an "Other" (in race, gender, class, age, or even species) as a fundamental working device: Aphra Behn's *Oroonoko* (1688), Montesquieu's *Les Lettres persanes* (1721), Defoe's *Moll Flanders* (1722), Françoise de Graffigny's *Lettres d'une Péruvienne* (1747), William Beckford's *Vathek: An Arabian Tale from an Unpublished [Arabic] Manuscript* (1786), Claire de Duras's *Ourika* (1826), Flaubert's *Madame Bovary* (1857), Joyce's *Ulysses* (1922), the novels of Ursula LeGuin, the parts of *Les Soleils des indépendances* (1968) where Ahmadou Kourouma writes from the point of view of a woman, Paul Auster's *Timbuktu* (1999, from the point of view of a dog), and countless other works of literature engage with otherness and even attempt to pass themselves off as *authentically* other (which is a special category and my subject here). The power of literature to impersonate is beyond dispute; the question is, How far can an author go? In the seventeenth and eighteenth centuries, the device or convention of the supposedly "found," preexisting manuscript—deployed in many of the cases I have just named—rose to prevalence. It forged a working understanding—an invisible contract—with the reader, who sometimes saw through it. The first and still most famous of these was Cervantes's *Don Quixote*. But some such works did pass as authentically foreign or other in some way and therefore can be considered hoaxes. The case of Diderot's *La Religieuse* provides an important milestone, as we will see.

Similarly, authors throughout history have used noms de plume or anonymity to protect themselves from retaliation and censorship. Kourouma, in *Les Soleils des indépendances*, changed the name of his country, Côte d'Ivoire, to Côte des Ebènes in a thin, parodic disguise that fooled no one because it was not supposed to. Undisclosed ghostwriting can be any number of things, from a mere convenience to a form of fraud designed to fool the public. The trend for a celebrity publication, for example, to say on the title page "by Donald J. Trump *with* Tony Schwartz"—thus revealing and crediting the helping hand of the writer—if applied retroactively, for example to Camara Laye, would produce a very different view of literary history—a question to which I will return in part 2.

All of these conventional devices—the roman à clé, the pseudonym or nom de plume, the found journal, the ghostwriter—are at least partially transparent and purposefully so; they exist within a socially sanctioned implied contract or pact with the reader. A real intercultural hoax violates those norms and conventions; its intent is not transparent but rather deceptive. It is one thing to be a writer of fiction, and quite another to be a fictive writer passing as real.

An intercultural hoax takes fictivity one crucial step beyond implied contracts, placing a fake *foreign or ethnic* name, or a name of a different gender or class, on the title page, thus attempting to pass the work itself (rather than just the fiction it contains) as the product of a genuine, real foreign or ethnic writer (who in fact does not exist, at least not as the stranger he/she claims to be). By radicalizing fictivity, by going rogue, these works may perhaps take us closer to exposing "the literary phenomenon itself" and a host of assumptions that we make about reading and culture.[32] And in doing so, they make a lot of mischief: violating boundaries, upsetting sensibilities, usurping identities, counterfeiting authenticity. An intercultural hoax is not necessarily a benevolent gesture or a victimless crime. As one journalist put it, these "fantastic deceptions" can produce "real victims."[33] In the course of this study, I will continuously explore the question of the "harm factor." Kevin Young writes, "The hoax is not measured by its maker, or intent, or its level of faking, but by its harm."[34] I would say it should be measured by all those things.

The pendulum may have swung against intercultural, interethnic, and interracial hoaxes in recent years. Some famous outrages, reviewed in the pages that follow, have no doubt propelled this reaction. Young says that we are in a "narrative crisis" that arose when "audiences began to mistake grotesqueries for reality, television talk for truth, hysteria for history, and spectacle for nature."[35] He cites the philosopher Harry G. Frankfurt's wonderful book on "the contemporary proliferation of bullshit."[36] But this centrifugal crisis of truth coexists with a centripetal trend that is further complicating representations of otherness in the present day: the vogue among young people in particular to abhor and denounce "cultural appropriation." Some of these cases have made headlines, provoking squirms on the left and glee on the right. When a college cafeteria, adopting and no doubt adapting Asian food, is denounced as "a culturally appropriative sustenance system"; when a white artist is told she has no right to paint a portrait of Emmett Till in his coffin because she is white; when an editor for the Writers' Union of Canada has to resign after "defending the right of white authors to create characters from other backgrounds" and to "imagine other peoples," it is safe to say that a line has moved.[37]

In academia, an essay in "defense of transracialism" (shifting identity from one race to another, along the lines of transgender shifting) that might have been considered unobjectionable twenty years ago now causes outrage: an open letter signed by hundreds of scholars called for the "retraction" of the article, claiming it does "harm to the communities" in question.[38] Adam Shatz suggests that there is a new "implicit disavowal that acts of radical sympathy, and imaginative identification, are possible across racial lines."[39] Subject matters and cultural materials now, in one view, belong strictly to their people of origin; border-crossing is verboten; a kind of essentialism is back. *Chacun chez soi.* Less controversially, this could be called a new identitarianism (Achille Mbembe refers to a "rebalkanization of the world").[40] After more than twenty years in which hybridity was the fashion and essentialism the bête noire—when everything in postcolonial theory militated for the deconstruction rather than reinforcement of borders—now the climate in academia and in the wider culture has changed. The perception of *harm* stemming from border crossing and appropriation is more easily triggered. We are closer to a world in which offense is automatically considered to be harm: if you do something I do not want you to do, you are harming me.[41] Many, but not all, of the cases examined in this book will, in fact, back up the idea that appropriation *can* have harmful effects. But what really *is* harm, in this context?

✳

The word "hoax" is funny and is of a surprisingly recent nineteenth-century origin, coming from "hocus" or "hocus pocus," which refers to a conjuror or a trick (*OED*). That derivation in turn may root the concept in Protestant mockery of the Catholic Eucharist, dismissing as mere trickery the words associated with transubstantiation: *hoc est corpus meum* (this is my body).[42] So the word contains within itself both play and truth, profane and sacred; and that is how hoaxes are structured: they are tricks that reveal truths, at least potentially, and eventually. If they don't, if they are worthless, they may be called *hokum*, also derived from "hocus pocus," combined with "bunkum," and denoting "pretentious nonsense," "foolish or untrue" (*Merriam-Webster*). A hoaxing author may write bunkum (Alan Sokal comes to mind), but it must pass as authentic for a time, or else there is no hoax.

Imposture—a word that has the advantage of working in both English and French—is "the action or practice of imposing upon others; wilful and fraudulent deception" (*OED*); it is the method by which intercultural literary hoaxes must work: the trick must fool *others*. Otherness is key. So an *impostor* is someone who crosses a line, "pass[ing] himself off as some one other than he really is" (*OED*). When an author does that *by means of a literary work*, the result is an intercultural literary hoax. All literary impostures are not necessarily hoaxes. When the element of play is lacking (as it seems to be in the case of Camara Laye), when the purpose is purely serious, then we should say it is an imposture but not a hoax.

*

My subject can be defined as literary "temporary visits" into imagined conditions of otherness of one kind or another.[43] A few guardrails align this inquiry. A pseudonym is necessary but not sufficient to make a literary hoax. Fictional hoaxes, recounted inside a novel, such as those one might find in Perec, for example, are not of interest here.[44] Fictional hoaxes set inside *real* hoaxes, however, are of great interest (something like that occurs in JT LeRoy's *Sarah*, when a male character passes as female). False hoaxes resulting from misperceptions—such as the Kenyan police trying to arrest Matigari, the protagonist of Ngugi's novel—are not included (if Ngugi had tried to pass Matigari off as real, it would have been a real hoax). Ancillary literary practices of inauthenticity such as ghostwriting, forgery, plagiarism, pastiche, parody, or heteronymity[45] may be of passing, but not defining, interest. The heart of this book is the identitarian hoax, where the author *as author* assumes an identity that is not his or her own, both in the world *and* in the literary work.

A word about method and procedure. Each of the cases that I will review is unique, but certain striking patterns and commonalities emerge. In each situation, I will consider the following aspects, more or less in this order: First, the who, what, when, where, and how of the hoax—the anecdotal facts that are essential for understanding the imposture. Second, the unveiling or unmasking of the true author, and what is known about his or her motivations. In a few cases, the author's identity remains a mystery, leaving many questions suspended in mid-air. Beyond these factual questions, I am most interested in exploring the identitarian implications of the hoax and their effects on any reading of the text. A literary hoax creates a rather dramatic before-and-after effect within the act of reading. The only way to recapture the reading process as it took place before the unveiling of the real author is to quote critics and readers who were, in effect, duped by the hoax. This also involves a certain amount of reverse engineering, pretending for a moment to "unknow" the true identity of the author and to relive the reading experience—the virtual reality, the spell—that the hoax created. (In only one case here—that of Camara Laye—can I quote my own earlier writing as that of a dupe.) The "after" reading attempts to come to terms with the ways in which the meaning of the text shifts—or is said to shift—once you know it was written by a different kind of person: a woman instead of a man, a white woman instead of a black man, a literate middle-class white man instead of an underclass teenager, and so on. How much does that shift matter, if the words on the page remain the same? This leads, finally, to the most difficult question of all: that of harm. As they say in law: *cui malo?* Who, if anyone, was hurt, offended, or misrepresented by each of these hoaxes? What damage, if any, was done? The opposite question can be equally relevant: *cui bono?* Who benefited from the hoax, and in what way? It is often obvious that the writer enjoyed the prank; but can readers learn anything from the vertigo of a hoax, once it has been unveiled? The answers to those questions will take us deep into competing, incommensurable assertions of truth and play: that is the afterlife of hoaxes.

*

In the remaining pages of this introduction, I will review two issues that are fundamental to this inquiry as a whole. The first is the role of anthropology, where debates about authenticity and fakery run directly parallel to those in literature and thus shed a useful light on this work. Anthropology does, however, sometimes exhibit different power dynamics, which should also help to establish a broader sense of context for the institution of literature. The second issue is the question of "telling," or what I will call forensic reading, which will come up in every hoax we examine: can you tell by reading alone what kind of person wrote a certain text? The remarkable case of George Eliot and Charles Dickens will help to establish some guidelines for that question.

*

Anthropology is literature's not-so-secret sharer in the business of ethnic hoaxes. As the science of otherness in the West, anthropology has been the arbiter and gatekeeper of non-Western ethnicity in the halls of academe and beyond; ethnographies and anthropologies are widely read and highly influential. So when anthropology (or archeology) is faked at any stage or any level, the consequences can be huge. Some of the most famous hoaxes—the "Piltdown Man," the "Gentle Tasaday,"—are not particularly germane here, except to the extent that they show how anthropology can be manipulated by powerful contemporary forces and exploited as a narcissistic mirror. Charles Lindbergh, who "met and lived with" the Tasaday, admired their "balance with [the] environment" and saw in their way of life the qualities that are "missing in the ways of civilized men."[46] (Kevin Young sees the case as "a dark if hopeful double for Vietnam.")[47] Many ethnic hoaxes will appeal to this same nostalgia. As one of our impostors will write: "Supernatural occurrences never happen up North."[48]

There is often a made-up urgency about ethnographic intervention: a world is on the brink of collapse and disappearance; if we do not capture it right now with our notepads, microphones, and cameras—and then preserve it in books and films—it will be lost. The preface to a recent, very popular, and enormous book of exotic photographs, Jimmy Nelson's *Before They Pass Away*, states the premise in guileless language: "If we do not document these last unspoilt men and their rituals, they will disappear without a trace. It will be too late to mourn when the last tribesmen are wearing suits and living in townhouses."[49] The power and persistence of that impulse to preserve dying civilizations ("the last original humans")[50] has from time to time induced Western adventurers to request, for example, that Africans take their clothes off before being photographed. Gide's companion, the filmmaker Marc Allégret, reportedly did that in the French Congo; and Gide himself suspected he was being hoodwinked by made-up "ceremonies."[51] Both sides were fooling with authenticity. The desire for an Eden that can be photographed and written about produces fakes and hoaxes.

*

A startling case of faked anthropology comes from a time long before the invention of the field as such: the early eighteenth century. George "Psalmanazar," as he called himself (from 2 Kings 17:3, an Assyrian king named "Shama-neser"), was apparently born "somewhere between Avignon and Rome," rumored to be Languedoc.[52] At some point he made it his life's purpose to be a cultural impersonator of an extreme variety, using his own body as well as his pen to create illusions. He traveled throughout Europe on false passports, passing as a Formosan convert to Christianity and exhibiting "outlandish customs" of his own invention.[53] In print, he invented a "Formosa" out of whole cloth, complete with a "lucid and regular" language and an alphabet: "Koriakera Vomera" is "The Lord's Prayer."[54] He was a highly successful phony ethnographer. His *Historical and Geographical Description of Formosa*, published in 1704, had thirty-two chapters on such subjects as religion, fasting, various ceremonies, clothing, and illustrations of fanciful Formosan currency (see figure 1).[55]

The book sold out quickly and was reprinted, then translated into French and German. It fooled a lot of people for a time (except for one William Innes, who saw through Psalmanazar, then entered into the hoax as a collaborator). Psalmanazar *performed* the identity he was describing, eating raw meat because he said that is what Formosans did. For a time he was the toast of Christ Church College, Oxford.[56] There were doubters, including Jesuits, whose good faith and knowledge Psalmanazar called into question. He eventually slipped into obscurity. Later he had a religious conversion experience, repented for his "base and shameful imposture,"[57] and wrote confessional *Memoirs* to be published only after his death (in 1764). He lived out the rest of his long life in piety. It has been argued that his confession influenced one of the most seminal texts in all of literature: Rousseau's *Confessions*.[58] It also anticipates the confessions of hoaxing that came from both Diderot, in the preface-annex of *La Religieuse*, and, in its posthumous design, Romain Gary. As Kevin Young says, Psalmanazar, by playing the race card as he did, helped "provide a map for the hoax of the twentieth century and beyond."[59]

Psalmanazar's success as a fake Formosan and ethnographer raises many of the questions that I want to focus on in this study, here in an early modern context. As Rodney Needham points out, the hoax was entirely dependent on Europeans knowing little or nothing about Formosa (80). Most of the hoaxes that we will see in this study depend on a similar dynamic: the targeted culture is relatively unfamiliar—and usually less powerful than—the culture of the presumed readership. And the Psalmanazar hoax provides a rather extreme illustration of a phenomenon we will see again and again here: exposing a hoax does not put an end to it. Even long after the publication of the *Memoirs* should have abolished the hoax, as late as 1896, Psalmanazar's phony *Description* was cited as authoritative.[60] Literary hoaxes do not

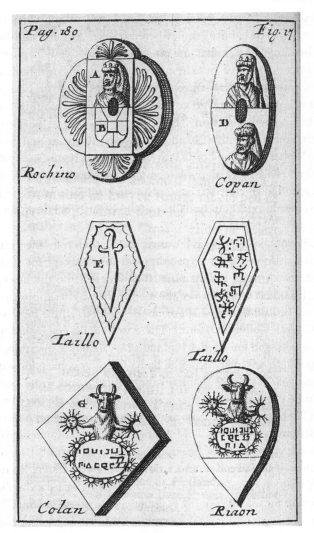

FIGURE 1. Formosan currency, from George Psalmanazar, *Description de l'île de Formosa en Asie* . . . (Amsterdam: Chez Pierre Mortier & Compagnie, 1708). Beinecke Rare Book and Manuscript Library, Yale University.

die, both because books stay on shelves and continue to be read and because the works continue to tell stories that people want to hear. Hoaxes can have "lasting persuasiveness."[61] One is left to wonder what Formosans (Taiwanese) might make of the *Description* now.

More properly speaking of real anthropology, the case of Margaret Mead is one to reckon with and keep in mind, because it allows us to consider the power dynamics of hoaxing from a very different and rare angle, from "below." It presents the hypothesis of the author from the developed world being hoaxed by her native informants or "traveling companions." Mead's assertion that Samoans have "an extensive tolerance of premarital sex relations," even "great promiscuity," was completely unfounded, in Derek Freeman's view, based on an examination of Mead's field notes and on the sworn evidence of her traveling companions.[62] Mead wanted to assert that unmarried Samoan girls were "*in secret* sexually promiscuous." The companions, Fa'apua'a and Fofoa, "conspiratorially pinched one another" and proceeded to tell Mead what she clearly wanted to hear; Mead did no further fieldwork on the subject (612). The two young women were engaging in the Samoan practice of *taufa'ase'e* or "recreational lying" (611). The rest is history: *Coming of Age in Samoa*, with its apparently fact-based image of a repression-free society, was highly influential in the United States, read by every college student, no doubt influencing the sexual revolution of the 1960s and 70s.[63] Until she died, according to Freeman, Mead remained "oblivious" of having been hoaxed (613).[64] Meanwhile, the "primitive youth" in Mead's book, her informants, might well have kept on laughing at the mischief they had made. A culture that she had labeled "uncomplex" and "uniform" eventually revealed itself to be anything but.[65]

This is reminiscent of what happened to American author Alex Haley, working at the crossroads of anthropology and literature, during his genealogical inquiries in West Africa that led to the publication of *Roots*. A local "griot" (in fact an impostor) heard that Haley was looking for an ancestor named Kunta Kinte and obliged by doing what griots do: making up a tale to fit the needs of the client, for remuneration.[66] Haley had hoaxed himself unwittingly.

Cases like this should be kept in mind as we move forward into literary hoaxes. A Western writer fooled by his or her local sources—resulting in published work that is seriously undermined from within—alters the power dynamic of the top-down literary impostures we will see. The writer is duped by knowledge or information that is itself false, which the writer cannot control, and which, in these cases, comes back to call the published work into question many years later. These are "time bomb" hoaxes: they sit on the shelf with false authority for decades, until someone exposes them. The informants could not have known that this would be the effect, but they did know that they were misleading the investigator, throwing him or her off the trail of the truth. Those informants are thus some of the most sophisticated hoaxers in modern history. The novelized memoirs of the great Ahmadou Hampâté Bâ are full of stories in which wiley, profiteering West African subalterns manipulate their colonial masters, hoaxing them on a daily basis.[67]

Turning to literature, the power dynamic is quite different, for the most part, for reasons that we will explore.

*

If I be wrong in this, then I protest that a woman's mind has got into some man's body by mistake that ought immediately to be corrected.
CHARLES DICKENS TO JOHN BLACKWOOD, January 27, 1858[68]

I turn now to a question that runs through every literary hoax and its exposure: can you tell? *By reading alone*, can you detect the identity of the author—what *type* of person is writing, if not what individual?

The question of ethnic impersonation has thus far been seen in the academy as predominantly an Anglo-American phenomenon, with a particularly rich history in the multicultural United States. Writing in the *New York Times* in 1991, Henry Louis Gates, Jr., explored the challenge to authenticity posed by such diverse American cases as nineteenth-century pseudo slave narratives, William Styron's *Confessions of Nat Turner*, "Danny Santiago" (the nonexistent Chicano author of a memoir in fact written by Daniel L. James, a white Anglo man), and the fake Cherokee autobiography *Education of Little Tree* (written by a white man with a history of racism).[69] Gates's essay was seminal.

Beginning with a disarmingly simple question, Gates raises an issue that haunts all of the hoaxes I will explore in this study: "Can you really tell?" By reading alone, can you detect a fake? Are the tools of sophisticated literary analysis able to uncover fraud and, in effect, act forensically? Could a computer do so? What if a hoax is, in fact, indistinguishable from the real thing in every aspect of its form? This is what critic Lia Brozgal has called a "blindfold test."[70] Mary Karr gets her students to read anonymized samples from two Holocaust memoirs, one real and one fake; she says "the proven fabricator gets the vast majority of votes for veracity every time."[71]

We all think we can tell, at least to a certain extent. Foucault himself stated the grammatical fact that underpins our hunches in his famous essay "What Is an Author?" "The text always contains a certain number of signs referring to the author."[72] But how reliable are those signs? Can they be used forensically, in order to identify the author? We will see many cases in which readers assert that the signs are adequate; that the repeated use of a certain phrase, for example, "outs" an author. In most such cases, however, the textual evidence itself, alone, is not probative.

There are few examples of actual "telling." The known cases seem to involve gender, not ethnicity or race or class. One of them establishes a benchmark of what I will call forensic reading. Charles Dickens, after reading the first fiction of "George Eliot," *Scenes of Clerical Life*, wrote to the author:

> My Dear Sir:
> I have been so strongly affected by the two first tales in the book you have had the kindness to send me . . . that I hope you will excuse my writing to you to express my admiration for their extraordinary merit. . . . In addressing these few words of thankfulness, to the creator of the sad fortunes of Mr. Amos Barton, and the sad love-story of Mr. Gilfil, I am (I presume) bound to adopt the name that it pleases that excellent writer to assume. I can suggest no better one; but I should have been strongly disposed, if I had been left to my own devices, to address the said writer as a woman. I have observed what seem to me to be such womanly touches, in those moving fictions, that the assurance on the title-page is insufficient to satisfy me, even now. If they originated with no woman, I believe that no man ever before had the art of making himself, mentally, so like a woman, since the world began.[73]

Dickens is playing cat and mouse with Eliot here: he suspects, and wants her to know that he suspects, that she is a woman. While dripping with admiration—and largely taken as a sign of pure benevolence on his part—,[74] his letter of course amounts to an implied threat: you have not fooled me with your cross-gender pseudonym, and I could expose you at any time. The possibility of blackmail lurks here (not that that was Dickens's intent).[75] Bearing in mind that she had not one but two secrets to hide—her identity and her out-of-wedlock cohabitation with George Henry Lewes, Mary Ann (or Marian) Evans was in a delicate position.[76] She had taken the name George Eliot for a solid careerist reason: to avoid gender bias and increase her chances of literary success; such was "the precariousness of her situation as a female."[77] But her "scandalous" life-style needed to be kept out of view as well. One secret—the pseudonym—was hiding another —the pseudomarriage. She valued secrecy in general; she called it "the iron mask of my incognito."[78] (Meanwhile there were published reports that the real author was a "ne'er-do-well" named Joseph Liggins.)[79] Dickens—then at the pinnacle of his fame—risked blowing her cover, ripping off her mask. George Eliot was "fiction itself" and wanted to stay that way.[80]

What exactly were "the womanly touches" that gave the show away to Dickens? In a second letter, he asserted that nearly all of Eliot's female characters "are more alive than the men," and "more informed from within."[81] Guessing at the exact textual signs that alerted Dickens—which he does not identify—would be an exercise in gender stereotyping. (Was the giveaway the narrator's confession that "Mine is not a well-regulated mind"? "The

home-made muffins glisten with an inviting succulence"? Was it this comment: "In bucolic society five-and-twenty years ago, the human animal of
the male sex was understood to be perpetually athirst . . ."? "Soothing, unspeakable charm of gentle womanhood! which supersedes all acquisitions, all
accomplishments"?)[82]

The salient point for our purposes here is that those writerly touches
alone, rather than any circumstantial evidence, apparently allowed Dickens
to deduce that Eliot—Mary Ann Evans—was a woman. He could tell *by reading alone*. In this study we will see many cases where readers *claim* they could
tell the author was not what he/she pretended to be, but they almost always
make this claim only *after* the imposture has been revealed.[83] ("I knew all
along; I just didn't say.") In the Eliot-Dickens case, we apparently witness pure
and accurate *forensic reading*. Such cases are exceedingly rare.

After the truth came out about George Eliot's gender, an unsigned review of
her *Adam Bede* accurately described how things had unfolded: "Now that we
are wise after the event, we can detect many subtle signs of female authorship
in *Adam Bede*; but at the time it was generally accepted as the work of a man."[84]

A real hoax, because it is not transparent, is a blindfold test for its readers:
Before you are "wise," *can you really tell* that the author is not what he or she
claims to be? Can you really tell where a wine comes from by the taste alone,
without seeing the label? These discussions are plagued by the use of certain
modal verbs: "would" and "could" in particular. What "would" a certain type
of person know? What "could" she have written and what could she not possibly have written? These may be matters of *likelihood*, but too often they
are stated as forensic proof. No white writer "would" say such-and-such; no
Arab immigrant "could" say something else. Such statements must be carefully scrutinized. Literary hoaxers are often enraged and provoked by—and
then set out to destroy—such essentialist expectations. One can assert that no
X writer "could" write or "would have" written A, but what if he or she *did?*
On the other hand, even if the proverbial monkey at the typewriter "could"
write *Hamlet*, he is not likely to, and questions of probability cannot be fully
dismissed.

✳

In *Slippery Characters: Ethnic Impersonators and American Identities*, Laura
Browder examines impostor tales, including "assisted" slave narratives; foun-
dational narratives of ethnic impersonation in nineteenth-century California
(*The Life and Adventures of Joaquin Murieta* and *Ramona*); and tales of be-
coming Indian, African American, and Chicano, including Forrest Carter's
The Education of Little Tree, John Howard Griffin's *Black Like Me*, and Danny

Santiago's *Famous All Over Town*. Browder argues that these books illustrate a "central paradox of American identity," a "belief in the fluidity of class identity and the fixity of racial, and, to a lesser extent, ethnic identity." Anyone can get rich, but no one can change their ethnic stripes—at least, not without consequences. Before seeing where this takes Browder, I want to point out that such an assumption would not hold in the French context, for the simple reason that ethnic stripes are not supposed to exist, not in the eyes of the Republic. If they do, they are to be subordinated to Republican universalism, even to the point of oblivion. Ethnic statistics are literally banned by the state.[85] The "right to difference" is not to be taken for granted and is, in fact, hotly contested (witness the ban on "ostensible signs of religion" in French schools). France has a problem with difference, which it historically "marginalizes," comments Françoise Vergès, who has studied the problem for decades.[86] "French universalism," writes Maurice Samuels, "is fundamentally opposed to minority difference."[87] This sets up a very different context for ethnic hoaxing, but does not make it either unthinkable or impossible, for the simple reason that the in-principle ban on *communautarisme* is, famously, itself something of a hoax.

Back in the US, Browder studies "what happens when people apply the [fluid] logic of class to a [rigid] construct of race and ethnicity."[88] In other words, what happens when authors cross lines that American society takes to be inviolable: those of race and ethnicity. These authors corrode the "polarities of race by moving along the ethnic spectrum" (8).[89] But that is only one possible effect. It may also be possible for an author to reinforce ethnic lines in the very process of crossing them. In part 1 of this study, I will review a series of exemplary American ethnic hoaxes, establishing a set of questions about literature and representation that I will then export and adapt to the French and Francophone context in parts 2 and 3 of this book.

PART 1

The Land of the Free and the Home of the Hoax

Slave Narratives and White Lies

Standing behind all American ethnic and racial impostures, the slave narrative establishes both a massive precedent and a series of questions. Narratives by Olaudah Equiano, Frederick Douglass, and countless others insisted in their titles that they were "written by himself," showing the importance of both literacy and authenticity. American nineteenth-century slave narratives insisted on their own truth for a very good reason: it could not be taken for granted. Because slaves were largely, but not completely, barred from literacy, demand for their writing was strong among abolitionists, but the status of any writing attributed to them was suspect. White hands often held the pen. And because those hands belonged to abolitionists, pressing for a political and moral imperative, the narratives needed to tell a certain kind of story. Henry Louis Gates, Jr., explains: "Two forms of imitators soon arose: white writers, adopting a first-person black narrative persona, gave birth to the pseudoslave narrative; and black authors, some of whom had never even seen the South, a plantation or a whipping post, became literary lions virtually overnight." Gates cites the examples of one Archy Moore (*The Slave*, 1836), actually a white historian named Richard Hildreth (the "white slave"), and the *Autobiography of a Female Slave*, written by a white woman named Mattie Griffith (who owned slaves at the time of her imposture).[1] These pseudo-ex-slaves, Gates says, "had to be authentic" in order for their stories to have any weight or influence; once unveiled as hoaxes, they surely undermined the credibility of the cause. Because it was known that some slave narratives were faked, it was common practice to include authenticating documents from trusted white people.[2] All of this was taking place in a United States that was deep into its "age of imposture," the nineteenth century: as Kevin Young describes it, "filled not just with tall tales and sideshows but also with con men and fake Indians, pretend blacks and impostor prophets, with masks and money."[3]

Laura Browder writes, "The only way [the abolitionists] could ensure the production of the slave narratives they preferred was to write them themselves."[4] A sort of "white lie" was thus key to certain fake slave narratives: the fakery served a high moral purpose, that of the abolition of slavery. Impostors of the twentieth century, including some in France, will sometimes stake an *ethical* rationale for their *ethnic* transgression. In the case of slave narratives, the high moral stakes might well justify the imposture.

The Forrest and the Tree

I now wish to leap forward to a golden age of ethnic hoaxing in America: our own times. The last quarter of the twentieth century and the beginnings of the twenty-first have produced a great new wave of impostures, a few of which I will review now.

The Education of Little Tree is an exemplary case of ethnic fakery framed by virulent American racism. The novel, a folksy Cherokee Bildungsroman, "tricked a generation of readers" with its soft-focus nostalgia for a lost world.[5] The cover bore the name Forrest Carter, who was supposedly half Cherokee, when in fact the book was written by Asa Earl Carter, a white man raised in Alabama who went on to a full career in racial hatred. The KKK was not radical or violent enough for him in the 1950s, so he formed a paramilitary splinter group; he authored the speech in which George Wallace called for "segregation today, segregation tomorrow, segregation forever." In the 1970s, Asa Earl Carter moved away from Alabama and reinvented himself as Forrest Carter, Cherokee.[6]

The Education of Little Tree "by Forrest Carter" was first published in 1976 and sold modestly.[7] Early editions bore the subtitle *A True Story by Forrest Carter*. Carter died in 1979, never having revealed the hoax. In 1985, the University of New Mexico Press reissued the book (minus the rubric "true story") with a dithyrambic introduction—"*Little Tree* is one of those rare books like *Huck Finn* that each new generation needs to discover and which needs to be read and reread regularly"—by a Cherokee legal scholar, Rennard Strickland. He describes the book as the "wonderfully funny and deeply poignant . . . autobiographical remembrances of [Carter's] life with his Eastern Cherokee Hill country grandparents." It is "a human document of universal meaning."[8] The commercial success began. *Little Tree* spent fourteen weeks on the *New York Times* best-seller list in 1991, and won the first American Booksellers Book of the Year Award that same year.[9] It was sold in souvenir shops on Indian reservations and was used "to rehabilitate youthful offenders" in Washington State.[10] *The Education of Little Tree* was widely taught, at both the secondary and college levels.[11] The hoax was definitively revealed in 1991, in the *New York Times*, by Dan T. Carter, a historian (and perhaps a distant cousin). "Readers have warmed to the uplifting story," he wrote, but "unfortunately, *The Education of Little Tree* is a hoax." Forrest Carter, a "new-age wise man for the greening of America" was nothing but a mask concealing Asa Earl Carter, a "home-grown American fascist and anti-Semite."[12] He was, a critic wrote later, a "redneck Paul de Man."[13]

But in fact, the true information about the author had been available for ten years. In 1976, the impostor "Forrest" Carter appeared on the *Today Show* with Barbara Walters to discuss his book; NBC received many phone calls from Alabama identifying him as Asa Earl Carter; and later that year, a piece in the *New York Times* by Wayne Greenhaw asked "Is Forrest Carter Really Asa Carter?," whom he identified as "a speech writer for George Wallace."[14] The hoax should have ended then, but amazingly—in a pattern we will see again and again—, it did not; it survived this initial exposure. Carter merely doubled down on his deceptions and cover stories, and the hoax went on even after his death.[15] (The republishing of the novel by the University of New Mexico Press may be compared, as we will see, to the new lease on life given to a novel signed by Camara Laye, *The Radiance of the King*.) As is often the case with literary hoaxes, the truth was hiding in plain sight; but something about the book and the "warm" story it told compelled readers to keep buying it and the publishing industry to ignore or suppress the facts. Forrest Carter was *good*, in the sense that he fooled a lot of people: Larry McMurtry endorsed one of his books as "the Iliad of the Southwest," nearly "the great American novel of the Indian."[16]

Critics and historians have asked, What did Carter have to gain *as a racist* by writing passages like these in *The Education of Little Tree*:

"It is The Way," [Granpa] said softly, "Take only what ye need. When ye take the deer, do not take the best. . . ." (p. 9).

How the government soldiers came. How the Cherokee had farmed the rich valleys and held their mating dances in the spring when life was planted in the ground; when the buck and doe, the cock and peahen exulted in the creation parts they played. (p. 40)

How the government soldiers came, and ringed a big valley with their guns . . . The Cherokees had nothing left. . . . The wagons could not steal the souls of the Cherokee. The land was stolen from him, his home; but the Cherokee would not let the wagons steal his soul. (p. 41)

How did "thinking Indian" (p. 123) advance the cause of white racism? As historian Gina Caison puts it, "It is difficult to reconcile" Carter's history of extreme and violent racism with "the imagined motives of the author of a book touted as a multicultural masterpiece of tolerance and respect."[17] Her typology of different answers to this riddle is useful. Why would a Southern racist write such a novel? To paraphrase Caison, readers have suggested three basic possibilities:

1. it reflects a genuine self-reinvention and atonement for previous racism;
2. the book actually conceals or smuggles in what Caison calls "a sinister narrative of white supremacy" (i.e., the Trojan Horse explanation);
3. the book is so salutary that its dubious origins are of little importance.[18]

Browder takes the first approach, seeing in *Little Tree* an attempt by Carter to find "a way out of the black/white binary."[19] The second theory is the most common among literary critics, as we will see below. The third case is succinctly stated by a reader's comment on the Goodreads website: "There is a lot of controversy and here say [*sic*] about the author of this book. Forget about it and enjoy this book with an innocent mind!"[20]

If Carter was the racist that he gave every appearance of being, and Carter wrote *Little Tree*, what does the book have to do with the author's ideology? *Was* his ideology in fact detectable—readable—in the book? A literary agent who had worked with Forrest Carter, struggling to deny the hoax in 1991, stated that "anyone who wrote *Little Tree could not have* worked for George Wallace. . . . I just don't believe it. I know it's not true."[21] The case of *Little Tree* flies in the face of the identity between self and work that we take for granted. Unless, of course, one subscribes to the second approach above, that of the Trojan Horse, in which case self and work are reunited: simply look at the text from a different angle, and its "true" meaning is revealed. One high-school teacher who had hailed the novel as "the hottest new text since *To Kill a Mockingbird*" and ordered one hundred copies for his students suddenly realized it was in fact a "manifesto for the message of states' rights."[22] *Since* the reveal, with 20/20 hindsight (which is, as Kevin Young calls it, "the hoax's best light"),[23] critics have found Carter's revival of the Lost Cause and his states'-rights agenda "obvious." Laura Browder points out that *Little Tree* had another very seductive agenda, which now seems painfully evident: an "inner child Indian" and "a way out of history" that appealed to post-1970s sensibilities.[24] Cherokee linguists have found that the "Cherokee" words in the novel are more like Klingon.[25] Dan T. Carter and Mark McGurl both point out that the convergence between Cherokee and Confederate had strong historical precedents.[26]

What does this case say about the possibility and power of forensic reading—the attempt to discern an author's true identity or true intentions simply by reading? Nothing good. There are very few Charles Dickenses out there, able to detect identity and imposture by reading alone. *Little Tree* would not and did not lend itself to that type of forensic reading: the reader "can't tell" and, more importantly, didn't tell, until the reveal. There were enough failures of reading to let the hoax fester for years, eventually producing "significant embarrassment for many Native Studies scholars who [had] extolled the book as 'authentic.'"[27] There is no hiding from the fact that authenticity suffered a stunning defeat at the hands of Asa Earl "Forrest" Carter. Even the initial revelation of Carter's true identity came up simply because people recognized the author on television.

In a deliberate or incidental attack on authenticity, an intercultural hoax violates what I will call the ethics of ethnicity: the unwritten code that says each group should represent itself, perhaps exclusively, perhaps only with permission.

This type of question comes up with striking force in the controversy surrounding a beloved if now dubious Francophone African novel, *L'Enfant noir*: Why would French colonialists write that book (if indeed they did)? Why would they, as opposed to an African, create a colonial Africa in which almost all signs of a French presence are invisible? If the text has certain traits, can we surmise who the author "must be"? There are some striking similarities between *Little Tree* and *L'Enfant noir*: the child's point of view, the depiction of a wise, timeless, "native" culture that is under threat from the outside, the use of iterative verbs and ellipses to suggest a cyclical, timeless mode of living. . . . I will return to those similarities in my discussion of *L'Enfant noir* in part 2.

Danny Santiago and the Ethics of Ethnicity

What nearly all these impostures have in common is that the real author comes from a higher socioeconomic stratum than the person he or she is pretending to be. "Danny Santiago," who "grew up in Los Angeles" according to the author's note in his novel *Famous All Over Town*, was actually Daniel James, an "aristocrat from Kansas City," a graduate of Andover and Yale (where he majored in Classical Greek), a black-listed Communist who, through this literary ruse, "escape[d] the strait-jacket of Americanism."[28] (The character of the "real sharp Ivy League" doctor, Penrose, who appears early in the novel, may be a stand-in for James.)[29] This Bildungsroman is narrated by Chato, a fourteen-year-old Chicano growing up in Los Angeles. For Browder, James's ruse was an act of "courage and self-liberation as much as one of presumption" (268). James said of Santiago, "He's so much freer than I am myself."[30] Fine for James, but what about those Chicanos whose story he appropriated? Focusing on James and his journey of self-fulfillment, Browder does not address that issue.[31]

Famous All Over Town, published in 1983, was for a time "a highly regarded contribution to Chicano literature"[32] (figure 2). The *New York Times Book Review* gushed: Santiago was "a writer endowed as though genetically with the sure, pure sense of how to shape his material . . . a natural."[33] The book was said to help students "connect with life in the barrio."[34] The *Los Angeles Times* said it was "a dark mirror-image of white East-Coast *Catcher in the Rye*."[35] Remaining unseen in person, James carried his hoax forward after publication in ways that anticipate the practices of Jack-Alain Léger as Paul Smaïl, such as written interviews in the voice of the fake author while his own body remained invisible. James/Santiago passed up a $5,000 literary prize because it required a photograph of the author.[36] Most literary hoaxers are reluctant to "produce a body," no doubt because doing so raises the stakes and the risks of the imposture considerably.

James's real identity as the author of *Famous All Over Town* was revealed in the *New York Review of Books* by John Gregory Dunne, a longtime friend, in August 1984; the hoax had lasted seventeen months.[37] In a simple but important assertion, Daniel James, after being exposed, told the *New York Times* that he had thought, in conceiving of the project: "Nobody's going to be hurt *if the book's any good*."[38] (This is an argument that we will see repeatedly in this study: what one critic calls "free-floating literary talent" has the capacity and the *right* to cross ethnic boundaries.)[39] The question of hurt or harm has legal implications: the "harm principle" says that only actions that do harm to someone should be banned. Ethnic impostors usually claim to have done no harm, but once exposed, the act can be seen differently by those whose identity has been usurped or appropriated. The *New York Times* commented dryly: "What complicates matters among Hispanic Americans is that some of them think the book . . . is quite good." The *Times* did not ask average, nonprofessional readers of the novel how they felt about the deception. But the editor of a Latino magazine "expressed mild annoyance" at the imposture; "consternation" and "anger" were reported; and the consensus at a San Francisco bookstore forum was "fraud."[40]

Another form of harm must also be considered: that done to readers who do not belong to the culture that has been usurped but who came to the book earnestly seeking information about it. They were expecting an "authentic" account of a foreign culture, but they instead consumed a fake; they were duped. When the hoax is revealed to them (if it is), they must go back and

FIGURE 2. Cover of Danny Santiago, *Famous All Over Town* (New York: Plume, 1983).

question everything that they thought they had learned about the target culture from that work. Do the X people eat/sleep/marry in the way that was depicted? Or does the hoax—the lie—stop at the boundaries of the work, the cover and title page? The second hypothesis is perfectly possible: the factual identity of the author is a lie, but everything inside the work, all or much of the cultural representation, is accurate, *juste*. From trick to truth, as in the word "hoax" itself. After a hoax is revealed, it is actually rare for such claims of enduring authenticity to be made by anyone except the author defending himself or herself. (It is not the case with the "Klingon" passing for Cherokee language in *The Education of Little Tree*, to be sure.)

Daniel James intended to continue writing as Danny Santiago, despite the unmasking, but he died in 1988 before publishing anything else.[41] The comments section of Amazon.com shows that some readers continue to be fooled, while others discover who the real author was. One reader commented in 2015: "The author did an amazing job of writing from inside someone else's skin."[42] The role that Amazon now plays in the afterlife of hoaxes is a subject to which I will return below.

In cases like this, two forms of "good" are thus in competition: on the one hand, the moral good of ethnic self-respect and self-representation, which is violated by the imposture; and, on the other, the aesthetic quality and/or representational power of the work ("if the book's any good"—"free-floating literary talent"). The stronger the quality of the work—the more it is convincing—the more harm it may do to *the ethics of ethnicity* and its requirement for *self*-representation. Both James and Léger created ethnic narrators who push back against the expectations of essentialism; but that gesture is *ethically* different when made from outside or above. Deconstructing someone else's ethnicity, these authors are Trojan Horses.

Browder concludes her chapter on Daniel James/Danny Santiago with an essential(ist) and closely related point:

> We read autobiographical texts in the comfortable knowledge that the narrator has gotten through whatever horrors he or she documents. We also read them not only to find out how other people succeed, but how we, too, can learn to prevail. The impersonator autobiography is a betrayal of this trust. Since the life documented did not really exist, there are, it seems, no lessons we can learn here.[43]

While recognizing Browder's logic (which is only one step in a larger argument), I have to disagree: *much* can be learned from lives that "did not really exist"—fictive, literary lives, by the thousands; and much can be learned from "writers [including anthropologists] familiar with and sympathetic to" a group

THE HOME OF THE HOAX

to which they do not belong.⁴⁴ Impostures and appropriations can do harm (example: minstrelsy as "theft").⁴⁵ But taking a hard line against fakes of all kinds can only lead to Plato's "be yourself only" policy, an impoverished realism, and a world of immutable divisions.⁴⁶ Jack-Alain Léger, for one, revolts against this idea, justifying his literary practice of constant disguise with a theory of lies that tell truths that otherwise cannot be told.

In reviewing several other American literary hoaxes of the twentieth and twenty-first centuries, I want to stress one point in particular: the internet has altered and prolonged the afterlife of hoaxes. The instant availability of "information" should have made untruths obsolete instantly, but we all know that the web has had quite the opposite effect, producing a new golden age of "alternative facts." Before the internet, it was entirely possible to be taken in by a fake text simply because its unmasking had escaped one's attention; in the age of the internet, it turns out, this remains the case. Both before and during the age of the internet, the exposure of a hoax often fails to put an end to it.

Go Ask Amazon

> Chris and I walked into Richie and Ted's apartment to find the bastards stoned and making love to each other. . . . Here I am peddling drugs for a low class queer . . . What a disgrace I am to myself and my family and to everybody.
>
> GO ASK ALICE

The case of a fake diary published anonymously in 1971, with the words "a real diary" on its cover, is exemplary. *Go Ask Alice* tells a paranoid cautionary tale about the dangers of drugs: a fifteen-year-old girl who tries LSD, then marijuana, then heroin, and is drawn away from home and family, raped by "low class shit-eaters" (78), eventually winding up dead. We can call this a case of intercultural hoaxing, if in a different sense: *Go Ask Alice* was written as a representation of a supposedly "alien" culture living in the midst of (and threatening) middle-class America: the counterculture, the "drug culture." The diarist (whom everyone refers to as Alice, although the name is never used in the book) complains: "I can't quite adapt or fit in. Every so often I even seem to be on the outside just looking in on my own family."⁴⁷ At one point she channels the threatening rhetoric of intergenerational war: "I can't believe that soon it will have to be mother against daughter and father against son to make the new world" (83). This was not any kind of honest ethnography of youth culture; it was a heavily tendentious, propagandistic representation, designed to scare children away from drugs. Our diarist drives the point home: "Anyone who says pot and acid are not addicting is a damn, stupid, raving idiot, unenlightened fool" (96). To make drug use even scarier, this

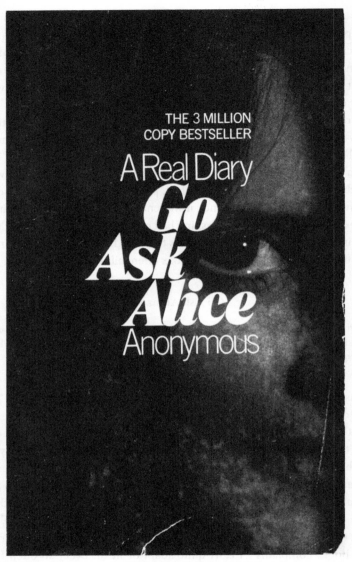

"establishment narrative masquerading as a countercultural one" wallows in what Susan Ziegler calls "generalized homosexual and gender panic."[48] The diarist memorably sums her life up: "Another day, another blow job" (112). She learns her lesson, "It isn't worth it!" (121), but it is too late. *Go Ask Alice* is an inadvertently hilarious camp classic (but only if you know it is a hoax).

The book has been enormously successful and influential, selling millions of copies both before and after it was revealed to be a hoax. Over the lifetime of the text it is said to have sold more than five million copies.[49] Meanwhile, the mere discussion of sex and drugs in the text has made it "one of the most-often challenged [i.e., censored] books in the country."[50] This may be due to something that Susan Ziegler points out: cautionary tales like *Go Ask Alice* "must dramatically flesh out the pleasures against which they warn, creating an interest that can blunt the moral's force."[51] Again, the unmasking of a hoax does not put an end to it: the book can keep selling and fooling at least some readers for years afterward.[52]

There has never been a proper, complete, or definitive exposure of the true authorship of *Go Ask Alice*. That fact alone is surprising, considering the wide circulation of the book.[53] The suspected author, Beatrice Sparks, came out, but only as "editor" of *Go Ask Alice*, and that is not the same thing. She continued to claim that she based the book on the real diary of a real teenage girl, conveniently "locked away at Prentice-Hall."[54] (Why did someone not ask for it to be "unlocked"?)[55] Copyright records list Beatrice Sparks alone as author.[56] Her obituary lists Sparks as the sole author of *Go Ask Alice* but neglects to mention it was published as a fake "real diary" of a teenage girl.[57]

If *Go Ask Alice* were actually based on a real diary, edited by Sparks and perhaps one other person,[58] then *Go Ask Alice* would be a case of plural authorship (albeit shrouded in mystery to the point of fraud). Visible signs of editing were left in the original and all other editions, although missing from the cover and title page: a short foreword claiming that *Go Ask Alice* "is based on the actual diary of a fifteen-year-old drug user" is signed "The Editors," and deep in the narrative, a footnote informs us that "there are no dates for the following material. It was recorded on single sheets of paper, paper bags, etc." (102n). And of course someone had to write the epilogue: "The subject of this book died three weeks after her decision not to keep another diary . . . Was it an accidental overdose? A premedidated overdose? No one knows" (214).

The shared authorial responsibility implied by an edited volume brings two comparisons to mind. The first is postcolonial anthropology, in which those previously known as "native informants" receive the recognition they deserve, including their names on title pages of published books. In *Go Ask Alice*, the dynamic is the opposite: it is the editor (or editors) who remain nameless. The second comparison is, again, the case of *L'Enfant noir*, the famous Francophone African novel whose authorship has been called into question; I will return to that issue in the second part of this study. Shared authorship can be a positive, legitimate, collaborative arrangement, or, if it is distorted

or disguised, it can simply be deceptive. Given the lack of transparency and
the absence of any original diary as proof of authentic shared authorship, *Go
Ask Alice* appears to be a case of simple—and spectacularly sucessful—fraud.
The most likely hypothesis is that Sparks's Plan A was to pass the book off as
an authentic diary, published as such; when that was called into question, she
moved to Plan B: a story of shared authorship based on a found diary (which
was conveniently unavailable). She never revised that claim. As one commen-
tator puts it, Sparks found a way "to carve a literary career out of the body
of a dead girl."[59] Or perhaps: out of thin air. Sparks died in 2012. The book
continues to be read "as pure fact."[60]

The real diary of a dead young girl would be, as Alleen Pace Nilsen suggests, "exempt from the regular kind of literary criticism."[61] It would be both
indecent and superfluous to critique the writing style of an authentic diary
written under duress. But suspicions about the existence of the diary have
opened the door to forensic readings of *Go Ask Alice*. (Here come the modal
verbs.) *Would* a teenager really use "polysyllabic terms such as 'gregarious,'
'impregnable,' 'conscientious,' and 'ecstatic'"?[62] *Would* she, on LSD, really
think she had found "the perfect and true and original language, used by
Adam and Eve"? (32). *Would* she comment omnisciently: "Adolescents have
a very rocky insecure time"? (87). Perhaps not, but those stylistic hints could
be merely signs of shared authorship—the hand of the "editor"—, and, in any
case, such evidence does not determine the true authorship of the text.

Go Ask Alice has never fallen out of print, and, in the world of Amazon, the
book remains completely available. In fact, a buyer could be taken in by the
hoax almost as easily now as in 1971. Amazon presents the book with this caption: "A teen plunges into a downward spiral of addiction in this classic cautionary tale." (Below, in small letters, Amazon requests: "Report incorrect product
information.") In the top "editorial review," the book is said to depict "the torture and hell of adolescence," and the book is hailed, now, in these terms: "Despite a few dated references to hippies and some expired slang, *Go Ask Alice* still
offers a jolting chronicle of a teenager's life spinning out of control."[63] Excerpts
from reviews in the *Boston Globe*, *Library Journal*, and the *New York Times* all
cite the work as important and authentic. It is only the customer reviews that
mention the "fictional" status of the text. In other words, this Amazon page—
the parts of it designed by the corporation—could have been created before the
hoax was exposed. Amazon is, in effect, perpetuating the hoax. So is Simon &
Schuster: the book that comes in the mail, printed in 2006, claims to be "the definitive book on the horrors of addiction."[64] (Such paratexts as jacket copy and
Amazon blurbs are essential ingredients in any hoax: as Kevin Young says, this
is "text that in its very authorlessness means to establish authority.")

If, as I suspect, *Go Ask Alice* is entirely fake and was never based on any authentic diary, what harm has been done? If millions of readers have been either edified—"scared straight"—or amused by the text, where is the damage? Because the group that is being (mis)represented here—the youth/drug counterculture of the late 1960s and early 1970s—is long since extinct, it would be hard to say that anyone is being harmed now by the continuing sales of the text (unless truth itself counts). But the paranoid vision of drug culture promulgated by *Go Ask Alice* certainly contributed, in some immeasurable way, to what would become the "war on drugs," with its mass incarcerations for nonviolent offenders. *Go Ask Alice* became "Just Say No."[65] So yes, harm was done by this hoax.

"I Never Saw It As a Hoax": JT LeRoy[66]

I will reclaim my tears, petrified by the terror of loss.
TERMINATOR (JT LEROY), "Baby Doll"

Sarah, by "J. T. LeRoy," the story of a transgender teenager from Appalachia, was published in 2000. The initials stand for "Jeremy Terminator." LeRoy was supposed to be seventeen years old when the book contract was signed.[67] His first publication, as "Terminator," was a "memoir" that appeared in 1996, in the volume *Close to the Bone: Memoirs of Hurt, Rage, and Desire*.[68] With that, the charade began. This would be much more than a pseudonym: it became a full-service hoax of massive proportions.

The author of *Fight Club*, Chuck Palahniuk, said *Sarah* was "everything a good read—or good sex, for that matter—should be." Joel Rose in his blurb said that he had known LeRoy "since he was sixteen years old" and that he "walks with God and writes like an angel." John Waters called LeRoy's writing "savagely authentic and appallingly beautiful."[69] In a pattern we will see time and time again, only *after* the exposure of the hoax does a critic find *Sarah* to be riddled with imperfections: in 2016, A. O. Scott wrote that *Sarah* was a combination of "pornographic content with greeting-card sentimentality."[70] That radical reappraisal came after the world found out that JT LeRoy was a fake. How could the same work be both so good and so eye-rollingly bad?

Thrusting the reader into an underworld filled with slang ("lot lizard," "pavement princesses," "the green bean run," "a faggot goodbuddy"),[71] *Sarah* spins a tale of a rough but somehow uplifting quest for identity. The first-person narrator, sometimes called Cherry Vanilla, is a transvestite male prostitute (a "lizard") in training at a truck stop diner in West Virginia. Like any number of literary impostures, this one embeds a tale of impersonation, *en abyme*, as if

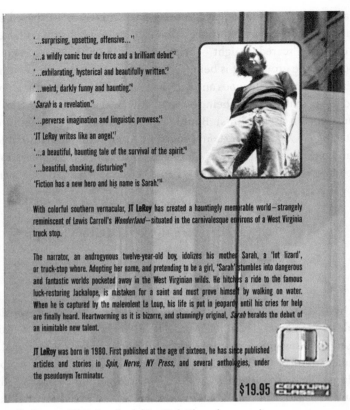

'...surprising, upsetting, offensive...'[1]

'...a wildly comic tour de force and a brilliant debut.'[2]

'...exhilarating, hysterical and beautifully written.'[3]

'...weird, darkly funny and haunting.'[4]

'*Sarah* is a revelation.'[5]

'...perverse imagination and linguistic prowess.'[6]

'JT LeRoy writes like an angel.'[7]

'...a beautiful, haunting tale of the survival of the spirit.'[8]

'...beautiful, shocking, disturbing'[9]

'Fiction has a new hero and his name is Sarah.'[10]

With colorful southern vernacular, JT LeRoy has created a hauntingly memorable world—strangely reminiscent of Lewis Carroll's *Wonderland*—situated in the carnivalesque environs of a West Virginia truck stop.

The narrator, an androgynous twelve-year-old boy, idolizes his mother Sarah, a 'lot lizard', or truck-stop whore. Adopting her name, and pretending to be a girl, 'Sarah' stumbles into dangerous and fantastic worlds pocketed away in the West Virginian wilds. He hitches a ride to the famous luck-restoring Jackalope, is mistaken for a saint and must prove himself by walking on water. When he is captured by the malevolent Le Loup, his life is put in jeopardy until his cries for help are finally heard. Heartwarming as it is bizarre, and stunningly original, *Sarah* heralds the debut of an inimitable new talent.

JT LeRoy was born in 1980. First published at the age of sixteen, he has since published articles and stories in *Spin*, *Nerve*, *NY Press*, and several anthologies, under the pseudonym Terminator.

$19.95 CENTURY CLASS

FIGURE 4. Back cover of JT LeRoy, *Sarah* (New York: Bloomsbury, 2000).

to hint at its own origins: the male narrator assumes the identity of his prostitute mother, Sarah; when his penis is revealed, he says, "I never asked for it to be there."[72] When they are not consuming "livermush fry topped with red-eye gravy," the characters spout homespun, Bible-steeped wisdom: "The Lord can give the curse of life to the most unlikely being."[73] The supposedly twenty-year-old author has the supposedly uneducated, rustic narrator say, "I determine myself to stoically brave my engulfing nausea."[74] Reversed regional condescension provides blue-state readers with a slight thrill of self-flagellation:

> "Supernatural occurrences never happen up North, because Yanks have no space left in their hearts, in their minds, and on their land for a miracle of the Lord to have a chance to take seed."
>
> Everyone nodded furiously in agreement.[75]

This is one of the most common tropes of primitivism; this is the same sentiment that Charles Lindbergh expressed about the "Tasaday." The developed world has lost touch with spirituality, which is still to be found in more remote, less developed regions. Knowing that this is a hoax makes such postures—the ventriloquizing of Northern nostalgia by fictional Southern mouths—easy to recognize.[76] After the unveiling of the hoax, such writing could of course be reinterpreted as a sophisticated, postmodern hipster parody of that very nostalgia—if one chooses to look at it that way. But before the unveiling, despite the novel's surreal aspects and stylistic flourishes, "it was widely believed that LeRoy's material was autobiographical," and it was taken seriously.[77] After the fact, the author described the publishing context of 2000 as "the time of the memoir craze," which demonstrates that she knew exactly what kind of literary market she was manipulating. Among the books she cited was Mary Karr's *The Liars' Club*.[78] Manohla Dargis wrote, "Given publishing's seemingly endless appetite for memoirs filled with sexual sob stories and kinks, a JT LeRoy was inevitable."[79] In the wake of this hoax, the James Frey affair, and other deceptions, "the fake memoir has become a genre unto itself,"[80] and the memoir is "a form under siege."[81]

JT LeRoy did not exist. The author was a woman from Brooklyn Heights named Laura Albert; she "had never been to West Virginia" and never saw a truck stop until one of her books was being filmed on location.[82] The author photo was a fake.[83] Laura Albert says she learned to write at the Eugene Lang College of the New School, so she was, at least to a certain extent, a trained writer.[84] But it wasn't just the text that made the novel a success; it was the performance called JT LeRoy. Public appearances were circuses, involving the real Laura Albert as "Speedie," a British-accented handler of JT LeRoy, who was played by Savannah Knoop, the half-sister of Albert's boyfriend. This JT was "a soft-spoken waif in a blond wig, dark glasses, and baggy, androgynous clothes."[85] In fact, the public JT most often wore dresses and looked completely female; he sometimes claimed to be undergoing gender reassignment, sometimes not. Savannah taught herself to pronounce "like" as "lack." At packed public events, famous friends, including Carrie Fisher, Nancy Sinatra, Heather Graham, Rufus Wainwright, the Pulitzer Prize–winning poet Sharon Olds, and Lou Reed—comprising a sort of "celebrity support group"—read aloud for the "shy" LeRoy.[86] Claiming to have AIDS and to be suffering the after-effects of sexual abuse, JT LeRoy milked all of them for sympathy. (Later, AIDS "was no longer part of his story"; it simply disappeared, and "no one ever questioned it.")[87] Susan Dey said she "wanted to heal this person . . . but I was healed."[88] Kids reportedly worshiped him. He published widely, and a film was made out of his second book, *The Heart Is Deceitful Above All Things*.[89]

Times reporter Warren St. John exposed the real identity of JT LeRoy after receiving a phone call from Albert's boyfriend in February 2006, revealing "an all-consuming web of deceit."[90] Two documentary films tell the story: *The Cult of JT LeRoy* and *Author: The JT LeRoy Story*, the latter being largely a vehicle for Albert's after-the-fact self-defense. Albert had been illegally recording her telephone conversations with her band of celebrity friends (including Courtney Love, Gus Van Sant, and none other than Mary Karr), recordings that are heard in *Author*.[91] Karr later characterized JT LeRoy as "a fine little prankster" who "weaseled me into taking a call by dropping Mary Gaitskill's name."[92] Although she does not say so, having been duped by this hoax must have at least partially motivated Karr to take her uncompromising position on truth in *The Art of Memoir*. As she wrote elsewhere, "I want to stay hamstrung by objective truth."[93]

This, then, was a hoax carried out on a larger stage, for longer (ten years), and with a lot more daring, than usual: a six-week European book tour, a writing assignment from the *New York Times*, and an interview with Terry Gross on NPR[94] (using a fake Appalachian twang) are high-water marks for imposture. Few literary hoaxes dare to "produce a body" in the world; doing so heightens the risk of exposure exponentially. With extraordinary daring and stamina, Laura Albert and Savannah Knoop managed to do it for years. (Romain Gary and his "nephew" will not be so successful.) "The greatest literary hoax in a generation," said the *San Francisco Chronicle* about JT LeRoy.[95] In the film *Author*, Albert described her methods without regret or apology, disdaining those who claimed to have been hurt by what she refused to call a hoax.

When it was all over, Laura Albert told an interviewer, "I'm sad I was so injured."[96] In 2016, she told the *Times*, "I meet a lot of young people and they're shocked that it was an issue to even have an avatar," and, "Today, it's such a blessing that people have the words 'gender-fluid.' "[97] In other words, she was ahead of her time, bravely challenging barriers of identity and gender, not simply running a money-making scam constructed out of the suffering of others. In fact, *Sarah* is intriguing and perhaps somewhat ahead of its time in its treatment of gender fluidity. As with all literary hoaxes, this text can be read on its own and appreciated, detached from the shenanigans of its author.[98] The embodied performance of Savannah Knoop as JT LeRoy was also a significant act of gender bending. (It is perhaps no coincidence that Barthes's reflections on the death of the author began with Balzac's tale of a gender queer, *Sarrasine*.)[99] From the perspective of writer Mary Gaitskill, the JT LeRoy hoax was "a very enjoyable one . . . expos[ing] the confusion between love and art and publicity."[100] But of course this hoax was not strictly literary, and it was not enjoyable for everyone.

The question of harm—cui malo—is often posed in the wake of a hoax, often rhetorically: what harm did it do? In this case, the question need not remain entirely speculative: the question was addressed in two different, very concrete ways. First, an actual trial took place. Unlike most literary hoaxers, Albert was sued, for fraud and breach of contract by the film company that had bought the rights to *Sarah*. She defended herself with the notion that JT LeRoy was both a pseudonym and, more impressively, "a sort of 'respirator' for her inner life . . . a survival apparatus that permitted her to breathe."[101] On the stand, Albert wove a tale of childhood sexual abuse that had left her "incapable of speaking as herself," leading to a series of impersonations as teenage boys; she was, in effect, defending her actions as grounded in a version of multiple personality disorder. As JT LeRoy, she supposedly "lost herself while reaching for the truth."[102] (Hoaxers, including Jack-Alain Léger, usually claim to be serving a higher truth, or their own truth.)[103] The relation between hoaxing and mental illness is not to be dismissed: as we will see in the cases of Romain Gary and Jack-Alain Léger, the consequences can be fatal.

But Laura Albert faced the paradox of the Cretan liar in her attempts to justify herself. If she claimed that her hoaxing grew out of sexual abuse at the age of three, producing a series of avatars who say false things—if that is her story—why would anyone necessarily believe her? The federal jury didn't buy it, and here, for once, the question of the harm done by a literary hoax was actually adjudicated and given a dollar amount. Laura Albert, labeled a "wily, venal hoaxer," was assessed $350,000 in legal fees and $116,000 in damages.[104] She later settled for an undisclosed sum.[105]

The second form of damage that came to light after the exposure of the hoax was the pain suffered by readers who had been deceived. "Kids who are really abused," and who had believed in the JT LeRoy story, were "shocked" and hurt.[106] A voice heard in the film *Author* tells Albert, "The whole transgender community is going to want to lynch you." This is not second-hand speculation: a group of twenty-eight young LGBT people, many of them survivors of abuse, clients of a drop-in center in San Francisco, wrote a statement, saying:

> We . . . are appalled by the exploitation of our real world struggles by the author JT LeRoy and company for the purpose of personal profit and celebrity. We expect an apology, not simply for defrauding the public into giving money to someone who they believed to be young, struggling, and seriously ill, but for repeatedly defaming our community both in articles and in interviews.[107]

Here, for once, is the voice of the reader who has been deceived and who feels the harm of the hoax. Defenders of the hoax as an art form should bear this testimony in mind. The feeling of harm is no doubt rooted in a sense of appropriation, of theft; but it also includes a sense of devaluation: real memoirs of real hurt (and rage and desire) are diluted and undercut by fake ones. Kevin Young states the problem bluntly: "Hoaxers erase those their story purports to represent."[108] Albert's glib response: "If you feel upset, I'm OK with that."[109]

The barriers of class and region that this hoax traversed—the invention and exploitation of a West Virginia underclass by a denizen of Brooklyn Heights and San Francisco—have barely been commented on, but should be. Laura Albert may have made "literature out of a terrible childhood"[110] (if she actually had one), but also out of Northern, middle-class notions of Appalachia, based on no actual contact. She "invoked transgenderism"[111] in ways that may have been simply exploitative, and, in "the most unfortunate part of all of this,"[112] she passed as a person dying of AIDS in order to elicit sympathy. JT LeRoy's now-you-see-it-now-you-don't case of AIDS represents the ethical nadir of this imposture. We will see this called "stolen suffering" in the next case, below. But the other significant deceit in all this is the phony "rags to riches tale," the notion that a person such as "JT" can, as Stephen Beachy puts it, "charm his way to the top, through diligence and talent," from the truck stop to Hollywood. In the United States, where false consciousness about social mobility runs rampant, this is hardly an innocent fiction. This, then, is a hoax in the service not just of a certain truth (gender fluidity) but also of a fundamental lie (rags to riches).

Something more than "free-floating literary talent" allowed Albert to do all this, something more daring and perverse. Delightful, devastating, and despicable, the JT LeRoy hoax was most certainly an elaborate and highly successful work of performance art.

Margaret B. Jones, Misha Defonseca, and "Stolen Suffering"

A white, middle-class woman who, in 2008, writes a fake gang memoir and succeeds—until she doesn't—deserves to be mentioned here. *Love and Consequences: A Memoir of Hope and Survival* was said to weave "stunning, forthright narration together with the distinctive, rhythmic slang of the street."[113] With that statement, this book became an open invitation to "tell"—for someone to detect by reading alone that this was not what it appeared to be. No one did. This hoax takes us squarely back to the question of ethnicity.

If the notoriously hard-hitting *New York Times* critic Michiko Kakutani found that some of the memoir "can feel self-consciously novelistic," she nonetheless thought the "remarkable" book as a whole was "deeply affecting," with its "anthropologist's eye for social rituals and routines." Margaret B. Jones had "borne witness to the life in the 'hood that she escaped."[114]

The pattern is familiar enough now. Before the exposure, the book looked like one thing; after, quite another. If a person named Margaret B. Jones, half Native American and half white, "at age eight, after many relocations, . . . landed in a foster home in South Central Los Angeles," she would have a certain story to tell.[115] A person named Margaret "Peggy" Seltzer, raised all white and middle-class in Sherman Oaks (Brady Bunch territory) and going to private school, presumably would have a different story, and, strictly speaking, no right to tell the story of Margaret B. Jones. But she did, with considerable success. True to the form, the "memoir" leavens the tales of hardship with uplifting sentiments, including this from the girl's "Big Mom": "I know it ain a lot, but it's home an we got each other, we got love and we got God" (37).

Seltzer was unmasked by her own sister, Cyndi Hoffman, who called the publisher after seeing a photo of the author in the *New York Times*. (The author should not have "produced a body," her own.) The story in the book was "entirely fabricated."[116] Nineteen thousand copies of *Love and Consequences* were recalled, and refunds were offered.[117] (But of course, you can still buy it.) Seltzer, unlike Laura Albert, was repentant—in a way. She gave a "tearful, often contrite" interview to the *Times*, while still justifying her caper in moral terms: "I thought it was my opportunity to put a voice to people who people don't listen to."[118] In 2015, Ishmael Reed wrote a letter to the *New York Times Book Review* to remind readers that *Love and Consequences* is "a fake memoir but is still on the market."[119]

✶

About ten years earlier, in 1997, a book titled *Misha: A Mémoire of the Holocaust Years* appeared under the name Misha Defonseca (with a cowriter, a former professor of French named Vera Lee).[120] It told a harrowing tale of a young Jewish girl's survival, trekking more than 1,900 miles through wartime Europe: "I kept telling myself, 'It only hurts if you think about it'" (46) . . . "I had perfected the art of being transparent" (76) . . . "Some day I would bear witness to what I had seen here this day" (112) . . . "Behind me I left . . . a line of closed and boarded up boxcars filled with human cargo bound for the gas chambers at Treblinka" (145) . . . "'I'm not afraid of you, *Boche*, I killed one just like you'" (219). The parts where she was taken in and nurtured by packs of wolves ("I shared my purloined meals with them, too," 97; see 156ff)—not to mention the unlikely nature of the entire narrative—might have served as a red flag, and did for some people, who warned the publisher about the hoax in advance and refused to endorse the book. But the publisher pressed on with a story that would sell, marketing it as real and true, with a blurb from

Elie Wiesel himself ("very moving") and the education director of the North American Wolf Foundation. Then, in a twist, the coauthors sued the original publisher for underselling the book in the United States; they were awarded $32 million by a judge. The French edition, labeled an "adaptation"—*Survivre avec les loups: de la Belgique à l'Ukraine, une enfant juive à travers l'Europe nazie, 1941–1944*—was published in a collection called "Vécu" or "lived experience" and sold over 30,000 copies. It was translated into eighteen languages, and was made into a film in Belgium, aimed at children: *Survivre avec les loups* (2007).[121] A new mass-market paperback—which, oddly was translated "back" into English from the French edition, itself a translation of the original *Misha*, labeled as a memoir—was issued in 2006 under the title *Surviving with Wolves: The Most Extraordinary Story of World War II* by Misha Defonseca.[122]

In an artful hall-of-mirrors effect that so often occurs in hoaxes, the fictional Misha is given a pseudonym by the Catholic family that shelters her; that name is Monique de Wael, the author's real name, which thus hides in plain sight inside the book, like an open invitation to be discovered (*Misha*, 13). The narrator claims that she "never knew" her real family name (*Misha*, 172). The French edition of the book changed the protagonist's pseudonymous family name to Valle, which threw researchers off the trail for years.[123]

Suspicions grew, and finally a genealogist named Sharon Sergeant uncovered the author's real identity.[124] Her name, she admitted in February 2008, was Monique de Wael: she was Belgian, Catholic, not Jewish, the daughter of Resisters killed in the war. In a statement to the Belgian newspaper *Le Soir*, she said, with echoes of Laura Albert: the story of Misha "is not actual reality, but was my reality, my way of surviving."[125] In a new height of hoaxing chutzpah, de Wael claimed the publisher "made me believe, and I believed it."[126] *Je me suis laissée convaincre*, "I let myself be talked into it."[127] And several years later she told an interviewer, "I lied, yes, but I did it to save us: to rehabilitate my father, to give meaning to my mother's death, and to save myself, so that I could breathe in this world. . . . I didn't kill anyone, *I didn't hurt anyone.*" This was her "Plan B" or fallback defense: she had invented the story in order to survive. French-language newspapers had some fun with the *supercherie* (hoax) in their headlines: "Elle a menti avec les loups" (She lied with wolves), quipped one. But condemnations rained down: "She exploited [*a instrumentalisé*] the Shoah. That is hateful."[128]

There is of course something particularly repellant about faking a Holocaust survival narrative and passing it off as real.[129] In such a case it is hard to stake an Aristotelian claim for the art of the hoax, no matter how successful it was. Blake Estin describes the affair as an "affront to those authentic Holocaust survivors with sad but not otherworldly stories, to the memory of those who did not live to document their own fate, and to those who take the study of history seriously." Again, not a victimless crime.

∗

These two cases together provoked an anguished statement from Daniel Mendelsohn in an op-ed in the *New York Times* titled "Stolen Suffering." That characterization, of course, haunts many of the cases we have seen already and casts them in a very negative light. Mendelsohn's essay provides a stinging rebuke to those who would claim that intercultural hoaxes are all victimless crimes. Reacting to the false Holocaust memoir *Misha* as well as to *Love and Consequences*, Mendelsohn deplores the fact that "a comparatively privileged person has appropriated the real traumas suffered by real people for her own benefit," and he suggests that there are proper limits to empathy. "We all have AIDS" may be a well-intentioned slogan, but it is simply not true; to pretend otherwise, Mendelsohn says, "debases the anguish of those who are stricken." "Slick identification" is not the same as true understanding; there is such a thing as "plagiarism of other people's trauma." While a Deleuzian practice of "becoming-other" (which, incidentally, includes "becoming-wolf") may be anything from a profound engagement to a parlor game—and while I may disagree with Mendelsohn when he asserts that identity is "precisely that quality in a person or group that cannot be appropriated by others"—there are clearly limits of decency that should be respected.[130] Identity *can*, we have seen time and again, be *appropriated*: the question is whether it *is appropriate* to do so, and what the consequences may be. As for the question of harm: if someone says he is offended, you can tell him he *should not* be, but not that he *is* not offended.

∗

Why does this keep happening? In economic terms, these ethnic or class-based hoaxes are, without exception, responding to the demands of the market. There is a dearth of authentic narratives "from below"—from socioeconomically and ethnically underprivileged groups who lack representation: "people who people don't listen to" (in other words, people who do not generally write and therefore are not read). "Cultures of the dispossessed usually, for better or worse, come to us mediated through dominant-cultural filters," writes Eric Lott.[131] About slaves, Native Americans, druggy teenagers, underclass youth, transgender or not: the literate overclass wants to *know*. Opportunistic authors rise (or stoop) to the occasion, filling in the blanks. Like blackface minstrelsy as described by Lott, some of these intercultural and interclass hoaxes "[open] to view the culture of the dispossessed,"—that is, to a view from above, looking down—while at the same time effectively denying the underclass access to the means of self-representation. Lott calls that a "truly American combination of acknowledgment and expropriation,"—what he calls love and theft—but we will see that it transcends borders.[132]

What would it take to eliminate the "need" for all this fraud? No doubt, full, unfettered, universally accessible opportunities for self-representation by all groups: then a Platonic literature of pure, nonimitative truth and self might reign. Or not. Would the human impulse to *play* and pretend to be Other bubble up, even in the absence of any real need, thereby perpetuating the endless tradition of hoaxes?

Minority Literature and Postcolonial Theory

I suggested earlier that the moral philosophy implicit in late twentieth-century postcolonial theory—which heavily valorized all kinds of mixing and melding over any kind of separation or division—may now have been superseded by a new identitarianism. Is there anything to be gained by looking back to those earlier sources? After all, the hoaxes that are of interest in this study, especially the Francophone cases yet to be reviewed, are utterly postcolonial.

We might indeed consider intercultural hoaxes as a form of hybridity (à la Homi Bhabha), blurring boundaries and disrupting essentialisms. If that is what a hoax does, then it overlaps with the principal goal of postcolonial theory: the deconstruction of essentialism. The intercultural hoax is an "interstice," no doubt, and may seem to be the very definition of Bhabha's hybridity as "the repetition of discriminatory identity effects."[133] This is literally the case with, for example, *The Education of Little Tree*: Asa "Forrest" Carter *repeated* as a (fake) Cherokee the "discrimination" of the North against the South that so defined his worldview. But we cannot for an instant say that that novel "unsettles the . . . demands of colonial power" or of essentialism (as Bhabha claims of hybridity): Carter wrote in *defense* of essentialism, simply disguising Southern racism as Cherokee nostalgia.[134] Once again, the temptation to celebrate the art of the hoax keeps running into the wall of inequality, discrimination, and power. The cases in which a hoax succeeds in unsettling colonial power—with a time delay—are those anthropological or historical inquiries that I mentioned at the beginning of this study: the fooling of Margaret Mead and Alex Haley by their informants.

An intercultural hoax also, indubitably, wreaks havoc with Gayatri Spivak's canonical postcolonial question, which is famously rhetorical: "Can the subaltern speak?" We have seen that to be the case almost without exception in the examples reviewed so far: the ventriloquism of hoaxes produces simulacra of subaltern voices. If a hoax deconstructs an identity, we have seen, the result may well be, in the end, a reinforcement rather than a destruction of unequal majority/minority power relations. Usurping a minority voice that has little if any bandwidth in the global economy of representation, the hoaxer may further contribute to, rather than remediate, the silence of the subaltern. Thus, difference ostensibly erased through hybridity becomes difference reinforced through inequality. Sad!

An essay by Jaime Hanneken takes us beyond those overused terms and helps define a better context for this study. In "Scandal, Choice, and the Economy of Minority Literature," Hanneken examines the place of "scandal"—of which ethnic hoaxing or impersonation is just one kind—in "the economy of minority literature." (As Hanneken points out, the category of "minority" literature of course requires adjustment and critique for the French context, since France is "notoriously averse to the politics of recognition," or *communautarisme*.)[135] Hanneken writes, "The archive of minority literature of the past half-century abounds with polemical cases of mistaken identity, literary pilfering and purported malfeasance." He cites Rigoberta Menchú, Yambo Ouologuem, Calixthe Beyala, and the American examples *The Education of Little Tree*, *Sarah*, and *Famous All Over Town*.[136] All defy Western notions of personhood and authority—the inseparability of identity and things, objects. "People are, in a sense, what they have" (51); I have, therefore I am. Extended into the domain of literature, this means, as Mark Rose explains, that with the dawn of copyright, "A work was also the objectification of a writer's self, and the commodity that changed hands when a bookseller purchased a manuscript or a reader purchased a book was as much personality as ink and paper."[137] The *equity* value of a minority life story in a majority publishing context—to adapt Hanneken's terms here—derives from the cultural capital of knowledge about *real* minority identities:

> The value of minority literature depends upon its representation of a culturally different, oppressed and/or exotic life, which is only valid if it can be attributed to the real life of a free, inalienable subject, who is free and inalienable because he or she made and sold the story.[138]

This is essentially the argument that was made in court against Laura Albert by the film production company: we purchased not just a literary property but a life, a real personality. In plain terms, exoticism sells, and exoticism requires (the illusion of) authenticity. People want to know about foreign lands (including West Virginia and East Los Angeles) and the peculiar habits of those who live there. Without that exotic capital and its foundations in identity and difference, the whole thing collapses. Intercultural hoaxes feed on this system like parasites, until they are revealed, at which point they threaten the system itself. How much fake exoticism can the system tolerate?

But to look at the problem from a different, more Aristotelian angle, if "all writers are cultural impersonators," as Gates asserts, then intercultural hoaxes are not a big deal. In this spirit, Rajagopalan Radhakrishnan "minoritizes the [entire] world" (as Hanneken puts it) by deconstructing the difference between majority and minority discourses.[139] An intercultural impostor like Paul Smaïl/Jack-Alain Léger is not so much appropriating or exploiting an identity different from his own as he is revealing what he considers to be the hoax of identity itself.

This puts us inside a classic conundrum of postcolonial theory: the world is divided between those who divide the world and those who don't. (Those who don't divide the world are morally superior to those who do.) Those who invest in distinctions such as majority and minority risk perpetuating colonial paradigms; those who don't, dismissing identity as a mirage, risk ignoring the persistence of those same paradigms in the postcolonial world. Hanneken's solution to this is to "refocus minority literature and scandal through the lens of economy," and more specifically through Amartya Sen's theory of rational choice.[140] While borrowing from that approach (to which I will return in my reading of the Paul Smaïl affair), I note that Hanneken did not take his analysis into a diachronic, before-and-after consideration of the Smaïl affair, to unpack the evolving and no doubt nuanced "choices" that readers made as the affair unfolded. It is in those details, I believe, that the true interest is to be found.

Long ago I examined the disruption of the modern Western literary system that was gleefully perpetrated by Yambo Ouologuem.[141] In *Le Devoir de violence*, he used writing itself, through plagiarism, as a means of wreaking postcolonial literary havoc. Here I am interested in authors who go about the business of disruption from a different angle: by twisting personhood itself, identity itself, through imposture—which Ouologuem did not do; nor Calixthe Beyala more recently. Those two authors retained their own names and personal identities even as they disturbed literary propriety and property. Their very existence was never called into question.

In part 2 I will turn to French and Francophone authors who created or were created as phantom others, through books that went out into the world to wreak havoc with cultural boundaries. In the context of French universalism, these hoaxes have a rather different flavor.

PART 2

French and Francophone, Fraud and Fake

What Is a (French) Author?

In the 1960s and 70s, when French theoreticians asked "what is an author?"—and wondered if he was "dead"—, they did not have impostors in mind. Throwing our question of ethnic hoaxes into the vat of vintage French theory produces some interesting results. Philippe Lejeune wrote:

> In printed texts, responsibility for all enunciation is assumed by a person who is in the habit of placing his *name* on the cover of the book, and on the flyleaf, above or below the title of the volume. The entire existence of the person we call the *author* is summed up by this name: the only mark in the text of an unquestionable world-beyond-the-text, referring to a real person. . . . But the place assigned to this name is essential: it is linked, by a social convention, to the pledge of responsibility of a *real person* . . . a person whose existence is certified by vital statistics [*l'état civil*] and is verifiable.[1]

Reading this normative description through the lens of hoax disturbs almost every element. Lejeune writes like a lawgiver; he uses strong language and italics to emphasize the importance of the author's genuine, authentic, state-certified existence outside the text; and he is at pains to define what a "real person" is. It all depends on the *name*. Lejeune writes later, "We know all too well how attached people are to their names" (26/14). But in a hoax, there is no "indubitable *hors-texte*" because the referent of the name on the cover is not a real person. (For Lejeune the "referential pact" goes along with the autobiographical pact [36/22].) Lejeune in fact anticipated just such cases, of "exceptions and breaches of trust"(23/11):

> Only cases of literary hoaxing [*supercherie littéraire*] . . . would escape this test [of the "fictional pact"]: they are extremely rare—and this rarity is not due to respect for someone else's name or to the fear of penalties. *Who would prevent*

> *me from writing the autobiography of an imaginary character and publishing*
> *it under his equally imaginary name?* It is exactly this, in a slightly different
> domain, that MacPherson did for Ossian! *This is rare, because few authors are*
> *capable of renouncing their own name.* [italics in original][2]

As this book demonstrates, the scarcity of hoaxes, including in France, is not
what Lejeune seems to think it is. Underestimating hoaxes and their importance, Lejeune has in these few lines described exactly how a hoax works,
while completely misunderstanding the motivations of literary hoaxers.
(They are never troubled about "renouncing their own name." They want,
sometimes desperately, to acquire *another* name.) As Nejiba Regaieg points
out, in the Paul Smaïl novels we are precisely inside the case discounted by
Lejeune, something "almost unheard of."[3] So we can begin from the premise that intercultural literary hoaxes of the kind that are so prevalent in the
United States are an exception to the (Lejeune) rule in France. But that is just
the tip of the iceberg.

Lejeune wrote that in 1975. We saw Barthes's death certificate for the author, written in 1968, in part 1; what it left in place was *écriture*, in which "the
voice loses its origin, the author enters his own death, writing begins." The
third major voice questioning authorship, perhaps the loudest of all, was of
course that of Foucault, who in 1969 gave a lecture that responded to Barthes:
"Qu'est-ce qu'un auteur?"/"What Is an Author?" If there is a gap between
what Foucault is saying here and what Barthes said about *écriture*, it is not
significant for our purposes. Foucault was not thinking about hoaxes (with
one exception), but much of what he says sheds light on our analysis here. His
most basic question, which he says is "ethical," goes to the heart of hoaxing:
"What does it matter who is speaking?"[4] It is a rhetorical question (borrowed
from Beckett). We have seen that defenders of impostures say that it does
not matter who is talking or writing: it's the work itself that counts; detractors claim the opposite and assert that rights of self-representation must be
respected. Foucault's aim in his essay was to show how little it matters who
is talking (or writing), to take the "transcendent" author down from his ped-
estal. But before he gets to that, he first writes in a constative, descriptive
mode, asking in effect, What has an author been? And in that context, which
involves questions of property, authority, and authenticity, he mentions one
very interesting French hoax.

In 1949 a supposedly "lost" text by Rimbaud, *La Chasse spirituelle*, was
published. The twenty-five-page prose poem was a fake. The forgery was
eventually called "the most extensive and remarkable *scandale littéraire* in the
history of Rimbaud studies and of French letters." It put criticism, specifically

that done by purely internal reading, "on trial" and revealed it to be "helpless to decide" about authenticity.[5] The case was peculiar because the perpetrators, Nicolas Bataille and Marie-Antoinette Emilie Allevy (known as Akakia-Viala), tried to put a stop to it before it even appeared in print, only to find that some critics would not let themselves be persuaded that the text was not real. The battle that ensued was a case study in the failures of forensic reading: textual "proofs" of one kind or another were deployed, but they could not demonstrate anything; some who claimed to have discovered the fraud by reading alone in fact had already learned that the text was fake.[6] Foucault comments about this: "When we discover that Rimbaud did not write *La Chasse spirituelle*, we cannot claim that the meaning of this proper name, or that of the author, has been altered" (6, AT). In other words, this hoax did nothing to affect a well-established brand. But, he goes on to say, if it turned out that Shakespeare did not write the sonnets attributed to him, that *would* "constitute a significant change and affect the manner in which the author's name functions" (7).[7] So impostures are not all created equal, and they can have consequences. *Ecriture* or not, the name of the author is not just "one element in a discourse," it plays "a certain role" and has "a certain status." That is nothing new. But one of the characteristics that Foucault attributes to the author-function resonates strongly with hoax texts: "It does not refer purely and simply to a real individual, since it can give rise simultaneously to several selves, to several subjects—positions that can be occupied by different classes of individuals" (113). The author-function of a hoax text answers to that description perfectly, including often the difference of social class that is collapsed by the imposture.

One other passing remark in the early pages of the essay deserves attention. Foucault says that the name of the author "is not to be found in the civil registry office, *nor in the fiction of the work*."[8] Not normally. But in a hoax, of course, the author's name *is itself* fictional and is intrinsic to the overall purpose of the work; that fact is concealed, creating a deliberate disturbance in the system that Foucault describes. This is the case that Lejeune called "rare," and it is our main concern in this study.

Moving beyond his description of what the author-function has been, Foucault shifts to a mode that is prescriptive and utopian; this is what made the essay famous. The author is an obsolete construct and almost a form of tyranny; it stands in the way of something new and better: "The author is not an indefinite source of significations which fill a work; the author does not precede the work. He is a certain functional principle by which, in our culture, one limits, excludes, and chooses; in short, by which one impedes *the free circulation, decomposition, and recomposition of fiction*."[9] In this passage on the "free circulation" of fiction—passed indifferently from subject to subject, group to group, without ownership—Foucault came close to writing a manifesto for imposture. No sooner does Foucault float this idea than he critiques it as "romanticism," but he does not drop it; he is positive that "the author function will disppear." His last word is "What difference does it make who is speaking?" ("Qu'importe qui parle"). Foucault does not know exactly what new creature will replace the author-function, but he is certain that it will dwell beyond questions of authenticity and realism. Instead of "Who really spoke?" we will ask, "What are the modes of existence of this discourse? . . . and, *Who can appropriate it for himself?*" As it happens, these are the very questions that we have been asking about hoaxes. But we ask them not because the author is dead; that is an exaggeration. We ask them precisely because the notion of authorship remains very much alive, and very much in dispute. Literary hoaxes are texts with more than one perceived author, more than one "mode of existence," more than one meaning. So it is interesting to see Foucault raise "our" question of appropriation; he sees this in the positive, countercultural spirit of free circulation. But we already have seen and will continue to see that *appropriation is not always free, is not always evenly distributed, and can wreak havoc.* Pace Barthes and Foucault, we still seem to care "who is speaking." Even in French.[10]

The French Paradox and the Francophone Problem

In order to explore French and Francophone intercultural hoaxes, one must confront the very different paths of identity and difference that run, initially, between France and the outside world, and, after immigration, between different groups inside France. The hoaxes that are of interest here, since they follow those paths and exploit French assumptions about identity, may shed a different light on the issues we have seen so far.

If Americans believe in "fluid" classes and "fixed" races, what do the French believe about identity, and what are they escaping through these hoaxes? The twin ideas of universalism and assimilation have permeated French Republican colonialism and postcolonial discourse. Frenchness is a universal category to which anyone may, in principle, accede, regardless of origin; whiteness is not supposed to be required. On the other hand, *communautarisme*, as the French call it (multiculturalism, ghettoization), remains anathema; this indicates the delicate status of difference itself. The center/periphery dichotomy is far from obsolete.

Centripetal forces pull colonial and postcolonial subjects toward the French language, Paris, and Republican Frenchness. French ethnic and cultural impostors work against that current, manufacturing strangeness at and from the center, disturbing Frenchness, and disrupting universalism. Or do they? Isn't it just as possible that these hoaxes, in the end, validate universal French culture by successfully "performing" otherness within certain frameworks and institutions, thereby weakening community boundaries? If so, they are Trojan Horses of phony otherness inside France.

A French critic wrote a tongue-in-cheek "Little Guide to Literary Fraud" in the magazine *Gulliver* in 1972. Gilles Lambert advised that the best approach may be to "invent" a person, then write his or her "memoirs." "Being non-existent, the signatory will never contest the document; any protests will be vague" and therefore not dangerous. This fairly describes what Jack-Alain Léger did in *Vivre me tue*, but in fact the exercise *did* prove to be rather risky. What Lambert's proposal fails to anticipate—perhaps because it is a blind spot in French Republican universalist culture—is a backlash against cross-cultural identity usurpation. When the invented pseudo-author is supposed to be from a constituted minority, when a culture seems to have been stolen or appropriated, some may object, even in France.[11]

France has an extremely rich tradition of literary hoaxes. Existing studies of French and Francophone literary hoaxes have not focused on the issue of intercultural posing, cultural impersonators, or "ethnic usurpation."[12] Among the few critics who have noticed the difference between the French and American contexts, Lia Brozgal describes a "lower incidence of so-called ethnic usurpation in French literature," and she goes so far as to assert that Paul Smaïl's *Vivre me tue* "may be the first of its kind in France" (3). In fact, further scrutiny reveals a far longer and deeper tradition of ethnic posing in French and Francophone literature. In the remainder of this book, I will explore that tradition, with a particular focus, in part 3, on *Vivre me tue* and its "*affaire*."

*

Francophone literature has been dogged by questions of authenticity since its beginnings. Because of the divide between colonizing and colonized cultures, marked in the early decades by the difference in French-language literacy—which alone counted—the field was full of doubts, impostures, and opportunities. France held an institutional monopoly on the French language, its literacy, and its literature, thereby creating a playing field that can be called, with some understatement, uneven. African literature was forged between two imperatives that were not necessarily reconcilable: on the one hand, to be authentic to Africa, and, on the other, to adhere to French notions of language, literacy, and literature (which, incidentally, snuck the ideology of universalism in with them).[13] The tension between those two needs created a space in which both African authenticity and French literacy could be and would be faked. Mischief done in this field can shake the ideas of "African literature," "Parisianism," and "authenticity" to their core.

Critics have taken various viewpoints on issues of inauthenticity in African literature, ranging from the accusatory to the defensive and the explanatory. A special issue of *Research in African Literatures* explored this history through the lens of "textual ownership," which is slightly different from the approach that I have been taking here; the work in that volume will be cited here frequently. Questions about authenticity, as the proper authorship and ownership of the text, have been raised about Bakary Diallo, Elissa Rhaïs, Camara Laye, Sembene Ousmane, Yambo Ouologuem, Calixthe Beyala, and numerous other authors.[14] I am concerned here only with those cases in which an intercultural imposture seems to have taken place.

Koffi Anyinefa addresses the "persistence of scandal in the history of Francophone African literature." Most of the cases he reviews involved plagiarism, which is not our main concern here, but which does help make an important connection. A "recidivist plagiarist" like Calixthe Beyala (who reproduced words written by Romain Gary, one of our subjects here, among others) was able to dress her literary practice in a theory of "free circulation" that is reminiscent of both Barthes and Foucault, on the one hand, and African traditions of orality on the other. That exact confluence is visible in this defense by Beyala, in which she plays both the race card and the theory card:

> As a backwoods, barefoot African woman, I have always thought—along with certain French intellectuals—that literature was in perpetual movement, that a text is never closed, but that, like a river, it found its interest and its place in the all-universal by enriching itself: upstream with its sources, and downstream with its encounters with other texts. . . . I come from a civilization of orality. . . . By that fact, history belongs to everyone and to no one, to the person who inhabits it, transmits it, makes it come alive! What is literature? Has it no movement, is it not transmitted?[15]

Plagiarism, the literal appropriation (or theft) of another writer's words, is not exactly the same as imposture, the appropriation of someone else's experiences and culture. But the parallels are nonetheless striking. Beyala's defense could be that of any number of the impostors analyzed in this study, many of whom claim to be following a higher truth and a more "fluid" model of culture than their detractors can possibly understand. And, as Anyinefa points out, her strategy has worked: she remains one of the few African writers to achieve commercial success, and she has paid little price for her plagiarism. It has been a "profitable strategy" (469).

There is an important distinction to be made between acts of plagiarism committed by African writers such as Ousmane Sembene, Yambo Ouologuem, or Calixthe Beyala, on the one hand, and the usurping of colonized, oral, or minority cultures by impostors such as Mérimée, Romain Gary, Jack-Alain Léger, and those who may have written works signed by Camara Laye. It is the distinction of a power imbalance that we have seen throughout part 1 of this study: impostures tend to work from the top down, appropriating voices and experiences (that of the slave, the prostitute, the youth, the colonized, the minority), trafficking in ersatz authenticity. Plagiarism, on the other hand, tends to reach "upwards," from colonized to colonizer, "borrowing" or stealing French literacy and literature: Yambo Ouologuem stole from André Schwartz-Bart and Graham Greene. I have identified only one moment of actual intersection between these two currents—when Calixthe Beyala plagiarized Romain Gary—to be explored below. Understanding those countercurrents helps to establish the context of colonial and postcolonial French and Francophone literature that we enter now.

The hoaxes and impostures that I have selected for this review do not add up to a complete survey by any means. However, I think the cumulative effect will be to demonstrate the existence of a rich French-language tradition of intercultural, differential imposture. I have used two main criteria of selection: the compelling nature of the intercultural hoax, and a need for new commentary that places the work in the context of this tradition. (As in part 1 of this study, I use the term "intercultural" to cover a wide variety of differences.) Moving from Diderot in the eighteenth century through Mérimée in the nineteenth, we will see how the groundwork is established for all the murky ethical questions that hoaxes generate in the twentieth century and beyond. I aim to remain attentive to issues of power difference between the colonizer and the colonized, as colonialism itself rises and falls over time. This journey spans "French" and "Francophone" literatures, the relations between which have preoccupied writers and critics for decades.[16] As African writer-names such as Bakary Diallo, Elissa Rhaïs, and Camara Laye emerge, the playing field is not level, and the stakes of fraud are high. Above all, this adventure requires a fluid perspective and an enjoyment of vertigo.

The Real, the Romantic, and the Fake in the Nineteenth Century

To give some sense of the volume and tradition of hoaxing in the long history of French literature, consider that in the middle of the nineteenth century, between 1845 and 1853, Joseph-Marie Quérard published *Les Supercheries littéraires dévoilées*—"literary hoaxes unveiled"—and it took him five volumes.[17]

Numerous fake aristocrats were exposed and cried foul, but the work was huge and solid, if still inadequate to cover the subject.[18] In his preface, Quérard practically threw up his hands in despair: "Who could possibly unveil all the mysteries with which half of nineteenth-century French literature has enveloped itself?"[19] (His corrupt object is thus *half* of the French literature of *half* of a century, and it is still too much.) Quérard's nearly obsessive effort was preceded by an important treatise on "questions of legal literature, plagiarism, . . . and hoaxes" by Charles Nodier in 1812.[20] (As a critic points out, while ostensibly condemning all literary shenanigans, Nodier managed to compose a veritable "how-to" guide for fraud.)[21] With the emergence of copyright and author's rights, literature was tightening up, and one way to do that was to stigmatize rogues. In 1872, Octave Delepierre published *Supercheries littéraires*, asserting that "literary hoaxes are frequent" in all periods, that Quérard's prosecutorial approach was too harsh, but that, at the time of Mérimée in the 1820s, "literary lies were found everywhere in France, even in sermons."[22]

Quérard's Javert-like detective work was done in defense of "*le bon goût et les saines lettres*" and in order to eliminate "*confusion*" in the archives. What he calls "*industrialisme*" (mass production), far from eliminating fraud, has only increased it: "*le travestissement*" is a "mode or fashion that is propagating itself more and more among our writers," although all their hoaxes "are not blamable to the same degree" (3). All are "*crimes de lèze-littérature*" (93).

To state the obvious: that is not the view I have taken in this book. If anything, there is something *particularly* literary about a hoax, because it is a fiction about a fiction. While the work of bibliographers and librarians may be complicated—sometimes to the point of madness—by anonymity, pseudonyms, and hoaxes, literature itself is enriched. But, as we have seen, some are indeed "blamable."

What was Quérard reacting to? Hoaxes are no doubt as old as literature itself. There were faked texts in circulation during Quérard's time whose real authorship was only revealed much later, in the twentieth century. The famous *Lettres portugaises* (1669), a book that was thought to be made up of real, authentic letters—contributing significantly to the rise of the epistolary genre—was, in 1926, alleged to have been authored by the man who had claimed to be merely the translator, the viscount Guilleragues. This also meant that the work belonged to French literature rather than Portuguese, and male instead of female. *Lettres portugaises* resembles and foreshadows the themes of Diderot's *The Nun*, which we will examine: confinement and the yearning for liberation.[23] If Guilleragues was the author, rather than the Portuguese nun Marianna da Costa Alcoforado—a fact that remains in dispute—then this was one of the longest-lasting impostures in literary history (257 years).[24]

Some form of fake name or status was the norm rather than the exception for French writers in the nineteenth century: Honoré "de" Balzac (fake nobility), Stendhal and Nerval (fake names), George Sand (fake name and gender), and so on.[25] In *Aesthetics of Fraudulence*, Scott Carpenter argues that the period beginning with the Revolution and "extending through much of the nineteenth century" was one in which "issues of falseness [were] particularly sensitive."[26] Fraudulence, he explains, "becomes all the more scandalous at times when authenticity is held in especially high esteem," such as during the rise of realism, originality, transparency, and sincerity in literature—all qualities that emerged and gained great credibility with Madame de Staël's *De l'Allemagne*.[27] The way of truth was ascendant, but embattled.

The word for hoax in French is playful and bizarre: *supercherie*. It is pronounced, exceptionally, with the accent on the second syllable, not the penultimate one; it is not "super-chérie." From the Italian *soperchieria* (*soverchieria* in modern Italian) meaning excess or affront, a *supercherie* is something over-the-top. Its meaning in French evolved from insult to fraud before 1694 (*Dictionnaire de l'Académie Française*). The *Littré* of 1873 defines it as *une tromperie faite avec finesse* (a trick done with finesse), emphasizing what we have seen and will see a lot more of in this study: a good *supercherie* is a work of art. (There is no noun to describe someone who performs a *supercherie*.) I will not insist on parsing distinctions between *supercheries, mystifications, canulars, impostures*, and other French terms roughly covered by the English term "hoax."

*

The fraud that cast possibly the longest shadow over European literature in the nineteenth century was that of Ossian. The great twentieth-century French hoaxer, Romain Gary, cited only one predecessor in his posthumous confessional narrative: Ossian, a fake third-century (CE) bard invented in 1760 by James MacPherson, a Scotsman.[28] According to Donald Rayfield, this fake "British Homer," "this massively successful misrepresentation of Gaelic oral poetry . . . altered the course of literature from England to Russia."[29] There were dozens of editions of *The Poems of Ossian* in English and translations into all the major languages of Europe. If the hoax was denounced relatively quickly, by Dr. Samuel Johnson, in England, it lived on, like a wandering zombie, throughout Europe. The Ossian phenomenon had a large impact in France, where Chateaubriand embedded its ideology and tropes in his thinking, thus implanting a fake element at the very roots of French romanticism. It is therefore no surprise that Chateaubriand's American Indians sound like MacPherson's fake Gaelic warriors. Diderot, Jefferson, Napoleon, and Ingres were all enthralled. William Hazlitt placed Ossian on a par with only Homer, the Bible, and Dante.[30] What was the appeal? Ossian's works appeared to be natural "savage" poetry, "free from the falsifications [ironically!] of . . . civilization."[31] This is therefore an early and important example of the dynamic that we keep seeing in this study: the market demand for works from beyond the realm of literacy induces impostures. Ossian no doubt inspired Mérimée's faking of an Eastern European oral work, a subject to be examined here soon.

The Single-Use Hoax: Diderot's *La Religieuse*

Our first French case study actually takes us back before literature was made "legal," tightened up, and controlled. The status of the author and of his or her text in the eighteenth century was much more loosely defined (although certainly subject to the whims and the censorship of the crown). Denis Diderot embodied a very complex set of "author-functions" (to use Foucault's term): he ghost-rewrote the works of others, including Raynal's *Histoire des deux Indes*; he borrowed and plagiarized "brazenly"; he edited the *Encyclopédie*, which justified its borrowings as "compiling"; he disrupted the conventions of the novel in *Jacques le fataliste*.[32] And he was the author of perhaps the most famous hoax in the history of French literature, which had only one real victim (and there is some doubt about him, actually). This is a special case. Diderot's novel *La Religieuse* grew out of a series of letters sent to a marquis in Normandy, seeking to lure him back to Paris with a *mystification*. He was apparently fooled, believing he was getting letters from a real nun in distress, when in fact Diderot was the author. But from the moment the letters were published as *La Religieuse*, and ever since, a "preface-annex" has explained the hoax and therefore prevented anyone who reads it (which is not everyone) from being fooled. So the hoax, strictly speaking, only had an audience of one, surely unique in this history. But no one can say how many readers have failed to read the preface or paid it no attention, thus leaving themselves open to thinking the nun was real.

The word *mystification* was coined in middle of the eighteenth century in French, and its importance for the Enlightenment's task of *demystification* is obvious.[33] In English and in French it can refer to specific acts and is thus a synonym for farce, practical joke, or hoax, anything designed to pull the wool over someone's eyes. For philosophes with a sense of humor, it was a rich vein, and they "co-opted mystification."[34] A literary hoax created in this context and in this spirit could be a mystification in support of demystification. That is in keeping with the etymology of *mystification*: the Latin *myste* indicated "he who was initiated to the mysteries." As Ora Avni explains, "A lie becomes a mystification *because* it is an initiation to a truth of a higher order."[35] The deeper meaning of mystification is thus is keeping with the pleas of many hoaxers we have seen: I was sincerely trying to communicate some higher or inner truth.

That is what Diderot's novel *La Religieuse* did, eventually. He who once wrote that "nothing is more contrary to the progress of knowledge than mystery"[36] used mystery in the service of progress and truth—and fun.[37] To understand this novel in its dimension as a hoax, it must be studied in the chronological order of its composition, publication, and reception. Written between August and November of 1760, the text was not originally conceived as a novel but as an elaborate ruse—Diderot called it a *mystification*—in the form of a series of fake-real missives from a fake-real nun, locked in a convent and subjected to all kinds of torment. It was set up to hoax the Marquis de Croismare, sixty-six years old and a denizen of Parisian salons. In 1758 he retired to his chateau near Caen, and after fifteen months his friends, including Grimm and Diderot, finding him "irreplaceable," conspired to lure him back. That is the genesis of *La Religieuse*. Remembering a real incident involving a nun, Marguerite Delamarre, who sued to be released from her vows, without success, and how compelling the marquis had found the case, Diderot composed a long letter to the marquis *as if* from a nun in the same situation of involuntary confinement, asking for his intervention and aid. The marquis suspected nothing; he was taken in by the hoax. But instead of returning to Paris, he invited the nun to Normandy to serve as chamber maid to his daughter. This was, then, a white lie in two ways: the real purpose was to inveigle the marquis to return to his friends in Paris, which is simply an expression of friendship; but on another, more lasting level, the text used in the original hoax, once published, became one of the great Enlightenment pleas for liberty. The nun's status as a virtual prisoner makes this hoax highly relevant to the context of inequality in which almost all impostures seem to arise.

The letters that the marquis received and read purported to be from one Suzanne Simonin, who said "no" to her vows but was made a nun anyway; she later says she was unconscious when taking her "profession."[38] She constantly resists injustice and is persecuted and tortured for it. She finds a way to sue for her own freedom, and her case has obvious echoes with other struggles for freedom in the eighteenth century such as the abolition of slavery. As her main letter (or "memoirs," 198/144) goes on, Suzanne becomes a mouthpiece for the values of the Enlightenment: justice and, especially, *liberty* (a word she uses constantly and which her lawyer calls "man's inalienable prerogative," 121/75). "Kill your daughter," she memorably tells the marquis, "rather than see her imprisoned in a cloister against her will; yes, kill her" (104/60, AT).

She proffers some powerful rhetorical questions, of a "protestant" nature and sounding a lot like a philosophe: "Are convents so essential to the constitution of a State? Did Jesus Christ institute monks and nuns?" (119/74). In her third convent, Suzanne is subjected to the constant advances of a lesbian "madwoman," the mother superior. The theme of lesbianism and its complex treatment has at times tended to overshadow the rest of the novel.

Suzanne affirms, "I am reporting nothing that is not true" (202/147). She flees to Paris and is working for a laundress at the time of writing to the marquis. This finally completes the hoax, setting the marquis up to come to Paris: "Monsieur, make haste to help me" (206/151). She wants him to "change her fate" (39/3, AT). The end of the novel consists of sixteen letters, three from Suzanne to the marquis and the others between an intermediary, Madame Madin (actually Diderot), and an increasingly distraught marquis, as he learns about the illness and, finally, the death of the nun.

Suzanne's tales of woe, like those in *Go Ask Alice*, have entertainment value. Both texts subverted their own ostensible purposes, which were twofold: first, anthropological documentation of an "alien" culture, and second, inducing aversion (to convents and drugs respectively); they went further by providing titillation to readers. The exploitation of same-sex desire in both novels is certainly no coincidence, conforming as it does to the dual purposes of repulsion and thrill. Both books have been banned or censored at times.[39] There is no ethnic differential in *La Religieuse*, but there is a considerable gulf between the class status, gender, and "estate" of the philosophe hoaxers, on the one hand, and the person whose voice they are appropriating, on the other: the nun (both the real Marguerite Delamarre and the fictional Suzanne Simonin). Convent culture was by definition walled off from society, and *La Religieuse* gave readers a forbidden glimpse through the walls. Writing as Suzanne—a "feminine image that Diderot has constructed to hide behind *and* to identify with"[40]—, Diderot was crossing the gender line and speaking as a woman. He was writing in what is called a "heterostyle"—a style not the author's own, as a form of disguise.[41] This involved code switching: adopting a "simple and spontaneous style . . . considered typically feminine" at the time; the fake Suzanne describes her own style as without "skill or artifice."[42] But by the time the novel was published, Diderot had given up on fooling anyone with the text, and on passing as a woman; identification with Suzanne and her plight became paramount. Although, as Béatrice Durand explains, with the annex printed at the *end* of the novel, "readers may still be fooled" by *La Religieuse*.[43] Like *Go Ask Alice* and so many other hoax texts, the possibility of being taken in does not die when the trick is unveiled. Knowing that the writer is a man allows critics to point to his "obvious presence as a male in the text," including a male voyeuristic interest in lesbianism.[44] But if they did not know, would they be able to tell—by forensic reading alone, like Dickens? The marquis did not. It is always easy to see "through" a mask after it has been removed. The purposes and effects of this gender-borrowing were complex, but I would say from the outset that if, on the one hand, the hoaxing of the marquis was a "sin," on the other hand, a novel giving voice to a young woman whose freedom has been denied was not.

If the hoax succeeded perfectly in creating a false reality—the marquis wrote letters seeking to free the nun and give her a stable and safe situation in his household—it failed to have the desired effect of luring the marquis to Paris. It was eight years later, when he finally returned, that the marquis was let in on the secret—and laughed.[45]

That was the end of the real hoax. But the text—the outpouring of a horrific and compelling story of oppression—still existed, and was deeply meaningful for Diderot, whose own sister had died, mentally ill, in a convent in 1748. So his engagement, unlike that of so many other hoaxers we have seen, was not exploitative: he was not stealing or appropriating the suffering of others (of another gender and another station in life). He was giving voice to the voiceless.

Scholars have not entirely failed to point out that the techniques of fakery deployed for the original hoax were carried over and expanded when the text was transformed into a novel.[46] If a hoax is a fiction about a fiction, *La Religieuse* is thus a real-life hoax turned into fiction, a fiction that reveals the working of a hoax. A revised version of the text, including the *préface-annexe*, was published in nine installments in a periodical between 1780 and 1782. The novel as such was not published in Diderot's lifetime; his hands were full with the *Encyclopédie*, and *La Religieuse* could have sent him back to prison.[47] It appeared in 1796, Year V of the Revolution, and bore Diderot's name, thus obviating any hoax: Suzanne was fictive. Still some critics admired the verisimilitude and "the *illusion* of reading authentic memoirs."[48] Georges May long ago dismissed the myth that Suzanne was taken for real in 1796, but that is not the whole story.

The *préface-annexe*—composed in 1770 by Grimm and written in his voice, but corrected by and therefore coauthored by Diderot—has been an integral part of the novel since 1780. (The title is certainly confusing: is it supposed to come before or after the text?) It is an important document in the history of literary hoaxes, a kind of how-to manual: it reveals how the prank was set up, referring to "the author of the preceding memoirs," Diderot, by name. The affaire is described as the morally dubious enterprise that it no doubt was: the group of friends sat around "with fits of laughter" reading "letters that would make the good marquis weep," along with his sincere and credulous replies. This was "wickedness," "knavery," "blackness," and "sin."[49] As this vocabulary shows, there is a tone of delighted pseudo-confession in this text ("our contrition," 211/155). The reader, invited behind the curtain of the hoax, is clearly meant to continue and perpetuate the laughter at the expense of the hapless marquis. The narrator says that the marquis took it in good humor when the hoax was revealed to him years later, but never spoke to Diderot about it. Diderot himself was captivated by the tale he had created, discovered crying over it by one of his friends (211/154). So if the hoax against the marquis was an exercise in cynicism, the hoax text itself was anything but, as any reader can attest.

The real letters from the Marquis de Croismare to the fictive Suzanne Simonin that are included in the novel called *La Religieuse* are a voice from inside the bubble of the hoax, the voice of the dupe. The annex tells us that they "are real and were written in good faith"—the very opposite of all the letters written by Diderot (211/155). The letters from the fake Madame Madin play him and manipulate his kindness, finally driving in the dagger of Suzanne's death. Here she (Diderot) kills off the nun, for whom the marquis has shown the greatest concern: "The dear child is no more, her sufferings are ended, and ours may last a very long time" (243/175, AT). The marquis replied:

> You knew her, and that is what makes your separation from her so hard to bear. Even without having enjoyed that advantage, I was keenly touched by her misfortunes and was able to anticipate the pleasure of being able to add to the peacefulness of her existence. . . . Everything related to the memory of our ill-fated friend has become extremely dear to me. Would it be asking too great a sacrifice of you to ask you to send me the memoirs and the notes that she wrote about her various misfortunes? I ask you this favor, Madame. . . . (244/176–77).

Did *those* words provoke peals of laughter from the assembled salonniers? In the annex, Grimm and Diderot congratulate the marquis for the role he played in the correspondence, "not the least touching aspect of the novel" (245/177), and claim that the group of hoaxers was as sad about the nun's death as was the marquis. But of course only the marquis thought she was really alive, and really dead.

Or did he? An essay published in 1962 suggested the possibility (shaky, in my view) that marquis was *not* a dupe, at least not for long; that he "saw through the joke from an early stage."[50] That would make him a tacit coconspirator in the hoax, which would in turn hoax the interpretation that I have been offering. Such is the hall of mirrors of hoaxes. This is a nonbinary hoax: it is not a simple choice of real or fake. The "truth" of *La Religieuse* is more complex than that. We can't know exactly "who was being taken in, and by whom, and for how long."[51]

So this novel allows us to ask—and demands that we consider—whether a hoax can march on like a zombie even after the author himself has exposed it: "If I show you on the one hand the real-life trick, and on the other hand the story it produced, can you still be made to believe in Suzanne and her touching end?" (as a critic paraphrases Diderot).[52] If readers could think that Rousseau's Julie and Saint-Preux were real and model their lives on them (and that Rousseau was just the publisher of their letters), they could certainly think that Suzanne Simonin was real.[53] Georges May explains the lengths to which Diderot went in order to make his novel believable, including the use of real convent names. The asterisks used in certain names of people (Madame la présidente de ***) only heighten the impression of realism—or, as recognizable artifice, can have the opposite effect on a savvy reader, "calling attention to the fictionality of the work."[54] But as readers, don't we often ignore inconsistencies that interfere with our enjoyment of a text through immersion in its illusions?

The novel ends with a "question for people of letters," which echoes one I have been asking about hoaxes since the beginning of this study. Grimm and Diderot claim, in this, the last words of the novel, that while concocting the hoax, Diderot threw out everything that would compromise its realism (*vraisemblance*); he did this under the advice of his wife and the coconspirators. His first drafts were "beautiful," but the final versions were "true"—to the artifice of the hoax. The "question" is, Which was "better"? *Quelles sont les bonnes [lettres]?* Time and again in this study we have seen competing versions of the "good." A good hoax is not always a good deed. The quality or artfulness of the hoax itself, our "Aristotelian" option, always seems to be at odds with the "Platonic" truth, violated by the hoax. By asking us, "Which were the good letters?" Diderot reframes that question for us, but does not answer. In fact, no answer is necessary: if we bracket the pain suffered by the marquis when he learned of Suzanne's death, the letters that we have are "good" from both points of view. And that makes this hoax exceptional in yet another way.

La Religieuse has lived on, mainly and not entirely accurately taken as an Enlightenment critique of religion and of convents in particular.[55] Its exceptional status in the history of hoaxes stems not only from its visible trickery but, perhaps more importantly, from the power of its cry for freedom and self-determination. No matter who was being hoaxed, by whom, or for how long, the voice of Suzanne Simonin, subaltern, continues to speak.[56]

Mérimée's Illyrical Illusions

Several factors contributed to the rise of the French intercultural hoax in the nineteenth century. Expanding colonial horizons made otherness or "local color" both more accessible and of greater cultural and political import. The institutionalization of literature as a legal phenomenon, subject to greater control, meant that practices that had been normative in the past, such as extensive borrowing, became transgressions like plagiarism. Literature became a legal question, subject to copyright and sanction, with increased emphasis on the single author and his/her identity and rights of ownership.[57] Now there was something to steal. Finally, there was the rise of the "generation of 1820"—Mérimée, Hugo, Delacroix, Sainte-Beuve. Chafing under the gerontocracy of the Restoration, these young men sought something more in exoticism, romanticism, and Orientalism. Bringing all these threads together, Prosper Mérimée had a burst of creativity in the late 1820s that renovated the relations between French literature and the outside world and raised new questions about writerly authenticity.

How many authors begin their writing careers as someone else, with a pseudonym or a hoax? Those French and English *women* writers who did this—from George Sand to the Brontës and George Eliot—made a straightforward, practical use of falsehood, in order to overcome gender barriers. But why would a male author, in the same period, do the opposite, disguising his literary identity in female drag, even going so far as to have a portrait made of himself as a woman? (figure 5). Mérimée invented himself in 1825 as Clara Gazul, a Spanish female playwright, and then in 1827 as Hyacinthe Maglanovich, an Eastern European male bard. Portraits accompanied both publications and helped to shore up the hoax.[58]

In previous work, I found Prosper Mérimée to be an extremely intriguing figure, with a unique role in literary history. In the novella *Tamango*, he created the most indelible image of the slave trade in French literature, an image that Francophone writers and filmmakers have struggled against ever since.[59] But more importantly for our present purposes, Mérimée was a fanatic for otherness. He sought it everywhere, and when he couldn't get to it—he didn't travel very much—he made it up. That is exactly what he did in the text that concerns us most here: *La Guzla*.

In *The French Atlantic Triangle*, I argued that Mérimée is in a very real sense the godfather of Francophone literature. This is not simply because of the genealogical ties—often agonistic ones—that are recognized between French exoticist literature and Francophone literature, although that is part of it. Mérimée's importance is rooted in his actual stylistic practices and specifically in his handling of foreign words in French, which lays the groundwork for the techniques that will be used by colonized and postcolonial writers. Colonialism brought languages into contact with each other, and Mérimée found new ways to accommodate new colonized languages, also known as basilects.[60]

FIGURE 5. Prosper Mérimée (by Etienne Delécluze) as Clara Gazul, in *Théâtre de Clara Gazul* (Paris: A. Sautelet, 1825).

But he began his literary career with a hoax (two, in fact), which is a very different way of engaging with otherness: by faking it. The first hoax is interesting largely because of the gender question; the second one is compelling because it succeeded in a way that the first one did not. Both *Gazul* and *Guzla* work across a North/South divide within Europe.[61]

✳

The title *Théâtre de Clara Gazul* contains the letters of the name "Delécluze." Etienne Delécluze, a friend and patron of Mérimée, also executed the sketch of Mérimée dressed up as a Spanish actress.[62] However, this was not a hoax of the kind that most interests us in this study, for the simple reason that Mérimée was not really trying to fool anyone: Clara Gazul was an allegory rather than an actual disguise. Ora Avni has argued correctly that Mérimée "wasn't trying to 'mystify' his public . . . He fooled no one," and that this was a bit strange, given the popularity of *mystifications* since the eighteenth century (as witnessed by Quérard's outrage and outcry).[63] Mérimée read his Gazul plays aloud before they were published, to assembled groups of friends, who no doubt spread the word about their authorship. Corry Cropper explains: "While Mérimée did not himself actively hide behind Clara, he did hide criticism of France behind Spain."[64] Like Kourouma's "Côte des Ebènes" in *Les Soleils des independances* (but real), Mérimées's Spain is a kind of nominal mask behind which the author was able to criticize his own country. (There was much to criticize: the conservative Restoration was about to get ultraconservative with the crowning of Charles X, only one day after the publication of *Clara Gazul*.)[65] That is a fascinating process, and a use of what Cropper calls literary "subversion" that is deeply resonant, but it is not our main interest here.[66]

*

After not even trying to fool anyone with *Clara Gazul* in 1825, why did Mérimée go to some lengths to create a real and effective hoax with *La Guzla* in 1827? Only his publisher was in on this secret, and, despite excesses of representation that seem obvious to us today (vampires and ghosts, for example), he fooled people with his fake "Illyrian bard." Mérimée's title seems to contain a hint that he is taking us to a land of poetic make-believe: *La Guzla, ou choix de poésies illyriques recueillies dans la Dalmatie, la Bosnie, la Croatie et l'Herzegovine.*[67] His portmanteau word *illyriques* combines the proper geographical term *illyrien* with the idea of the poetic lyric, while suggesting, as Laura Abramson points out, that these poems are *"not* lyrical" (as in "illogical").[68]

The book was graced by a portrait of the fake bard himself, Hyacinthe Maglanovich (figure 6). Mérimée, an armchair traveler, constructed his work by pillaging everything from the Bible to contemporary travel accounts; "so many books," exclaims one scholar.[69]

Years later, in his preface to the second edition of *La Guzla*, Mérimée told a story—itself likely apocryphal—about the origin of *La Guzla*: that he and his friend Jean-Jacques Ampère, hungry for "local color," wanted to travel to Trieste and beyond, but didn't have enough money. So Mérimée took it upon himself "to write our travel account in advance," supposedly to finance the trip. They abandoned the plan for the trip, but Mérimée wrote the book "in two weeks," having learned "five or six words of Slavic." (This kind of after-the-fact bragging about a hoax—how easy it was both to write the fake text and to fool people with it—is something we will see from Boris Vian, Romain Gary, and Jack-Alain Léger.) Mérimée goes on to say what a "brilliant success" the hoax was, and to comment on the effect it had on him: it made him "doubt the merit of *local color* itself."[70] I will return to that change of heart later.

This much is true: he used all the techniques of a hoaxer, including the employment of an intermediary who dealt with the publisher in Strasbourg.

Hyacinthe Maglanovich.

FIGURE 6. Hyacinthe Maglanovich. Frontispiece, Prosper Mérimée, *La Guzla, ou choix de poésies il-lyriques recueillies dans la Dalmatie, la Bosnie, la Croatie et l'Herzegovine* (Paris: F. G. Levrault, 1827). Beinecke Rare Book and Manuscript Library, Yale University.

But unlike some literary identity hoaxes, this one cannot be dismissed as a money-making scheme, nor can it have paid for any trip, because the arrangement with the publisher stipulated that the author would not be paid anything.[71] Mérimée said later, "The result was a small volume that I published in deep secret and that fooled [*mystifia*] two or three people."[72] He was being modest: he fooled everyone (although low sales may have made that easier) for about one year. *La Guzla* "mystified the press, even the most respectable," and was quite well received. The work of translating this "half-savage" bard was compared to Madame de Staël's *De l'Allemagne*; the volume was found to have originality, "richness of imagination," and a "naïve simplicity" that was "biblical or homeric."[73] Reviews in England were full of praise.[74] The hoax was working perfectly. All aspects of it were covered in a 566-page volume devoted to *La Guzla* by a Slavic scholar, Voyslav M. Yovanovitch, in 1911: *"La Guzla" de Prosper Mérimée: étude d'histoire romantique.*

∗

If Victor Hugo was the first to reveal that Mérimée was the true author of *La Guzla*, he apparently did so only orally, in a salon.[75] It was Goethe who really blew the whistle, in March 1828. An avid Francophile, Goethe eagerly took in literary news that made its way from Paris to Weimar, where Mérimée's friends Jean-Jacques Ampère and Albert Stapfer sometimes called. In his article, Goethe begins by putting *La Guzla* in the exact context that is appropriate here in this study: as part of a relatively new trend, of French writers looking beyond their own borders, to the outside world, seeking "local color." As I said earlier, Mérimée was one of the leaders of that movement. Goethe puts it this way:

> [*La Guzla* is] a striking work from the first glance. If one examines it more closely, it poses a mysterious question.
>
> It is only recently that the French have studied with interest and passion different poetic genres from abroad, granting them certain rights in the empire of aesthetics [*ihnen gewisse Rechte innerhalb des ästhetischen Kreises zugestanden haben*]. It is also only recently that they have felt compelled to use foreign forms for their own works. Today we see the strangest new thing: they are donning the mask of foreign nations, and in works that they pass off as ours [*untergeschobene Werke*], they make fun of us with clever wit in the most amusing way. First we read a problematic work as a new original, with pleasure and admiration, and, after discovering the ruse, we again find new delight in the skillful talent that proved itself capable of such serious jokes [*solchen ernsten Scherzen*].

Goethe is claiming that he could "tell"—that he did tell—by reading alone. By his own account, no outside information influenced him; he is, with Dickens, another rare forensic reader. He says that the name *Guzla* reminded him of *Gazul*, so he did some "research," which he does not explain. He emerges with this declaration: "Monsieur Mérimée will not think ill if we declare him the author of the *Théâtre de Clara Gazul* and of *La Guzla*, and if we try to find out, for our own pleasure, all the clandestine children [*eingeschwärzten Kindern*] that it may please him to bring into the world."[76] According to Mérimée himself, Goethe was trying to make himself look smarter than he was in this case: Mérimée had sent a copy of *La Guzla* to Goethe, inscribed "from the author of *Le Théâtre de Clara Gazul*." In other words, the two anagrams were put into Goethe's hands by Mérimée: a dead giveaway, since Mérimée was known to be the author of *Clara Gazul*. It seems clear, therefore, that Mérimée planned this hoax in order to see it exposed. He gave the means of his own exposure to Goethe, and did not protest afterwards. (As Abramson says, he intended this to be a "temporary deception.")[77] "[Goethe] put on the airs of a great discoverer so as to appear more clever," Mérimée wrote to a friend.[78]

The anecdotal sniping raises a larger question: by perpetrating the hoax of *La Guzla*, did Mérimée make a mockery of the very project for which he would become famous, the new outward orientation of French literature, its engagement with foreign traditions? That is quite clearly what Goethe is suggesting, and Mérimée himself returns to that hypothesis years later. But writing again in several years, Goethe softens his judgment, praising Mérimée's tireless efforts to familiarize himself with a world that was foreign to him.[79] By then, after the publication of Mérimée's revolutionary explosion of short stories in 1829, that was easier to say.

As we have seen many times, the unveiling of a hoax does not put an end to its web of deception. The same year as Goethe's revelation, a German translation of *La Guzla* in verse was published; the translator, Wilhelm Gerhard, was truly duped and victimized by the hoax. It was reviewed in France and Germany as a genuine South Slavic work.[80] In an interesting and exceptional twist, Pushkin proceeded with a translation of *La Guzla* into Russian, even after learning about the unveiling of the hoax by Goethe. Pushkin shrugged off the inauthenticity of its origin, making the poetry his own; the result was *Songs of the Western Slavs* (1835). Mérimée, apparently amused, called it the equivalent of translating the Spanish-themed French novel *Gil Blas* into Spanish.[81] Or perhaps it's like building a Kunta Kinte museum in Gambia. A volume of *Contes de la Bosnie*, some plagiarized from *La Guzla*, was displayed in the Bosnian pavilion at the Universal Exposition in Paris in 1900, bringing the hoax full circle, in a sense.[82] All in all, *La Guzla* was a very fine blue-chip if short-lived intercultural literary hoax.

✶

But on the textual level, this hoax is particularly hard to understand: how could readers be taken in by something so over the top? Ora Avni asks, "How could the reader of 1827 let himself get caught in such a crude trap . . . where vampires and ghosts are on parade?"[83] As the editors of the Pléiade edition (which does not include *La Guzla*) said, "It is hard to take seriously customs that are so savage, beliefs that are so superstitious."[84] The explanation, at first blush, appears to be simple: like Psalmanazar's Formosa, Mérimée's Illyria must have been almost completely unfamiliar to French readers, leaving him free to make up whatever he liked. It was a blank slate, the very opposite of what is stated in the preface ("the Illyrian provinces . . . are well enough known"). Oscar Wilde quipped, "Where there is no illusion there is no Illyria."[85] Jennifer Wallace sheds light on this context, explaining that Illyria has "always been a threshold between the known and unknown world . . . a liminal space which dramatizes the problems of our conventional polarizations of ethnic identity."[86] Thus for staging an ethnic hoax, Mérimée seems to have headed directly for some extremely fertile ground; was this just by chance?

Anyone who has read him knows that it is hard to catch Mérimée writing about France directly; he preferred the "local color" of other lands. But if, when he wrote ostensibly about Spain in *Clara Gazul*, he was really writing about France, what was he up to with Illyria? It is an ancient name for western parts of the Balkan Penisula, including parts of what are now Croatia, Bosnia and Herzegovina, and Slovenia. (Illyria was the setting for Shakespeare's *Twelfth Night* and Sartre's *Les Mains sales*.) But on closer inspection of history, it turns out that Illyria was, if distant, *not* unknown to the French: it had recently been part of their empire. In Mérimée's lifetime, the name was revived by Napoleon for provinces on the eastern Adriatic that were briefly taken over, under the Treaty of Schönbrunn in 1809.[87] The *Provinces Illyriennes*, a veritable "Tower of Babel,"[88] with a million and a half inhabitants, were together a kind of French colony, when Mérimée was a child aged six to twelve. (Napoleon's "reawakening" of the Illyrian myth is said to have contributed, later, to "a new nationalist purpose.")[89] The Napoleonic period in Illyria is in fact represented in *La Guzla*, as we will see.

In a letter of November 13, 1810, Napoleon wrote, "Assure my subjects in Illyria of my imperial protection."[90] He saw the province as strategically necessary and as a bargaining chip; but based on French notions that the Illyrians were related to the ancient Greeks, he also had a full civilizing mission in mind, as he explained: "I wanted to introduce and enracinate our doctrines, our administration, our codes; this would be one step further toward European *regeneration*."[91] That is very loaded language, especially coming from the emperor himself. Historian Barbara Jelavich explains the special status of Illyria, which was "incorporated directly into France": "In setting up the new government, the French officials did not take into consideration the local customs, which they regarded as *primitive and barbarous* [as will Mérimée], and they proceeded to introduce the French administrative system intact."[92] For a time, the country seemed "Napoleonized" (all that was lacking was the guillotine).[93]

But Napoleon's Illyria was, of course, not to last. His grand strategy was falling apart and the Illyrian Provinces had to be ceded to Austria. Charles Nodier, who had previously written *Questions de littérature légale*, moved to French Illyria and ran a newspaper there. He recalled later that the French despaired of Illyrian civilization and left "with little confidence in the perfectibility of conquered nations."[94] After only a few months in Ljubljana, Nodier returned to France and played a continuing role as a cultural intermediary between France and Illyria. He "introduced Illyrian literature into France," starting in 1814, and "implant[ed] certain Slavic elements in the mind of the ordinary Frenchman," putting Illyria on the French literary map.[95] And he did this for real, thirteen years before Mérimée did it in a hoax; his was the real coin that Mérimée counterfeited. Nodier represented literary legitimacy and propriety, which Mérimée sought to disrupt. Mérimée took his ideas about Illyria from Nodier, whom he then went on to vilify when accepting the deceased Nodier's place in the French Academy.[96] Nodier's work was part of a large infusion of information about Illyria that came into France during and after the Napoleonic period: travel accounts, geographical descriptions, and linguistic studies—all grist for Mérimée's future mill. The Abbé Fortis's *Voyage en Dalmatie* (translated from Italian in 1778), to name one example, was an enormously important source for Mérimée.[97]

What was this Illyrian literature that Nodier brought home and Mérimée imitated? The area called Illyria includes the territories, then in Yugoslavia, where Milman Parry and Albert Lord "solved" the Homeric Question in the mid-twentieth century and revolutionized the study of oral traditions; they did this by recording *guslari* or players of the gusle, the instrument from which Mérimée takes his title.[98] So Mérimée, with this hoax, was in fact trampling on some of the most fertile ground in the world for oral epics—but only as a joke and only in his imagination.

The first paragraph of the anonymous preface to *La Guzla* places the work very squarely at the heart of our concern with *unequal* intercultural hoaxes, operating across a Great Divide. But in this case, Mérimée has complicated the structure of inequality by making his editor-translator a son of this soil:

> When I was busy assembling the anthology [*le recueil*] of which you are about to read a translation, I imagined myself the only Frenchman (and I was at the time) who might see any interest in these artless poems, products of a savage people. And publishing them was the last thing on my mind. (vii)

This factitious Frenchman goes on to explain that his mother was a "Morlaque" (an "inhabitant of Dalmatia who speaks Slavic or Illyric"). He says

that he "for a long time spoke Illyric more often than Italian" (viii). Then
he announces that he is in fact Italian, naturalized in France. Anonymous,
protean, and apocryphal, this editor-translator positions himself as both native informant and participant-observer, thus endowed with considerable
ethnographic authority. Without mentioning Napoleon or the Empire specifically, he alludes to the recent history: "I imagine that the Illyric provinces,
which were *for a long time* [sic] under French government, are sufficiently
well known, so there is no need to preface this anthology with a geographical
or political description, etc." (x, emphasis added). With this gesture, Mérimée's avatar editor overstates both the length of the French occupation and
the knowledge of the region that could be expected among French readers.
This has the effect of throwing the reader off balance and keeping him/her in
the dark, the better to surprise him/her with the shock of the primitive exotic.
The rest of the preface goes on to describe the one-stringed gusle and the
practices of the bards who sing along with it—in insulting terms. "The habit
of hearing it alone can make this music tolerable" (xii). Mérimée thus presents us with a repulsive "savage" cultural object that he has dragged back to
France—in fact, merely conjured up—thereby piquing in the reader a strange
mixture of interest and disdain. In his paratextual materials, the editor displays lots of conscientious attention to detail: what is a fragment of a larger
song, what is whole, what is the meaning of this or that cultural practice or
term, and so on. The formatting and structure of the book imitate other im-
portations of foreign, exotic literature into France of the same time period:
Claude Charles Fauriel's *Chants populaires de la Grèce moderne* (Fauriel was
a friend of Mérimée's), Nodier's works, and Baron Jacques-François Roger's
Kelédor.[99] Working almost simultaneously with Mérimée, Roger used a similar approach in order to import oral literature from Senegal, "harvesting" an
epic and annotating it heavily. Fauriel, Roger, and Mérimée all use the term
recueilli (collected) in their titles; Fauriel calls himself the "translator-editor"
of the oral works. But Fauriel had real credentials as a linguist; Roger had actually lived in Senegal, and his book has been taken seriously ever since.[100] So,
very effectively, Mérimée made his *Guzla* look like numerous authoritative
books that were making the rounds at the time, parasitizing their credibility.
All of this took place in the midst of a burgeoning literary interest for popular
songs and tales, from Greece, Illyria, Provence, and Scotland.[101] The shadow
of Ossian loomed over all of this.

In *La Guzla*, a fake biography of the apocryphal Maglanovich ("son of the
fog")[102] follows, full of the bard's adventures: religious conversions followed
by flights across borders; abducting his wife and killing his rival; and eventually settling into domesticity. The narrator-editor meets him and describes

the scene of the bard's performance in terms that foreshadow the practices of ethnographers of the twentieth century, who disclose the conditions in which their recordings were made. In one of his notes, the narrator also anticipates the idea of salvage that will be a central gesture in modern anthropology: this culture and its customs are fast disappearing; I the ethnographer will save what I can.[103] Thus he claims:

> It is unfortunately quite rare today to find Illyrian poets who don't copy any-one and who try to conserve beautiful language, *the use of which is diminishing every day.* [46–47, emphasis added]

The book of exotic photographs *Before They Pass Away* is only one recent illustration of this premise.[104] Camara Laye, whose work we will examine presently, says something very similar in his preface to a work of the same structure, a transcription and translation of an oral epic, *Le Maître de la parole*.[105] Maglanovich, like an African griot, promotes himself and brags about his skills (173–76).

✳

What was the appeal of *La Guzla?*—if not to vast numbers of French people, then at least to Pushkin? There must have been some literary merit. To take one example, "The Morlaque in Venice" contains this stanza, which has considerable Romantic effectiveness (negative capability, perhaps) . . . if you bracket the imposture:

> Women laugh at me when I speak the language of my country, and here the people of our mountains have forgotten theirs, as well as our old customs. I am a tree transplanted in summertime: I dry out and die. (45)

Again Mérimée foreshadows Francophone literature, with its concerns for language, difference, the fear of the loss of identity in exile, and ultimately, cultural extinction. In this and perhaps a few other passages, this work of fakery in fact achieves real poetry and genuine feeling. The mystification contains a hidden truth.[106] And to the extent that *La Guzla* was written in a literally postimperial period, in the aftermath of Napoleon's "Illyrian Provinces," a passage like this suggests some eerie connection to postcolonial literature.

Such passages are not, however, what has attracted the attention of critics. How could they, when other parts are so sensational, on several different levels? One agenda is to let the French reader feel morally superior to these Eastern "barbarians." "One sees at every instant new proofs of the contempt that the Illyrians have for their women," we are told in a note (65). Another large category of distraction is the fantastic: armies of ghosts (66n5), a severed head that talks (87), the evil eye (91–100), and lots of vampirism (68–69, 135–56, 189–91, 217–23). The editor-narrator remains outside the belief system and superior to it, recounting how he hoaxed a young peasant woman who thought she had been attacked by a vampire: he recited Racine to her as a fake "conjuration" (154).[107]

Like other hoaxes (Defonseca/de Wael, for example), this one contains a peek-a-boo appearance by the real author, although still in disguise: a note that speculates that "the author of the theater of Clara Gazul"—Mérimée's previous hoax—must have gotten "her" idea of "African love" from a version of one of these tales that was published "in an English magazine" (231n4).

One short piece in the volume has not received the attention it deserves, perhaps because it is so enigmatic. Ora Avni chuckles over the bizarre irruption of Frenchness represented by the name "Jeannot" (French for "Jack" or "Johnny") in *La Guzla*.[108] But what about, much later, the appearance of Napoleon's troops—and words—in the section called "Les Monténégrins" (245–48)? The editor's note appended to the title clashes slightly with what Napoleon himself wrote on the subject ("I wanted to introduce and enracinate our doctrines, our administration, our codes"). The editor opines:

> There is no small people [*petit peuple*] that does not imagine the gaze of the universe upon them. I further think that Napoleon never gave much thought to [*ne s'est jamais beaucoup occupé des*] the Montenegrins. (248n1)

Napoleon's own words, quoted earlier, show that in fact his gaze *was* at least briefly on Illyria. The aspirational universalism represented by the emperor's attention was not just a fantasy on the part of this small people. Maglanovich's ballad begins:

> Napoleon said, "What are these men who dare to resist me? I want them to come throw their guns and their *ataghans* [swords] decorated with *nielles* [enamel] at my feet." Suddenly he sent twenty thousand soldiers up the mountain. (245)

So here, late in this large volume, Frenchness finally asserts itself, not just in a name, but in full imperial and historical fashion. What is Mérimée up to now? For one thing, as with "Jeannot," he may be planting a deliberate strain on credulity, as a tease and a hint: how did the bard Maglanovich have access to this quotation from Napoleon? The fiercely independent, tribal Montenegrins were leading opponents of the French in Illyria before making peace for a time—then revolting and helping to drive the French out in 1813. The French defeat was the subject of genuine ballads in the region.[109]

"Les Monténégrins," recounting a fictitious battle, reads like a reverse "Marseillaise":

"Les Monténégrins"

> Ils sont partis: leurs armes luisaient au soleil; ils sont montés en ordre pour brûler nos villages; ils sont montés pour enlever dans leur pays nos femmes et nos enfans.

> They left. Their weapons gleamed in the sun; they went up in formation to burn our villages; they went up to abduct to their country our wives and children.

"La Marseillaise"

> Ils viennent jusque dans vos bras
> Egorger vos fils, vos compagnes!

> They are coming into your midst
> To cut the throats of your sons and consorts!

In "Les Monténégrins," *they* are the French enemy: twenty thousand of them against "five hundred brave Montenegrins." Writing from the point of view of a defeated "small people," in this instance, Mérimée slips an anti-imperial message into French literature.[110] As the work of a Frenchman, this is saying: We are doing to this small people the violence that was done to us earlier. So, as with *La Religieuse*, this prank literary text is at the same time, at least briefly, an unlikely conduit for unheard voices. The ventriloquism of the oppressed is, however, partially undermined by the note that the editor appends at this point: "The habit of warring with the Turks made the Montenegrins think that all nations practiced the same atrocities in the military campaigns" (248n4). Again there is a stark divide between the voice of the bard and that of the editor-translator (both fake, of course). The editor assures the reader here that the only French atrocities are those imagined by the Montenegrins. Between the ballad itself and the note, Mérimée has hedged his bets and left the reader to decide about French "civilization."

Like the Napoleonic occupation itself, this song doesn't last long. (The piece is interrupted by a blank line indicating a "missing stanza," a nice *effet de réel*.) If this were the work of a Montenegrin or Illyrian bard, wouldn't he be a bit more fulsome about this victory by David over Goliath? The "gaze of the universe," represented first by Napoleonic conquest and second by Mérimée's hoax, passes quickly. This piece and the entire volume of *La Guzla* can be seen, in fact, as an after-image of the Napoleonic era and empire, lingering, as so many things would, into the Restoration. The Empire was gone, but the cosmopolitanism that it had enabled (by violent means, to be sure)—in contacts between places such as Egypt and Illyria on the one hand and France on the other—survived and progressed. *La Guzla*, of course, occupies a highly ambiguous position, because it makes a mockery of the cosmopolitan intellectual spirit represented by Nodier and others who brought knowledge of Illyria back to France; and more widely, of the whole body of imperial knowledge-collecting (*La Description de l'Egypte*, Baron Roger's *Kelédor*, and so on). The imposture must be seen as a deliberate ridiculing of the sincere and authentic work of "learning from the Empire." Gibson argues that Nodier wrote about Dalmatian Illyria as "a region of primitive contentedness, superstition and song, as an antidote to the confusions of his own day."[111] But I think that Mérimée produced *La Guzla* in order to *reestablish* some confusion and to disturb both Romantic pieties and the notion of literary propriety that Nodier had helped establish. Two years later, still disruptive, he will do something similar: in *Tamango* he undercuts abolitionism at a crucial moment in its evolution.

*

Seen in this context, as an intervention in the knowledge-importing and -processing industry in France, *La Guzla* can be compared to another hoax, perpetrated on the "theory industry" in the United States in late twentieth century: the infamous Sokal hoax.

Alan Sokal was a professor of physics who set out to make the language and assumptions of postmodern theory-speak in the humanities and social sciences look foolish. He submitted an essay to the journal *Social Text* that was a pile of nonsense and hokum: "Transgressing the Boundaries: Toward a Transformative Hermeneutics of Quantum Gravity." It was accepted.[112] He wanted to see, as he explained later, if a leading journal would "publish an article liberally salted with nonsense if (a) it sounded good and (b) it flattered the editors' ideological preconceptions."[113] Thus he declared that "physical 'reality' . . . is at bottom a social and linguistic construct." He wrote later: "Any competent physicist or mathematician (or undergraduate physics or math major)" could have realized that it was "a spoof." It cannot be denied that he exposed what he called "the intellectual arrogance of Theory." Any sense of embarrassment was not avowed by the duped editors, however: they wriggled and dodged blame, claiming they had always thought the piece "a little hokey," "not really our cup of tea," and "outdated."[114] But they had condescended to publish what they thought was an "earnest attempt to seek some kind of affirmation" from themselves, the priests of theory, and claimed to be glad they had done so. They refused to admit that they had been hoodwinked. Twenty years later now, after decades of right-wing attacks on, for example, climate science, and with a person in the White House who has claimed that global warming is a "Chinese hoax," Sokal's guerilla defense of "objective," nonsilly science seems more important than ever.

It is not clear that Mérimée's intentions were as serious as Sokal's; there is no reason to think that he wanted to entirely discredit the early ethnographic work that he parodied. But that had to be an effect, and he said it was, in his preface to the second edition, published thirteen years after the hoax, in 1840:

> Such a brilliant success didn't distract me [*ne me fit point tourner la tête*]. Strengthened by the testimonies of Mr. Bowring, Mr. Gerhart, and Mr. Pushkin, I could claim to have made *local color*. But the process was so simple, so easy, that I came to doubt the value of *local color* itself.[115]

La Guzla demonstrated that information apparently coming into France from the outside world, wrapped in scholarly garb, could be faked and yet pass for real. For Mérimée, if for no one else, this meant that the cultural currency of the day—local color—was devalued, perhaps worthless. So there was truly something intellectually subversive about this hoax. It was not an empty stunt.

Yet no one cared: not Pushkin, not Gérard de Nerval, who based a libretto on songs he knew to be fakes. The way of play prevailed. If there was any discrediting of the knowledge- and poetry-importing industry, it has left no traces except in the statement from the author himself, which does need to be taken seriously. Mérimée went on, two years later, to produce his explosion of local color, the short stories of 1829. The disillusionment, the *demystification* that he had wrought, and the true meaning of his own hoax perhaps dawned on him only thirteen years later.

And what about the "Illyrians"? What did they think of this forgery of their own oral literature? The only reaction that the exhaustive Yovanovitch reports concerns the allegation in the preface that Illyrian bards customarily interrupt their tales to ask for money: that "false assertion" was bitterly resented by "Serbian critics in 1827" (241). Those same critics apparently did not realize that the whole thing was fake. Later, Yovanovitch devotes a chapter to the reception of *La Guzla* in "the Slavic countries" (498–522), but he covers only Pushkin and two Polish poets, and says nothing about the fortunes of *La Guzla*, *after* it was revealed as a hoax, among Serbian, Croatian, Bosniak, or other peoples of the former Illyria. He points out that Pushkin was no more qualified to judge the authenticity of the volume than Musset was to judge a book of Catalan folklore (499–500). We are left with only one trace, itself worse than dubious: those fragments from *La Guzla* that Bosnians (we assume) put on display in their pavillion in Paris in 1900—in a French-language book. That may mean that Mérimée's artificial limb was not entirely rejected by the body from which it had *not* originally come—a slim connection indeed.

In the end, I think *La Guzla* had two effects: on the one hand, it hoaxed the scholarship and poetry of otherness that was then being produced by Fauriel, Nodier, Roger, and even Hugo in *Les Orientales* (which was written in the same year). In that vein, it could even be said that Mérimée pranked his own future as the very serious Inspector of Historic Monuments, which he became a mere seven years later. On the other hand, it gave a voice (a small one) to those who had been conquered by the Empire: the relatively voiceless. Those two effects are in tension with each other and cannot necessarily be reconciled. But that, in turn, is in keeping with the idea that mystifications can contain hidden truths.[116]

Bakary Diallo: Fausse-Bonté

If most of the hoaxes seen so far in this study have reflected a top-down power dynamic, with authors from a dominant culture masquerading as authors from a nondominant one, the rise of colonialism will bring new challenges, motivations, and payoffs for those who might be tempted to perpetrate a literary hoax. It is strange but literally true to say that *La Guzla* was a postcolonial work, representing the oral literature of a former French possession. Now, in leaping forward by almost a century and from Europe to Africa, how much changes? When, in the wake of the Congress of Berlin, France came to possess large parts of Africa, the stakes of such representations were raised. This was very different from the brief French colonization of Illyria. Millions of Africans were now French subjects, and their cultures (as well as their crops and minerals) were considered to be available for harvesting. The colonial enterprise was never deeply popular inside the metropole; consequently there was a need for representations, if not for actual propaganda favoring colonialism. This was a perfect setup for fakery.

In Africa, a new French educational system worked toward the closing of the supposedly great divide of literacy. Those who mastered the French language in school would be the new intermediaries, explaining their culture to the outside world while advancing the French cause, civilization, in Africa. Ahmadou Mapaté Diagne's *Les Trois volontés de Malic*, a reader for schoolchildren, blandly invites Senegalese children to abandon the underpinnings of their own culture and to adopt careers (smithing, for example) forbidden by tradition but useful to the new state. This small book was written, as far as anyone knows, entirely by Diagne, who worked for the French educational system.[117] This text establishes a baseline of self-representation in French, the "normal" path of Francophone authorship. (Diagne's procolonial stance was not intrinsic to writing in French; his opposite and counterpoint was Lamine Senghor, the radical communist author of *La Violation d'un pays*.)[118] Diagne was memorably called one of the "thurifers of French colonialism."[119]

But most Africans remained nonliterate or of very limited literacy, and therefore subject to appropriation by literary means: they could not represent themselves, not adequately, not in literature, so they had to be represented or "aided." There was apparently not a sufficient supply of authors like Diagne, so, as with slave narratives in the United States, white hands sometimes held or guided black pens. The first several decades of Francophone African literature were haunted by suspicions of inauthenticity, which have carried over into the postcolonial era.

Bakary Diallo's *Force-Bonté* (1926) has been considered to be "the first autobiography written in French by a black African author from Senegal."[120] Like *Les Trois volontés*, this work supported colonialism and in fact has been called the last of its kind: "the end of a series" of procolonial writings and the beginning of the Francophone African autobiographical novel. Despite its unrelenting collaborationism, critics have managed to find "nuance" in its pages, and a certain documentary value.[121] Even as the *mouvements nègres*, led by Lamine Senghor and others, were stirring aggrieved African veterans of World War I, the last words of *Force-Bonté* are "Vive la force-bonté de la France!" [Long live the strength-goodness of France!]. Despite republication in the 1980s, *Force-Bonté* has remained in a "hard eclipse."[122]

But the "problem of the paternity"[123] has overshadowed questions about the content of *Force-Bonté*. The original preface, by Jean-Richard Bloch, undermines the credibility of the text attributed to Diallo by stating: "He is not even an educated Negro . . ." but "started to stutter in French"—a language that is still "foreign" to him—while in the army.[124] Yet the language of the text is perfectly correct and fluent. How did that happen? No explanation is offered. Questions about the authenticity of *Force-Bonté* were raised, perhaps not for the first time, by Robert Pageard in 1966. "It is difficult to write a novel by proxy," he wrote, pointing toward Lucie Cousturier, a French patron of Africans, as the likely author of this "harvested autobiography."[125] (Others suggest that editors "ghosted" the text.)[126] If that is true, Cousturier was a white *nègre* or ghostwriter, and the text was an "as-told-to" product.

Mohamadou Kane, reviewing the evidence of Diallo's heartfelt belief in the colonial project (widely shared among his compatriots at the time), concludes that "Bakary must have produced the raw material, the first spurt" for the book, but perhaps no more. But Kane then proceeds to discuss the work as Diallo's own, thus erasing the complex polyvocality of shared authorship. More recently, Abiola Irele has stated that *Force-Bonté* is "the clearest example of a work whose text in French as we have it could not possibly have been created by the person whose name is advertised as its author." Alain Ricard has called it "supervised literature."[127] Without stretching the definition too far, and without knowing exactly what took place, we can consider *Force-Bonté* to be one of our intercultural literary impostures.

Like all such hoaxes, *Force-Bonté* paints a picture that appeals to a certain public: in this case, it is an image of a sweet-natured, pastoral, apolitical Africa eager for French civilization:

> Starting in my earliest childhood, my parents expected me to do my job as a shepherd. Among my people, a guardian of cattle, sheep, or even goats, is a noble person. . . . Respect will be due to those men and women whose efforts will one day lead to the elaboration of the principles of universal understanding. . . . O you, Frenchmen of France, you whom God has long since chosen to be our masters . . . you will see the absolute proof of our attachment to you. (7, 68, 98–99)

Force-Bonté is a significant literary signpost, as much because of what we don't know about it as because of what we do know. We cannot transport ourselves back to the time when Diallo was either writing it himself or dictating the text or its ideas to someone else. We cannot recover or measure the lost polyvocality, if indeed there is any, without wandering off into what Irele calls "the realm of pure speculation."[128] Methodologically, we are dealing with a "known unknown": we know that we don't know who wrote this book. We are left to wonder exactly how much of the collaborationist ideology in the text is due to African thinking and how much is due to European ventriloquism. The structure of this literary mystery will be reproduced quite exactly, with much higher stakes, in the controversy that now surrounds one of the best-known authors of Francophone African fiction, Camara Laye. *Force-Bonté* thus sets the stage for both the emergence of Francophone African literature and questions about its authenticity. The book has been easy to purge from the canon of African texts because its procolonial ideology has become repugnant. But what if an inauthentic text (perhaps Camara's *Le Regard du roi*) seemed to embody Africanness? What would then be said and done?

Elissa Rhaïs, Literacy, and Identity

There is no better way to describe the case of Elissa Rhaïs than in these semi-facetious phrases of Mireille Rosello: "Elissa Rhaïs was the first francophone Algerian Muslim woman writer. The only trouble is that she could neither read nor write, that she was Jewish rather than Muslim, and that the author was probably not a woman either."[129]

In 1919, a woman named Rosine Boumendil moved from Algiers to Paris, wrapped in Oriental garb (figure 7). She wrote (or didn't) and published large numbers of Orientalist tales, which appeared in various journals, all under the name Elissa Rhaïs. They responded to and stoked a certain vogue for colonial exoticism during the interwar period, the high-water mark of which was the Colonial Exposition of 1931. The image of Elissa Rhaïs was carefully constructed by her publisher, Plon, one of the oldest houses in Paris, known for its traditional Roman Catholic values and conservatism, enjoying new prosperity in the interwar period. Some of that fortune was due to signing the Tharaud brothers, the anti-Semitic authors of works such as *Petite Histoire des Juifs* (1927), as well as more mainstream writers including Georges Bernanos and Denis de Rougemont. One of its great successes, now forgotten, was *Mon oncle et mon curé* (My Uncle and My Priest, 1889), by Alice Cherbonnel, writing under the male pseudonym Jean de La Brète; a novel for young women, it was reprinted 244 times by 1927. In the early 1930s the house joined in the celebrations of colonialism associated with the Paris Colonial Exposition and the centenary of the French conquest of Algeria, issuing a series devoted to "Les Grandes Figures Coloniales."[130] (As we will see, Plon later published the works of both Camara Laye and Chimo.)

Plon's history of promoting anti-Semitism (which goes back at least as far as the Dreyfus affair)[131] sheds some light on their casting of Rhaïs as Muslim, not Jewish. Plon's press release stated: "A Muslim woman from our Algeria, who attended French schools until she was twelve, then took the veil of the women of Islam and left the harem to tell stories in French."[132] Plon was just plain lying: they knew that "Elissa Rhaïs" was not Muslim. This had several effects, if not purposes. On the one hand, it protected a Jewish author from anti-Semitism and the house from the perception of having published a Jewish author. On the other hand, it enabled the groundbreaking appropriative representation of an identity with little to no voice in French literature at the time: the Muslim North African woman.[133] The status of *écrivain indigène*, in its masculine form, barely existed at the time, so a woman author was truly something new.[134] Elissa Rhaïs was supposed to be "the George Sand of Islam."[135]

FIGURE 7. Elissa Rhaïs (ca. 1920?).

And as we will see, this was not the last time that Plon would support colonialism by using a proxy "native" author (I am referring to the case of Camara Laye). Modern colonialism was, of course, a product of the Third French Republic, whose warm embrace we will see numerous times in this part of *Impostors*. In *Le Mariage de Hanifa*, a "kindly, generous French woman" teacher tells her rainbow tribe of pupils, "We are all equals, my dears."[136]

That these works later fell into obscurity is no surprise. Then, in 1982, came the sensational publication of a book entitled simply *Elissa Rhaïs*, by Paul Tabet. Claiming to be a "true account," but taken to be a novel by some readers, this narrative biography purported to expose the truth about its subject: Rhaïs was not a product of French schools but illiterate, and her books were written by her nephew, who was also her lover, her "slave," and her ghostwriter: Raoul Tabet (who happened to be Paul's father).[137] Rosello points out that Paul Tabet does not even consider the "as-told-to" possibility: of an oral/written collaboration between Elissa Rhaïs and Raoul Tabet, which we saw with Diallo and will see again with Camara.[138] In the wake of Tabet's revelations, as Rosello points out, there is something odd about the republishing of the Rhaïs novels—six between 1996 and 2007.

The initial impression created by the works of Elissa Rhaïs, in the 1920s, was of authentic subaltern speech, rendered through writing: the very thing that the market keeps demanding. It was supposed to be the voice of an Arab-Muslim woman telling us, for example, that "the first concern of an Arab entering a house that he will inhabit" is to count the beams in the ceiling, or exactly what a women's mourning procession looks like in this culture.[139] Her success as a writer, as Plon makes clear, is a credit to "our" colonial system: so long as it can produce exceptional *writing* subjects like Rhaïs, we must be doing something right in Algeria. Rhaïs wrote in a style that Emily Apter calls both "a commercialized Flaubertianism" and an "updated Romantic Orientalism," which contributed to her success.[140] Apter also suggests that the doubts about Rhaïs's authorship ("For all we know, the novels could have been written by a French colonial officer") cannot be dispelled "on the basis of the writing alone."[141]

There are actually three hypotheses about the authorship of Elissa Rhaïs. The first is what Plon advertised, as seen above: a Muslim woman from Algeria who went to French school and wrote books herself. The second possibility emerged in the 1930s through the anti-Semitic "outing" of Elissa Rhaïs as Jewish: she wrote her books, but she was not the Muslim Arab she had claimed to be. That shift was crucial because Arabs and Jews had different legal and social positions in French Algeria after 1870: Jews were allowed in French schools, Muslim Arabs were not.[142]

The third theory is that of Paul Tabet: that Elissa Rhaïs wrote nothing. He claims that she was born to a Muslim father and a Jewish mother, making her Muslim by Islamic law and Jewish according to Jewish law. (That claim about the father is not supported by other sources.) Tabet says that Plon prevented Elissa Rhaïs from receiving the Légion d'honneur, revealing her as an "illiterate," Jewish impostor and Raoul Dahan ("dit Rhaïs") as the real author; she was devastated and died soon thereafter.[143] It is true that Rhaïs was exposed as a Jew in a virulently anti-Semitic publication of 1934, Charles Hagel's *Le Péril juif.*[144]

The three steps in this sequence of authorship thus move across boundaries of both gender and religion, and from a position in which literacy in French is highly unlikely (Muslim female) to one in which it is likely (Jewish male). Identity and literacy track each other on this sliding scale. The other interesting characteristic of this case is that there were two unveilings: the first, moving Rhaïs from Muslim to Jew, and the second, moving the writings from female to male. The first is universally accepted, but the second allegation is widely rejected by scholars.

We know that exposing a hoax does not put an end to it. The revelation is often poorly circulated, disbelieved, or simply ignored. The actual republishing of novels that had supposedly been exposed as hoaxes is somewhat rare, although we saw it in the case of *Little Tree*, and we will see something like it again with Camara's *Le Regard du roi*. The fifteen-year gap between Paul Tabet's book and the first of the new editions of Rhaïs may be one part of the explanation; the other part is that Paul Tabet was not believed. Those who defended the Rhaïs novels after their reappearance rejected his story; some also cited various versions of the "way of play": it's the text that counts, not the author, nor his/her identity; the scandal itself is unworthy of a self-respecting reader; or it's Paul Tabet who is the scandal.[145] Both those who defend Elissa Rhaïs as author and those who credit Raoul Tabet, of course, find evidence in the texts to support their positions.[146] Charles Dickens, or the gender-detecting computer that we saw in part 1, is perhaps needed here. (Does it detect religion?)

One of the recent editions of Rhaïs demonstrates, again, how the truth can hide in plain sight after the unveiling of a hoax. The author's name on the cover of the Archipel edition of *La Fille d'Eléazar* is simply Elissa Rhaïs. But on the back cover, at the end of a description of the work, is this disclosure, easy to miss: "Published for the first time in 1921, this novel is . . . one of twelve works published between the wars by Elissa Rhaïs. Behind this pseudonym was Leila Boumendil, an illiterate woman who, by signing the novels of her nephew and lover Raoul Tabet, fooled [*mystifia*] the literary world for twenty years."[147] (One notes the slight contradiction between illiteracy and "signing.") This publisher thus has it both ways: cashing in on the ethnic-representational value of the novel, and revealing it as a hoax. It is also interesting to note that this wording attributes the agency in the affaire to Rhaïs rather than to her writer-lover-nephew Raoul. His son Paul, in his preface, makes the new relevance and marketability of the novel explicit: Raoul "could not but denounce . . . the intransigence and the devastating effects of fanaticism or of what one would call nowadays fundamentalism."[148] Thus the novel is repurposed for the needs of the present, and its authorship—now taken (by Paul Tabet at least) to be Jewish male rather than Muslim female—hardly matters.

Or does it? If authorship is flipped from one identity position to another, what impact does it have on the reading of the text?[149] Judith Roumani interprets the dangers of that double flip, of both religion and gender: "Muslims would be particularly incensed at having their cultural soul bared by

Jews. French critics would have been embarrassed because of the 'feminine' qualities they had detected in the work."[150] The first of those possibilities was confirmed by the director the *Revue des Deux Mondes* in 1939, when he wrote that the "Arab community" would be "agitated" to learn that a writer they had seen as a "heroic spokesperson for their interests and their culture" was actually Jewish.[151] In other words, an impostor and a cultural appropriator. It is a matter of dispute as to whether any Muslims actually expressed outrage about Elissa Rhaïs.[152] What remains is French anxiety about what the reaction of the "Arab community" might be.

Rosello briefly compares the Elissa Rhaïs case to that of final subject in this book, Jack-Alain Léger and his alter ego Paul Smaïl. The difference is that in the Rhaïs affair, as with both Bakary Diallo and Camara Laye, there is no satisfying moment of what Rosello calls "triumphant definitive demystication" (which both Romain Gary and Jack-Alain Léger provided, in subsequent publications). The facts about Elissa Rhaïs remain in dispute, circulating endlessly without resolution, and "doubt is the only survivor."[153] In the larger history of intercultural identity hoaxes, this one stands apart for a number of reasons. First, the literary-critical establishment, such as it is, has largely rejected Paul Tabet's allegations and retained Elissa Rhaïs as the legitimate author of the books that bear her name (while recognizing that she was Jewish, not Muslim). But second, sufficient doubt has been introduced to complicate the reading of these texts from now on: the bell can't be unrung.

Sex and Temperament in Postwar Hoaxing:
Boris Vian and Raymond Queneau

In the bleak but percolating years of postwar France, two polymaths with cleverness to spare, two devoted practitioners of the way of play, engaged in a couple of closely linked literary hoaxes, which I want to review briefly now. The first one takes us back across the Atlantic, to black America, but only in pretend; the second takes us to Ireland and across the barrier of gender, also in make-believe. Together these impostures contributed to a renewed spirit of play in French literature. Boris Vian (born 1920) and Raymond Queneau (born 1903) were both impressed by Anglo-American hard-boiled fiction, as were plenty of French writers, including famously Camus.[154] The sex and violence of that genre would serve their hoaxes well, in different ways. In 1946, Vian disguised his writing as that of one Vernon Sullivan, supposedly translated from the American English by Vian, in a novel called memorably *J'irai cracher sur vos tombes* (*I Spit on Your Graves*). A year later, Raymond Queneau became Sally Mara, author of *On est toujours trop bon avec les femmes*

(*We Always Treat Women Too Well*), supposedly translated from the Irish, published by the same racy publishing house, Les Editions du Scorpion. Due to its explicit sexual content, each work was supposedly unpublishable in its prudish native land. But beyond these similarities and connections, are the two cases the same? How do these two novels handle the violence against women that seems intrinsic to the genre of noir fiction?

*

The class, race, and national differences could hardly have been greater for Boris Vian: he took a leap from his own status as a rich white kid from a leafy suburb of Paris to that of an African American passing as white.[155] As a teenager, Vian fell in love with jazz, and that no doubt set him on his course of admiring affection for and mimicry of African American culture. But he was no dilettante. He went on to play the jazz trumpet semiprofessionally, leaving behind a number of recordings as well as voluminous writings about jazz.[156] One of his songs, to take an example, "Je bois" ("I Drink"), is pure blues and pure appropriation. Like armies of other white boys, from Elvis to Eminem in the US, Vian was both an appropriator and an appreciator of African American culture. His articles and essays showed a genuine preoccupation with race and civil rights in the United States, and he joined a league against anti-Semitism and racism. In a coincidence that brings together two of our authors, Vian attacked the racist Asa Carter (the future author of *The Education of Little Tree*) in print.[157] Vian began publishing under pseudonyms in 1944, even as he kept a day job as an engineer. *J'irai cracher sur vos tombes* was the top-selling book of 1947, beating Sartre, Beauvoir, Camus, and Malraux; Vernon Sullivan made Boris Vian rather wealthy.[158]

The book was written in response to a very literal market demand. The Série Noire had been created at Gallimard in 1945 and was bringing hard-boiled fiction to a wide French public. Jean d'Halluin of Editions du Scorpion asked Vian to find an American thriller and translate it into French. Instead Vian, genius that he was, wrote it himself, in two weeks, and presented it as the requested translation.[159] Vian had never visited the United States. He described himself in a preface as the translator (like Cervantes and Guilleragues) of *J'irai cracher*, not as the author; this was the hoax. The author, Vernon Sullivan, was supposed to be an African American who considered himself more black than white even though he, like his protagonist, Lee Anderson, was passing.[160] So this was a hoax (Lee Anderson passing as white in the plot of the novel) within a hoax (the supposed author Vernon Sullivan passing as white in life) within a hoax (Vian passing as translator, not author). It was also a spectacular case of cultural, racial appropriation: what Rebecca Ruquist

called " 'writing in blackface,' . . . the French jazzman picking up his pen like
so much burnt cork and performing a literary act as an African American
subject."[161] Vian published three more novels as Vernon Sullivan: *Les Morts
ont tous la même peau*, *Elles se rendent pas compte* [*sic*], and *On tuera tous les
affreux*.[162] In a fun twist, Vian and an American collaborator also translated
J'irai cracher "back" into the language in which it was supposed to have been
written in the first place, English.[163]

The hoax lasted for about a year and a half, until the secret leaked out.
Meanwhile, Vian went to some lengths to protect the imposture, publishing
a preface to the second Sullivan novel in his own name, in which he denied
being the author on the grounds that he was "too chaste and too pure to write
such things." The preface turns into a full-throated defense of the way of play,
the death of the author, and *écriture*: the identity of the author should count
for nothing, Vian argues; it's the work that counts. "When will you stop demanding to know, in advance, if the author is Peruvian, schismatic, a member
of the Communist Party, or a relative of André Malraux? When will you dare
to talk about a book without surrounding yourselves with references to the
author and all his ins and outs? . . . When will you allow for freedom?"[164] (This
is the position taken by Jack-Alain Léger.)

The harm factor is very evident in this case. Following complaints from a
"cartel for moral action," Vian was prosecuted for the first two Sullivan novels
in 1949 and, in May 1950, was assessed a considerable fine (100,000 francs)
for "offense to good morals." The books were to be "put outside the reach of
young people . . . withdrawn from circulation and destroyed." Because they
were ostensibly written by an American, they were actually "forbidden" in
France and not just "seized."[165] The hoax had come home to roost. Vian responded with a sarcastic newspaper piece titled "I Am Sexually Obsessed"
(and should no doubt be locked up).[166] He was amnestied in 1953, but it was
another twenty years before *J'irai cracher* was reprinted.[167] It is now ubiqui-
tous in French bookstores, along with the other Vernon Sullivan novels.

J'irai cracher expects the reader to believe that the African American
DNA of a mixed-race man with blond hair and fair skin, passing as white,
can be detected by such characteristics as "sloping shoulders" (48–49/34, AT)
and a deep voice (117/94). The protagonist Lee Anderson grew up black but,
after time in Europe, moves to a new town in the South, where he hangs out
with privileged white teenagers; his sexual attributes and skills drive young
women wild with desire, and one of them gets pregnant. True to the noir
genre, Lee plans to "demolish" that woman and her sister, Jean and Lou As-
quith, as part of a larger plan for racial revenge against whites for lynching
his brother (167–68/139–40). Lee's plot is very much like a hoax: he is passing

FIGURE 8. Vernon Sullivan (Boris Vian), *J'Irai cracher sur vos tombes* (Paris: Editions du Scorpion, 1946). Original French edition passing as translation from English. Beinecke Rare Book and Manuscript Library, Yale University.

as something he is not (white) and getting away with it. But after he kills the Asquiths, he will reveal Jean's pregancy and his race to the parents, so that they will know "their darling daughter had got it from a 'nigger'" (168/140). Like many *literary* hoaxers, Lee's satisfaction will come from the unveiling of his imposture; then he will move on and repeat the procedure. He kills Lou in a frenzy of sex and violence mixed together (but not before she shoots and wings him). He reunites with the pregnant Jean and reveals that he has "more than an eighth colored blood in me" (201/166), as he strangles, then shoots her. He then rapes her dead body. This is therefore a deliberately, shockingly toxic, murderous moment of unmasking: the truth of Lee's identity in exchange for Jean's life. But his larger plan is foiled because a white friend detected his race, and the cops are in hot pursuit of the "damn nigger" with blond hair (204/169). The last chapter reads, in its entirety: "The townspeople hanged him anyway because he was a nigger. Under his trousers, his crotch still protruded ridiculously" (213/177) (*Sous son pantalon, son bas-ventre faisait encore une bosse dérisoire*).[168] It doesn't take a Fanon to diagnose this hypersexualization of the black male body and the wanton "demolition" of the white female body. What Fanon did not write about was the exploitation of this formula for fun and profit, through products like this novel.

We will see several cases, most notably that of Romain Gary, in which hoaxing and death cross paths. The first death associated with the Vian hoax

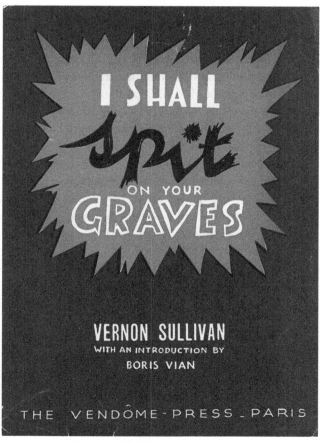

FIGURE 9. Cover of translated novel *I Shall Spit on Your Graves* (Paris: Vendôme Press, 1948), passing as original English text. Beinecke Rare Book and Manuscript Library, Yale University.

was a sensational case of murder for which *J'irai cracher* was blamed; the murderer had underlined gory passages of the novel before strangling his mistress. Shrieking headlines in the Paris newspapers made the novel a best-seller, even as Vian defended himself as translator; said he was the "first to be sorry not to be Sullivan"; and denied any causal link between the novel and the murder.[169] If that *affaire* wasn't enough, death called again. In a bizarre twist, Vian, aged thirty-nine, ten minutes into a private screening of the first film made from *J'irai cracher*—a movie he had contributed to but disapproved of—, rose and violently objected to the inauthenticity of the French actors playing Americans: "Those guys are about as American as my ass!" were his last words. He had a heart attack and died on the spot.[170] (The film is preposterous and inadvertently hilarious in its representation of America—with Trenton, New Jersey, looking exactly like Nice, France; but then the novel itself is not known for its hyperrealism.) A critic comments: "Vian would have to die to escape from Vernon Sullivan" (as Gary would have to die to escape Emile Ajar).[171]

This novel was both a hoax and a parody. All hoaxes involve some amount of parody and pastiche, in the sense that the author is writing as someone else, often in a heterostyle. But by doing so, the real author is producing a fake object that, with any luck, will *pass* for the real thing. And as we have seen many times, the work can then live on as the very thing it was created to imitate; the irony and the parody can melt away. This seems to be the case with Vian's *J'irai cracher*: the book lives on to this day as the noir potboiler it was born to imitate, enjoyed as such by many thousands of readers. A book that, if placed on a syllabus, might get an American professor in trouble with Title IX, is on sale widely in France without controversy (but no doubt not taught in French universities, either, if for other reasons).

In my reading, even if he was the "first to put quotation marks around the 'hardboiled' thriller,"[172] Vian did nothing to undercut the genre he was pastiching; *au contraire*. And for that reason he stands in interesting contrast to Queneau.

*

Raymond Queneau is known to posterity by a number of extremely clever works, including *Exercices de style* and *Zazie dans le métro* (made into a famous film by Louis Malle). For Queneau, "the life of the mind was . . . a great *ludic* activity," and literature was "festive potlatch."[173] In 1947, he invented a female alter ego. She was Sally Mara, an Irishwoman, the author of *On est toujours trop bon avec les femmes* (*We Always Treat Women Too Well*) (figure 10).[174] The title in French was followed by the explanation *roman irlandais*

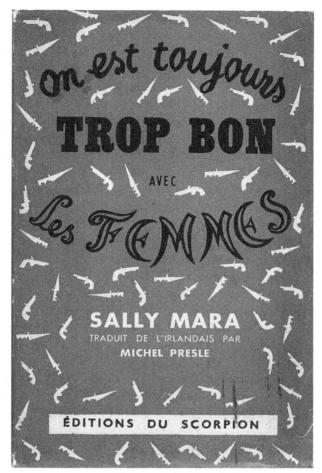

FIGURE 10. Original edition of Raymond Queneau (Sally Mara), *On est toujours trop bon avec les femmes* (Paris: Editions du Scorpion, 1947). Beinecke Rare Book and Manuscript Library, Yale University.

(an Irish novel), "translated from the Irish by Michel Presle," and a wrapping band that announced: *Inédit de la chaste Irlande* (something unheard-of from puritanical Ireland).[175] So Queneau's hoax, like Vian's, was a fake translation; but Queneau's had an extra layer of deception, since Presle did not exist.

Queneau had serious credentials as a wordsmith. He was one of the founders of a literary group exuberantly devoted to the way of play, in fact institutionalizing that approach to writing: OULIPO, organized in 1960 at a colloquium that was, in fact, devoted to Queneau's work. It is no wonder that he was later suspected of being the real Emile Ajar: he had hoaxed before, and he was capable of chameleonic changes of writing style. That was the whole point of *Exercices de style*: he was a virtuoso who could write anything, in a plethora of heterostyles, ninety-nine times over, apparently without effort; *Exercices* was published in the same year as *On est toujours trop bon*. One of Queneau's long-term goals was to bring oral and written French closer together again, forging a written "neo-French" that broke a lot of grammatical and orthographical rules.[176] Such a project has strong resonances in the context of intercultural—and particularly interclass—hoaxing: one of the prime tricks of impostors like "Alice," Danny Santiago, JT LeRoy, and Emile Ajar is to write in a more oral or "street" style. (The free-indirect discourse and interior monologue used in *On est toujours* are prime tools for that project.) In short, Queneau had all the makings of a world-class hoaxer. Recent work on the Sally Mara books has tended to ignore the initial hoax, treating the name as a transparent pseudonym.[177] But it was not that at first, nor, officially, for fifteen years: Queneau's name appeared nowhere on the first edition, because he was careful to sign his editorial notes as "M. Presle" and to erase all traces of his own name from the manuscript.[178] Although his authorship was mentioned in the press as early as 1948,[179] it was only in 1962, with the publication of the "complete works of Sally Mara" that Queneau's name appeared on the title page of this novel.

True to the tradition of fake translations and "found" manuscripts, *On est toujours trop bon* begins with a "note from the translator," Michel Presle (originally signed by Queneau, who removed his name entirely from the proofs before publication).[180] Presle traveled in Ireland between 1932 and 1939 and met Sally Mara. A poet friend of Mara's gave the manuscript of a novel—not a memoir, exceptionally in this context—to Presle after her death in 1943. She wanted him to publish it in French, knowing that its sexual content would never see the light of day in Ireland. Buyers of this book in 1947 had no reason to disbelieve any of that. Queneau will gradually introduce many new layers of complication, as Sally Mara later claims to be alive when she issues her *Journal intime* and complete works. But for our purposes, the period from 1947 to 1962 constitutes a time of actual (if imperfect) hoax.

The uses and abuses of sex and violence in this novel—"unique in Queneau's work"[181]—are complicated. In an interesting contrast to what we will see in the would-be Beur author Chimo, one critic describes Queneau's use of sexual content "as a pretext for linguistic innovation" and play.[182] Some play: the novel depicts seven sex acts, both voluntary and involuntary, involving an Englishwoman named Girtie Girdle, held by rebels inside the Dublin Post Office during the Easter Rising. It has nonetheless been described as "gut-bustingly funny."[183] (Girdles, by the way, are for Queneau "always . . . a symbol of culture's highest aspirations.")[184] Girtie is another Lolita in that she is a sexualized virgin, but unlike Chimo's Lila, Gertie uses her quickly acquired sexuality as a weapon. The writing of the novel toys with issues of consent and rape in perverse ways that are almost impossible to parse. Gertie is the first to initiate—to "provoke"—sexual contact with her one of her captors, Chris Callinan, who is described (from her point of view) as virile and attractive (108–113, 116/83–87, 90). After the first act, she says "Take me" (123/95); and after the second, she is "radiant with satisfaction" (129/100). Callinan later says it was "rape . . . Or maybe she had *me*" (170–71/134–35). With a second rebel, Gertie is inert, and the act is clearly rape, as she labels it later.[185] She repulses the third, O'Rourke, and a shell mortally wounds him; he hands his severed penis to her and dies. " 'Poor little thing,' she murmured" (209/165). Gertie then seems to encourage one of the two rebels who is gay to have sex with her, then withdraws consent; the two anally rape her (216–17/170–71). Her British commodore fiancé arrives to save her. Overall it is clear that Gertie has been able to use sexuality against her captors, even as she is also victimized by them. "That's one less," she says to herself with satisfaction when one of them dies.[186] She wins in the end. She has the two gay rebels executed for trying "to look at my ankles" (220/173), and she goes on to marry her boring British officer. The language of the novel is full of bilingual puns, allusions to Joyce, and parodic English-in-French à la Ionesco's *Bald Soprano* (which came three years later). Some of the narration is interior monologue from Gertie's point of view, in neo-French like Molly Bloom's neo-English.

Now let us recall what critics have sometimes forgotten: that this tale was supposedly concocted by one Sally Mara, Irishwoman, writing in Irish. The sexual politics of the novel would in that case seem very easy to read: this is a kind of female-sploitation story that ends in sexual empowerment. Gertie Girdle is a Foxy Brown before her time. But what about the question of nationality? Why would an Irishwoman make an Englishwoman, a fierce opponent of the IRA, her heroine? That would be hard to explain unless Sally Mara was, long after Irish independence, a loyalist to the British crown, which seems unlikely.

Knowing that Queneau is the author, of course, puts these questions in a different light. Jordan Stump says that Queneau's "perversely and relentlessly playful language renders his novel useless as pornography, as history, or as gorefest . . . ," and the result is "a perfectly undefinable whole."[187] But there may be something more stable underneath the surface. As Valerie Caton points out, Gertie *defeats* the rebels by means of her sexuality: all of them are dead at the end, making the novel a "calculated act of literary sabotage" against the genre it was pastiching, the hard-boiled novel and its violent exploitation of women.[188]

Three years before publishing *On est toujours*, Queneau wrote an article attacking James Hadley Chase's *No Orchids for Miss Blandish*, calling it "fascist."[189] That was his motivation. The novel is the opposite of what it appears to be. In other words, Queneau wrote this in order to destroy, not to reinforce, the idea that is reflected in the title, or, as one male character voices it to another: "Women suffer all the time. You might even say it's what they're made for" (192/151). The Sally Mara hoax allowed Queneau to sabotage the genre from the inside, disguised as a woman, without leaving his own fingerprints behind.[190] The perfect crime. He defeated not only gender essentialism, but also "fascism."

My feeling is that these two hoax texts, despite all their similarites, differ in fundamental ways. Vian exploited exploitation under guise of fighting (American) racism; he left the hard-boiled genre intact and perhaps even improved by his extremely lucrative use of it.[191] Queneau, on the other hand, undermined the genre, failing commercially, but leaving behind a bizarre text that deserves more attention than it has received.

Did Camara Lie? Two African Classics Between Canonicity and Oblivion

What if one of the most beloved classics of African literature turned out to be a fake, written by white hands? How about two classics? This is going to be painful.

The Cameroonian novelist and critic Mongo Beti, who lived in exile in France for decades while contesting power in his home country, told a story about the Guinean writer Camara Laye, whom Beti had long disdained as a producer of "rose-colored literature." Attending a conference in Berlin in the summer of 1979 that brought together a who's-who of African writers, Beti says he met Camara for the first time and found him to be a "little old man" with a sweet smile. In conversation, Camara tried to persuade Beti that the place for an African writer was in Africa; otherwise "we run the risk of false writing" [*nous risquons d'écrire faux*]. On June 24, a "significant incident" took place. Camara did a reading from his latest book, *Le Maître de la parole*; the South African novelist Lewis Nkosi spoke from the floor to ask a question, making a favorable passing mention of Camara's first novel, *L'Enfant noir*. Beti writes:

> Absolutely nothing would have let me predict what then happened. Suddenly Camara Laye stood up with an angry grimace and rage in his eyes, walked through the assembly, and came up to me; he took my hand and solemnly declared: "Professor, you can attest, can't you, that I wrote my own novel *L'Enfant noir* myself?"[192]

It was "a scandal," Beti writes; the room filled with murmurs. Camara had apparently misunderstood Nkosi's spoken English, in which there was nothing but praise. The anecdote leaves the distinct impression that Camara, ailing and with only seven months left to live, was tormented by rumors and doubts about the authorship of his own works and unnecessarily made a spectacle of his feelings. The surprise is that he mentioned *L'Enfant noir*, whereas the doubts had always focused on his other famous novel, *Le Regard du roi*. By publishing this anecdote in 1979, before Camara died, Beti blew the lid on questions that had been circulating under the surface for decades and expanded the cloud of suspicion.

Camara Laye lived from 1928 to 1980. Four books were published under his name, two of which achieved lasting international fame: *L'Enfant noir/ The Dark Child* (1953) and *Le Regard du roi/The Radiance of the King* (1954). The status of *L'Enfant noir* has been almost without peer among Francophone African texts. One of the most readable and lyrical depictions of African village life, this Bildungsroman poignantly and with understatement tells the story of a young man's nonviolent rupture from a culture that he never fully mastered. No survey of Francophone African literature has been complete without *L'Enfant noir*, and enormous amounts of scholarship have been devoted to this small novel. *Le Regard du roi* has a different, more complicated history, but it too has attracted a great deal of scholarly atttention, of a largely different, more ambitious, kind. Now, largely thanks to a new introduction by Toni Morrison in a new edition by the publishing arm of the *New York Review of Books*, *Le Regard du roi/The Radiance of the King* is again prominent, important, and problematic. The two books have distinct histories and need to be reviewed one at a time. Together, they have had considerable influence on the idea of Africa in the larger world.

The study of these novels was revolutionized by Adele King's book *Rereading Camara Laye* (2002)—although one would not necessarily know that from reading the scholarship that has followed, much of which simply ignores her revelations. Using exhaustive research in several countries, King originally "set out to disprove" longstanding rumors about Camara's authorship, the notion that "*L'Enfant noir* was written by a white woman," and the direct testimony of the founding critic of Francophone African literature, Lilyan Kesteloot, who said that Camara told her "that a white man had written *Le Regard du roi*."[193] Kesteloot had written in 1981: "Camara Laye died in 1980. He had told me (and it must finally be indicated here) that *Le Regard du roi* had been written by a *white man*. This takes nothing away from his worth as a person, but it should call a halt to the learned speculations of European critics about the soul and the black mystique in this novel."[194] As we will see, one of the problems here is that Kesteloot's report of Camara's confession has been widely ignored, or dismissed.[195]

Instead of the exonerating evidence about Camara that she expected, King found a web of doubts and strong evidence that Camara was not the sole author of either novel. Thus King not only confirms Camara's confession to Kesteloot about *Le Regard du roi*, but, more surprisingly, argues that *L'Enfant noir* was the result of "a collaboration among [Camara Laye] and four other people" including two women, Aude Joncourt and Marie-Hélène Lefaucheux, aided by the Ministry of France Overseas. Camara was "groomed for a role supporting French colonial policy for some time," and *L'Enfant noir* was advanced as a part of this strategy.[196] King believes that *L'Enfant noir* likely tells Camara's own story, but in words that are not entirely his own; it would thus be an "as-told-to" autobiography. For one of Africa's most-loved literary works to be the product of the French colonial propaganda machine—a Trojan Horse, part of an effort to "retain control of Africa"—is truly a scandal and highly disheartening.[197] As for the writing process itself—whether Camara only spoke as someone else wrote, or if he at least wrote some of the manuscript in some form—King found no physical evidence.

On the other hand, King says that *Le Regard du roi* was a manuscript that Camara was given and to which he "contributed little." (This may explain how the second book followed so closely on the first.) According to King, the principal author of *Le Regard du roi* was one Francis Soulié, "a Belgian with a passion for Africa and an unsuccessful literary career," who had been condemned to death for journalistic collaboration (à la Paul de Man) with the Nazis. During the war he had written to his mother: "The Belgium of tomorrow will be a National-Socialist dictatorship. I am a royalist." King argues that Soulié, in the aftermath of the war, having found safe harbor in Paris and with a private income, "wanted to justify his actions during the war by criticizing the system of justice that had condemned him and by imagining a world in which he could find salvation." That world is the Africa of *Le Regard du roi*. What were Soulié's ties to Africa? He had apparently read a great deal and could speak about Guinea with ease. Michel Leiris's *Afrique fantôme*, which had a new edition in 1951, may well have served as a sourcebook for Soulié in his writing of *Le Regard*.[198] Camara and his wife lived in Soulié's Paris apartment in the mid 1950s, and it was said that "Soulié wanted to adopt Laye." He did adopt another Guinean young man, Kelefa Keita, who refused to cooperate with King's inquiry. Soulié's papers remain unseen. Soulié and Kelefa Keita may have done some writing together, but it is lost; Soulié died in 1976 without ever having seen Africa.[199]

Simon Bolivar Njami, the father of the writer Simon Njami, was a Protes-

tant pastor living in Switzerland in the 1950s. King says that "Laye had con-
fided the story of *L'Enfant noir* and *Le Regard du roi*" to Njami *père*, namely
that the first book was a collective collaboration and that Camara was simply
not the author of the second one. Despite the fact that he supposedly possesses the manuscript of *Le Regard*, Simon Bolivar Njami will not discuss
the matter, because, King says, "he regards any research into this question as
damaging to the validity of African literature." But he must have passed on
Camara's confession to someone, apparently his son, who passed it on to King
in 1994.[200]

Between fascism on the one hand and colonialism on the other, and with
the reputation of one of Francophone Africa's best-known authors at stake, it
is no wonder that many of those with knowledge of this affair were reluctant
to share it with King. As with other impostures that we have seen, manuscripts
are either missing—there was supposedly a flood at the publisher's—or kept
unavailable out of fear of damaging the reputation of African literature. What
little has been written about King's work has sometimes been inaccurate. The
introduction to the special issue of *Research in African Literatures* devoted to
"textual ownership" stated in plaintive tones that "even a canonized author
such as Camara Laye is not immune to the scrutiny of the plagiarism detec-
tives," suggesting two things: first, that Camara perhaps *should* have been immune to scrutiny because of his canonical status; and second, that King alleged plagiarism. Neither of those ideas is valid. If anything, canonical status
calls for heightened scrutiny rather than immunity; and King alleged imposture by persons other than Camara, not plagiarism by him. That special issue
of *RAL* would have been the perfect context for a full examination of the
implications of King's work and of Camara's legacy, but instead it contained
only a dismissive, defensive review by Abiola Irele.[201]

Both Camara novels were published by Plon, the same house that issued
the first works of Elissa Rhaïs in the colonial era and the two books by Chimo
in the postcolonial period. We have already seen the background of conservatism, anti-Semitism, and procolonialism associated with Plon. During World
War II, the house had aligned itself with Vichy and published collaborationist
books, making substantial profits; its directors were put on trial after the war
(the charges were dismissed). When the first two books signed by Camara
Laye came out in the early 1950s, Plon still had a distinctly backward-looking
reputation.[202] The pastoralism of *L'Enfant noir* in particular was right at home.
Asa "Forrest" Carter comes to mind.[203]

King's revelations have been, as I said, largely and widely ignored, but also
actively disputed by some critics. In order to discredit King's work, it would
be necessary to show significant flaws in her research or in her thinking, or to

find countervailing evidence of some kind, demonstrating that Camara Laye actually wrote *L'Enfant noir* and *Le Regard du roi*. The most forceful critique of King's book (in fact one of very few) came from the eminent critic Abiola Irele, writing in *RAL*. While conceding that King has produced "an impressive work of scholarly research and investigative zeal," he calls her conclusions "unproven" and "unconvincing." The basic problem with Irele's argument is that he cannot refute the evidence about publishing that King has produced; he can only argue, as King does herself, that it does not add up to a smoking gun; and he can say, as he does, that he is not happy about the results. Citing Diallo's *Force-Bonté* as an example of a work that "could not possibly have been created by the person whose name is advertised as its author," but in which Diallo's "voice [nonetheless] comes through the French text," Irele invokes Alain Ricard's concept of "supervised literature." The methodological problem here is that Irele is attempting to disentangle "voices" and "hear" a Diallo, or a Camara, distinct from the voice of the amanuensis or ghostwriter. That can only be what he himself calls "pure speculation." Moving on to *L'Enfant noir*, Irele examines the ideology of the text, looking for signs of its origins; but that, too, is a faulty approach: anyone *can* write anything, and "likelihood" is not proof. It is important to remember: it was not clear why a Klansman would write *Little Tree*, but deeper examination showed, first, that he had, and second, why. *L'Enfant noir* depicts a happy childhood in Africa, with scant influence of French colonialism: does that favor or discredit the *mission civilisatrice*, and what would that, in turn, say about authorship? Irele argues that because *L'Enfant noir* may possibly have an anticolonial subtext and "bears a polemical import," it *must* have been written by Camara, an African.[204] I do not find that convincing.

Irele's attempt to refute King's book is undermined by his own reliance on speculation, hunches, could-haves, and would-haves. To say that Camara "could not but have benefited" from the French education system is not to prove he wrote his own books. Irele's emotional claim that King has "tarnished the memory of Camara Laye" does nothing to repair Camara's literary legacy.[205] Irele is right to say that King sometimes indulges in attempts at after-the-fact forensic reading (discerning a "European sense of literary form"[206] or citing the use of the imperfect subjunctive as evidence of European "help"). But those moments are only in addition to her detective work about the actual origins of the novels. Another critic attacks King, groundlessly ascribing to her an intent to "restore the authority of the European author," while ignoring her actual findings about the publication of *Le Regard du roi*—not to mention Camara's confessions to Njami and Kesteloot.[207]

What remains in the end is King's research, which amounts to a massive and largely convincing accumulation of circumstantial evidence, by a scholar with decades of bona fides in African literature. She is honest and forthright about what she was able to learn and what remains either unclear or unknown.[208] Her case for the prosecution would not hold up in a court of law, but literary history is not a court of law.

Irele's closing argument is based on his visit to Camara Laye's deathbed: "I recall having been struck by the similarity between Laye's speech patterns and his writing style: the short, hesitant phrases and repetitions that are a hallmark of his texts, a fact that settled for me once and for all the questions of the provenance of the novels that bear his name" (123). It is surely far-fetched to conflate the speech patterns of a man who is dying with a writing style, his or someone else's; it simply cannot be considered as conclusive evidence. Furthermore, the last book published by Camara, Le Maître de la parole, whose authorship has *not* been called into question, is written in a style that is not particularly marked by "short, hesitant phrases."[209]

Before proceeding, I want to repeat what I took away from reading King's book when it first appeared: her work should motivate us to reread and reconsider all previous interpretations of "Camara Laye," and perhaps to rethink our notions of what "can" and "cannot" be written by a person from any particular background.[210] If the two principal works signed Camara Laye are intercultural impostures, how can they be read now? I cannot take the space to perform two complete (re)readings. What I think is most called for now is an assessment of the impact and implications of King's findings. Camara's two best-known novels have been left in a state of unhealthy ambiguity, suspended between canonical status and oblivion.[211] Clearly, an ongoing silence is not good enough.

In the analysis that follows, I will proceed with the working assumption that King's research is valid, for two reasons: first, no one has refuted her evidence; and second, doing so is the only way to explore the implications of her findings. In the absence of absolutely conclusive proof, however, I will proceed with caution. King acknowledges the aporias in her research. And there is a clear distinction to be made between the two novels: on the one hand, King has raised serious questions about the authenticity of L'Enfant noir, but she was not able to prove definitively that it was written by someone else. So we must examine it as a liminal, shadowy case, and ask, What if? On the other hand, it is widely admitted that there is little chance that Le Regard du roi was written by Camara Laye, and we can look at it in a much sharper light.[212] Even if his authorship of both novels were miraculously to be definitively demonstrated at some point in the future, these questions about authorship, identity, and imposture are worth asking now.

✶

With few exceptions, this study has found stylistic evidence and forensic reading to be less than probative, interesting only as an after-the-fact exercise. I do not think it is possible to produce smoking-gun evidence about authorship by reading the style alone. The case of Camara Laye is somewhat different from others we have seen, in that the two novels published in rapid succession in 1953 and 1954 were so divergent in style and content. It was hard to see how the same author could have written both. Style was therefore the first clue in the minds of many readers, who found the discrepancy strange. The first novel is placid, sincere, realistic, specific, and nostalgic; the second is "singular," mystical, vague, and surreal.[213] King reviews the style question in detail, using a before-and-after approach, while maintaining, as I do, that "it is not possible to prove or disprove authorship by examining the style of a work of art" (75).

Numerous times in the course of this study I have quoted critics who were duped by hoaxes. Now it's my turn. In an earlier book, I made *L'Enfant noir* one of the linchpins of what was supposed to be a study of Mande (or Malinké) culture, in a chapter called "*L'Enfant noir*, Totemism, and Suspended Animism."[214] My goal was to reinsert the novel into what I thought was its proper original cultural context:

> To state it simply, *L'Enfant noir* may be closer to traditional Mande art than has been suspected; there may be a concrete sense in which Camara was a *literate griot*. The fact that Camara was born into *nyamakala* status [the hereditary caste of those designated as artisans and bards], as the son of a smith, forces us to confront the question of the transformation and retention of traditional aesthetics within new media such as the francophone [African] novel. (125)

If the novel was written by French people, with any degree of participation by Camara—if this is, as King herself maintains, "still Laye Camara's story" (173)—, then some shreds of this project may be salvageable. The text may well recount his life with some fidelity and thus bear a relation to Mande culture. But the whole idea is severely compromised, as can be shown by simply substituting the name on the cover: if the author were listed as Aude Joncourt or Marie-Hélène Lefaucheux, would I or anyone else have looked to *L'Enfant noir* as an important artifact of Mande culture?[215] Unlikely. My eager analysis of the word "totem," which fit into my anthropological scheme all too well, now seems particularly abject. If the hands doing the writing of the novel were those of Aude Joncourt, an anthropology student, did she slip this term of art into her transcription of Camara's spoken discourse, just for the fun of it? For Mongo Beti, "totem" was a red flag from the beginning, in 1955: "The evocation of the totem is so artificial as to not be credible. One had the impression that someone had prompted him." Beti called it "pathetic."[216]

If Joncourt was the writer of *L'Enfant noir*, or if it was "a team of ghostwriters," as Beti suspected,[217] what can we now say about the novel's putative "art of auto-archaeology"? *L'Enfant noir* as a "vibration of the soul"? The "spiritual journey" of goldsmithing? Can *L'Enfant noir* still be considered "a legitimate Malinké voice," as King herself says?[218] If the names of Joncourt or Lefaucheux had appeared on the cover, the novel would always have been read from a very different angle: as the image of a certain Africa that the French government wanted to maintain and promote. Any relation to Mande culture or the African soul would have been seen as incidental and deeply suspect. Rightly or wrongly, the book, as lovely as it is, would have long since been relegated to the footnotes of colonial history.

*

If King is right, and the whole establishment of Francophone African literature was fooled by the *Enfant noir* imposture for decades, the story of *Le Regard du roi* is different, in two principal ways. First, there seems to be very little likelihood that Camara wrote any of this novel; second, suspicions about it have circulated publicly, in print, since soon after publication. This is, therefore, a spectacular occurrence of a phenomenon that we have already seen numerous times in this study: the resistance of both the literary establishment and readers to bad news about a text that is admired. In the case of *Le Regard du roi*, the recent high-profile revival of the novel by a Nobel prizewinner, Toni Morrison, and a leading journal/publisher, the *New York Review of Books*, makes for strange reading indeed.

Le Regard appeared with two significant European signposts on its opening pages: an aesthetic one (an epigraph from Kafka's *Zürau Aphorisms*), and a political one (a dedication to the High Commissioner of the Republic in French West Africa; there is no sign of a colonial government anywhere else in *Le Regard*). The novel recounts the story of Clarence, a white man shipwrecked on the coast of Africa, who declares, if not in so many words, "Take me to your leader," the king. But the king has moved away, and Clarence must undergo an archetypal journey seeking him, overcoming obstacles such as his own white hubris. True to the genre—which is as old as literature—his quest takes him through numerous tests, including simply finding his way.[219] (The names of the two "interchangeable" helper figures, Nagoa and Noaga, are anagrams of each other, and, partially, of *agon*, Greek for struggle.)[220] As in Conrad's *Heart of*

Darkness, as in Céline's *Voyage au bout de la nuit*, and as in Kafka's *The Castle*, "there is no possible means of orientation" here. "The South is everywhere," and "one corridor [is] just as good as another" (*Regard*, 88, 90, 158/*Radiance*, 94, 96, 172). Clarence's personality and will must dissolve and fade away before he can gain wisdom. The discourse of the novel itself gives no specificity to this Africa: no geography except North and South, no history, no distinct culture, nor language—hardly even any names.[221] But the Africans are all wise; they say portentous things like "all truths are not necessarily good to say, nor good to hear" (188/206, AT). This Africa is blank, a backdrop for an allegory. Ultimately, Clarence is embraced by the king and his salvific *regard* or radiance, thereby attaining knowledge and wisdom and love—all provided by "Africa."

Despite (or perhaps because of) the blankness of this artificial Africa, critics have been able to perceive in the pages of *Le Regard* "a lesson in African wisdom," "animist metaphysics," "traditional oral sources and traditional metaphysics," Sufi mysticism, "Africa's own home-grown values," and a host of other deeply African traits.[222] It's enough to make one wonder if literary texts do not function largely as Rorschach tests. Some of these interpretations may well retain at least a part of their validity: if the seven phases of Sufi purification are really present in the text, they will remain present, no matter who did the writing. But interpretations based on the identity of the author (such as "home-grown values"), as so many are, need to be revisited.

Meanwhile, if Francis Soulié, the Belgian war criminal—with the "odor" of those crimes still clinging to him—, was really the author of this novel, the overall scheme of redemption through a process of forgetting, surrendering to naked nothingness and shame, makes perfect sense and resounds in these closing lines:

> "My lord! My lord!" Clarence kept whispering. "Is it true that you are calling me? Is it true that the *odor which is upon me* does not offend you and does not make you turn away in horror?" . . .
>
> "Yes, no one is as base as I, as naked as I," he thought. "And you, lord, you are willing to rest your eyes upon me!" Or was it because of his very nakedness? . . . "Because of your very nakedness [*dénuement*]!" the look seemed to say. "That terrifying void that is within you and which opens to receive me; your hunger which responds to my hunger; your very baseness [*abjection*] which did not exist until I gave it leave; and the great shame you feel . . ." . . .
> Then the king slowly closed his arms around Clarence, and his great mantle enveloped him forever. (*Regard*, 252/*Radiance*, 278–79, AT, emphasis added)

Another phrase leaps off the page with possible echoes of Soulié's situation: "Clarence . . . you are not one of the 'righteous'" ("Clarence . . . tu n'es pas parmi les 'justes'" [*Regard*, 248/*Radiance*, 274, AT]). In the context of Belgium and France in the 1950s, the term *juste* has a very obvious meaning, listed in the *Robert* dictionary as "a person who hid or saved Jews during the Second World War." The "Righteous among the Nations" (*Justes parmi les nations* in French) is a status created by a decree of the Israeli Knesset in 1953, around the time that *Le Regard* was likely being written. *Juste* is precisely what Soulié was not.

Going back to the first appearance of the novel, there was some "telling" in this case. Due to the remarkable difference between this text and the novel published just one year earlier, readers raised questions: could these be the work of the same author? The editor of both novels at Plon was Robert Poulet, yet another Belgian collaborator, also condemned to death in Belgium but thriving in France.[223] Perhaps hinting at something suspicious (in which he was himself involved), Poulet said in a pseudonymous review that we have "the black child promoted to the status of avant-garde writer"![224]

Mongo Beti played a key role in shaping and complicating the reputation of Camara Laye from the beginning. In a searing seminal essay published in 1955, Beti attacked Camara's complacent production of a "rose-colored literature" that can only sink into "the quagmire of the picturesque." In the same journal issue, he reviewed *Le Regard du roi*, calling it a "cock-and-bull story" (*une histoire à dormir debout*) and mocking its surrealism: "Going in this direction, anybody can write anything anytime for any reason." One sentence in particular leaps off the pages of that review: "One can no longer recognize the author of *L'Enfant noir*."[225] Did Beti already suspect something about the authorship of the second novel, if not the first? If so, he was very discreet. In any case, his condemnation of both books on ideological grounds could not be clearer.

From the opposite end of the ideological spectrum, Léopold Sédar Senghor raised questions about *Le Regard* in 1955: "I had to skim dozens of pages in order to get interested in the story. I didn't feel Africa." He cited expressions that an African "would not" use, including "don't blush." But nonetheless, Senghor is finally able to find Africa in "the Negro rhythm" of the style, thereby saving the "authenticity" of the book (for now) for his brand, Negritude: "Indisputably [*nul moyen de s'y tromper*] a European does not write like this."[226] But the worm of doubt was already in the apple.

In 1956 an English translation of *Le Regard du roi* was published: *The Radiance of the King*. That same year, a French Africanist journalist named Claude Wauthier interviewed Camara in Cotonou, Benin, and Camara told him that "rewriters" working for Plon had helped him with his books. Wauthier did not publish the interview, only telling King about it in 1992.[227] But Wauthier went public with doubts about Camara's authorship in 1964, in his seminal book *L'Afrique des Africains*, translated as *The Literature and Thought of Modern Africa* in 1966: "The difference in tone, style, and, doubtless, intention between these two books by Camara Laye is such that one is led to wonder whether they are really both by the same hand."[228] Wole Soyinka, the future Nobel laureate, in 1963 accused *Le Regard/Radiance* of "imitativeness," a kind of inauthenticity that did not call Camara's actual authorship into question, but certainly his integrity: "I think we can tell when the line of mere 'influence' has been crossed."[229]

The critic Lilyan Kesteloot, meanwhile, had her own doubts. It is significant that her foundational work of criticism, published in 1963 and later translated as *Black Writers in French*, mentions Camara Laye numerous times, but omits any reference to *Le Regard du roi*; the dean of Senegalese critics, Mohamadou Kane, did the same in his magnum opus of 1982.[230] Kesteloot waited until after Camara's confession to her—the date of which she did not report—and his death, before she went public, in the quotation from 1981 that I cited above. Then in an issue of the journal *Notes africaines* published in July 1982, the Guinean intellectual Mamadou Traoré, known as Ray Autra, stated flatly that *L'Enfant noir* was the result of a "collaboration" between Camara and "a young Frenchwoman, a professor of literature" to whom Camara recounted his life.[231] Kesteloot wrote in the same issue; she raised no questions about *L'Enfant noir*, but made this point about the other book: "For my part, a conversation with [Camara] on this subject [the authenticity of *Le Regard*] convinced me once and for all that he had lent his name in order to provide cover for the work of a French friend."[232] An interview with Mongo Beti was published in 2006 in which he summed up his suspicions about Camara Laye: "a team of ghostwriters wrote *L'Enfant noir*," a text that was "an apologia for tradition," and an obstacle to independence.[233]

Other writers and critics, both African and European, joined in after Camara's death, to express their belief, even their conviction, that *Le Regard* was not written by its listed author. Birago Diop wrote that it was "not ours" (*non de chez nous*).[234] That might have been the end of *Le Regard du roi/The Radiance of the King* as an "authentic" work of African literature; it could have simply faded away (and in fact it has faded away, in French). But then something extraordinary happened.

★

On August 9, 2001, the *New York Review of Books* published an essay by the Nobel laureate Toni Morrison: "On 'The Radiance of the King,'" with a photo of Camara dating from 1954. Morrison's reading of the novel was seismic:

Coming upon Camara Laye's *Le Regard du roi* in the English translation known as *The Radiance of the King* was shocking. This extraordinary novel ... accomplished something brand new. The clichéd journey into African darkness either to bring light or to find it is reimagined here. In fresh metaphorical and symbolical language, story-book Africa as the site of therapeutic exploits or of sentimental initiations leading toward life's diploma, is reinvented. . . . This extraordinary Guinean author plucked at the Western eye to prepare it to meet the "regard," the "look," the "gaze" of an African king. . . . In his portrait of Africa, Camara Laye not only summoned a sophisticated, *wholly African* imagistic vocabulary in which to launch a discursive negotiation with the West, he exploited with technical finesse the very images that have served white writers for generations. . . . We never expect what Camara Laye offers: an African answering back ... Deep in *the heart of Africa's Africa* is more than the restorative gaze of the king.[235]

By the year 2001, when Morrison wrote this, Africa had of course been "answering back" for decades, and there was every reason to "expect" this; that is one problem. More generally: everything that Morrison claims about the novel depends entirely on Camara's identity as both African and author. That identification alone allows her to stake this claim about *Radiance* as a savvy act of post/colonial pushback, an answer, and a deeply emblematic artifact of *Africanness itself.* Replace the name Camara with that of Soulié, and Morrison's assertions crumble and fall. A Belgian war criminal seeking redemption by fictional proxy in Africa is not the same thing as an African novelist offering redemption, through transcendent Africanness, to a white fictional proxy. We have to wonder if recognizing Soulié as the author does not place us right back where Morrison said we started: in a "story-book Africa as the site of therapeutic exploits or of sentimental initiations leading toward life's diploma." *Le Regard/Radiance* may take Africanist literature back to its origins, in "blank darkness"—but with a Hollywood ending.[236]

King's book did not appear until one year after Morrison's essay, so it was not hard for Morrison and the *New York Review* to overlook (or ignore) the more obscure scholarly work—some but not all in French—that had raised questions about *Le Regard*, cited above. Morrison gestures toward and briefly quotes, dismissively, what she calls "much of the novel's appraisal" in "the language of criticism applied to Laye's fiction," suggesting that she has reviewed the scholarship. But she does not say whom she is quoting, and she quickly passes on.[237] Better scholarly diligence—in fact minimal research—would of course have prevented this enormous gaffe. Advertised in the same issue, the *New York Review* itself issued a new edition of *The Radiance of the King*, with

Morrison's piece as its introduction, as part of its new series of books, *New York Review Classics*. The edition remains on the market now. This imposture thus has had a spectacular new lease on life.

On August 10, 2001, I sent a letter for publication to the *New York Review*, in order to alert the readers of Morrison's piece about the questions surrounding *Le Regard/Radiance*. Despite repeated remailings over a period of months, the letter was never published, nor answered in any way except for a printed postcard, referring to the "thousands of letters and comments" received. In November 2002, I notified the editors about the publication of King's book and again received no response.[238]

*

In part 1, I suggested that Camara might be considered as a case of undisclosed ghostwriting or "as-told-to" literature. That is close to what Irele and Ricard see in *Force-Bonté*—"supervised literature"—a label that may be applicable to *L'Enfant noir*. But *Le Regard du roi* is not even that. Why was this whole thing done? As King says, and as we have seen many times in this study, "Where there is a demand, it will be met." There was demand for African literature in French *among French readers*: it is well to remember what Mongo Beti wrote in 1955: "Among Africans the consumption of the staple food known as literature is statistically negligible. . . . We are left with a European public."[239] Camara Laye was apparently willing to be the benign, nonthreatening face of that literature.

Meanwhile, of course, genuine self-authored African literature began to burgeon and has since come fully into its own. These two dubious novels could have been left behind. But they were not, for different reasons in each case. With *L'Enfant noir*, no one knew, and the novel was broadly appealing. With *Le Regard du roi*, the doubts were circulating for years but were kept quiet for reasons of discretion; and then along came Toni Morrison and the *New York Review of Books*, and the rest is history.

*

What, then, is left of Camara Laye? Of the four books that bear his name, he apparently participated in the creation of three (all except *Le Regard*) and seems to have written two on his own: *Dramouss/A Dream of Africa*, an autobiographical novel universally thought to be politically brave but of poor literary quality; and *Le Maître de la parole/The Guardian of the Word*, a scholarly transcription and translation of the Sunjata epic as performed by a griot. *Le Maître*, produced while he was in exile and in residence at the IFAN research institute in Dakar, is highly valued. It appears that he "spoke" the story of *L'Enfant noir* to a writer; that seems to be the most likely scenario. *Le Regard du roi* seems to be a case of outright fraud, about which Camara lied for decades, sometimes quite awkwardly. Yet he also leaked his own truth and stoked doubts about his authorship repeatedly: to Wauthier, to Simon Njami, to Kesteloot, and to Mongo Beti in front of an audience.[240] So it is a complex and troubled literary legacy. Camara's agency in the affair cannot be totally bracketed: if he was a very young man, and taken advantage of in 1953 and 1954, he went on through decades of cover-up, apparently ending in the partial disclosure of the truth. It seems that, in the end, he wanted people to know.

The question of harm or appropriation is particularly difficult to ask and answer in this case, because the facts are in dispute and are likely to remain so. Despite Camara's confession to Kesteloot—which is curiously overlooked—critics seem to think that there has been no moment of "triumphant definitive demystication." But if King is right and Camara was *not* the legitimate author of either *L'Enfant noir* or *Le Regard du roi*—or even if he was the author of only one of them—, then a vast conspiracy has polluted the waters of African literature for decades, with no end in sight. Counterfeit Africanness, now billed as "the heart of Africa's Africa," continues to be sold. In the end, is this a hoax? Because there is no element of play—because all of this was done in dead seriousness, in a conspiracy to manipulate the image of Africa, using Camara Laye as the front man—"hoax" does not seem to be the right term. It was and is a tremendous imposture. The real authors of these books were posing as an African author, by proxy, with Camara as the public face of their work. Camara himself was apparently posing as an author he was not, or not entirely.

Reviewing King's book, Janis L. Pallister concludes with a casual version of the Aristotelian "way of play" and a post-Foucaldian attitude toward authorship: "Ultimately . . . everything depends on whether one regards a literary piece as autonomous. If one does, then authorship becomes irrelevant."[241] Kyle Wanberg offers a more elaborate version of this argument, pressing a Derridean case for subversive "ghostwriting."[242] (That argument has more credibility in cases of guerilla plagiarism like that of Yambo Ouologuem.) While superficially seductive, these arguments cannot resolve a problem such as that of Camara Laye, not as long as literature is seen by so many as a vessel for identity. The identity of the author either counts or it does not, and reports of the author's death have been, so to speak, greatly exaggerated.[243] For defenders of Camara's authorship as well as for doubters, clearly identity does still count.

Should these two books be repudiated, suppressed, or forgotten? No. They should be read and studied, but with asterisks, and perhaps not as vessels of "Africa's Africa." Instead, we should appreciate them for what they now appear to be: cautionary tales about the relations among literature, authorial identity, and cultural authenticity in a colonial context.

Gary/Ajar: The Hoaxing of the Goncourt Prize
and the Making-Cute of the Immigrant

In the long history of literary hoaxes in French, Romain Gary deserves a special place and posthumous accolades for the sheer magnitude and beauty of his caper. A saint and a martyr in the world of hoaxes, his long, prolific, and convoluted literary career has been well analyzed by numerous scholars, including David Bellos, Myriam Anissimov, and Ralph Schoolcraft. My aim here is to review this hoax with a focus on its intercultural dimensions, which have largely eluded analysis. To do this I will focus on one of the novels that Gary wrote as Emile Ajar, *La Vie devant soi*, known in English as both *Momo* and *The Life Before Us*. The enormous paper trail that he left behind will allow us to go deeper into the methods and motivations of a consummate impostor.

Born in Moscow in 1914, he grew up in Vilnius (in Lithuania) as Roman Kacew; he moved with his mother to Nice in the 1920's. He took the name Romain Gary de Kacew and then became Romain Gary in 1944.[244] Gary is Russian for "burn" (in the imperative).[245] Naturalized French in 1935, Gary served heroically in World War II in the Lorraine Squadron of the Free French air force. After the war he became a diplomat associated with de Gaulle (eventually becoming the French Consul General in Los Angeles) and a prolific author, part of a wider trend of "intra-European *francophonie*."[246] His fifth novel, *Les Racines du ciel*, won the Goncourt Prize (France's top literary honor) in 1956 and was made into a film with Errol Flynn.[247] He famously married the actress Jean Seberg and was divorced from her; both of them committed suicide, she in 1979, he a year later. Through all of this, he embraced and refracted any number of identities, as Polish, Russian, Jewish, Catholic, and, most of all, French. And he was, as Nancy Huston wrote, an "inveterate liar."[248] To enter into Gary-land is to find oneself in a zone of, on the one hand, well-heeled French-Republican Gaullist respectability and, on the other, what David Bellos aptly calls "bullshit."[249] Hokum.

By the 1970s, Gary's fame of the '50s had faded, and the *nouveau roman* had displaced his kind of writing. "The public is forgetting me," he lamented; he was thought of as a has-been.[250] His novels were getting little notice; he seemed to represent the old Gaullist order of things and a middlebrow kind of writing. In 1965 he took a stand against both contemporary schools of writing in French: Sartre's engaged literature on the one hand, and the *nouveau roman* of Robbe-Grillet on the other, both of which subject the reader to a "totalitarian truth" that is "incompatible with the novel."[251] *Pour Sganarelle* was an unreadable five-hundred-page defense of the traditional novel. But his solution would itself be rather postmodern: an escape from the self through what he called the "total novel," the very opposite of totalitarian. This would embrace "a constant change of identity" and "a totality of experiences that would let [the reader] decide the dominant meaning of the work . . . [according to] his own preoccupations."[252] Total fiction would "create its own author."[253] Consistent with this theory, Emile Ajar will claim to be both father and son of his own works.[254] But Gary's defense of characters and plot made him seem reactionary—a label that haunted him. *Pour Sganarelle*, which Nancy Huston calls "un flop total," was ignored.[255]

In an act of dazzling cleverness, Gary published an allegory of his own condition of decline simultaneously with the launch of his hoax avatar. In *Au-delà de cette limite votre ticket n'est plus valable* (*Your Ticket Is No Longer Valid*), the narrator Jacques Rainier, a French businessman nearing sixty, suffers from "andropause" and erectile dysfunction, in a commentary on how critics were seeing Gary (not how he saw himself). A remedy that is proposed in that novel bears a striking resemblance to the hoax that Gary was hatching:

> [Jean-Pierre, an elite politician who is thirty-two years old] knew how to play a certain seduction that young men can exercise on older men. It stems from an unconscious quest for a "substitute," the man whom you would choose when you are about sixty, as an image of yourself, if you could start over and become something else again [*redevenir*].[256]

Gary was sixty-one in 1975. What is described here in sexual terms he *performed* through the art of a literary hoax: he created his own substitute, Emile Ajar, who was thirty-five and who would be seen by critics to have the prowess that Gary, "the tired stallion of the Gallimard stable,"[257] had lost. In *Au-delà de cette limite*, the surrogate for Rainier is a dark, virile, dangerous, and handsome stranger named Ruiz—someone similar to Ajar. This novel created a perfect distraction from the caper that it described in its own pages allegorically: critics saw *Au-delà de cette limite* as confirmation of Gary's decline, which cleared space for the rise of his substitute.

So Romain Gary invented Emile Ajar, giving in, not for the first time, to what he calls "the oldest protean temptation of man: that of multiplicity" (29). "J'étais las de n'être que moi-même," he sighed: "I was weary of being merely myself."[258] And he adds this famous, nongrammatical sentence: "Je me suis toujours été un autre" (I have always been myself an other) (*Vie et mort*, 30). It was parthenogenesis, giving birth to himself, by himself, as an other. Four Emile Ajar novels were published in five years: *Gros-Câlin* (Big Hugs, not translated) in 1974, *La Vie devant soi* (*Momo* or *The Life Before Us*) in 1975, *Pseudo* (*Hocus-Bogus*) in 1976, and finally *L'Angoisse du roi Solomon* (*King Solomon*) in 1979. In the same period, Gary published four other novels under his own name and one as Shatan Bogat.

"Ajar" means "live coals" or "burning embers" in Russian, and is thus a coded version of "Gary." That was the story, anyway, debunked by David Bellos as further game-playing.[259] It also means "left partly open" in English, as Gary/Ajar pointed out.[260] In his posthumous unveiling of the entire hoax, published as *Vie et mort d'Emile Ajar* (The Life and Death of Emile Ajar), Gary made it clear that a certain revenge against the literary establishment, "the professionals," motivated him. (We will see that again from Jack-Alain Léger, a certain "I'll show you" spirit from a writer who feels that he has been snubbed; this was also what motivated the hoaxers who wrote the fake Rimbaud text in the 1950s.)[261] He loathed their incestuous, logrolling "Parisianism" (25), which left him with "a profound disgust for publishing" (26). Gary quoted an unnamed "brilliant essayist" who pontificated, after the publication of works by Ajar, that "Romain Gary was incapable of writing that."[262] Ha. Vengeance is dish that Gary ate cold, very cold, in his grave.

But there was another motivation for writing the novel that most interests us here, *La Vie devant soi*. Beyond both resentment and the innate quest for self-multiplication, Gary, despite his wealth and success, felt a long-standing sense of identification with the downtrodden and an ethical engagement with the question of immigration.[263] This was not a casual one-time junket into a ghetto—or not only that. As David Bellos explains, the mid-1970s in France saw President Giscard d'Estaing's government abolish the right to citizenship of immigrants' children born in France; Gary "realized that if he were to live his life over again as a fourteen-year-old immigrant in 1974 he would be an illegal, without a chance of ever becoming French." So he "acquired a new self-image as a clandestine member of the underclass." Here then, is a classic—and apparently profoundly ethical—motivation for a top-down intercultural, interethnic, and interclass imposture. But it also must be said that there was a gap between Gary's intentions and his methods. In order to write *La Vie devant soi*, Gary needed to speak for *and as* an Algerian teenage boy. But Gary "didn't know any Algerian teenage immigrants."[264] So he did "research" in the manner of a real limousine-liberal novelist. This consisted of leaving his residence in the fancy rue du Bac and spending a couple of hours, guided by a black friend of a friend, in Barbès—not even the neighborhood he would write about, Belleville—simply looking, not even eavesdropping.[265] (On the Métro, he could have taken a direct line from Saint-Sulpice and arrived at Barbès within twenty minutes.) That was enough. This was indeed a "temporary visit." He would be taking a leap into the dark, culturally and linguistically . . . and emerging triumphant.

Emile Ajar was originally supposed to be a thirty-five-year-old French doctor from Oran, Algeria, who had known Camus; he was not using his real name because of legal trouble linked to providing abortions. The manuscript was sent to Gallimard by a friend in Brazil.[266] *Gros-Câlin* appeared in 1974, was a hit, and was "subjected to surprisingly little probing analysis."[267] Its success was, in fact, a threat to Gary's plan: the public was demanding to see Emile Ajar, for a body to be produced. There were certainly doubts about the Ajar-Algeria-Brazil story, and rumors flew about who the real author might be. Louis Aragon? Raymond Queneau? In an act of hoaxing audacity that remains without equal (except, of course, for JT LeRoy), Gary produced a live body: that of his "nephew," Paul Pavlowitch, who would "be" Emile Ajar in interviews and on television.[268] The details were all spelled out in a contract, which obliged Pavlowitch to keep the arrangement secret and which established, for posterity, that Gary was the real author. Pavlowitch, who was remunerated handsomely (40 percent of the proceeds), later signed contracts for books and movies as Ajar.[269] He appeared in public just as *La Vie devant soi* was published; the book became an enormous success: half a million copies were sold, and it won the Goncourt Prize, the ultimate achievement in French literature. Total sales would eventually exceed one million, rare for any book in French—and many millions more around the world in translation.[270] David Bellos reports that *La Vie devant soi* "is generally reckoned to have sold more copies than any other French novel in the history of the French book trade."[271] It is worth pausing to consider that notion: more than *Les Misérables* (Emile Ajar's favorite book), more than *Madame Bovary*. And yet *La Vie devant soi* has virtually no academic status.[272] How and why did this come to pass?

At first, Emile Ajar's "real" name was supposed to be Hamil Raja; it said so on papers he (Gary) filled out for the publisher and on his fake driver's license.[273] Would a "French" doctor from Oran have such a name? "Raja" is "Ajar" spelled backwards, so obviously one pseudonym was hiding another behind a cryptonym, and neither would disclose anything about the author's real identity.[274] Ajar is a rare Hindu name, but no one noticed. And what about Hamil, a real Arab name? Was he supposed to be an Arab? No one seems to have asked. The ethnic and religious identity of "Hamil Raja" received no attention. Hamil became Emile (very French, with undertones of Rousseau). Gary later told Pavlowitch that he, Pavlowitch, had made a big mistake by dropping the fake biography of Raja and going with his own.[275] By the time he was interviewed by *Le Monde* in late September, Hamil Raja was no longer

FIGURE 11. Paul Pavlowitch as Emile Ajar. This photograph was published in several French national magazines. Reproduced by permission of Paul Pavlowitch.

mentioned; Emile Ajar, played by Pavlowitch, had a new birthplace: Nice, and new ancestry: Jewish and Eastern European, just like both Pavlowitch and Gary.[276] The interview (which is now conspicuously missing from the on-line archives of *Le Monde*) is bizarre reading. It took up an entire page of the newspaper. With minimal prompting from the interviewer—she speaks exactly fifty words—Pavlowitch unleashed a stream of (it can only be called) bullshit, spinning out an autobiography, then meandering philosophically between profundity and nonsense: "Women are more Jewish than men. . . ." Momo, the narrator of *La Vie devant soi*, "is a Jew because he is an Arab. . . ." "Writing is . . . unlivable."[277] (In fact, this was a very good parody of the speech patterns associated with Momo.) That same month, a photograph taken some years earlier, supplied by Pavlowitch, was printed in various national magazines; it showed a dashing youngish man, running in a white t-shirt (figure 11).[278]

In *Pseudo*, Gary/Ajar explained the rationale for taking the risk of an interview: "The best way of proving you don't really exist is to show yourself openly. . . . There's no better token of being a nonentity" (*Pseudo*, 73/*Hocus-Bogus*, 51). It worked almost perfectly. *Le Monde* raved that *La Vie devant soi*, a "story full of wise lucidity," made Emile Ajar "the herald of the hopeless" (*le héraut des paumés*).[279]

Because of the photograph that he had provided (against Gary's advice), Pavlowitch was identified as Ajar, Gary's cousin, on November 21, 1975. There was a hubbub: Pavlowitch was assaulted by papparazzi in the streets.[280] But the hoax was simply adjusted—Pavlowitch was now the public face of Ajar, while Gary continued to write—and things moved forward on that new basis. Now that the riddle of Ajar's identity was supposedly solved, there was much less attention and noise.[281] In a spectacular achievement of imposture, Gary's authorship of the Ajar novels remained secret until after his death. Best of all, the entire hoax was Gary's demonstration of his theory of the "total novel," articulated in *Pour Sganarelle*: he had become someone else.[282]

The perennial resistance to the unveiling of a hoax is further demonstrated by a story Gary tells in *Vie et mort*. A friend of his, Lynda Noël, saw the clearly labeled manuscript of *Gros-Câlin* on his desk and surmised that Gary was Ajar; when she tried to tell people later, no one wanted to hear about it. And Gary was confident that forensic reading would fail to unmask him, despite using "the same sentences, the same turns of phrase" under both names: "I never feared that a simple and easy textual analysis would destroy my cover" (*Vie et mort*, 18). Literary critics were simply too blind, he implies, too incompetent, and simply unwilling to read the texts.

Gary did not do all of this *in order* to win an illicit second Goncourt, as has been suggested,[283] although he was thrilled to have fooled the literary establishment in this way. After the prize was announced, he reluctantly followed his lawyer's advice and wrote as Emile Ajar to the Goncourt committee to decline.[284] But the academy would have none of it: "The Goncourt Prize can neither be accepted nor refused, no more than birth or death can be refused."[285]

According to both Gary and Pavlowitch, the charade was not fun for very long. Pavlowitch got a bit too enthusiastic and spun autobiographical tales about Ajar for the delectation of the media, and to keep himself in the spotlight; but "the charm wore off."[286] Gary began to see Pavlowitch as a rival and an enemy. Pavlowitch demanded to take possession of the manuscripts. Pavlowitch took over Ajar, and Gary, like Dr. Frankenstein, lost control of his monster. (Gary had predicted this in *Au-delà de cette limite*: the surrogate wants to become the master.)[287] Pavlowitch, credentialed by the false idea that he had written the Ajar novels, got a job as editor at Mercure de France and now wanted to write books of his own as Ajar, which was out of the question for Gary.[288] Gary was, he said, "dispossessed"; "someone else was living the fantasm in my place" (*Vie et mort*, 42, 33). According to Gary's theory, he was supposed to be both father and son of his "total novels," but Pavlowitch was now trying to usurp both of those roles. Pavlowitch thought Gary was a "dangerous metaphysical leper."[289] The "wonderful hoot" of the Ajar adventure, as David Bellos puts it, became "a murky farce."[290]

Then things got even crazier. The third Ajar novel, the aptly titled *Pseudo*, appeared in 1976; it is narrated by none other than Paul Pavlowitch, who happens to be *dingue*, "nuts," and who refers to his famous writer uncle as "Tonton Macoute."[291] Nancy Huston calls this book an "absolute literary hapax."[292] It is the story of the Ajar hoax, in a funhouse mirror: Pavlowitch is the real author of the Ajar novels. I do not know of another case in which a fictional hoax (*Pseudo*) is perpetrated *inside* an existing, real hoax (the Ajar caper). It is hard to keep things straight when reading *Pseudo*: this is Gary, writing as Ajar-as-Pavlowitch, which in turn provides Gary with a perfect framework in which to get his revenge on his upstart nephew. In so many hoaxes, we have seen peek-a-boo gestures in which the real author plants a glimpse of his/her real identity inside the work (Monique de Wael, for example, or Danny Santiago). By using the real name of his fake stand-in for Ajar, Gary dangled a hint of the truth in front of everyone—but the hoax would be disrupted only if someone uncovered the real authorship of the Ajar books, which no one did. The cover story was the best lie of all: the truth; Gary and Pavlowitch were relations. Bellos describes the gesture Gary was making here in all its twisted glory: "Masquerading as the conscience of a schizophrenic pretending to be someone else in order to authenticate the real existence of a fictional author and the strictly autobiographical nature of his work, Gary can at last say what he means."[293] What was that? Perhaps the process described in this sentence: "I began to invent characters I was not every day so as to have less and less of myself" (*Pseudo*, 154/*Hocus-Bogus*, 116). Compulsive self-multiplication asymptotically diffuses and dissipates the self, until there is almost nothing left. Writing can stop when the suffering of being yourself ends (*Pseudo*, 178/ *Hocus-Bogus*, 137).[294] *Pseudo* has been seen as a genuine illustration of the discourse of "psychosis."[295] I will return to *Pseudo* later, for the light it sheds on *La Vie devant soi*.

This story does have a Charles Dickens, in fact two: readers who were able to "tell" by reading alone. Gary says that the literary critic for *Paris-Match*, Laure Boulay, after interviewing him, "demonstrated" in a few words that Ro-

main Gary and Emile Ajar "were one single person." She did this by pointing
out that the catch-phrase "Je m'attache très facilement" (I get easily attached)
occurs in both *Gros-Câlin* (by Ajar) and *La Promesse de l'Aube* (by Gary); that
Madame Rosa's signature line, "You don't need a reason in order to be afraid,"
appeared in Gary's *La Tête coupable*, and in his film *Les Oiseaux vont mourir
au Pérou* (*Vie et mort*, 36–37).[296] Gary had been plagiarizing himself under a
new name. Apparently another young woman, a professor named Geneviève
Balmès, had previously shared similar observations. Gary was ready with an
explanation in both cases: "Ajar is influenced by me," and these cases amount
to "virtual plagiarism" (*Vie et mort*, 38). But magnanimously, he would take
no action against such a young author. Nothing came of these conversations,
and the hoax lived on. Responding to another allegation that he was Ajar,
Gary signed a sworn statement that was published in *Le Monde*: "I affirm that
I am not Emile Ajar and that I have not collaborated in any way on the works
of that author."[297] This put Gary on very shaky legal ground.

Gary's *Vie et mort d'Emile Ajar* is dated March 21, 1979 (five months before Seberg's suicide), with a note addressed to his publishers saying that the
timing of publishing "these revelations" should be determined by them and
by his son after Gary's death. (Careful planning for the posthumous unveiling of the hoax had started years earlier.)[298] If it is tempting to represent his
suicide as the happy conclusion of a gloriously successful hoax, we should
remind ourselves that depression, paranoia, and terror were also behind it.
"He was terrified of being found out as a fraud," writes Bellos (loc. 5810); Pavlowitch described him as obsessed and terrified.[299] But Bellos also says, as
seems fitting, that if depression was a factor, an artful sense of closure was
also involved: "He brought all his work to the best close he could manage,
then did what he had always planned to do" (loc. 5985.) Having put everything in place, Romain Gary committed suicide on December 2, 1980. *Vie et
mort* was prepublished in *L'Express* on July 10, 1981, but Pavlowitch, violating
the agreements he had signed, had beaten the late Gary to the punch: he got
his own tell-all book, *L'Homme que l'on croyait* (The Man Who Was Believed),
into print on July 1, and he appeared on television's *Apostrophes* on July 3.[300]
Le Monde, royally hoaxed and peeved, said the revelation of this "magisterial
imposture," perpetrated by the "monstrous" Gary, was "shocking."[301]

There is one precedent for the posthumous unveiling of a hoax among
those we have reviewed: Psalmanazar. But his was an act of contrition for an
act he regretted, a "base and shameful imposture."[302] Gary's *Vie et mort*, on the
other hand, was a declaration of victory over his adversaries and detractors.

Who killed whom?, critics have asked. Did Romain Gary kill Emile Ajar
or vice versa?[303] Emily Apter points out that Gary converted "the ultimate

piratical act—self-theft—into a ritual of authorial self-repossession."[304] In his suicide note, Gary wrote: "This can be attributed to depression. But then it has to be admitted that this has been going on since I reached maturity and has permitted me to have a successful literary career . . . I have finally expressed myself completely."[305] Depression, self-duplication, and creativity are linked. We will explore these issues further in the case of Jack-Alain Léger.

No one was harmed in the making of this hoax. I would have liked to write that, but with a suicide and a legal mess left behind, the idea is hard to maintain. As for the question of harm, who was *lésé* in this affair? The Goncourt committee for sure. They had been hoodwinked into giving a forbidden second Goncourt Prize to the same author. Parisian literary critics had egg on their faces, their incompetence was unmasked; Gary had seen to that in *Vie et mort*. But what about the question of cultural appropriation?

LA VIE DEVANT SOI

The dazzling technical beauty and complexity of this hoax could make it easy to miss the fact that *La Vie devant soi* is a fable about immigration and integration in France and thus belongs in the same category of intercultural hoaxes that make up the bulk of this study. The real writer, Gary, is a Jewish immigrant, posing initially as a *pied noir* doctor, who assumes the voice of a Muslim Arab boy in a poor quarter of Paris. Strangely, the novel was understood by some to be autobiographical, even though the public face of Ajar, Pavlowitch, was not presented as Arab.[306] So the whole hoax is built on a cultural aporia that was never addressed head-on and never resolved. *La Vie devant soi* was understood to be part of a *littérature de dénonciation*, documenting and protesting against the treatment of immigrants in France: "a moving and cruel portrait of racist segregation," according to *La Quinzaine littéraire*.[307] Myriam Anissimov says that the novel, through the motherly figure of Madame Rosa, a survivor of Auschwitz, "renew[ed] novelistic writing on the Holocaust."[308] There were some dissenters, including one critic who called the novel a "pretty gadget,"[309] and another who (mistaking Jewish humor for anti-Semitism) thought that Vichy would have loved it.[310] But, in a sign of how ambiguous the discourse of the novel was—a question to which I will return below—*Les Nouvelles littéraires* cited Ajar as a successful leftist writer.[311]

La Vie devant soi is the story of an Arab boy, Momo, and an old Jewish woman, a Holocaust survivor named Madame Rosa. She was played in the film version, *Madame Rosa*, by Simone Signoret, who won the César for best actress. The book and the film thus come early in a series of feel-good intercultural,

interracial, or interreligious comedy-dramas, specific to France, that continues to the present day. Such works include: *Monsieur Ibrahim et les fleurs du
Coran/Monsieur Ibrahim and the Flowers of the Koran* (François Dupeyron,
2003); *Les Intouchables/The Intouchables* (Olivier Nakache, Eric Toledano,
2011); *Bienvenue à Marly-Gomont/The African Doctor* (Julien Rambaldi, 2016);
and *Qu'est-ce qu'on a fait au bon Dieu?* (Philippe de Chauveron, 2014, with a
sequel in 2017). Some of these have been spectacular box-office hits. I believe
that that success, in literature and in film, is related to a certain making-cute
project that they all share. I will argue in the next part of this book that Paul
Smaïl's novel *Vivre me tue* and the film made from it, while not exactly cute,
belong to a school of Republican fables that protest against discrimination
while at the same time domesticating and making cute or funny the problems of immigration and integration. They usually, but not always, come from
"above," from nonimmigrant authors.[312] Making cute is not necessarily a bad
thing, not when it actually helps to ameliorate problems and defuse tensions;
but I will argue that the cuteness in this novel is a very complicated thing.[313]
Gary was doing several things at once.

La Vie devant soi is not a classic intercultural hoax because Momo was
never supposed to be Emile Ajar, nor vice versa. Momo is an allographic narrator (not the same as either the fake author Ajar/Pavlowitch, nor the real
author, Gary). But before Paul Pavlowitch became the public face of Emile
Ajar (not of Momo), the author's identity was amorphous and protean, and
the exoticism of the "Emile Ajar" name induced readers to forget the difference between him and Momo; this was all part of Gary's plan. What held
sway was the compelling voice of the immigrant boy narrator. I consider the
novel to have perpetrated an intercultural hoax because of the effects it created. Momo became "real"—fake real.

La Vie devant soi is built on the appropriation of a voice across ethnic-
religious lines: the narrator is a Muslim-Arab boy; Gary was Jewish, as was
the (second) persona of Ajar. According to the strictest rules of ethnic self-
representation—the new essentialism, if you like—the book is therefore already a violation. And there is some tension between the implicit ethic of
representation in the novel (it is fine to cross ethnic lines) and the narrator's
ambition to protect Madame Rosa from being moved out of her apartment,
citing the "sacred right of peoples to self-determination" (234/156). The right
that Momo alludes to of course dates to World War I and the body of international law that emerged in its aftermath; it has nothing to do with an individual's health-care rights, nor with literary representation. This misprision—
along with his confusion between abortion and euthanasia—is part of his
endearing cuteness. His vocabulary is off, but the reader understands that his

moral intentions are pure and sound. And the book was noted as an early call for the right to die according to one's own terms.[314]

Coming in the name of Madame Rosa, we will see, this "right of peoples to control their own affairs" could not possibly be a call for *communautarisme*, of which she is the antithesis. By crossing ethnic and religious lines, by daring to speak in the voice of an Arab boy, Ajar/Gary implies that there are values other than simple autonomy. What are those values?

In this case, no one complained about the cultural appropriation: the book was so seductive, so obviously well-intentioned that no one was offended on those grounds. In 1975, there was no Beur literature to usurp, as there would be in the case of Jack-Alain Léger/Paul Smaïl more than twenty years later. Set in the Belleville section of Paris, full of "Jews, Arabs, and Blacks," the milieu is comfortably and colorfully multicultural. Ethnicity is omnipresent but always ready to be transcended. Madame Rosa's identity as a Jew is mentioned in the first paragraph; she speaks Arabic because she lived for a time in North Africa. She has survived both Auschwitz and prostitution. Her foster-mothering of Momo quickly emerges as the backbone of the tale: "I was the dearest thing in her life" (10/2, AT). The making-cute project comes up very quickly: "My name is Mohammed but everybody calls me Momo because it sounds littler," Momo tells us (11/2). Thus Islam, represented by the name of the Prophet, is made cute and nonthreatening.[315] This comes naturally in the linguistic universe of the novel, written in what Bellos calls a "street-slang kiddy-speak," which was taken by critics as "the authentic tongue of contemporary Belleville."[316] Both ethnic and adorable, Momo's language, full of malapropisms, was simply irresistible. "Purposefully incorrect language," carefully guarded by Gary, was a trademark of an Ajar novel, starting with *Gros-Câlin*, and here again it is highly amusing.[317] "Aren't you the cutest thing!" exclaims a shopkeeper (16/5). (Later, having learned more about the world outside Madame Rosa's protective embrace, he angrily resists being called Mohammed, because "Mohammed in France sounds like 'Arab asshole' . . . a street sweeper or a day laborer. . . . Mohammed sounds idiotic" [222/148]). The hoax that Rosa plays on Momo—making him believe he is four years younger than he is—is part of this same pattern: "I was afraid you would leave me, Momo," she tells him. "So I diminished you a little bit" (229/152, AT). The entire enterprise of the novel depends on Momo's irresistible cuteness.

In this harmonious multiethnic stew, there is only one "original French" boy, Antoine (27/13–14), although Momo, with his brown hair and blue eyes, is pretty sure that he could pass as French: "My nose isn't Jewish like an Arab; I could have been anything at all without changing my face" (87/55). That is surely significant, because it makes difference dispensable. Despite poverty,

prostitution, and broken families, there is an air of near-utopia in this Belleville: Arabs, Jews, Blacks, and even a few "French" people love and support
each other.[318] Madame Rosa, raising a rainbow tribe of orphans, makes sure
that Momo is instructed in the Koran and fasts during Ramadan (40/22,
53/31). The narrative voice being that of a child, grave events like the Holocaust are evoked in simple, flat, and compelling tones.

It is no exaggeration to say that Madame Rosa is the Republic. This is not
to say that she is France, which is not the same thing: France outside of Belleville is racist. But all in Madame Rosa's embrace are equal, as all are equal
before the Republic:

> Madame Rosa . . . wasn't bringing me up to be an Arab for the fun of it [*pour
> son plaisir*]. Anyway, she said that as far as she was concerned those things
> didn't matter, *all men were equal* [*tout le monde était égaux*] when steeped in
> misery and shit, and if the Jews and the Arabs clobber each other it's because
> whatever you may say to the contrary *the Jews and the Arabs are no different
> from anybody else*, which is the whole principle of *brotherhood* [*fraternité*]. . . .
> She respected the beliefs of others. (52/31, emphasis added)

> Madame Rosa hadn't one drop of patriotism in her veins. It was *all the same to
> her* if you were North African or Arab, Malian or Jewish, *because she had no
> principles*. (170–71/111, AT, emphasis added).

The last sentence is a good example of Momo-Ajar's talent for self-consuming
sentences that leave nothing but a chuckle behind: Madame Rosa's egalitarian,
Republican principles make her, precisely, a patriot, but are the very reason
why Momo says she has "no principles." Gary's own mother, the model for
Madame Rosa, saw France as "the homeland of all justice," and Gary's views
may well have been rooted in Polish Romanticism and its image of France.[319]
In his autobiographical interview late in life, Gary said that his mother had
"raised him as a Catholic" ("a fait de moi un catholique") despite being Jewish herself—to be "polite," he says—, just as Madame Rosa raises Momo as a
Muslim.[320]

In the quotations above, two of the three key terms of Republican universalism are visible: equality and fraternity (liberty is not mentioned).[321] Not
by coincidence, the rejection of difference is also of paramount importance
in this passage: we must not think that Arabs and Jews are *different* from
other peoples; they can be assimilated and integrated because they are *not*
different. Difference must recede before the Republic, hence the making-cute
or making-small of differences. Madame Rosa says, "Identity can be deceptive . . ." *L'identité, vous savez, ça peut se tromper* . . . (198/131, AT). She switches
Arab and Jewish boys at will, with that rationale. Rosa is the direct descendant

FIGURE 12. Simone Signoret as Madame Rosa and Samy Ben Youb as Momo, in Moshe Mizrahi's film *La Vie devant soi* (1977).

of the benevolent Papa Mélé in the Josephine Baker film *Zouzou*, an embodiment of *la plus grande France*, "clasping all its children in an egalitarian embrace."[322] Madame Rosa's embrace in the film of *La Vie devant soi* is the same (figure 12).

Momo has a Muslim mentor as well, Monsieur Hamil (as in Hamil Raja, supposedly Emile Ajar's real name), who is the perfect Republican Muslim, a model minority: he teaches Momo both the Koran and Victor Hugo. (Jack-Alain Léger's Muslim narrator will be a good Republican as well.)

Trouble darkens Momo's world only when Madame Rosa lapses into dementia and thinks she is being deported to Germany by the French police. Momo thinks it may be because "the Arabs didn't want the Jews around" (165/107). When the utopia created by Madame Rosa falls apart—when Momo's father shows up and wants to take him away; when Momo finds out he is fourteen, not ten; is called "Arab"; and ultimately, when Rosa dies—he calls it a "national catastrophe" (172/120). She is the nation, Gary's idealized vision of France. Her autonomous death, refusing to be taken away to the hospital like a "vegetable," a refusal defended by Momo as a "sacred right of peoples to self-determination" (234/156), can be seen as a triumph of the Republican nation over the State. As it draws to a close, the novel works the sentimental attachment between Momo and Rosa to the maximum, driving home the plea for Arab-Jewish harmony. The last words of the novel are: "One must love" ("Il faut aimer," 274/182).

The *appeal* of that ending must not, of course, be taken at face value. Gary, as Ajar, was working, manipulating, and subverting the literary system by making this book so widely appealing. Roger Picard stated a principle in 1945 that Gary followed in 1975: a mystification must be "in harmony with the state of mind of the milieu in which it occurs. . . . The public's psychology must be prepared to receive it and believe it."[323] Otherwise, there would be no buyers of the hoax. Gary "read" both the critics and the larger public and knew what they would fall for: a cute immigrant child. Gary took Picard's principle beyond mere success, into an apotheosis of appeal. The enduring value of the image he conveyed in *La Vie devant soi* can be seen in the popularity not only of the novel, but of the movie that was made from it, then remade for television in 2010.[324] And let us not forget, the novel has apparently sold more copies than any other French novel. Momo was the bait in the trap. Once the trap was closed so definitively and violently by Gary, and the entire hoax exposed, "the dirty business of French literature," wrote *Libération*, "lies agonizing in the public square."[325] Ralph Schoolcraft attributes to the Gary/Ajar caper some credit for undermining, if not toppling, the old literary order of "Parisianism."[326] But Momo and Madame Rosa live on in the minds of readers.

Did Gary/Ajar do the same to the stereotype that he did to the literary establishment? Mireille Rosello's reading of *La Vie devant soi* suggests that Momo's odd use of language is a form of *esquive*, dodging and subverting harmful clichés, while refusing to deal with them on their "own turf."[327] Momo destroys "commonplaces that [he] apparently believes in" (132). Many of his utterances take themselves apart in front of the reader's eyes. Rosello says that his nickname itself "functions like a ghost, redoubling [his] identity, revealing and playing with arbitrary conventions." This may be so, but the reading I proposed above is also plausible; this novel, like all hoax texts, can be doing more than one thing at once. Seen purely at the level of the text and its discourse, *La Vie devant soi* may be subtly subversive of convention. But taken within the wider perspective of the hoax, as the work of Romain Gary, its French Republican values are hard to overlook. The hybrid identity ("nonbelonging," "anti-identity," 148) that Rosello sees in Momo and in Madame Rosa, *is also* the anticommunitarianism of the Republic. If Gary undermined the literary establishment with his hoax, he did not, in the text of this novel, "decline the stereotype" of the cute immigrant child; he exploited it and sold it to a huge worldwide audience.

Although much has changed in postcolonial France since 1975, much has remained the same. A statement that Romain Gary wrote in 1980 explains his attitude as a successful, assimilated Jewish immigrant, war hero, and famous writer: he had lived through his "starvation years,"[328] but he would not be made into a poster boy for any identity. Like all good French Republicans, then and now, he feared and loathed "the disintegration of the great traditional values"—those of the Republic—and their devolution into the "tribalism" of "small corporeal identity positions."[329] After his death, he was hailed as a "French writer," *tout court.*

All of this is reflected and refracted in *Pseudo.* The narrator Paul Pavlowitch's girlfriend, Alyette, tells him that she had dreams of being a writer, too, but that writing about "true things" is no longer allowed: "It's taboo."

> We can't imagine true things any longer. To get at them, to unearth them, *you have to cross unbelievable cultural barriers* [*des barrages culturels inouïs*], have to dig as deep as *an archeological expedition,* and then they call you a fascist [*réac*] because what is permanent never changes and is therefore regressive. (*Pseudo,* 66/*Hocus-Bogus,* 46, emphasis added)

Gary is speaking here, behind several layers of masking, with echoes of the resentments that drove him to invent Emile Ajar. It was his project in *La Vie devant soi* to "cross unbelievable cultural barriers"—like all the hoaxers we have examined. We know he didn't exactly "dig deep" in his literal "archeological" research, that trip to Barbès. That part is hokum. But he did dig deep inside himself, and my reading, if not Rosello's, has tended to confirm the basically conservative but multicultural French Republican but certainly not "fascist" permanency of the result: conservative in the sense of being devoted to the liberal, universalist values of the Republic. This is consistent with Gary's broader thinking, as far as it can be discerned: his commitment to "a genuine fraternity of different communities," his opposition to racism, and yet his skepticism about anticolonialism, and his unapologetic embrace of bourgeois status.[330]

*

This was a spectacularly successful hoax: fooling almost everyone, maintaining nearly total control of the public transcript, adapting nimbly to suspicions and leaks, winning Gary an illicit second Goncourt, and even shaking the foundations of the Parisian literary establishment. Only after Gary's suicide was the hoax uncovered, and only *because and how* (with one deviation) Gary wanted it. Gary was the undisputed author of both the means of his own death and the unveiling of his hoax, in *Vie et mort d'Emile Ajar.* (The only violation of Gary's plan was that Pavlowitch published his own *L'Homme que l'on croyait* a few days early.) For the revealing to take place only in a suicide note is perhaps the ultimate gesture of discipline and authorship. This raises the question: did Romain Gary commit suicide, at least partly, *in order* to complete this hoax? To make it a hoax quite unlike any other, a hoax worth dying for? To laugh at everyone from beyond the grave, as he does in *Vie et mort*: "I don't want to go into an exegesis of my works here; days and days after my death, I have other fish to fry" (*Vie et mort*, 40)? If there were to be any legal fallout from the hoax—he could have been sued by the Goncourt Academy, or by *Le Monde* for that falsely sworn statement—it would be mooted by his death. The triumph—by apotheosis—of the Emile Ajar hoax was one effect of Romain Gary's suicide, if not a motivating factor. His last note said, "I have finally expressed myself completely" (*Je me suis enfin exprimé entièrement*).[331] This has the same tone as the last words of his confession/unveiling, *Vie et mort*: "I had fun. Goodbye and thanks." The quest for meaning is finally completed by the literal erasure of the self, of its suffering, and of its hoaxing self-multiplications.[332]

*

A postscript is necessary here, in order to connect a couple of dots. At the beginning of part 2, I touched on plagiarism as one element in a general context of literary tension, if not warfare, between French and Francophone literatures. We have seen how the preponderance of hoaxes have been "top down," as in the case of *La Vie devant soi* (even as we duly note that Gary was simply an earlier-generation immigrant who had assimilated to French literacy, literature, and Republican culture; he said he had changed culture four times).[333] When Calixthe Beyala plagiarized *La Vie devant soi* in 1992, in her very similar novel *Le Petit prince de Belleville*, the dynamic was ostensibly the opposite: a recent African immigrant author was stealing from a decorated hero of the Republic and Goncourt Prize winner.[334] Here we see, therefore, a rare case of *intersecting, dueling* practices of inauthenticity: a "French" hoax that is in turn plagiarized by a "Francophone" author. I reviewed Beyala's unconvincing defense earlier. The "petit prince," the Momo figure, is Loukoum (French for Turkish delight), and he is, by the way, cute. If Suzanne Gauch is right, and Loukoum "entertainingly complicate[s] optimistic theories of hybridization, cosmopolitanism, and globalization by slyly pointing out the continued importance accorded to nation, ethnicity, religion, class and gender," then Beyala is doing more than plagiarizing Gary; she is undermining his Republican optimism.[335] But if, as Gauch also says, Loukoum is, after all, a "new emblem of French universality" (210), then *plus ça change, plus c'est la même chose.*

Who Is Chimo? Sex, Lies, and Death in the *Banlieue*

With the possible exceptions of Bakary Diallo, Elissa Rhaïs, and Camara Laye, all the hoaxes we have examined in this study have been definitively unveiled. That is how we know they are hoaxes. The case of Chimo is different: it is in all likelihood a case of imposture that has not yet been solved and may never be. Or perhaps there is a posthumous unveiling in the works.

But unlike most hoaxes, this one flourished inside a cloud of suspicion that surrounded it almost immediately. The publisher, Plon again, marketed the book teasingly, as a mystery (but not necessarily a hoax), asking on the back cover, "Who is Chimo? A talented unknown? A great writer behind a mask?" An editor's foreword takes the unusual step of casting doubt on the authenticity of the text being published, as if this very uncertaintly were a selling point:

> The story behind this book manuscript is worth telling. . . . The manuscript came to us via a lawyer and was delivered by hand. The author, Chimo, the name that appears in the text, wishes to remain anonymous. We have never met him and we know nothing about him. . . . Chimo's handwriting, done with a Bic pen, was difficult to decipher. . . . Though the narrative voice of the book is clearly sincere, we did consider the possibility that it was a hoax [*mystification*]. The publishers are divided on this question. Is this the work of an established author or the first novel by a young, talented writer (in the book, Chimo says he is nineteen)?[336]

"No matter," because of the "astonishing literary quality" of this narrative [*récit*], "a flower sprung up from the concrete of the housing projects" (back cover of the French original edition). The word *récit* is ambiguous; it suggests that this might be nonfiction, the real life story of a real person, even as it allows for the possibility of fiction and imposture. By reproducing in facsimile a page of the handwritten manuscript, and inserting some fussy footnotes about the physical details of the writing,[337] Plon further reinforces the idea that this might be the real thing. But the director of Plon, Olivier Orban, went on television to say, "I am among those who think this is a mystification."[338] Plon has found a way to have it both ways: the book is both "naïve and sophisticated," genuine and fake, you decide. Orban himself was rumored to be Chimo, and it's worth stopping to consider that possibility.[339] Publishers are usually among the "victims" of hoaxes; for a publisher to be the perpetrator would be new ground and would throw a new light on the question of "cui bono." Plon, whose history we have seen in association with both Elissa Rhaïs and Camara Laye, was no longer in the hands of the same family as it had been

until 1962. But it was the same house. By now deliberately generating an imposture, Plon would be casting a strange light back on those other two dubious authors it had published long before.

When *Lila dit ça* appeared, the Emile Ajar affair had already made the
entire French publishing industry wary of hoaxes. So there was no cover-up
this time; the questions of authenticity were out in the open. Plon's act of
publishing this book was an investment in the way of play, the theory that
"it's the work that counts," not the identity of the author. However, if Chimo
was "a great writer behind a mask"—Michel Tournier, Yann Moix, and Daniel
Pennac were all rumored—, this ruse was quite elaborate: to write the whole
manuscript in longhand, hire a lawyer, and, most challenging of all, to keep
the secret. Plon went so far as to hire a handwriting analyst, who concluded
that the author had "a high level of culture" and "painful affect."[340] This takes
forensic reading to a new level, but with the same results: inconclusive.

Lila dit ça gave a shot in the arm to French literary hoaxing, if for one
reason only: profit.[341] The book sold heavily in France and was picked up by
eight foreign publishers within a month, for a total haul of 1.4 million francs,
"unheard of for a first novel in French," according to *Le Monde*. Cui bono,
indeed. In 2004 it was made into a film, directed by a Lebanese-born filmmaker, Ziad Doueiri.[342] This was "an economic victory for French publishing," all built on an apparent hoax, openly avowed by the publisher if not by
the author.[343]

As for the novel: you know the story. "Chimo," the author-narrator, is only
nineteen years old, a child of immigrants in a Paris suburb. This is a French
would-be JT LeRoy (simultaneous with that hoax, which began in 1996): a
very young member of the underclass who has a way with words. He has
never been inside a bookstore, but he can recite poems he has only heard
once (139/129) and can remember every word that Lila—the object of his tu-
mescent attention—says. He is a natural writer.

Published only one year earlier, *Lila dit ça* sets the stage for Jack-Alain
Léger's *Vivre me tue* and establishes an atmosphere of suspicion about Beur
fiction that Léger will strive to overcome. Unlike Léger, who was always discreet with sex in his fiction, Chimo revels in long, lurid passages of near-
pornography. (Something that strains credulity happens while Chimo and
Lila are riding a bicycle; it goes on for seventeen explicit pages [33–50/23–40];
the back cover art coyly alludes to this, showing a bicycle laying on the ground,
as if spent) (figure 13).

Chimo's perspective is in fact largely a device for voyeurism, as he listens
to and lusts after a sixteen-year-old blonde Lolita named Lila. This is not a
making-cute by any means; it is a making-dirty. Like a porn site Scheherazade,

Plon

FIGURE 13. Chimo, *Lila dit ça* (Paris: Plon, 1996). Back cover (detail).

Lila spins lurid tales about filming pornography and numerous other sex acts as if she has done it all. Plon has come a long way since publishing and republishing the moralistic Catholic *Mon oncle et mon curé* (My Uncle and My Priest, 1889), by Alice Cherbonnel, writing under the male pseudonym Jean de La Brète. (In the interim Plon published Camara Laye, Claude Lévi-Strauss, and Mouloud Mammeri, and has since gone on to publish erotic works by Nedjma, a pseudonymous, supposedly North African woman writer.)[344] Lila is, as they say, *pas très catholique*.

Lila wants Chimo to film her having sex with other men. The quest of our narrator-hero is for the money that will allow him to buy a camera, which will in turn make that form of closure with Lila possible; she promises him a blow job. For pages, he catalogues the numerous hustles that *banlieue* youth can run in order to raise funds, thereby providing majority-culture readers with the insight they are seeking in a book like this: how the other half lives. But our narrator, of course, is different, a hybrid creature whose writing sets him at a slight remove from the world he is reporting on: "I go away and write this, I write slowly just to be somewhere else at that particular moment, to escape on my own" (97/87). He is both of and better than the "useless timewasters around me, the association of failures and headcases" in his world (99/89). He has no path, he is "lost" (103/93), he thinks; but we know better: he is a born writer. Lila knows it too.

Chimo shares a worldview with Léger's Paul Smaïl, as we will see, a kind of hip nihilism: life is "a long wait for nothing" (101/91)—as in "living kills me"; this stance may in turn have been borrowed from Azouz Begag's *Quand on est mort, c'est pour toute la vie* (When You Die, It's For Your Whole Life).[345] And Islam does not hold him in thrall, for "no one has seen the name of Allah written by a laser on the clouds" (112/103). He is a disaffected Arab Muslim in France, but with a good heart and strong secular values. Another model minority and, what really counts: a writer, someone able to record and report from one "invisible level" of the world to another (158/148). It's "you up there, me down here," but writing bridges the gap (or hoaxing pretends to). Almost ten years later, the 2005 riots in the Paris suburbs highlighted the distance between the privileged center city and the poor communities beyond the Boulevard Périphérique; those two "invisible shelves" were made very visible. When Chimo wrote in 1996, "Ça va taper dur bientôt" ("There's soon going to be one hell of a rumble," 158/148), *Lila dit ça* acquired a certain prophetic value. We are far from the Republican optimism of *La Vie devant soi*. The various communities thrown together in the housing project "don't mix as well as the concrete, the more you want them to be the same, the more they stay one thing or another, so in the end they rub each other the wrong way" (158/149–49). Lila's mother, Catholic and bigoted, is no Madame Rosa.

Lila tells Chimo she had a dream about being "gang-banged" by a hundred men who all looked like him. Then she recounts a long sexual encounter with the Devil, in a meticulously detailed description of fellatio and anal sex that goes on for many pages and seems to have no purpose except to excite both Chimo and, potentially, the reader (127–41/117–35). It appears to be significant that Lila's vagina remains intact, despite everything, up to this point.[346] The story about the Devil spreads around the housing project, and the various faith communities react with exorcisms and sacrifices that lead to violence and torchings. The riot is said to be her fault, based on what she later admits was a fabrication—a hoax within this hoax. Chimo borrows a video camera, which makes him wonder if he really wants to achieve the promised closure with Lila. He goes to her apartment and finds his friends brutally gang-raping her; Chimo interrupts them but Lila thinks he is one of the attackers and falls to her death. Lila's discourse has been the condition of possibility of the entire narration and of Chimo's coming to writing; but the book leaves a distinct impression that her dirty talk led to a riot, her rape, and ultimately her death.

This plot leaves disturbing questions in its wake. Female sexuality has driven the entire novel, but somehow had to be destroyed at the end, leaving only straight male sexual desire standing, . . . and literature.[347] To make matters more complicated, much (but not all) of Lila's sex talk was only talk. The story about the Devil was a fraud that led to Lila's violent death. Was this book a much-needed unheeded cry out of the disadvantaged suburbs of Paris, a true Beur voice? True or fake in culture, was it sexist to create, use, and destroy the Lila figure this way? In the sequel novel, *J'ai peur* (I Am Afraid), Chimo lives on as a young, accomplished writer.[348]

Seeking answers to those questions, we cannot fall back, as we usually do, on the author's "real" identity, because we do not know who the author is. We don't know if this writer comes from "up there" or "down here," to use the terms in the novel itself. Our ability to make judgments—for example, that Romain Gary sympathized with immigrants in *La Vie devant soi* because he had been one, but decades earlier, so he was not exactly au courant—is cut off. What if Chimo turned out to be a woman? Would my judgment of the work as sexist have to change? *Lila dit ça* therefore confronts us with our own weaknesses as readers. As Romain Gary derisively pointed out: we can't tell.[349]

Conclusion to Part 2

It would be impossible to attribute a single common purpose to all of these hoaxes. Each occupies a different position on the spectrum between truth and play. I hope to have demonstrated that there is, after all, a certain French-language tradition of differential, intercultural imposture, and that some of these impostures are every bit as entangled in problems of identity as their American counterparts. But at the same time, French universalism and Republican anticommunitarianism have clearly played a tremendous role in these cases as well, providing both a beacon of harmony toward which a character like Momo might aspire and a roadblock to any impulse for difference he might feel. As we now turn to our final hoax, that of Jack-Alain Léger, those dueling tendencies will be again very much in sight.

PART 3

I Can't Believe It's Not Beur: Jack-Alain Léger, Paul Smaïl, and *Vivre me tue*

Denise Glazer: *Qui êtes-vous? Qui êtes-vous?* [Who are you? Who are you?]
Dashiell Hedayat [Jack-Alain Léger]: [laughs] *C'est tout de suite un piège. Personne n'a vraiment une identité.* [Right away it's a trap. No one really has an identity.][1]

Introduction

On July 18, 2013, a strange thing happened. As I was getting deep into my work on the author who is the subject of this concluding part of my book—I felt like I was the only academic critic in the world to be working on him at that moment—I accessed *Le Monde* on line and found that he had committed suicide the day before, throwing himself out of his apartment window in Paris and thus succumbing to decades of bipolar disease.[2] Stupidly, I felt as if my patient had died on the operating table. That day I began reading Jack-Alain Léger's ("homosexually incorrect") coming-out narrative, *Autoportrait au loup*, published in 1982, when few French authors "assumed" (embraced) homosexuality. Describing his psychic relationship with a brother, Louis, still-born (*mort-né*) two years before him—and for whom he thought he was conceived as a replacement—, Léger wrote: *Un mort-vivant ne peut se tuer vraiment.*[3] The play on words is lost in translation: a living still-born can't really kill himself. But finally he did. In his penultimate book, *Zanzaro Circus*, published in 2012, he had described in painful detail the bipolar disease from which he had suffered since childhood.

He (let's just call him that for the moment) entered the literary scene in 1969 as Melmoth (a name likely taken from Oscar Wilde, who in turn had borrowed it from a novel written by his uncle).[4] Melmoth was the author of a poetic novel, *Being*. Two years later *he* became Dashiell Hedayat, author of *Le Bleu, le bleu* (1971), *Selva obscura* (1974), and *Jeux d'intérieur au bord de l'océan* (1979), and translator of Bob Dylan's *Tarantula* (1972).[5] Hedayat was already more than a mere pseudonym, since the back cover of one of his books provided a fake biography: he was half "Mediterranean" and half English; he was planning to translate *The Divine Comedy*.[6]

FIGURE 14. Jack-Alain Léger as Dashiell Hedayat with Denise Glazer on *Discorama* (January 30, 1972).

Both Melmoth and Hedayat were rock musicians as well as authors, and in performances took the pose of being someone else far beyond a mere name change. Hedayat's album *Obsolète* has been called "one of the best French records of the post-1968 period," now selling for "up to €500."[7] His hit "Chrysler Rose" is noisy and full of sexual double entendres, an ode to a smashed-up car in which the narrator makes love to women, telling them "we're *all* smashed up" (figure 14).[8]

In 1973, the author began publishing as Jack-Alain Léger, the name he settled on and which I will use for general purposes here; it was under this name that the bulk of his work appeared, and his friends called him Jack-Alain.[9] But this was still a pseudonym, a mask, and never his legal identity. His first work as Léger, *Mon premier amour*, actually featured a dialogue between Jacques and Alain (like Rousseau and Jean-Jacques), so his new literary identity was already multiple; it was devoted to what he later called the "chaste incest" between himself and his mother, whom he mourns.[10] His works often include doublings of his voice and his self. In 1988 he published one novel, exceptionally, under a female name, Eve Saint-Roch. (All of these author-personae were supposedly born in 1947.) Then, between 1997 and 2001, he went beyond mere pseudonym or pose, to create one of the great hoaxes of twentieth-century French literature, as Paul Smaïl.[11] How and why he did this, how he both followed and deviated from the French tradition of intercultural hoaxes, and what the consequences were: these are the topics I will discuss in this part of my book. This was the first "American-style" ethnic hoax in French literature, because it targeted a recognized, constituted minority living inside the French Republic. Unlike the rest of this book, this section will be an in-depth study of one case.

✳

Daniel-Louis Théron (born in 1947) seems to be the original real name—if not the core "identity"—of the author who eventually became Jack-Alain Léger.[12] He was referred to in some of his book contracts as "Daniel Théron, dit Paul Smaïl." He came by the habit of pseudonyms honestly: his father, whom he "detested," was a literary and music critic for *Paris-Match* in the 1960s and 70s, officially named Ernest Théron, but known as "Yorrick" to his friends, who—perhaps to avoid confusion with the magazine's longtime editor, Roger Thérond—used the noms de plume Jean Buèges for literary criticism and Louis Séranne for music.[13] The name of the father was thus, for our author, always/already a fraught issue: both father and son, for different but comparable reasons, dropped the name Théron, and both were seeking to distinguish themselves from a superior, an elder.[14] In *Autoportrait au loup*, Léger writes: "I never conceived of myself [the pun intended, no doubt] as my father's son," and he describes his father as a "domestic tyrant," constantly at war with others.[15] The son's tempestuous relations with literary critics were no doubt rooted in these "daddy issues."

As of the time of his death in 2013, Léger had published a total of 38 discrete books (including translations but not including reprintings, articles, or unpublished works). He produced this body of work under five different names. "Léger," with its suggestion of lightness, compensated for his being taunted in school as "*la grosse*," the fat girl.[16] But *léger* has other connotations: flighty, frivolous, superficial, brazen—a perfect name for the way of play. It was both a nom de plume and a nom de guerre, he said. War against what? Against publishers and critics, against guilt, against death, against moralizers, "communitarians," falsifiers, and conformists.[17] He claimed that his fictions and lies served larger truths.

Jack-Alain Léger was without doubt one of the great hoaxers and impersonators in the history of French literature. But how could a deliberate liar constantly claim the moral high ground? This is one of the central enigmas of the author's career. His grandest achievement was inarguably the invention of the author-persona known as Paul Smaïl (supposedly born in 1970), whose novel *Vivre me tue* (1997) was (mis)taken—by his design and calculation—as the voice of a generation of Beurs in France. This was not a perfect hoax; it was almost stillborn, but like so many other hoaxes, it survived and triumphed nonetheless. Léger put an end to it in 2003. But even in 2006, suspecting that

Jack-Alain Léger was the real Paul Smaïl, a critic could not shake the sheer verisimilitude of *Vivre me tue*: "All indications, even the language used by the author, mixed with the vocabulary of Barbès, seem to reflect the life of a young Parisian Beur, even if the identity of the author seems debatable."[18] In 2012, nine years after the hoax was exposed, *Le Magazine littéraire* still cited two Paul Smaïl novels, *Vivre me tue* and *Ali le Magnifique*, as among the "best" texts "to come out" of the *cités*.[19] And after the suicide, Walid Salem, while deploring Léger's Islamophobia, admitted that *Vivre me tue* "feels real"—that the novel evoked the banlieues of the late 90s "like nothing else."[20] This is a hoax that has outlived itself and its perpetrator. It is a hoax with a legacy.

This was among the most audacious acts of intercultural impersonation in France in the twentieth century, and once exposed it provoked outrage. And it is at this point that the French tradition of ethnic hoaxing joins the American one: now, in France, despite universalism, there was an identity *inside the Republic* to be hoaxed and appropriated. For the first time in France, there was pushback on identitarian, cultural, and ethnic grounds. How dare a white, middle-class French guy usurp the experience and the identity of a generation of immigrants? What right did he have? The enduring ability of the novel *Vivre me tue* to overshadow fiction written by real Beurs raises questions about authenticity and representation in literature. As Lia Brozgal has argued, *Vivre me tue* is "a complex literary enterprise that toys with notions of universality and of authenticity."[21]

Meanwhile, the literary coup that Jack-Alain Léger effected in the fall of 1997 was not limited to the publication of *Vivre me tue* as an intercultural hoax. In order both to create a distraction (as Gary had done with *Au delà de cette limite*) and to "thumb our noses at the small world of Parisian publishing," Léger and his editor published a second novel on the very same day, under Léger's name: an autobiography, *Ma Vie, titre provisoire*.[22] The similarity of the two titles was itself a provocation, as if daring critics to uncover the secret. Léger later reported that there was far more eager interest in his Beur manuscript than he was used to for his own work, even if one publisher reportedly told his people not to offer Smaïl "too much money."[23] To Léger, this proved the existence of a double standard, a racist one: French publishers were fighting over an exotic author, but wanted to get him on the cheap.

The full measure of Léger's double literary coup can be seen in the pages of the magazine *Le Point* in that fall of 1997. The September 13 issue featured a full-page, favorable review of Jack-Alain Léger's autobiographical *Ma Vie, titre provisoire*, with the author's photograph and a partial list of his previous works. *Vivre me tue* was not reviewed immediately, but it began appearing on *Le Point*'s bestseller list on October 4 and stayed for a month. In early November, the magazine reviewed *Vivre me tue*, with admiration.[24] Léger had doubled himself, and both of his personae were succeeding.

Despite publishing with almost all of the most prestigious houses (Gallimard, Christian Bourgois, Flammarion, Denoël), Léger thrived on controversy and could not maintain relationships with those he called "*les salopards de l'édition*" (the sons-of-bitches of the publishing industry).[25] (For their part, editors found him "unmanageable.")[26] His autobiographical works are filled with bitter complaints about the supposed ill treatment he received at the hands of his editors. Consequently, he would "fire himself," said his lawyer and legal guardian in his last years, Emmanuel Pierrat.[27] "In the china shop of the French literary milieu, he [was] a baby elephant," wrote Yann Moix.[28] He never won any of the most highly coveted French literary prizes, although he came close with *Jacob Jacobi* in 1993, and *Wanderweg* won the grand prize of the readers of *Elle* in 1987.[29] His novels were actually fairly well received among critics, overall, but not well enough to satisfy him: "A literary season would not quite be worth its salt," he whined, "if Léger were not insulted."[30] As we will see, if it had not been for a leak from a publicist, *Vivre me tue* might have won a prize for the best first novel.

Before "Paul Smaïl"

It is not impossible to give a global account of Léger's entire oeuvre, despite its volume, since he repeated himself constantly. Themes and obsessions circulated continuously like the water in a fountain, and his works form a genuine totality or oeuvre.[31] As he said himself, after writing only twelve books, "In their apparent diversity, all these works tell the same story: my story."[32] (But who was he?) That remained true for the rest of his life and career, as reiterations and reinventions accumulated in his books.

Léger wrote in a number of different generic registers, and he played with literary conventions. He published novels, autofictions and autobiographies, children's stories, translations, cultural criticism, and commentaries on art and opera. . . . In many of his novels, under several of his names, one gets the impression that he was reaching for or attempting to reproduce the commercial success that he achieved only twice, with *Monsignore* in 1976 and *L'Heure du tigre* in 1979.

His narrator/protangonist is always male, sometimes straight (*Capriccio, Monsignore, Vivre me tue, L'Autre Falstaff*), sometimes gay (*Autoportrait au loup, Ali le magnifique, Maestranza*).

He often has a brother who was stillborn, an "angel" in his mother's eyes, whom he can never equal or replace. One of his first books was called *Le Livre des morts-vivants* (The Book of the Living Dead), and his principal autobiography, *Autoportrait au loup* (Self-Portrait with Mask) began with these words: "I was born still-born" (*Je suis né mort-né*).[33] In one of many poignant retellings of his own origins, Léger wrote: "My mother, all love and tenderness, mourned in front of me an older brother who died while being born two years before my own coming into the world, a brother I was supposed to replace."[34] He is haunted by the image of his mother calling and searching for this "other child, a child she lost before I was born"; "the dead child."[35] This unreachable br/other, who must constantly be displaced, bears some version of his name.[36] The dead brother is the source of all the doublings and otherings of this author, who, in turn is "always the shadow of an other, of a dead child."[37] Wrongly diagnosed with spina bifida as a child, he feels "doubled, two children: the still-born one and me, or the dead one and the one who wants to live and writhes in folly."[38] He is truly always "the shadow of an other." (A child conceived and raised as a "replacement" for a deceased sibling is a current running through recent French literature, including works by Annie Ernaux and Philippe Grimbert.)[39]

The narrator is often an amateur boxer. The boxing gym is an important element in *Vivre me tue*, a site of masculine belonging.

He is often a curmudgeonly critic of the world around him, deploring (for example, in *Ma Vie, titre provisoire*) "the exemplary spinelessness of the malefactors who govern us, the disappearance of all moral instruction in the schools, the ignoble economy-obsessed propaganda served up to us day after day on television, the continual on-screen celebration of the most sordid petit-bourgeois values."[40] He is preoccupied by the ironies and idiocies of the *société du spectacle* described by Guy Debord, which has in the long run led to a "religion of the festive and the spectacular" and has produced "a false France."[41] (He shares many preoccupations with the novelist Michel Houellebecq, who, in works such as *La Possibilité d'une île* and *Soumission*, implies that his fellow men are all sheep, blindly following false leaders, duped by appearances.)

How could such an inveterate poser, impostor, and showman, so devoted to the way of play, be so opposed, in the name of truth, to a society of spectacle? In his view, his inventions were the *cure* for the false consciousness of mass culture. He would create "no longer the false true but the true false."[42] Léger's stated reasons for writing include the search for truth; to oppose all attempts to "appropriate my person"; "to deny that I am the reincarnation of a brother who died before my birth"; to "escape the machinations of a spirit sect"; to battle "against fanaticism, against obscurantism"; and of course, to denounce publishers and critics.[43]

In 2007, he opined that the society of the spectacle was obsolete, replaced by the internet and its endless circulation of nothingness and falsehood.[44]

Fiction, he repeats again and again, is "the only weapon against universal falsification."[45] Perhaps flattering himself, Léger claimed in one of his later books that he had had such "increasing difficulty finding acceptance for my novels," in effect, because they told too much truth, by creating "illusions that deny the illusion that society maintains about itself," thus throwing a disruptive stone into Narcissus's pool.[46] Along with this (easily rattled) confidence in the truth-value of his own books, Léger articulates a general defense of literature based on the idea that "One can remake the world only in novels."[47] Overall, Léger walked a tortuous line between truth and falsehood.

His narrators are all disdainful of identitarian prisons. They cry out in opposition to all forms of *communautarisme* (communitarianism in Frenglish)— the word expressing a peculiarly French aversion to all forms of identitarian conformism (except Frenchness itself). Most pertinently for our reading of *Vivre me tue*, the Léger worldview abhors all forms of totalitarianism, while tending to place them all on the same level and, in moments that approach paranoia, to conflate community with totality and religion with fascism.

The narrators are obsessed with the Parisian literary milieu and can never find enough bad things to say about publishers and editors—their alleged treachery and perfidy. They are filled with a resentment that stems from "the silence that has greeted so many of [their] books."[48] Diatribes targeting the Parisian literary establishment ("that little Parisian Mafia that tries to rule literature by terror")[49] and the denizens of the Brasserie Lipp can go on for pages. Writing as himself in 2000, Léger lamented going into his second *rentrée littéraire* (the beginning of the French publishing season in the fall) without a new book, and he claimed that one of his novels (*Hé bien, la guerre!*) will never find a publisher because it has been "censored" in advance.[50] (It was published in 2006.) Léger and his narrators mixed a persecution complex with delusions of grandeur in toxic proportions.

His mind is rich in culture, animated by a small pantheon of writers, artists, and composers: Dante, Cervantes, Melville, Conrad, Proust, Schumann. Leitmotifs crop up with regularity and great continuity: Mozart's "Exsultate, Jubilate," Schumann, the Cure.

With rare exceptions, the narrators have little taste for descriptions of sex ("May the reader allow me to avoid the licentious scene that follows," says the narrator of *Jacob Jacobi*).[51]

And above all, the narrators of Léger's works are increasingly preoccupied by depression and bipolar disorder. Léger's later works are like a prolonged flirtation with death and, ultimately, a suicide note. "He who wants life wants death," he wrote in 2000.[52] His illness, as he described it in 1997 in *Ma Vie, titre provisoire*, was "incurable" (218). Convinced that he was in some sense a living stillborn, he sees suicide not as the end of life but as the end of life-as-death: "If I put an end to myself, it will not be to kill my life, but to kill the death that infected me" (*Si je mets fin à mes jours ce ne sera pas pour attenter à ma vie, mais à la mort qui m'infectait*).[53] It should already be clear to what extent he intertwined, even conflated, "life" and "death."

Ultimately, all of these narrators are unreliable, even—or especially—when one of them claims, "I know who I am."[54] I want to review three of Léger's most important works published before the Paul Smaïl hoax in order to shed some light on this devilishly complicated author.

*

Monsignore (1976) stands alone in Léger's oeuvre as the only international blockbuster, selling more than 300,000 copies in France alone, translated into twenty-three languages, and made into a Hollywood film.[55] It was obviously written with that kind of market in mind. The story of a corrupt, virile Irish-American clergyman who becomes a cardinal and head of the Vatican bank, the novel covers all the expected bases in this genre. The film (1982) starred Christopher Reeve and Geneviève Bujold, and its publicity was lurid: "Forgive me, Father for I have sinned. I have killed for my Country, I have stolen for my Church, I have loved a Woman, and I am a Priest."[56] Alongside and despite its obvious soap-opera thematics—clearly written with a parodic intent, reportedly as the result of a dare—[57]the novel's focus on financial corruption in the church actually resonated with the various scandals that have plagued the Vatican bank over the years. It was, said one critic, "perfectly realistic."[58]

The money that he made from *Monsignore* and its sale to Hollywood allowed Léger to live the high life for a time in the early 1980s, hosting champagne-soaked parties on the rue de Lille, until his funds were exhausted.[59] Some say the success was his downfall. He then lived for a time in Montreal. His writing continued at a furious pace.

Autoportrait au loup (1982) is a coming-out narrative, and it provoked the first "scandal" of Léger's career. A *loup* or wolf is the type of mask used in masquerade balls; it covers only the upper part of the face. Léger substitutes the mask for the closet as a symbol of nonliberation for gays, but in his case, of course, his very name and identity are already complicated. (*Masques* was the name of a new gay magazine, founded in 1979.) In the early 1980's in France as elsewhere, coming out as gay was not the banality that it is now; it was an event. The first gay antidiscrimination law was not passed until 1985.[60] Any writer who did come out was likely to be placed in an identitarian box and left there as "a gay writer," the last thing on earth that a protean, contrarian trickster like Léger wanted. So this book was genuinely risky for him.

The early 80s saw the rise of a new gay male culture in Paris; "a veritable gay 'citizen' was born."[61] *Autoportrait au loup* both is and is not part of this history. On the one hand, it was scandalous and brave to be gay and to write about it. On the other, for the emerging gay community in France—of which Léger wanted no part—coming-out narratives were often expected to be constructive and to contribute to the ongoing quest for respectability.[62] *Autoportrait au loup* unfortunately represented homosexuality as one among many neuroses, "perversions," suffered by the narrator. As Murray Pratt puts it, Léger refused "to buy into the American model of coming out with regard to his sexuality."[63]

Having shown himself previously only behind masks, silent about himself and his unavowed sexuality, he was a "fetishistic, masochistic pervert living in secrecy and solitude" (*Autoportrait*, 25). This book thus promises to drop all the masks and reveal the truth. But the truth will not be pretty; his sexuality, which he analyzes through a thick, archaic Freudian lens, is indissociable from fetishism and voyeurism. It is *un mal* (98)—a "disorder," as Pope Benedict XVI would later put it—whose "causes" are to be found in his childhood. He loves women but lusts for men; he could never love a gay man; and in the ultimate provocation, he asserts: "love between two men cannot exist" (106, 207, 208). His friend Cécile Guilbert said "he could only have sex with men but only had feelings for women."[64] Relations with men he described as "love without love."[65] In Proust and Mishima—"two men whom I wanted as brothers" (159)—and in their visions of homosexuality as perversion, he sees himself.[66]

He also wrote: "Through a perverse reversal, which nonetheless seems right to me, it seems to me now that the disorder that affects my morals [*le mal qui me frappe dans mes moeurs*] has earned me, on the other hand, greater moral well-being . . . . My weakness is also my strength" (159). So there is redemption here, but not for homosexuality itself, which remains a perversion. Ten years after publishing *Autoportrait*, Léger continued to say that homosexuality "remains a damnation."[67] No wonder he "keeps [his] distance from the homosexual scene" or "ghetto." This is his way of "living [his] difference . . . living with my contradictions, living in the contradictions." "I refuse to assimilate myself completely to the people of Sodom and thereby lose my identity . . . Man first and then gay; not gay *tout court*" (189). (What identity, one might ask, is that?) Speaking about *Autoportrait* on the must-see literary television show *Apostrophes*, Léger said of homosexuality: "Whatever happens, it is a damnation. . . . I do not want to be reduced to that dimension."[68] Nor did his view soften over time: never one for understatement, in *Ma Vie, titre provisoire* he denounced "gay conformism, gay stalinism" as "insidious terrorism."[69] While subscribing to the slogan "Out of the closets! Down in the streets!" Léger simply refuses to declare Freud's pathological view of homo-sexuality obsolete.[70] An embrace of perversity is intrinsic to his writing:

> Stillborn.
> To be perverse is to engender yourself [*s'enfanter*]. It is to give birth to yourself. But is it is also endlessly to kill yourself. To be perverse is to be still-born. (197)

In his parents' eyes (by his account at least), Léger was always the mask of his stillborn brother. In the end, he writes, "I have finally chosen to be what I have always been: stillborn . . . . But it can no longer be seen: I am wearing a mask [*loup*]" (224).

Léger described *Autoportrait* after the fact as a "refusal of all indoctrina-tion" (*refus de tout embrigadement*), which left him "rejected from the Same, [but] neither wanting to only be the Other."[71] His abstinence from tribalism and *communautarisme* earned Léger condemnation as "homosexually incor-rect."[72] Moving toward Léger's imposture as a phony Beur writer, it is impor-tant to keep in mind that he held this attitude of rigorous refusal and noncon-formism with regard to what should have been "his own" subculture: the gay community. Later, we will see, he will make no distinction for Arabs or Islam.

In 1990 he bitterly recalled that *Autoportrait au loup* and *Ocean Boulevard* had made him the victim of "an abject cabal." "I don't forget the hatred."[73] In a later version of things, he claimed that *Autoportrait* had been attacked from all sides—as "vomit," "navel-gazing," "exhibitionism," "the sound of a toilet flushing"—and it even provoked, he said, death threats.[74] The year before he killed himself, he brought this "filthy press campaign" against *Autoportrait* back up, in his penultimate book, *Zanzaro Circus* (30)—thirty years after *Au-toportrait* was published.

There is some irony in the reaction to Léger's anticommunitarian stance, since this is France, after all, where *communautarisme* is a dirty word; where, as Scott Gunther explains, the term "*ghetto* is used by some French gay political actors to describe what in the American context might respectfully be referred to as a *community*."[75] So Léger's independent stance should have brought ac-colades. (Ten or more years later, it might have.) There is a further irony in the consonance that can be discerned between Léger's embrace of perversity on the one hand, and on the other, the "radical deviancy" and "permanent refusal of fixed values"—a refusal of identity—espoused by the French founder of queer theory, Guy Hocquenghem.[76] So Léger's position was perhaps not as deviant as it appeared; its very deviancy was in fact fashionable and should have placed him near the mainstream of French postmodern ideology. The air was thick with a general deconstruction of identities (Deleuze and Guattari) and origins (Derrida). I suspect it was the terms of Léger's exceptionalism—his retrograde adherence to Freud, for example, and his recourse to Proust and Mishima, as well as his bad attitude—that cast him into outer darkness.[77] He seemed to want nothing else. *Autoportrait au loup* has been shunned by critics and historians of French gay literature (it is not mentioned in any work on French gay literature that I have seen), as has Léger's remarkable, compelling narrative about a friend dying of AIDS, *Les Souliers rouges de la duchesse*. According to Léger, the latter book was denounced by a gay critic until he found out Léger was gay: "Why didn't you tell me? It changes everything!"[78] Léger saw that same double standard in the Paul Smaïl affair: *Vivre me tue* was "magnificent" if it was by Paul Smaïl but "shit" if by Jack-Alain Léger.[79] This merely hardened his bitter opposition to identity politics in literature.

*

Jacob Jacobi (1993) was one of Léger's most successful works, lauded by critics and nominated for all of the most coveted French literary prizes. It may be his most readable and engaging novel. *Le Monde* said it was "bursting with life," making the reader move "constantly from laughter to tears."[80] The narrator is a ghost writer (*nègre*) who calls himself Zanzaro. Reprising a familiar trope, he is born fifteen months after a stillborn brother, supposed to replace him and to bear his name: Daniel. But the new baby/narrator is fat, angry, and odd—a poor substitute, so he is hastily given the name of the saint whose feast day it is: Saint Léger. He becomes "Léger Lazare," a name that appears to be backwards, and the confusion about his identity leads to his choice of métier as both a ghostwriter and an author whose own works are ignored.[81] He is thus his own doppelganger, nemesis, and rival.

The novel is the story of how he fraudulently authors the books that are supposedly written by a famous survivor of World War II, a Parisian Jew named Jacob Jacobi, who won the Nobel Peace Prize—largely based on the books he did not write—in "198*." Jacob (born Jacques) Jacobi escaped the infamous Paris raids in which French police removed Jewish families for deportation: his yellow star fell off his coat, and he denied knowing his mother. He fled to Spain, then returned to his family's empty apartment in Paris, where he hid during the rest of the war and occupation. As an adult, Jacobi tells this story at a dinner party, and an editor invites him to publish it; the editor—claiming that Jacobi has the stuff of a great writer, and that is why we need a ghostwriter!—hires Lazare to write Jacobi's books (727–29). "A willing slavery," Lazare calls it, playing on the meanings of the word *nègre*, as both ghostwriter and slave (696). Zanzaro/Léger Lazare fears that Jacobi is a better writer than he, even though he is the sole author of Jacobi's books, which are a huge international success (604). (If Francis Soulié was the author of *Le Regard du roi*, and therefore in effect the *nègre* of Camara Laye, there is a loose parallel between Soulié and Lazare.)

After Jacobi's death, the editor orders up a posthumous last book, which provokes a case of existential writer's block in Léger; he eventually finds his true calling as "posthumous ghostwriter, faithful impostor, false counterfeiter, and real author" (*le nègre posthume, le fidèle imposteur, le faux fraudeur, le vrai auteur*, 819). The final phony Jacobi book is written in what the horrified editor calls "ppppppoetry!" With Jacobi's name on the cover, it provokes a revival of poetry in France.

Questions of identity, falseness, and resentment all contribute to this clever double portrait of an artist (Léger Lazare) and his mask (Jacob Jacobi). *The mask alone succeeds.* (There is a parallel to the relation between Romain Gary and Emile Ajar.) Perhaps that explains why Jack-Alain Léger, after the notable success of *Jacob Jacobi*, took his game to the next level, going beyond the representation of a hoax in fiction to produce a real and significant hoax of his own. There is a logical progression.

Vivre me tue (Living Kills Me, or *Smile*)

Paul Smaïl came into the world when *Vivre me tue* was published for the *rentrée littéraire* in late August 1997. The cover and paratext are very discreet. There is no photograph, and the only biographical information that follows is, in effect, a plot summary of the book (figure 15):

> He is French and twenty-seven years old now. His grandfather died for France; his uncle was assassinated by the French police in October 1961. He boxes, rages, reads books, loves. Head over heels for Myriam, the "Jewish princess." Devoted to Daniel, the "little brother," who can't cope with being Beur, Arab [*sidi*], *nardène*.[82] Crazy about literature: Melville, Conrad, Stevenson . . . Adventure! "The green shores of the Promised Land. . . ." He lives in Barbès, for now. Excellent education, but no job worthy of the name: he delivers pizza . . . for now. What is he waiting for? He knows that words alone can save him from hatred. The first words of the novel that he hasn't finished are: "LIVING KILLS ME." [VIVRE ME TUE].

The book is identified as a novel on its cover and title page, but the narrator of this "novel" bears the same name as the author. Normally, when the author's name and the narrator's are the same, the work is considered autobiography. So already there was a riddle, a fairly common one (*A la recherche du temps*

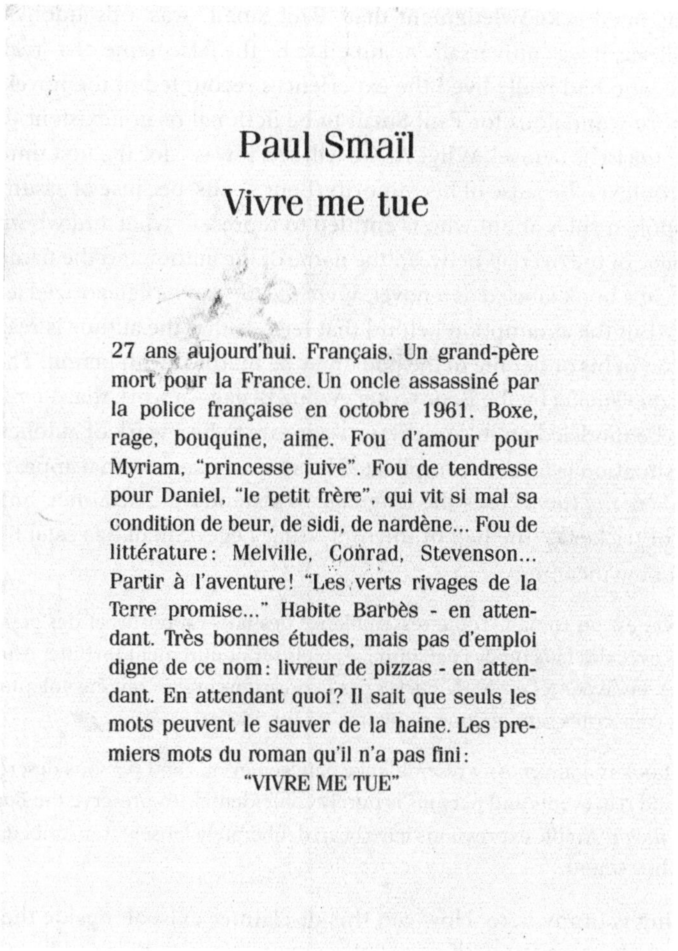

Paul Smaïl
Vivre me tue

27 ans aujourd'hui. Français. Un grand-père
mort pour la France. Un oncle assassiné par
la police française en octobre 1961. Boxe,
rage, bouquine, aime. Fou d'amour pour
Myriam, "princesse juive". Fou de tendresse
pour Daniel, "le petit frère", qui vit si mal sa
condition de beur, de sidi, de nardène... Fou de
littérature : Melville, Conrad, Stevenson...
Partir à l'aventure! "Les verts rivages de la
Terre promise..." Habite Barbès - en attendant. Très bonnes études, mais pas d'emploi
digne de ce nom : livreur de pizzas - en attendant. En attendant quoi? Il sait que seuls les
mots peuvent le sauver de la haine. Les premiers mots du roman qu'il n'a pas fini :
"VIVRE ME TUE"

FIGURE 15. Jack-Alain Léger (Paul Smaïl), *Vivre me tue* (Paris: Balland, 1997). Back cover.

perdu, *L'Enfant noir*, and *L'Amant* are all seen as novels: autobiographical novels or autofiction).

In the book that unveiled and ended the Paul Smaïl hoax in 2003, *On en
est là*, Léger reminds his readers that *Vivre me tue* "was explicitly preferred
as a novel, accompanied by the traditional disclaimer"—as if to say (as Laura
Albert said), You had fair warning; it was right there in black and white.[83]
The word "novel" alone, in fact, might have prevented the entire hoax: if this
was simply a novel, why fight over its fictional contents? The answer to that
question, as we have seen, lies in *the name of the author* and *its* fictional status. In the publicity for the book and in various statements made about it,

there was open acknowledgment that "Paul Smaïl" was a pseudonym. But, as we will see, it was universally assumed to be the false name of a "real Beur," someone who had really lived the experiences recounted in the novel. It was much more scandalous for Paul Smaïl to be fictional or nonexistent than for *Vivre me tue* to be a novel. Why? As we will see, it was—for the first time in the French context—because of his minority/Beur status, because of assumptions and unspoken rules about who is entitled to represent what and whom.

Because of the overlap between the name of the author and the name of the narrator, in a book labeled as a novel, *Vivre me tue* can be categorized as "auto-fiction."[84] But the assumption behind that term is that the author is real, while the version of his or her life in the book may be marbled with fiction. The novel *Le Gone du Chaâba* by the Beur writer Azouz Begag—a work that *Vivre me tue* seems to be modeled on in some ways—appears to be a work of autofiction.[85]

The situation is further complicated by an *avertissement* that appears at the end of *Vivre me tue*. It uses the language of a standard disclaimer, but in the context of trickery—the hall of mirrors—that Léger/Smaïl has established, it takes on new meanings:

> Ce livre est un roman. Toute ressemblance des faits rapportés et des person- nages avec des faits ou des personnages réels serait purement fortuite. Afin de garder sa saveur à l'*arabe de Barbès*, les expressions arabes ont été volontaire- ment transcrites sans aucune rigueur — "à l'oreille."

> This book is a novel. Any resemblance between events and persons described in it and real events and persons is purely coincidental. To preserve the *Barbès Arab flavor*, Arabic expressions have been deliberately loosely transcribed, the way they sound.[86]

Something is funny here: How can this disclaimer exist alongside the nomi- nal identity between the author and the narrator (suggesting autobiography)? How can any resemblance be purely fortuitous when the author and the nar- rator are the same? And how can a book with only "coincidental" ties to re- ality come to represent—for a time—a *culture* (an agenda that is supported by the claim of linguistic authenticity in the final sentence)? In a book that otherwise appears to conform to Lejeune's autobiographical pact (identity of author, narrator, and character: all Paul Smaïl),[87] the disclaimer jars. It should have alerted readers and critics to some trouble in the house of autobiography and authenticity, but it mostly did not. *Vivre me tue* promulgates a twisted, dizzying version of the autobiographical pact, claiming authenticity (in the third sentence above) while simultaneously stepping away from it (in the first two sentences). The terms of any operable contract between the author and the reader are difficult to discern.

Incidentally, the claim made in the second sentence quoted above is utterly false if Léger in fact—in one version of things that he provided—gleaned the street and banlieue vocabulary that he used in the novel from dictionaries—what could be less "authentic"?[88] (In the other version, he eavesdropped in cafés.)

At the time of publication and for several years thereafter, even as—in the absence of a body called Paul Smaïl—doubts arose and circulated, Paul Smaïl was taken to be real. (The closest he came to having legal status was a post office box that Léger took out in Smaïl's name.)[89] But for that time—the time of the hoax—*Vivre me tue* could well have been considered autofiction. Since the exposure of the ruse, perhaps it can only be called *fictional autofiction*.

For the purposes of this reading, I will consider the time of the full, active hoax to extend from publication of *Vivre me tue* in August 1997 until the moment when Jack-Alain Léger revealed himself as Paul Smaïl (confirming the rumors) in *Libération* and in his book *On en est là* in 2003.[90] During those six years—no matter what they said later—no one knew in any concrete way who Paul Smaïl was. But the interplay of things known and unknown about his identity was in fact highly complex. Rumor, suspicion, open secrets: these are all ways of knowing and not knowing at the same time, and all circulated around the figure of Paul Smaïl.[91] (Bruno Tessarech comments, "In publishing, everything is known and nothing is known.")[92] When I speak about the "success" of this hoax, it must be seen in this context. But there should be no mistake: this was a successful hoax because it fooled a lot of people. And, as we have seen with other hoaxes, it can still continue to take people in: anyone can pick up a Paul Smaïl novel now and unknowingly read it as "authentic."

*

The controversy that would surround *Vivre me tue* was proportional to the *culturally and politically specific* audacity of this literary coup. A real and present ethnic minority—a huge one—was being (falsely) represented, appropriated, and hoaxed. That is what sets this apart from other French literary hoaxes. When Prosper Mérimée invented Hyacinthe Maglanovich, when Romain Gary invented Emile Ajar, or when Boris Vian wrote *J'irai cracher sur vos tombes*, the otherness that was being manipulated in each case was non-French, distant, and therefore safe. Gary/Ajar's Momo was, in fact, a Beur, but before the *mouvance* of the 1980s that propelled this group of immigrants' children to the status of a recognized minority. Léger, as Smaïl, was trifling with the identity of many thousands of native-born Arab French people, people with a stake in both the French Republic and French literature and who were at the time looking for "the true Beur novel."

Straining credulity and with stunning braggadocio, long after the fact, Léger claimed that he had written the novel in one day, after spending only three
afternoons in a Barbès neighborhood café in order to "capture" an authentic
Beur tone.[93] There is a direct line connecting Léger back to his literary predecessor of the nineteenth century, Prosper Mérimée, who similarly bragged
about dashing off *La Guzla* in two weeks, knowing only five or six words
of "Slavic," and to Boris Vian, who said he had written *J'irai cracher sur vos
tombes* in two weeks of vacation. In both cases, the subtext is: look how easy
it is to fool people, to counterfeit authenticity and sell it.

Vivre me tue passed as a Beur novel, but what is that? A Beur is an Arab
(in French backward slang or *verlan*), but of the second (or third, or fourth)
generation living in France: a French citizen marked by difference. Mireille
Rosello explains the context: "By the 1980s, the single male migrant worker of
the 1950s and 1960s had been replaced by a whole generation of *Beurs* (children
of Maghrebian immigrants), whose relationship to France, to French culture,
and to French laws needed to be rearticulated."[94] Although born in France and
therefore a citizen, Azouz Begag wrote, "I am of that generation that experienced humiliations."[95] In 1991, a former minister of the interior asserted that African and Maghrebi immigration was a threat to the very survival of France.[96]
Hervé Tchumkam shows to what extent the obsolete paradigm of "immigration" continues to mask the real problem for Beurs and their children: racism
based on physical appearance (or, more relevant for the opening of this novel,
name).[97] Part of the "rearticulation" of Beurs' relation to their native country
was effected in a wave of novels that started in the 1980s, with authors such as
Azouz Begag, Farida Belghoul, Mehdi Charef, and Leïla Sebbar.[98] Paul Smaïl
was supposed to be an addition to that group of writers, already established but
still struggling for recognition after nearly two decades. One sign of deviance
was that Beur authors in 1997 were "without exception of Algerian descent,"[99]
and Paul Smaïl's family was supposed to be from Morocco. Kathryn A. Kleppinger further helps to explain the unique status of the Beur novel in France:

> This category of "*beur* writing" is the only French literary subgenre defined
> specifically in terms of ethnicity and social milieu, perhaps because the North
> African population is the only ethnic minority in France to reach a critical
> mass strong enough to produce writers identified by a label. It is also the only
> French literary category to receive extensive but highly codified attention in
> the national audiovisual media.[100]

Vivre me tue was a perverse intervention in—and exploitation of—that context in its early years.

The novel begins with an epigraph from *Moby-Dick*, thus establishing a strong intertextual link and raising questions about what or who the white whale will be in this story—and who the Ahab. The elusive whale is most likely, as Kleppinger says, a legitimate position in French society.[101] A small library of literary intertexts—from Shakespeare to Conrad to Baldwin and Genet, but with an emphasis on maritime literature—will accumulate during the course of the narrative.

The first line, "Appelez-moi Smaïl"—is hilarious and already indicates that a winking metaliterary game is taking place.[102] (The first line of *Moby-Dick* in French translation is "Appelez-moi Ismaël.") Melville's narrator is addressing the reader when he says, "Call me Ishmael," but "Call me Smaïl" here is addressed to a potential employer in a job interview that is taking place by telephone. The play of language may be amusing, but the novel is immediately confronting the enormous social issue of employment discrimination against Beurs. "Smaïl" sounds like the English word *smile*, Paul points out, but a boss later pronounces it *semelle* like the sole of a shoe (and sounds like "smell") (20/10). The "banal" Christian first name, Paul, was a "good idea" his father had at his birth in 1970. Good because it allows the narrator to *pass*— "je peux faire illusion"—as what, he does not say, but it is clear: as something other than Arab. "Paul," and his brother's name Daniel, are "white masks." The cultural ambiguity between the names Paul and Smaïl serves to hide, for a moment, his status as "*bougnoule*," "*bicot*," and a string of other anti-Arab epithets (10/2). So, here on the threshhold of this novel, we are watching a French author passing as an Arab author who is telling his own story of passing as . . . something other than an Arab.

But that was not apparent to readers before the hoax was revealed. What leapt off the page was a story documenting a social situation that has endured in France for decades: employment discrimination against those perceived as "other."[103] In a Republic allergic to difference and wedded to universalism, the very existence of discrimination is hard to acknowledge. The absence of an official governmental and intellectual apparatus for handling otherness— something that in the United States takes the form of check boxes indicating race, for example—leaves the problem in limbo. Farid Laroussi points out that "a national non-governmental agency, HALDE (*Haute Autorité de Lutte contre les Discriminations et pour l'Egalité*), established in 2004 and terminated in 2011, found itself overwhelmed from the beginning by complaints, 50 percent of which were associated with workplace issues or complaints about job applications."[104] In 2013, 71 percent of banlieue residents reported job discrimination.[105]

No agency like HALDE exists in *Vivre me tue*. As the narrator says, "There'll always be another applicant less swarthy than me, hair less frizzy, skin not so rough, nose less hooked" (10/2). His view is dire: "we're at war," passing is impossible, and only extermination awaits. In the meantime, he works as a night watchman in a brothel and writes this book. His process of writing, it turns out, is his "adventure," his quest for a white whale (14/5). Sometimes he writes that he is writing (13/5). The book is something he promised to his dying brother (12/4).[106]

Vivre me tue is fast-moving and highly readable. The story of Paul Smaïl emerges in thirty-two short chapters, skipping artfully among the various phases of his life. He was bullied in school, caught between rival factions (like the Hutus and the Tutsis, he says [25/15]), and detested because his schoolwork was outstanding and hailed by his teachers.[107] To toughen him up, his father takes him to a boxing gym, where Monsieur Luis teaches him not to be a *maricon* (31/19). The boxers look like "a United Colors poster," "a so-called fraternity" (39/25). "All brothers," but a hint of trouble comes from a group of Arab Muslim boxers who get serious about religion:

> Virility and religion ever since Fouad, Farid, Taouif, Samir-the-welterweight and Samir-the-heavyweight all started to play at being devoted Islamists, chanting to us, at the first excuse, the five or six suras they finally managed to memorize, *refusing wine with much ado, hands raised—the Fascist salute, or as good as* [*le salut fasciste, ou tout comme*]—waving away the kirs the owner wanted to offer us.
>
> —Stupid bastards! As if Arab pride [*la fierté du melon*] meant acting like our caricature on TV! (40/26, AT, emphasis added)

The narrator's rejection of Islam is made very plain here. First he conflates Islam with "Islamisme," the term used not for faith but for the political exploitation of the religion; that is not an innocent substitution but rather a gesture of stigmatization. The next sentence is much worse: characterizing the gesture of raising a hand to refuse alcohol—which an observant Muslim is required to do—as tantamount to "the fascist salute" is an act of hysterical hyperbole and paranoid secularism. And to make matters worse, in Paul's view, this is all a game that these young men are playing; there is literally no good faith in Islam. In this passage it is easy (with hindsight) to see the anticommunitarian, antireligious hand of Jack-Alain Léger, who wrote in a note to himself: "I thank God for having let me be born a citizen of a country where I can choose not to believe in him."[108] In this, Léger and his alter ego Smaïl are part of a larger pattern among French writers who, as Hélène Jaccomard puts it, "want to show that Muslims can, and want to, integrate into French society" and who reassuringly "downplay the role of Islam in Muslims' lives."[109] With a minority like this, the Republic can relax.

Moments of transparency like this in the narration—where the real writer is suddenly visible behind the fake one—seem to be obvious giveaways, but only *after* the unveiling of the hoax. No critic raised an eyebrow about this incendiary passage.

Paul's only real friend is Bernard Diop, whose name suggests he might be a Senegalese Christian; the others call him an "Oreo cookie" (*Bounty*) behind his back (40–41/27, AT). He is washed up as a boxer but continues to practice the sport as a "religion without any god" (42/28). This contrasts starkly with the practice of an actual religion, Islam, which the narrator has just condemned.

Paul's own life is intertwined with the life and death of his brother, Daniel. The original identity or *état civil* of Jack-Alain Léger, Daniel-Louis Théron, is thus embedded in the novel, in this brother figure, and his death harks back to the primal story of Théron/Léger's dead sibling. Although it has been commented on very little, much of the book is in fact devoted to the close relationship between the two brothers—one an altered double of the other, one dying, then dead. Intertwined with *Moby-Dick* and other maritime texts, *Vivre me tue* taps into the homosociality of that genre—"the brotherhood of the sea."[110] The brother's nickname is Queequeg, which makes Paul his Ishmael and thus his loving partner. The brother's death is, in turn, doubled by the father's, making this novel truly a work of mourning. All of this in turn suggests that *Vivre me tue* was as much about Léger's own "issues" as it was about the intercultural hoax; it was both.

Gay and wasting away of "immunodeficiency" in a hospital in Hamburg, Daniel appears to have AIDS, although in fact he is succumbing to the effects of anabolic steroids, taken to enhance his competitive bodybuilding and his work as a performer in a peep show (157/127). Paul is perfectly fine with his brother's sexuality (55/40). Together, they were both "unemployment fodder" (*de la chair à chômage*, 69/50, AT), finding work only delivering Speedzza pizzas. A bookstore owner overhearing Paul's talk of *Moby-Dick* hires him to join her "mission" for the love of literature, with exploitative wages (82/62). Madame Moriot is delighted to have "a Maghrebin" on board; it is "an opening out to the world" (83/62). Full of condescension and hypocrisy, this character earns more of the narrator/protagonist's scorn than anyone else in the novel. Paul behaves insolently, then explodes when the store owner has the audacity to suggest that he might enjoy the works of authors from the Maghreb: Driss Chraïbi, Mohamed Choukri, Rachid Mimouni. "What does Arab literature have to do with me?," he rages. For him this is literary apartheid, "Each to his own!" "Chacun chez soi!" (93/71). This reflexive conflation of racial identity with fascism echoes his reaction to a Muslim's refusal of alcohol previously: both are somehow, for him, outrageous acts of oppression. He quits. Paul Smaïl, in his resistance to ghettoization, is reminiscent of Chato, the narrator-writer of *Famous All Over Town*, who, in Laura Browder's words, wants to "carve out an identity for himself free of others' conceptions about what should be culturally determined."[111] And behind both narrator-writers is the real writer, a white guy suggesting that that kind of assimilationism is a good idea.

Paul's father is a model employee of the SNCF, the French national railroad, an immigrant who is a constant reader with a tremendous reverence for books. Here, as in Margaret B. Jones's *Love and Consequences*, the heavy emphasis on literary culture among working-class or under-class people seems (in retrospect) to give away the ventriloquism of the hoax: the real writer is placing his/her own literary values in the minds of the characters. Bernard Diop's favorite book is Joseph Conrad's *The Nigger of the "Narcissus"* (41/27); later he reads James Baldwin's *The Fire Next Time* (184/149).[112] Paul's French teacher and mentor intones: "It's all in literature. It's all been said. In some book or other there is always an allusion to what's happening, the proof that others have suffered what you're suffering; that you're alone in the world" (104/81). He shows Paul how to find consolation in literature for discrimination in society. Arriving at the teacher's apartment after being detained and abused by the police, Paul's pride is regenerated by words from Shakespeare that the teacher reads to him: "If you prick us, do we not bleed? If you poison us, do we not die? And if you wrong us, shall we not revenge?" (105/82). These lines from *The Merchant of Venice* will return at the end of the novel. Paul tries to find courses about love and literature at Nanterre (the University of Paris X), but there is nothing, not even anyone who loves to read (131/104). Literature is appreciated only by readers, not critics.

Paul falls in love with Myriam Fink, a fellow employee at the bookstore. She and her parents, who are Jewish, provide an antidote to both the "fascist" Muslim boxers on the one hand and the segregationist bookseller Madame Morin:

> I was touched by their kindness, and my gratitude was somewhat effusive. These people didn't feel obliged to talk, like so many people do, about our origins, our cultural differences, the problems facing young people trying to get a foothold [*s'insérer*] in our society—right? And all it would take would be a little goodwill—right? And blah-blah-blah. I wasn't taking some exam. The Finks were good people. (127–28/101)

The Finks get high marks for their good manners but also for their lack of condescension, for their refusal to ask prying questions. They represent the best of French universalism: they don't ask about origins because they simply don't care. Momo would say they have no "principles."

There is an irony here. Despite Paul's resistance to identity politics, to religion and to stereotypes, *Vivre me tue* is best known for giving voice to the grievances of a *community*, of Arab immigrants in France and their children. Paul's uncle was killed in an event that often preoccupied the mind of Léger: the massacre of Arabs by the Paris police on the night of October 17, 1961 (102/79–80, 177–79/143–45). Paul's father, who dies of stomach cancer, is buried near Muslim soldiers who died "for France" but also near the common grave of the victims of that massacre (175/140).[113] Paul has an advanced degree in literature but can only find a job delivering pizza or sitting at the front desk of a brothel all night. In the end he can only take off for Morocco, going "back" to a country he has never seen (181/147).

*

What is behind this successful representation of Beur life by a non-Beur French writer? How did Léger pull this off in literary terms? In another book that he published during his Paul Smaïl years, but as Léger, *Maestranza* (2000), he describes an incident from his childhood that may explain (or at least serve as an allegory for) his concern for Arabs in France and his hatred of discrimination. Eight or nine years old, the boy was living with his parents in the thirteenth arrondissement in Paris, then an Arab neighborhood. When a nurse came to school one day to delouse the students, the school director separated out the Arab children—based solely on their first names—for special attention. The child who would become Léger, unable to support the injustice, rebelled and lined up with the Arabs, shouting "We all have lice!" (*Maestranza*, 132). True or fictive, this story shows how the author wished to present himself: in the *beau rôle*, as a defender of the downtrodden but also a scourge of all forms of identitarian segregation.[114] But this passage may have another function as well: to torment Azouz Begag, Léger's nemesis, who wrote of a similar scene of hygienic inspection in his autobiographical novel *Le Gone du Chaâba*.[115] We will see much more about the relations between these two novelists and their two novels—one "real" and one "fake."

Conrad, in his preface to *The Nigger of the "Narcissus,"* asserted that "a work that aspires, however humbly, to the condition of art should carry its justification in every line."[116] *Vivre me tue* justifies itself and Léger's hoax at various points in the narration. Paul, sounding exactly like Léger, believes:

> The only way to get by in this life is to play a role. People don't want to know
> who you really are in this world, they want you to look as much as possible like
> the ready-made image they have of you. (19/10)

The existential error, the false selfhood, represented in the second sentence—
the trap of living your life in conformity to someone else's stereotypical view
of you or your group—is exactly what the narrator accuses his Muslim fellow
boxers of (for the simple act of refusing alcohol).

Inside the universe created by the hoax, Paul Smaïl is a real Arab/Beur
in France, trying to find his way, his "truth," navigating his way around the
traps of identity and stereotype, to escape the expectations of others.[117] The
fact that, in the end, he could only do so by leaving France stands as a powerful reproach to the Republic, for a radical failure of "hospitality."[118] That cry
for justice is what readers initially saw, and that is what provoked waves of
recognition and admiration. *Vivre me tue* was an eloquent, deeply literary
appeal for equal rights, most apparently so in the passage from *The Merchant
of Venice* quoted earlier and brought back at the end of the novel. About to
board the plane that will take him to Morocco, Paul is ordered to open the
urn containing Daniel's ashes, provoking these eloquent thoughts:

> If you're continually suspicious of us, aren't we going to take offence? If you
> talk down to us, isn't that going to annoy us? If you ask us for our papers for
> the slightest thing, aren't we going to become exasperated? . . . And if you
> refuse to give us jobs that you'll give to others who are less qualified but less
> swarthy [*basané*], too, won't we finally rise up in revolt? Doesn't an Arab have
> feelings, emotions, and passions? If we're like you in every other way, we'll be
> like you in this, too: We'll get our revenge. (186/150)

This paraphrase of Shylock's famous speech was a *cri de coeur* that captured
the attention of readers and critics and made the reputation of the book.

On the other hand, seen in its most subversive potentiality, as a Trojan horse,
Vivre me tue was an attempt to massage, contain, and control a rising immigrant culture in France, similar to Gary/Ajar's making-cute, but with more serious implications because a constituted Beur literary culture had arisen in the
meantime. The secular Republican values espoused by the narrator of *Vivre me
tue* are those that the nonimmigrant majority want. A comment by Eric Lott,
discussing minstrelsy, comes to mind here: "It is obviously in the interest of
the dominant class to have a measure of control over the culture of those they
dominate."[119] This novel, among other things, was certainly such an attempt.

Outside of the illusion of hoax, all of this was quite different. I will return
to these questions after attempting to measure the impact of the imposture in
the popular press, among readers, and in academic publications.

But before moving on, I want to sum up the many parallels between this hoax and that of Romain Gary/Emile Ajar. Léger's was, to some extent, a copy-cat crime. The motives of the two authors, rooted in deep resentment of the Parisian publishing establishment, were similar. They both created distractions by publishing another book under their usual name at the same time as their first hoax. Their research methods, involving cursory field trips to an ethnic neighborhood or café, were the same. Both authors invented an ethnic alter ego, who wrote in a casual but masterful and highly successful form of underclass speech; and both wrote four hoax novels. Gary and Léger also shared French-Republican values, which they staged in allegories of Jewish-Muslim harmony and love. And both authors, finally, ended their lives in suicide. But Léger also raised the stakes of imposture considerably by writing an autographic narrative: unlike Momo, Paul Smaïl was both the author and the intradiegetic narrator of his own story. The fake reality of Paul Smaïl was central to the endeavor.

The Popular Press Reads *Vivre me tue*

The stakes of the novel's claim to cultural representation were pitched at a maximum, and the full measure of the success of this hoax can be seen in the review by Jean-Luc Douin in *Le Monde*. (Douin went on to play an interesting role in the hoax, as we will see.) His review was short—only three sentences—, but it ended with large claims: "Aside from its hard-hitting social realism (a sharp description of the backrooms of the Speedzza business), Paul Smaïl's novel, which is full of quotes from Melville and Genet, is an anthem for literature as a means of asserting identity and of fighting hatred."[120] Such a statement, in France's most prestigious newspaper, truly represents a high-water mark for intercultural hoaxing in French literature. In fact, there are two claims here: affirming identity and confronting hatred. The first assertion is hardly anodine in the French literary context, and may be something of a left-hand compliment: literature as a vehicle of identity is suspect and marginal; canonical, "universal" literature is thought to operate on a higher plane (with greater cultural capital). The second claim seems to soften the controversial implications of the first; if such literature reduces hatred, perhaps it should be tolerated. But there is an irony in Douin's assessment: the narrator of *Vivre me tue* himself is outraged by the very notion of ethnically confining literature.

In *Libération*, the Moroccan journalist Maati Kabbal wrote, "Of Paul Smaïl, we know almost nothing, except that he is Franco-Moroccan and that he lives in Casablanca."[121] (Everything in that sentence would, of course, turn out to be untrue, except "we know almost nothing.") Kabbal understands

Vivre me tue to be an autobiography, "full of bumps, corrosive. . . . Paul Smaïl writes in your face and without embellishments: the identity problems and sexual problems, the 'hechma' [shame], the shame and the fear of admitting his homosexuality [*sic*], the misery of ghetto kids, rejection, racism." It is a considerable error to claim that the narrator of *Vivre me tue* (rather than his brother) is gay, since much of the book revolves around his relationship with his girlfriend, Myriam Fink, "a Jewish princess" (90), and his full sexual history is recounted (121). In a letter to the editor of *Libération*, signed Léger, Léger claimed to have faxed Kabbal's review to Paul Smaïl, who "gasped" (*s'est étranglé*) at the number of untruths in it; "a correction would be welcome."[122] (Meanwhile, by acting as Smaïl's go-between with a major newspaper, Léger was playing fast and loose with his secret.)

In the second Paul Smaïl novel, *Casa, la casa*, published a year later, the narrator mocks *Libération* for publishing a review riddled with so many errors, and Léger/Smaïl seizes the opportunity to drive home his larger point about autofiction: "You understand why I insist that they label my works *fiction*? Novelists are the ones who say the least idiotic things, who stick to reality the most. Or at least they try."[123] As we will see time and again in the Smaïl case, the defense of the hoax serves a second purpose, that of promoting Léger's vision and brand of literature—and his literary products.

Paris-Match, Léger's father's old employer, gave prominent attention in its glossy pages to *Vivre me tue*. An outtake from its review, by Gilles Martin-Chauffier, ran along the side of the page, proclaiming in bold face: "French literature has finally found a Beur writer with talent," in contast to Chimo, he says. Finally? The premise that no Beur writer of talent had been seen before Paul Smaïl was of course a gesture of complete disrespect and disregard for writers such as Farida Belghoul, Mehdi Charef, and Azouz Begag, who had produced noteworthy and compelling works starting in the early 1980s.[124] (The slight will not go unanswered.) A review in *Le Devoir* (Montreal) repeated the idea that "with Paul Smaïl . . . we have perhaps, finally, the novelistic testimony of an authentic Beur."[125] The *Paris-Match* review began, provocatively, by raising the specter of cultural difference: how alien Beurs are, how hard to understand. "It's as if they were incapable of forgetting their origins, and us ours." There, in a nutshell, is the problem to be solved, the problem to which *Vivre me tue* in fact provides a comforting answer, in what another critic described as a "model of integration."[126] (There is an irony here because Léger, writing after the hoax was over, claimed that readers had liked Paul Smaïl for his *refusal* to "play the model Beur.")[127] Much of the appeal of the novel—among mainstream critics especially but not exclusively—might be attributable to this simple formula, which Léger/Smaïl manipulated:

- thesis (France)
- antithesis (immigrants, Beurs)
- synthesis (integration, as manifested by this model Beur, the narrator/author Paul Smaïl).

Thus is the problem of difference "resolved." But it isn't of course, because this is all a hoax.

The reviews were almost universally enthusiastic. All the reviewers knew that "Paul Smaïl" was a pseudonym, but as *Elle* put it, the name was a mask for a real Beur, "a young man born of Moroccan parents," "a Parisian novelist." *Elle* said that *Vivre me tue* was "the book we needed so as to not give up hope for French writers put off by the present times. Incredible. Beautiful, brutal, funny, and desperate."[128] *Le Nouvel Observateur* said that *Vivre me tue* was "the (happy) surprise of the literary season" (a phrase used by numerous reviewers), selling at a rate of six hundred copies per day in October.[129] Catherine Janvier wrote that *Vivre me tue* was "the surprise guest of the literary season . . . with [its] overwhelming sincerity and ferocious humor."[130] *Le Figaro* said in early October that the novel had "conquered the critics and the public," even while coyly asking "Is this a new literary hoax?" "Rumors suggest a confirmed author," meaning someone established and known . . . like Jack-Alain Léger.[131] (I will discuss such holes in the fabric of the hoax below.) The Communist newspaper *L'Humanité*, in a breathless review, brushed aside the questions surrounding the identity of the author as trivial matters; *Vivre me tue* "leaves a mark on your memory with its burning, scorched words."[132] In 2000, a web site recommended the book for "adolescent readers starting at fifteen or sixteen years old" and for the libraries of lycées.[133]

The right-leaning weekly *Le Point* only reviewed *Vivre me tue* after it had been on the magazine's own bestseller list for several weeks. The critic praised Smaïl for being neither the "reporter of banlieues in flames [an unwitting foreshadowing of 2005] nor a cheerleader of racial resentment" and cited his use of "the oral Arabic of the cafés of Barbès." Making this political reading even clearer, he concluded: "[Smaïl] was right to choose a pseudonym: the sirens of the 'politically correct' will write to him in Casablanca, where he is living, care of *poste restante*."[134] In other words, the novel was grist for the mill of a French preoccupation of the 1990s, a general rejection—by both the right and the left—of (dimly understood) American-style political correctness and multiculturalism. For *Le Point*, Paul Smaïl was a very useful Beur indeed.

It was one thing to fool the popular, mainstream, majority French press into thinking that *Vivre me tue* was authentic and Paul Smaïl merely the nom de plume of a real Beur writer. But the full measure of the hoax and its success can be seen in the reactions of more specialized journalists and reviewers. One such is Fayçal Chehat, an Algerian journalist who had been long established in France by the time *Vivre me tue* was published. Writing in *Africultures* in December 1997 Chehat hailed the novel as "fascinating," and "breathless," with "snarling humor and exceptional freshness." More significantly, he identified the author as "the young Paul Smaïl, Franco-Moroccan *by his birth certificate* [*de son état-civil*]."[135] So here was a North African reader—a cultural critic, who, based on both his background and his long experience in France, was presumably in a strong position to judge the text and detect any cultural or linguistic mistakes—who could not, did not, see anything inauthentic about *Vivre me tue*. Quite the contrary. He was hoodwinked. So was Hélène Morin, writing in *Qantara: Magazine des cultures arabe et méditerrannéenne* (and therefore presumably a reader of some expertise). She quoted *Vivre me tue* at length as an example of a Beur novel that negotiates the gap between France and North Africa through *language*, "the eternal vector of uncertain, fluctuating, and protean identity."[136] Yet another such example comes from the journal *Algérie Littérature/Action* in early 1998. Dominique Le Boucher, presented as a specialist of Maghreb literature, discussed "the literary enigma of 1997," *Vivre me tue*. While acknowledging rumors about its authorship, Le Boucher nonetheless reads the novel at face value and finds in it "an oral language made up of slang words, *verlan*, an updating of the language of 'neighborhoods,' the language that one can actually hear nowadays," all of which produces an effect of "cinematic immediacy." Paul Smaïl's writing is "brutal and sharp as a blade."[137] *Vivre me tue* was passing as a Beur text very successfully, *among Arabs and Beurs and specialized readers*.

Another triumph of the hoax occurred when *Vivre me tue* was cited as a source of authentic Barbès language in a dictionary of slang, and two authors of genuine Beur origins were thought to have copied the language of Smaïl.[138] The fake author bragged about this in his third novel, *La Passion selon moi* (137). In 2001, Farida Abu-Haidar published a detailed appreciation of Paul Smaïl's "code switching" in his first three novels, "recreating the polyglossic 'youth-speak' of Parisian multi-ethnic suburbs."[139] If Léger was able to pull off this linguistic charade—fully convincing to qualified scholars—after three afternoons in a café, he certainly deserves some credit.

Further confirmation of the success of the hoax can be seen in the invitation that Smaïl received from the Association de Solidarité avec les Travailleurs immigrés, or ASTI (an organization that still exists), whose representative asked for a meeting with the author because "his words are the echo of things said and lived by many members of our association."[140] In 1999, *Pote@*

Pote: le journal des banlieues invited Paul Smaïl to join their committee of patrons and proposed to publish a feature on him.[141] An organization called the Sons and Daughters of the Immigrants of France (Les Fils et Filles des immigrés de France) reportedly named Smaïl as honorary president.[142] In January 1998, Monique Cerisier-ben Guiga, a French senator who had lived in North Africa for a long time and served to represent overseas French citizens, quoted *Vivre me tue* during a debate on nationality laws; a passage from the novel supported her claims about discrimination in France.[143] These are all strong endorsements of the novel and its powers of representation. But as Kathryn A. Kleppinger also argues, the success of the hoax was utterly dependent on readers' expectations of what a Beur might be and how such a person might think—or at least what they hoped for among Beurs: a sense of injustice, yes, but also a commitment to Republican values like anticommunitarianism, secularism, and integration.[144] *Vivre me tue* played to those expectations and hopes, masterfully.

✳

Meanwhile Léger, like Gary before him, faced a practical problem, created by the success of his literary coup. Newspaper, radio, and television all wanted to interview Paul Smaïl and show this phenomenon to the world. But there was no Smaïl to show, nor a Paul Pavlowitch nor a Savannah Knoop to play the role. To protect his false identity, and also to promote the Paul Smaïl brand, Léger promulgated a high-minded code of authorial integrity that would be violated if he stooped to the level of in-person meetings and interviews.[145] In an undated fax, supposedly coming from Morocco to the magazine *Les Inrockuptibles*, signed in Arabic letters as Paul Smaïl, the author explained his stance, which is worth quoting in its entirety:

> It seems I was supposed to call you on the phone. But I told my editor, and had it included explicitly in my contracts: I refuse once and for all to *communicate*. No photos, no interviews, nothing. What I have to say, I write. I try, at least. It is by my writing, and only by my writing, that I want to be judged. I refused the offer of the first publisher who proposed a contract when I understood that he wanted to make me into the Beur on call, the Beur to be gossiped about in cafés, the fashionable Beur, the TV Beur, the barf Beur [*le Beur de service, le Beur sujet de société, le Beur à la mode, le Beur pour la télé, le Beur beurk*]. No way! I have no cause to defend. I am a writer, or at least I try. And that's all. I think that Salinger and Pynchon have it right: you have to hide. If I am thought to be horrible [*puant*], I don't care. If you liked my book, say so. If not, say that. If you don't want to talk about it because we haven't talked about it,

well, don't talk about it and let's not talk about it. I don't have to explain myself. And as for involving myself, I want to be involved in what I write and nothing else. Sorry to disappoint you, if that is the case.[146]

Laying down an ethic of authorial privacy and integrity, Léger—who in previous iterations of himself was far from publicity-shy—as Smaïl, attempts to puff up his own reputation by associating himself with two high-prestige Anglophone authors. Responding to an invitation associated with his nomination for the Prix des Lycées Professionnels du Haut Rhin, Smaïl declines, saying that meetings and discussions kill literature itself. So the defense of the Smaïl hoax has been given a second purpose by Léger: increasing the aura and status of the Paul Smaïl brand. He wants to be alone. His writing is all that counts. His only cause is literature itself. Paul Smaïl repeated variations of this message to anyone who wanted to meet him, interview him, or otherwise see him. To one reader, he responded, "I am deeply convinced that it is not a good idea for a writer to meet his readers. . . . I am committed to my fierce isolation [*ma sauvagerie*]."[147] To Elisabeth Helfer-Aubrac he wrote, "I hope a writer is not obliged to exhibit himself in the press or on TV."[148] To Dominique Noguez, a well-known writer, he expresses fear of the "take-over of the real by those in power" [*la privatisation du réel par le pouvoir*].[149]

On the practical level, the fiction that Paul Smaïl had moved to Morocco—as represented at the end of *Vivre me tue*—helped to maintain invisibility. Léger took various other concrete steps to promote and defend his hoax. He had stationery printed with the name Paul Smaïl in both Roman and Arabic letters. (He bragged in a letter to one of his editors, "Look, I can sign my name in Arabic, too!")[150] And he had cards printed with the following message: "Because of the large volume of mail that I am receiving, I am unable to respond to you personally, but I thank you very sincerely for your attention to my work."[151]

Smaïl Speaks (by Fax)

There was one major exception to Léger/Smaïl's stance (which he reiterated in a letter to *Le Nouvel Observateur*): "I refuse to *communicate*."[152] Despite the refusal, the author apparently could not resist, so he came up with a way to let himself be interviewed in writing by the same *Nouvel Observateur*, through an exchange of faxes. A friendly (bribed) bartender in Casablanca—where Paul Smaïl was supposed to be living—acted as intermediary, relaying the faxes back and forth.[153] Published on October 9, when *Vivre me tue* was brand new, the interview, entitled "Smaïl [note that no other identifier was necessary]

Writes to Us from Morocco," took up a whole page and shows the hoax to be working smoothly. Jack-Alain Léger had found a way to draw one of the most prominent French magazines into his hoax and make it an instrument of his deception. In the interview, Smaïl says he is forced to respond to the "insane rumors" about him that have been circulating. The reporter, Anne Crignon, sets up the interview by characterizing *Vivre me tue* as "the (pleasant) surprise of the literary season," a "testimony to the difficulty of being a child of the Maghreb in France," and "the voice of a generation condemned to casual employment" (*la voix d'une génération promise aux petits boulots*). Crignon further emphasizes the raw realism of the novel, its "impressive mouth-to-ear quality." Thus, while recognizing that "Paul Smaïl" is a pseudonym ("a homage to Melville"), *Le Nouvel Observateur* nonetheless thought it was interviewing the authentic and highly talented new voice of French Beurs.

Crignon's first question goes directly to the question of autofiction: if this novel is autobiographical, why did you insert the disclaimer stating that "any resemblance with real facts or persons would be fortuitous"? Smaïl responds that there is a lot of both real life and fiction in his book, that "the novel [as a genre] is freedom, and my ambition was to make a novel out of my life." Again Smaïl deflects questions about both fiction and secrecy by comparing his work and himself to great texts and writers: Was *David Copperfield* really a novel? You have never seen either Salinger or Pynchon, so why should you see me? Léger/Smaïl gets the best of both worlds in this interview: presented as the voice of a generation by *Le Nouvel Observateur*, and thus profiting from false verisimilitude, he nonetheless professes to be offended when *Vivre me tue* is called "the novel of the banlieues." "I want to smack somebody," he says; but he is not surprised by this reaction, because such people "live behind screens" and "know nothing of the real world, not even where Barbès is located." The irony of the hoax is at its maximum here, and Léger is manipulating the situation masterfully. Smaïl claims to be "as French as Le Pen, alas!" and of course, he (Léger, not Smaïl) is![154] Léger's goal—of shoring up a hoax that was already in danger, "proving" (by fax) that Paul Smaïl existed—was realized.[155]

A year later, in the second Paul Smaïl novel, *Casa, la casa*, the narrator rewrites the story of this exchange with *Le Nouvel Observateur*, adding a new layer of fiction to the mischief of his hoax, depicting himself writing the fax under a Moroccan palm tree (146). The paratext of *Casa, la casa* deepened the hoax by adding something that was missing from the cover of *Vivre me tue*: a biographical note that makes Paul Smaïl appear to be a real person: "Paul Smaïl is twenty-eight, a Frenchman born of parents from Morocco. He holds a DEA degree in comparative literature. He lives and works in Paris. *Casa, la casa* is his second novel [*son second roman*], after *Vivre me tue*."[156]

Situated as it is on the back cover, this statement exudes a kind of authority
that is different from anything inside the narrative. It stands as the publisher's
certification that there is a real Paul Smaïl, born in 1970; a real live Beur. The
publishers are guaranteeing the conformity of this text to the autobiographical pact described by Lejeune. The stakes of the Smaïl hoax are thereby raised
(by comparison to the paratext of *Vivre me tue*) and reinforced. This is all
the more intriguing because a significant leak had already taken place and
informed readers—which is not to say all readers—had reason to doubt that
Paul Smaïl existed. Doubling down on the hoax in *Casa, la casa* and two other
Smaïl novels, Léger was able to keep readers thinking that Paul Smaïl—or
someone very much like him—was real.

The Leak

We have seen many times that rumors and even revelations do not necessarily
end hoaxes. The Smaïl hoax was threatened almost from the outset and came
close to being spoiled. A publicist working for Editions Balland, Cécile Rol-
Tanguy, suspected there was something not quite right about Paul Smaïl and
Vivre me tue. When the novel was nominated for a prize that is specifically reserved for first novels, Rol-Tanguy seems to have passed on to the prize committee her suspicions about *Vivre me tue*: that Paul Smaïl didn't exist; that this
was the work of an experienced author, perhaps Jack-Alain Léger. Léger and
the editor, Jean-Jacques Augier, found evidence that Rol-Tanguy had notified
a major publication about her doubts by fax. The situation was extraordinary,
even among hoaxes, with an employee of the publisher blowing the cover
from inside the house. As Kleppinger puts it, this was "remarkably like a soap
opera."[157] Augier sued and fired Rol-Tanguy, who countersued for wrongful
termination and won in court. But first she issued her own press release, under the title "Smaïl m'a tuer" (Smaïl Kill Me), saying she was forced to resign,
claiming good faith, but not at all denying that she had leaked doubts about
the existence of Paul Smaïl to the press.[158]

Léger was furious. Writing as Paul Smaïl to Anne Crignon of *Le Nouvel
Observateur*, he referred to Rol-Tanguy (without naming her) as *une salope* (a
slut).[159] He wrote to Augier on September 4, 1997, complaining of Rol-Tanguy's
"malevolence and ill will," and the next day sent a tirade about the "plot" and
the "sabotage" that was coming from inside the Balland house:

> When I signed with you, and you *contractually* accepted the rules of the game,
> we agreed that *the only way* to play was from "above": like Salinger, like Pyn-
> chon, Paul Smaïl would refuse the media game, period. Those in on the secret

were (other than my friend Ahmed, who is light years away from the literary world): Salvy, you, and me. I can't suspect any of those four—nor Richard Millet, despite his suspicions about the real author of *Vivre me tue*—of screwing up the publishing of this book that was destined for success.[160]

In September, Léger had a close call, no doubt caused by the Rol-Tanguy leak. As he wrote to Augier: "ALERTE MAXIMUM." He had bumped into the literary critic for *Le Monde* Jean-Luc Douin, who, perhaps scrutinizing Léger's face for any sign of discomfort, repeated the rumor that he, Léger, was in fact Paul Smaïl. Léger told Augier that he believed he had been "absolutely convincing" in his denial. Douin would actually become a co-conspirator in the hoax before it was unveiled.[161]

In November, Léger was still in a rage about "false promises," and his anger now turned on his editor and publisher. He wrote to sever relations with Augier and the Balland house (which nonetheless published the second Paul Smaïl novel, *Casa, la casa*, the following year).[162] Léger continued his tempestuous peregrinations through Paris publishing houses until he died. The third Paul Smaïl novel, *La Passion selon moi*, was published by Laffont, and the fourth and last, *Ali le Magnifique*, by Denoël in 2001. Pocket editions—a sign of success—of three Paul Smaïl novels were released in 2003. Paul Smaïl, despite all the doubts and rumors about his real identity, had a very successful run through the French publishing establishment. A movie deal was signed during this period, and a very good film called *Vivre me tue*, with prominent actors Sami Bouajila, Jalil Lespert, and Sylvie Testud, came out in 2003. The film—to all appearances an "authentic" representation of Beur life—was supported by grants from the Ministry of Culture and antidiscrimination organizations, and sold nearly 40,000 tickets.[163]

When the second, third, and fourth Paul Smaïl novels were reviewed, whose works were they thought to be? At the beginning of the 1998 literary season, Anne Crignon reviewed *Casa, la casa* in *Le Nouvel Observateur*, and she reported the rumor that Jack-Alain Léger was the real author of *Vivre me tue*, but said "no matter" and went on to discuss the second Paul Smaïl novel as if Paul Smaïl were a real person behind the pseudonym.[164] It was as if the virtual reality of Paul Smaïl, Beur author, once released into the world, could not be killed. The cyborg marched on. In Montreal, *Le Devoir* claimed that *Casa, la casa* "confirms the presence of a true author," a Beur who prefers to remain anonymous.[165] But *Le Temps* printed a photo of Léger with the caption, "Is Paul Smaïl Really Jack-Alain Léger?"[166] The accompanying article by Isabelle Martin came closer than anything else that was published to "forensic" detection of the true authorship of the Smaïl novels, by citing a formula that is repeated in the other novel just published by Léger, *Ma Vie, titre pro-visoire*. The sentence that is repeated is *Je ne suis pas une ressource humaine* ("I am not a human resource").[167] The journalist asked, "Is much more than this necessary in order to qualify *Casa, la casa* as a true false second novel?"

Actually, yes. This perception by Martin is impressive, but with only six words of evidence, it could not and did not come close to demolishing the hoax. And her suspicions began with the "persistent rumors" that originated with Rol-Tanguy. Without those rumors to put a critic on the trail of Jack-Alain Léger—purposefully "looking for a hint" as Martin was—would anyone have discovered those six words? It seems highly unlikely. No one could tell—no one did tell—by reading alone, and it seems clear that without the head start provided by the leak from Rol-Tanguy, no one would have suspected Paul Smaïl of being anything but a Beur. It remains true that no one published a purely linguistic or stylistic unveiling of this hoax in the popular press. Rumors remained rumors; it was reasonable, for example, for one professional literary critic to dismiss them, despite their persistence, as "scurrilous."[168] We can only wonder how much farther the Smaïl hoax—which succeeded despite this handicap—might have gone without Rol-Tanguy's betrayal.

The Rol-Tanguy leak laid the basis for doubts that would swirl around Paul Smaïl for the duration of the hoax. Léger kept a letter that reads like a veiled threat, mailed to him care of Gallimard at the end of the year 2000:

> On t'a reconnu Daniel THERON alias Melmoth, Dashiell Hedayat, Jack-Alain Léger ou encore Paul Smaïl; Théron n'est pas léger . . .
>
> ni lettre d'injures ni courrier homophobique
> Ce que tu voudras[169]
>
> You've been recognized, Daniel Théron, alias Melmoth, Dashiell Hedayat, Jack-Alain Léger, and even Paul Smaïl; Théron isn't Léger [light] . . .
>
> This is neither an insult nor a homophobic message
> Whatever you like

According to Léger, in one of his most expansive reflections on the hoax:

> If the identity of [Paul Smaïl] was an open secret and had been for a while, so be it. But it was still I who pulled the strings, and I knew more than anyone about the question. I could say how the myth was born, how novelistic creativity had gradually given substance to another reality, how the author had been, so to speak, bypassed by his character, how the character had led him into a parallel universe where readers were writing to him, claiming to have known his father and his brother, asking him for advice and help! I also knew how this paper—not straw—man started to pull the strings himself; even though

he was imaginary, he took the power away from his creator: how I was willingly manipulated by him, thrown into other, riskier adventures, morally pressured to the point of giving myself over in real life to clandestine acts of solidarity with the victims of the very real tyrant who rules Morocco [Hassan II]. Until the day when . . . No, it was no longer a game: I made myself into a relay man [*un passeur*] for resisters, human rights workers who, in their own country—but I can't say any more, for obvious reasons. (*Les Aurochs*, 75)

I have quoted this passage at length because it may offer the best insight into Léger's odd combination of self-aggrandizement and self-deprecation. He follows this passage by calling the entire story of Paul and himself "quixotic," but only after claiming to have, under the spell of the hoax, entered into World War II–style *real* acts of clandestine resistance to an implacable regime (that of Hassan II in Morocco). He thus takes the do-gooder justification for intercultural hoaxing (seen, for example, in the case of Margaret B. Jones) one step further, into the realm of cloak and dagger. It is hard not to see in this some measure of *la folie des grandeurs*.

I will comment on the plausibility of some of these claims, those about readers' responses, below. As for the "acts of solidarity," well, they were clandestine. Léger's point is that the hoax took on a life of its own, and that, despite the rumors about the real identity of Paul Smaïl, the fake reality of the hoax lived on. It is important for us to consider how this can happen.

In this case as with other literary hoaxes, a secret can be both open and closed at the same time. Those who read the literary pages of the magazines and newspapers would be aware of the rumors suggesting that Paul Smaïl was actually Jack-Alain Léger; but not everyone reads those pages, nor necessarily remembers, nor cares one way or the other. To this day, anyone can pick up a Paul Smaïl book and be completely taken in. This is what allows the hoax to go on. And, as Léger is saying here, he was still in control of the process, directing the evolution of this parallel universe in which Paul Smaïl *existed* for readers.

Léger was not truly unmasked as Paul Smail until he unmasked himself in 2003 in a "sort-of" novel, *On en est là*.[170] As Kleppinger points out, on the inside covers of that book, Léger brought together all his pseudonyms, listing all thirty-three of his previous works together for the first time, including the Paul Smaïl novels.[171] So the hoax was over. Or was it?

Did "Hundreds" of Readers Write to Paul Smaïl?

The effectiveness of any hoax should be judged not just by the reaction of the press nor of the small, insiders' world of Parisian publishing. Readers' reactions count, and in Jack-Alain Léger's after-the-fact defense of the Paul Smaïl caper, he placed enormous emphasis on the validation he received from Arab readers in particular.

The key role that Léger attached to readers' responses was in fact prepared by claims that he made in the other Paul Smaïl novels, which were, after all, the continuation of the fake life of that fake author, after the publication of *Vivre me tue*. In *Casa, la casa*, Smaïl, after returning from Morocco to Paris, receives "a big bundle of letters," including many from Beurs "who tell me their misfortunes."[172] In the third novel, *La Passion selon moi*, the narrator begins to amplify his claims, saying of *Vivre me tue* that "thousands read it, hundreds wrote to me; they recognized themselves in it," and he brags about the novel being cited in a dictionary of urban slang.[173] In the fourth and final Paul Smaïl novel, *Ali le magnifique*, the eponymous narrator, a Beur serial killer, says he is "reading and rereading *Vivre me tue*," and that "all Beurs who read are reading it. . . . Finally a book where one of us talks about us."[174]

In *On en est là*, Léger claims that he received "mail in a wave that has not let up . . . dozens and dozens, hundreds of letters from readers, which, to this day, fill four large boxes in my home. . . . Love letters, really. . . . Fraternal letters. Testimonies sent to me by victims of everyday French racism. . . . No one reproached me for my hoax." According to Léger, this outpouring of responses to his Paul Smaïl novels constituted a remarkable historical archive: "An entire treasury that I want to archive as a historian, and, who knows, if the authors allow it, to publish."[175] A second work—not fictional in any way— *Tartuffe fait Ramadan*, published in the same year, gave a similar account of the hoax and repeated the claim that "hundreds of readers who recognized themselves in Paul Smaïl" became his friends.[176] In 2006, Léger maintained the idea that he had received "hundreds of letters from Beurs thanking me for being their mouthpiece."[177] He hammered on this theme in all his accounts of the affair; his Arab readers were "crazy about the book . . . grateful to see themselves reflected in this fraternal character" (*reconnaissants parce que se reconnaissant dans ce personnage fraternel*), he wrote in *Hé bien! la guerre*.[178]

One would not want to take his word on this (nor frankly on anything). After Léger's death, his papers were deposited at the archive for contemporary French literature, IMEC, just outside of Caen. Examining all of those papers (twice) has allowed me to gain some perspective on Léger's claims about the success of the hoax and the ability of *Vivre me tue* to convince readers of its authenticity. Unless Léger threw away a large number of letters (which is hard to imagine, since he placed such emphasis on them), it can safely be said that he greatly exaggerated both the scale of all reactions and, specifically, the outpouring of reactions from Beurs. In the archive, the number of letters from writers with North African names, or who identify themselves as Arabs, dating from October 1997 through the end of 1999, including all such letters commenting on *Vivre me tue*, is *nine*. The total number of letters reacting to *Vivre me tue* found in the archive is no more than thirty-five.[179]

Generally speaking, the letters from readers who identify with Paul Smaïl say what Léger claimed they said. They express gratitude, specifically for the sense of self-recognition that *Vivre me tue* offered them. One reader from the region of Bordeaux wrote to say, "My life resembles yours so much. I have been asking myself for a long time about my place in this country. Thanks to you, I have been able to get an answer, and I understand better what I am doing here. *Thank you.*"[180] A young man of Moroccan origin, working toward a degree in engineering—and thus someone living a life parallel to that of the narrator Paul Smaïl, even including a job as a night watchman—wrote to the author in early November. Living in Toulouse, he wrote in faulty French to thank the author for asking the right questions and for confronting "despair." This letter is particularly compelling: the reader fears he has "made a mistake" in reading the novel, "because despair is really starting to invade me, but as a practicing believer, I take confidence in the destiny that Allah has prescribed for us. A thousand times, thank you." In other words, *Vivre me tue* was so real as to produce hopelessness, and only religious faith has helped this reader keep himself on track. But he is grateful for the difficult questions that the novel raised, and he wants to meet Paul Smaïl.

The following June, a woman congratulated Paul Smaïl for his accurate representation of "reality, of truth in general and my life in particular." Another reader said that when she discovered the novel, "I felt like I was reading the title of my own life, as if you had discovered it instead of me." A retired teacher "of Algerian origin" found the tone of the book "comforting and consoling."

Smaïl received a questionnaire from a group of lycée students in Mulhouse, all with Arab-Muslim names. He responded to them kindly (which he didn't do with all his correspondents) and generously, but his letter contains flagrant proof of his French-Republican Trojan horse agenda. He says that he has been subjected to racism, but he goes on to admonish these young Beurs against "reverse racism"—"a certain Beur racism against those with Christian names, or [someone] who drops his religion or wants Western-style freedom for women."[181] Thinking that this sermon on Republican values was coming from a Beur writer, the students may have been very impressed and influenced. If and when they found out that they had been fooled by an impostor, how did they react? The full measure of the deception—and, potentially, the harm that was done—can be felt in this exchange of letters.

There is a gap between what Léger claimed in print and what is to be found in the archive. The letter from someone named Assia that Léger quotes in *On en est là* (189)—with the particularly compelling (and suspiciously Léger-sounding) message *Restez romanesque* (stay novelistic)—is not in the archive. Nor are there any letters in which readers claim to have known Paul Smaïl's father or brother. In his self-proclaimed Islamophobic essay of 2003, *Tartuffe fait Ramadan*, Léger made another claim that is not supported by the archive: that he had received numerous letters from Arabs frightened by the rise of "Islamist totalitarianism."[182] Nor are there other letters that Léger mentions in *Hé bien! la guerre*, from Ahmed in Colombes, nor Ali in Stains (64). Nor something mentioned in Léger's next book, *Les Aurochs et les anges*, a letter from Moustafa in Lille who detected "a strange echo" between Smaïl's writing and that of Léger, "which no professional critic has revealed so far."[183]

Critics, in turn, even after the hoax was unveiled, were forced to concede that the "chorus of presumably real Arab friends" who identified with Paul Smaïl constituted a "backing group of authentic Beurs," an "essential" element in "authorizing [Léger's] impersonation." And that in turn "implies that anyone can create a meaningful Beur character irrespective of their actual identity."[184] The number of letters from "authentic Beurs" supporting the novel is thus an essential element in Léger's claim that *Vivre me tue* was "*un livre juste.*"[185]

Assuming that "hundreds" of letters have not been lost or left out of the archive—and IMEC officials are clear about having collected all of Léger's papers from his apartment quickly after his death—we have to entertain the idea that Léger continued the hoax by other means even after it was revealed, by making these exaggerated claims about the reception of *Vivre me tue* among the people it claimed to represent. *Hundreds* of letters would indeed have been highly compelling proof of the value of the work, of its success both as literature and as hoax. The archive of those letters would indeed be the kind of historical resource that Léger claimed: a library of testimonies concerning discrimination and integration in France. Nine letters is still proof of something—of a certain effect that was created—but it is not the same as the "wave" of reactions that Léger described.[186]

*

Supposing for a minute that Léger lied about the "hundreds" of letters that he received, we can say that this fiction served a number of purposes. It defended him against accusations—which came along after the unveiling and which I will examine in detail below—that the text of *Vivre me tue* was, after all, not credible as a Beur novel. If it was fully convincing to *hundreds* of

Beurs, if it was good enough for them, then any such objections could be silenced. By promoting this version of things in 2003, as he was in the very act of "coming out" and ending the Paul Smaïl hoax (and thereafter), Léger both defended his practice of writing as someone other than himself and sought to continue his campaign against French racism (and Moroccan tyranny). Those dual purposes—of self-promotion on the one hand, and social justice on the other—make for an uneasy alliance. That double stance, we have seen, is common among intercultural hoaxers. The problem is that now, after his death, his archive does not support his claims about the power of his novels to testify about racism or to provoke testimonies from readers—not nearly as well as he said it would. And that calls his entire enterprise, revolving around his own virtuoso performance as a writer—Look at me! I spent three afternoons in a café and wrote this in one day! And it fooled *hundreds* of readers who wrote to me!—into question.

Truth and Lies à la Léger

Beyond self-promotion and perhaps even self-delusion, was a larger, nobler purpose served? Even Léger's prolonged and often-repeated defense of (his) fictions and his hoaxes as "truth lies" cannot completely resolve this issue. Why did he pose as Paul Smaïl? In one of his coming-out texts of 2003, *Tartuffe fait Ramadan*, he said it was for no reason at all, just for "my own pleasure" (*mon bon plaisir*)—purely for the way of play.[187] But of course it was not really as simple as that. He also claimed that *Vivre me tue* was "*un livre juste*," meaning correct and true. Several years later, in *Les Aurochs et les anges*, his thinking runs like this: the society of the spectacle (now largely replaced by the internet) in which we live generates so many lies that they cannot all be countered:

> It is a wave of falsehoods against which I will always hold up, in vain I know, my literary fictions, *my art of truth-lying* [*mon art du mentir vrai*], inventing as needed a double who writes for a moment, who relieves me, distracts me, and leads me to another adventure, testing my skills; an imaginary ghost-writer [*nègre*] who is also a brother, a friend, and—why not?—a successful author and a financial backer for me![188]

On the one hand, Léger is defending the role of fiction as at least a *quest* for truth in the midst of a virtual world dominated by "obscure idiotics" created by "uneducated strangers, all connected." Down that road lies facism, or, perhaps more likely now, the nothingness of excess, of consumption for its own sake (*Les Aurochs*, 14, 16). Such is the argument that Léger made in 2007.

In *Les Aurochs et les anges*, he characterized his masquerade as "quixotic," but then cleverly went on to associate his hoax with that of Cervantes himself. After all, didn't the great Spanish author "plagiarize, page after page, the manuscript of an Arab historian, Sid Ahmed Benengeli"? (76). Actually, no; Cervantes *wrote* the manuscript, he didn't "plagiarize" it, except within the fiction. The "existence of [Sid Ahmed Benengeli] is a joke," writes a critic, and "no one is for an instant deceived."[189] The convention of claiming that a novel was actually a "found" text written by someone else may have been given new life by Cervantes, but it was Cervantes's name on the title page.[190] So the analogy is imprecise, even as it serves, again, to associate Léger's literary practices with those of great authors. The larger point, the idea that Léger was desperate to communicate, was that "fiction [is] the sole weapon against universal falsification," even if it is merely quixotic.[191] Cervantes—who helped clear the way for modern, secular literature by maintaining that (in the words of a critic) "poets never intended to be liars but rather veilers of truth," and that "in literature, truth was what an audience can be persuaded to believe"[192]—was truly his spiritual ancestor.

But Léger's rationale—of producing truth lies in order to fight against the mass distortion of reality perpetrated by those in power—runs into trouble if it produces or justifies *actual* lies (as opposed to truth lies) such as those that Léger appears to have told about readers' responses to the Paul Smaïl novels. To radically exaggerate those responses is perhaps not to serve a larger truth so much as it is to brag.

And it is important to go back to the point that this hoax was and remained—despite the increasingly open secret about the author's identity—a success. *Le Figaro* reported that Jack-Alain Léger was Paul Smaïl as if it were news in February 2009.[193] And still in 2012—nine years after Léger fully disclosed the hoax—an article in *Le Magazine littéraire* that sought to identify, 150 years after Hugo's *Les Misérables*, the voice of "the people" in French literature, cited *Vivre me tue* and *Ali le magnifique* as among the best (if "apocryphal") texts to come out of the *cités*.[194] (In fact neither novel had anything to do with the banlieues; *Vivre me tue* takes places entirely inside the Boulevard Périphérique.)[195]

The Scholars Weigh In

I now want to circle back to the question that always animates discussions of intercultural hoaxes: can you tell? We will see one spectacular case of someone (Azouz Begag) claiming he could, or could *have*, all along. We have seen that no critic writing in the popular press unveiled the hoax in any definitive way by investigative reading alone. How did academic critics—who presumably work more slowly and methodically, with more sophisticated tools—fare?

Some of course were "caught by the hoax," to use Murray Pratt's term. I do not cite these examples in order to embarrass anyone—no more than my own old work on *L'Enfant noir* embarasses me, at least. I have found fewer than two dozen academic treatments of the Paul Smaïl novels. Of those, only six were published before the unveiling of the hoax in 2003; among those, only one critic was not taken in by the hoax, and I will turn to her remarkable work presently. Four critics were caught by the hoax before 2003.[196] Remarkably, a certain number of critics continued to fall for the hoax after it had been revealed.

Najib Redouane, a professor of literature, hailed *Vivre me tue* in the pages of *Le Maghreb littéraire* in 1999, as "in fact the first novel of a young Beur. . . . Paul Smaïl is the pseudonym of a young Moroccan born in Paris. . . . The author asserts his Arabness without evasions or reservations."[197] Dayna Oscherwitz was one of the first professional critics to publish on *Vivre me tue*, in 2001. She sees Paul Smaïl as a Beur writer, comparing him to Azouz Begag, Mehdi Charef, and Leïla Houari. Her concluding statement can be read in two different ways, from either inside or outside of the hoax: "*Vivre me tue*, then, is a plea for the opening up of paradigms of French identity beyond a monocultural model."[198] Inside the hoax, the novel is thus a straightforward call for multiculturalism; but outside, it might take on a different purpose, as some would go on to assert: its appeal to Republican values makes it a Trojan horse.

Ziad Elmarsafy's 2001 essay on Paul Smaïl represents a moment of triumph for the hoax, and it begins by reporting on an earlier high point, perhaps the ultimate marker of success: "On October 26, 1998, the audience at New York University's Maison Française was treated to a rare spectacle: Tahar Ben Jelloun reading extracts from Paul Smaïl's novels."[199] For the most famous Moroccan writer to give a dramatic reading like this, at a high-profile "debate on Francophone fiction" with Maryse Condé at NYU, was indeed a rare spectacle, but not of the kind it appeared to be. Elmarsafy cites it as a sign of the new acceptance of Arab literature in the West, and in a further irony, he argues for Smaïl's acceptance as "French, not Arab—historic connections to North Africa notwithstanding." But of course the scene at NYU was something else: a spectacular "gotcha" moment for Jack-Alain Léger ("French, not Arab," indeed) and his hoax. Elmarsafy dismisses the rumors about Paul Smaïl's identity and existence, emanating from Rol-Tanguy, as "scurrilous," merely a sign of disrespect for "writers of Arabic origin."[200] This protective reaction echoes the defenses of Camara Laye that we saw earlier.

In 2001 and 2002, Michel Laronde, who had already published a book about Beur literature, wrote about the three Paul Smaïl novels that existed at that point, as examples of "the Arab-French novel." Like Elmarsafy, Laronde recognizes and discusses the fact of the pseudonym, but sees the author as an "Arab-French writer" whose posture of anonymity and invisibility reflects a struggle not to become "the scapegoat" usually associated with that role (what Smaïl called the "Beur de service").[201] But of course the anonymity—Paul Smaïl's apparently principled refusal to play the role of "Beur author"—in fact served another purpose: the hoax itself.

One critic, known for her particularly acute readings of postcolonial Francophone literature, was not fooled, even if she could not say for certain that there was a hoax afoot. In 2002, soon after the publication of the last Paul Smaïl novel, Mireille Rosello took a unique approach. Admitting that she was "seriously (and literally) thrown off track [déroutée] by the 'Smaïl' phenomenon" (Rosello, "Paul (Smaïl) et le loup," 41n2)—which posed "an infernal labyrinth of traps" (41)—Rosello proceeded to examine the author's public statements about anonymity as an "important paratext." How is ethnic identity related to masking, and to the use of pseudonyms and anonymity? And what kind of light can Paul Smaïl shed, since, from the beginning, he has "succeeded in attracting attention to his identity by systematically refusing to construct it in a traditional fashion" (through television appearances, interviews, etc). He has made "anonymity itself into a spectacle" (46). The result is a personality about whom "questions remain without definitive answers," and "his 'real' name remains a mystery" (43–44). This statement by Rosello shows that, despite the reading she is about to perform—which ultimately associates Smaïl with Léger—the hoax was still operational and would remain so until Léger himself ended it one year later.

Rosello reads the history of Smaïl's public statements, including the farce of the faxed interview with Le Nouvel Observateur, with a skeptical eye. She doesn't know for certain who the real author is, but she knows that Paul Smaïl is fake, a "fiction" (45). Going back to the text of Vivre me tue, Rosello detects precisely the stereotype of the "good Beur," the "model of integration" that Paul Smaïl claimed to be demolishing (46). Further, Rosello makes the excellent point that anonymity and pseudonymity are not exceptional in literature but rather perfectly normal postures of professional identity or branding: a pseudonym by itself is "not a fake" (47). It is rather the fabric, the text, of Smaïl's posture that raises questions: he would have us believe that there is a real Beur behind the mask called Paul Smaïl, but that, for some reason, "we are not worthy of knowing the truth" (48).

This brings Rosello to the playful suggestion that "Smaïl" might as well be named, for example, "Léger." Citing the press reports, she opens her reading to this possibility and asks what would change if Smaïl were, openly, Léger. The "ethnic illusion"—the intercultural hoax—would die, but Rosello says, "so what?" The hoax works only "if one expected something from the [cultural] capital known as 'Beur'" (51). That expectation, of course, is the basis of the entire enterprise: readers certainly *did* expect something from the author's (false) Beur identity position. Without a Beur name (of sorts) on the cover, *Vivre me tue*, signed by Léger, would not have provoked the same reaction; it could not have been said that "French literature ha[d] finally found a Beur writer with talent" (*Paris-Match*). For Rosello this leads to insights not only about the "right" to maintain a pseudonym (claimed by Smaïl and his publisher) but also about "the role of the mask in the life of an author" (53). And who had written about that? Jack-Alain Léger, in his early book *Autoportrait au loup* and in his repeated claims about fiction as "the sole weapon against universal falsification." Thus Rosello's net tightens around Léger, as his published statements converge with those of Smaïl; "the Jack-Alain Léger phenomenon becomes the explanation for the Smaïl phenomenon" (54–55). Still, she admits, suspicion is not proof, nor is the kind of linguistic "coincidence" (*ressource humaine, nuit grave*) cited by Isabelle Martin and Christian Laborde. Rosello suggests that we read suspicion itself as a text and a literary tactic. She thus substitutes the uncertainty of a postcolonial/postidentitarian subject position for the (false) certainty of either the hoax itself, from the inside (Smaïl as Beur writer), or the hoax unveiled, from the outside (Léger as impostor). That, of course, is exactly what Léger was going for.

Rosello claims that, if it could be proved that Smaïl was in fact Léger, it would not solve anything: "the substitution of one name for another is in no way an end in itself" (*un aboutissement*) (58). While this is true, while the case of Jack-Alain Léger in particular makes it clear that masks conceal other masks, I do not think that the cultural import of the borrowed identity position Beur can be discounted. If Léger has "no identitarian heart," no "solid core" (59), his masquerade as Paul Smaïl was not, for many readers, just a play of signifiers; it was an identity position that needed representation. Rosello was entirely right, and somewhat prescient, to suggest that Léger had created Smaïl as a "multicultural literary cyborg" (59). My emphasis here is on the work that that cyborg accomplished in the world, inside the hoax.

Mireille Rosello thus came closer to "telling" than anyone. But it is important to note that Rosello's reading, as full of insight and skepticism as it is, is not (and does not claim to be) an act of pure forensic detection based on the language or the style of the novels; she in fact dismisses the idea of such "proof" as false. Her reading relies on the existing rumors associating Smaïl with Léger and on the paratext of Smaïl's and Léger's public statements. It thus does not provide a definitive example of someone who could "tell" by reading alone. In the case of Paul Smaïl's novels, there is none.

The work of the cyborg did not stop with the unveiling of the hoax in 2003, even among academic critics. Two dissertations on the work of Paul Smaïl were completed in 2005, one of which was caught entirely inside the hoax, praising the "French Arab novelist" for his "eloquent anonymity" and his "his ambivalent desire to embrace and redefine *la francité*."[202] The second dissertation consisted of an appraisal of the published translation of *Vivre me tue* and a new annotated translation of *Casa, la casa*. The translator, in an afterword, says he found out about the hoax "while completing the final pages of my own *travail d'archiviste*. . . . The knowledge was initially somewhat disheartening; but then I thought, Why not?" "Technically," he says, "Léger's Smaïl succeeds on every level."[203]

In a thoughtful article comparing *Vivre me tue* to Rachid Djaïdani's *Boumkeur* (1999), Laura Reeck refers to Paul Smaïl as an "author-character," but in a note identifies the novel as authored by "Paul Smaïl [Jacques-Alain [*sic*] Léger]."[204] She explains in another note that "Smaïl is a known French author by the name of Jacques-Alain Léger who has used pseudonyms in the past" (52n6). It is strange that she discusses the existence of Léger, behind Smaïl, only in the notes, when in fact the added complication would seem only to reinforce her point: that, "without the author at the center, [Smaïl/Léger] shows the boundaries between texts themselves to be non-authoritative" (57). Taking Léger's hoax fully into account, the point would, in fact, have to be broadened: since the hoax succeeded, one has to acknowledge that the boundaries between *cultures* are apparently not "authoritative," either. Léger, as Smaïl, demonstrated that. Reeck does not make that point, and in her comprehensive book *Writerly Identities in Beur Fiction and Beyond*, published in 2011, there is no mention of Léger, Smaïl, or *Vivre me tue*. This hoax, which raises such troubling questions about identity and representation, was thus expelled from Beur literature.[205] Similarly, Kathryn A. Kleppinger eliminated her excellent dissertation chapter on Léger and Smaïl—including rare information that I have cited here—from the book version of her work: *Branding the Beur Author*.[206] Henry Louis Gates, Jr., mused that "maybe Danny Santiago's *Famous All Over Town* can usefully be considered a work of Chicano literature."[207] *Vivre me tue* is not receiving that treatment.

The opposite approach was taken by Touriya Fili in 2003. While fully cognizant of the "open secret" of the hoax (because of the publication of *On en est là*), and thus knowing that Paul Smaïl was in fact Jack-Alain Léger, Fili nonetheless placed *Vivre me tue* firmly within Beur literature "despite the identity (birth certificate/origin) of the author." Fili agrees with Léger; when reality lies, fiction must tell the truth: "Is it not the truth of fiction to denounce the lies of reality?"[208] This postessentialist, open-minded approach places Fili at odds with those critics who have excluded the Paul Smaïl novels from Beur literature, and with Azouz Begag, as we will see.

Azouz Begag's Outrage and the Right to Write

"What did I do wrong?" asked Jack-Alain Léger, as he revealed the hoax.[209] Are literary hoaxes victimless crimes? How does the harm principle—which suggests that only actions that do harm should be banned—come into play in a case like that of Jack-Alain Léger/Paul Smaïl? Cui malo? The *Vivre me tue* affair allows us to examine these questions in depth. According to one unconfirmed report, some Beurs were so outraged by the hoax of *Vivre me tue* that they threatened Jack-Alain Léger with bodily harm.[210] A full-throated case for the prosecution was articulated by a famous real Beur. Azouz Begag, born in Lyon, was among the first Beur authors, publishing his début novel, the autofictional Bildungsroman *Le Gone du Chaâba*, in 1986. So Begag was one of those most likely to be insulted by the hailing of Paul Smaïl in 1997 as "*finally* ... a Beur writer with talent." Begag has had a distinguished career as an author of fiction and nonfiction, and, for two years, as minister of equal opportunity in the government of Nicolas Sarkozy and Dominique de Villepin (he resigned in April 2007, denouncing the "token" position).[211] He has published numerous books and essays on immigration, identity, and discrimination in France.[212] If anyone is qualified to speak about the Beur condition, it is Azouz Begag. So his reaction to the scandal of *Vivre me tue* is particularly significant. In an essay published in *Research in African Literatures* in 2006—thus well after Léger revealed himself as the author of *Vivre me tue*—Begag mounted an eloquent protest against the Smaïl hoax and a passionate defense of literary authenticity. I see this as a point where we can see, in precise terms, how American-style multiculturalism was brought to bear on a French ethnic hoax. (It is perhaps no coincidence that this came in the pages of an American publication.)

Writing while he was minister for equal opportunity, Begag launched an indictment of the Paul Smaïl hoax that included two charges: "imposture and incompetence."[213] Those are two different kinds of offense, and they need to be discussed one at a time. The first charge could be considered moot, since Léger had admitted the hoax three years earlier. But the ethical implications of imposture—bearing on the right to write—require further consideration. Can a hoax produce "*un livre juste*"?

The second accusation is different. Begag claims: "Far from representing the triumph of *free-floating literary talent* over minority ethnic bonds, *Vivre me tue* flounders in a sea of artistic incompetence fed by the author's inability to divest himself of a majority ethnic mindset clouded by racist prejudices" (Begag, "Of Imposture and Incompetence," 56, emphasis added). Begag invokes his own background as "an established Beur writer with a long personal experience of immigrant milieux and the *banlieues*" (56). So his own authenticity and authority were threatened by an impostor like Smaïl/Léger and his "attempts to 'steal' the terrain of minority ethnic writers" (56). This was a complaint against "cultural appropriation" years before the current vogue. Like counterfeit money or fake Rolex watches, the Smaïl novels diluted and contaminated the Beur literary stock, of which Begag was a prime stakeholder. Begag's critique is important as an examination of what he compellingly calls "free-floating literary talent" riding roughshod over "minority ethnic bonds" (56). The distinction is worth scrutinizing, since it goes to the heart of the ethical issues that haunt intercultural hoaxes. And the stakes are indeed raised, as Begag states, by the open Islamophobia of Jack-Alain Léger (which he vented in print after the four Smaïl novels were all published).[214]

What is the threat represented by "free-floating literary talent"? If any author with talent can convincingly represent any point of view and any lived experience, then "minority ethnic" authors have no unique role to play: "Anyone can create a meaningful Beur character."[215] Léger stated the claim plainly after the unveiling: "You don't have to be a Beur to know what a Beur feels!"[216] A simulacrum like *Little Tree*, or *Famous All Over Town*, or *Love and Consequences*, or *La Vie devant soi*, or *Vivre me tue* can be just as good (just as *juste*, one could say) and perhaps even better than a bona fide authentic narrative; they can do the same work of representing ethnic identity and experience, and readers will be just as convinced. Authenticity, sincerity, and legitimacy (Begag's terms) are all at stake. So, if Smaïl can be shown to be not simply an impostor—which is done—but also a *bad* impostor, trafficking in an obviously, visibly, *readably* false product, then literary authenticity, sincerity, and legitimacy will be saved.

Pursuing the charge of incompetence, Begag is at pains to show that Léger *did not succeed*; that *Vivre me tue* was a failure *as representation and as literature*. This will be a tough line of argument, since the book had already—as I have shown—succeeded in fooling a lot of people. No one was able to "really tell." But it is interesting to see how Begag mounts this ex post facto critique.

He claims that certain details in the novel "rang false" when he "first read" it. He implies, although he does not say, that that first reading took place in the six-year period before the hoax was revealed (56). By remaining vague on this crucial point of timing, he creates confusion. Some of Begag's critique is based on premises that seem retrograde and simplistic: he professes to be shocked to see an author sow "all manner of confusion" about who is speaking in his work (56). He seeks to impose clarity: "We need to distinguish clearly between the author of the text (Jack-Alain Léger) and the narrator-protagonist (Paul Smaïl)" (57). He points to the "mixing of languages and linguistic registers" as "suspicious"—although that term seems superfluous after the unveiling. He finds "outdated words and expressions dating from the 1960s and 1970s that can only belong to the now middle-aged author, Jack-Alain Léger, and not to the Beur narrator-protagonist, Paul Smaïl" (56). Misplaced, out-of-date slang can of course be an easy giveaway, and I do not discount Begag's expertise. (However, Lia Brozgal, in her thorough critique of Begag's arguments, later refuted considerable elements of his linguistic evidence.)[217] But it is easy, even facile, to engage in that exercise *after* the revealing of the hoax; there can be no honest blindfold test after the unveiling. And I would say that it is wrong to think that certain expressions "can only belong" to certain people; *Vivre me tue* proves the opposite. Begag is confident about what "a Beur would have written" and what a Beur "would never have said" (58). In "this mess," "Paul Smaïl is utterly incoherent as a character" (60). He documents very numerous lexical and cultural anomalies and anachronisms, including a confusion of things Moroccan and things Algerian. He also detects "a whiff of racism" (65).

Begag published nothing about this until three years after the unveiling. If Begag had published this critique *before* Léger was unveiled as the author, marshalling all this linguistic and cultural evidence and "demonstrating" that *Vivre me tue* "could not" be the work of a Beur author—even if he didn't know who the real author was—, it would have been an amazing defeat for "free-floating literary talent." It would also have been a spectacular act of "telling" or forensic reading. The hoax would have been a failure. But if *Vivre me tue* was so transparently phony—if so much of its very language screamed inauthenticity—, why did Begag not denounce it at any point in the nine years between its publication in 1997 and that of Begag's article in 2006? As Lia Brozgal has argued, Begag's criticism of *Vivre me tue* "hinges on the sole tenet that it could not have been written by a Beur because it is simply not Beur enough," which in turn creates a literary straitjacket for Beur literature.[218] Coming only after the unmasking, Begag's critique cannot accomplish what he seems to want: to *undo* the hoax and to prove that authenticity is always *discernable, readable.*

Begag writes as if he were Dickens figuring out by reading alone that George Eliot was a woman; but he is not.

The success of *Vivre me tue*, if nothing else, vitiates Begag's claim that Léger was "incompetent." The proof was in the reception—before, during, and even after the reveal. Begag claims that the novel "cannot be credibly read . . . as an autobiographical text" (61); but, precisely, it *was* read that way—and still can be by those who don't know about the hoax. The charge of "incompetence" is dismissed; the book was *juste* enough to fool many people. In terms of sheer literary effectiveness, we must, pace Begag, acknowledge a triumph of "free-floating literary talent"—the way of play. Point Léger.

But Begag's other line of argument, about ethics and imposture, is not so easy to discount. He is at pains to say that he is *not* saying "that a majority ethnic writer has no right to write about minority ethnic milieux" (56); "anyone has the right to write about the Beurs without being a Beur themselves" (66). He is not, he says, defending the logic that is explicitly attacked by the narrator of *Vivre me tue*: "chacun chez soi." So Begag ostensibly agrees with Léger's statement, after the reveal: "You don't have to be a Beur to know what a Beur feels!"[219] Still, Begag is outraged that an author whom he perceives to be racist could enjoy a "commercial success . . . in mainstream French society," and he asserts that it was precisely the "anti-Muslim, secular, republican Beur" character of the narrator that accounted for the success (66). In other words, Léger had manufactured a more palatable Beur for the enjoyment of the French majority: "So here we have a so-called Beur asserting that his ethnic origins are unimportant while simultaneously reminding us of those origins to underscore the uniqueness of his literary achievement" (68). That is no doubt true. But of course plenty of minority writers and artists exploit "caricatural prejudices" in all kinds of ways, often to undermine them, perhaps to wear them out. The famous scene on the tramway in Aimé Césaire's *Cahier d'un retour au pays natal* is an illustrious example.

Begag mentions but does not dwell on another of Léger's outrages: the resemblance between the title of the first Smaïl novel and a work by Begag published three years earlier: *Quand on est mort, c'est pour toute la vie*. Begag, in his essay, deadpans, "The similarity is perhaps fortuitous" (70). But it is of course more than that. The narrators in both novels are quixotic Beur intellectuals. In *Quand on est mort*, Amar is a "chercheur en sciences sociales et humaines" and a published, famous novelist (24, 48); he has a brother who dies (shot by a taxi driver). Married to a Frenchwoman, he reads *Madame Bovary* after naming his daughter Emma; he takes a "return" journey to the unnamed country that people are always telling him to go "back" to, a country he was not born in, to find his *arabe généalogique* (34). There the resemblances end.

Quand on est mort turns into a journey of discovery, exploring the distance between a Beur and his parents' troubled homeland. Begag stages a moment of epiphany during a long bus trip that echoes Césaire's tramway scene. The narrator, seated next to a friendly, foul-smelling peasant, accuses himself of feeling superior (52)—because France has "got him" (84). In his essay, Begag also quotes a sentence from *Vivre me tue* that is clearly modeled on *Le Gone du Chaâba*.[220] These are brazen literary provocations on Léger's part, thumbs in the eye of Begag and by extension of authenticity itself.

Begag's final gesture is to quote some choice insults of himself that appeared in *Ali le Magnifique*, published five years before Begag's article: "Azouz Begag. A iech! [What a shit!] Top of the class, a real touch-me-not ass-licker. Self-righteousness pushed through heavy-handed secondary school French. He thinks he's pleading our cause to the Franco-French by adopting the plaintive, cheap piety of the Good Beur. Where does that leave our honor, hey?"[221] To which Begag responds: "What right does Paul Smaïl/Jack-Alain Léger have to enunciate in such a bastardized form of French this poetic message of tolerance and universalism for the sake of 'our honor'?" (70). What right indeed? And from whom or what is such a right derived? Begag's authority and right to speak "from the point of view of a committed Beur writer born of illiterate immigrant parents" and in the name of "authenticity, sincerity, and legitimacy" (69) cannot be argued with—not on those terms. The Paul Smaïl novels are an aggressive, purposeful affront to that entire edifice of cultural self-representation—and to Plato's idea that "each man does one job. . . . A shoemaker is a shoemaker and not a ship's captain." Begag is "appalled" to see that *Vivre me tue* is being taught as Beur literature (just as *Le Regard du roi* is being marketed and taught as African literature). This is nothing short of usurpation. Authenticity has suffered a serious defeat. By pulling the wool over readers' eyes—even for a few years—Léger unveiled the shaky foundations, perhaps the hoax (he would say), of identity itself. He certainly demonstrated that identity can be faked in literature, and in France.

If someone tells you they are offended, you can't respond, "No you're not."[222] So the charge of imposture sticks; but of course Léger copped to that. Imposture, impersonation, appropriation—that was the whole idea. The "right" of self-representation that Begag defends cannot be refuted, but here it comes into competition with another, incongruent and equally irrefutable right: that of "free-floating literary talent" and liberty. Kwame Anthony Appiah, paraphrasing John Stuart Mill, explains what might have been Léger's point of view: "the mere fact that I do something you do not want me to do does not *eo ipso* count as my harming you."[223] Harm is only in the eye of the beholder. It is in the conflict between those competing sets of rights that the offense arises and lingers.

Reading: A Choice?

Vivre me tue, like all hoax texts, reads very differently depending on the reader's awareness of the hoax or lack thereof. In order to fully appreciate the hoax, the reader who already knows about it must try to project him/herself back into the time before it was revealed, to erase knowledge of the author's real identity and perform what Pratt calls a "crypto-reading."[224] This is like unringing a bell, of course, but it is nonetheless necessary for the retrospective reading of a hoax. A two-step reading process is required, and a certain vertigo can occur between the one and the other. That intellectual floating sensation can be disconcerting, but it can also be pleasurable. It is like the drawing that appears to be either one goblet or two profiles (figure 16); but here the "choice" appears to be between "real" and "fake." Does seeing it one way "prevent" you from seeing it the other way, as some say about that drawing?[225]

If that familiar analogy offers one model for reading, another might be the idea of choice as it was borrowed from Amartya Sen by Jaime Hanneken and which I reviewed earlier in this study. Do readers have a "choice" of readings? (Hanneken's article drops consideration of that in favor of economic-theoretical concerns.) What "choices" were readers able to make in approaching *Vivre me tue* (and the other Paul Smaïl books), both before and after the unveiling of the hoax? How did Léger manipulate and disrupt assumptions about "choice" in literature? Hanneken sets up Azouz Begag (the defender of Beur authenticity) against Henry Louis Gates, Jr. (who says all authors are impostors). Hanneken then says these are two sides of same coin—that coin being "the propagation of minority as a category of capital" (Hanneken, "Scandal, Choice, and the Economy of Minority Literature," 60). The Smaïl affair suggests "the surreptitious resurgence of the universal individual"— the super-author—"in the place of the culturally different particular" (61). Hanneken describes the scandal as requiring readers "to vote for or against writers like Smaïl" (63).

The very pronoun *je*/I is subject to dispute: in the "inside" reading, it belongs to a Beur citizen of France, going by another name, of course, but authentic nonetheless and speaking for himself and his experiences. This is the story of a life, perhaps somewhat fictionalized, but a life nonetheless. Seen from outside the hoax, the first-person pronoun of *Vivre me tue* reads as a clever trick, likely to induce a smile (smaïl), a shake of the head, and perhaps either outrage or admiration. A reader who is fully aware of the hoax can still lend some credence and sympathy to the narrator's story, his life—as one does all the time in reading plain old fiction. But something fundamental has been lost, because, as Jaime Hanneken put it (in a quotation we saw earlier in

FIGURE 16. Two profiles or one goblet?

this study): "The value of minority literature depends upon its representation of a culturally different, oppressed and/or exotic life, which is only valid if it can be attributed to the real life of a free, inalienable subject, who is free and inalienable because he or she made and sold the story."[226] So Jack-Alain Léger and anything he has to say are not the moral equivalent of Azouz Begag, as indeed Begag is at pains to make us understand.

To examine this dual reading process, let us take, for example, Smaïl's outburst at his employer the bookstore owner: "What does Arab literature have to do with me?" "Each to his own!" ("Chacun chez soi!") (*Vivre me tue*, 93/*Smile*, 71). Inside the hoax, this is a startling rejection of communitarian, identitarian literature—the backbone of the postcolonial canon. But it is surprising only because it is supposedly coming from a Beur; that was something new and different. Switching to the outside perspective, knowing that Paul Smaïl is a fake Beur, the tirade is entirely different: it suggests to Beurs that their preoccupations with identity are somehow unworthy; that they should aspire to and integrate into the general culture; it casts aspersions on Beur literature as it has existed up to this point. Why should an Arab read "Arab literature"? Everyone should read everything, no doubt. Identity itself is the fraud. These two readings are in opposition to each other, but both are fully present in the text, and since the unveiling of the hoax, both are necessary. The same goes for Smaïl's responses to the lycée students' questionnaire.

The same procedure can be used to shed more light on a passage that I highlighted earlier: the scene of the "fascist salute" used to decline an alcoholic drink. Inside the hoax, this is again a remarkable statement of extreme secularism (*laïcité*), astonishing in fact, because it suppposedly comes from an Arab. If there are Beurs like this in France, the reader might think, then the Republic has succeeded in instilling its "universal," secular values. But knowing that this is a fraud—coming from a writer who went on to profess his own brand of Islamophobia in later publications—makes this scene appear to be very much a farce, offensive, and not credible. As Murray Pratt wrote, "For Léger, the politically correct and communitarian attitudes informing France's apocalyptic retreat from the values of the Republic is nothing less than a capitulation to fascism."[227] In these two examples, then, the reading process would appear to be Manichean: like the goblet and the profiles (see figure 16), you can't see both readings at once; it's one or the other. A choice.

However, I would also suggest that, with regard to the essential message of the book—concerning discrimination and the civil rights of Arabs in France—the hoax makes little if any difference. In his final plea on this subject, Smaïl, paraphrasing Shakespeare, asks: "And if you refuse to give us jobs that you'll give to others who are less qualified but less swarthy, too, won't we finally rise up in revolt?" (186/150). If anything, this message may be more powerful and meaningful coming from a white Frenchman like Jack-Alain Léger than from a Beur like Paul Smaïl. And from a more contemporary perspective, influenced by the riots of 2005, the question "Won't we finally rise up in revolt?" (like Chimo's warning) is striking and prophetic, no matter who wrote it. So it is no coincidence that Smaïl's friend Bernard Diop appears again at this very point in the narration, branishing his copy of Baldwin's *The Fire Next Time*, and that Smaïl recalls that title (and biblical allusion) to himself as he is being blocked from entering the airplane: discrimination breeds fire.[228] I want to suggest, therefore, that a unified, overarching significance can and does accompany the dualistic, mutually exclusive readings I proposed above. It is hard to say whether such a reading survives the trial "by fire" of Jack-Alain Léger by Azouz Begag—whether any such message can withstand the burden of authorial inauthenticity. That would be another choice to make.

Readers in fact have many chances to vote or choose, diachronically: from the moment they decide whether or not to buy the book, through a reading before the revealing of the hoax and perhaps a second reading thereafter. These are all moments of choice, each with its own coloration. The full spectrum remains open: it is still possible to buy a copy of *Vivre me tue* or its translations and be completely fooled by the hoax, because nothing you see tells you different. It is also possible to read the novel in full knowledge of its inauthenticity and yet appreciate its remarkable qualities.

The Parts He Played

How each of us decides
I've never been sure
The part we play
The way we are
How each of us denies any other way in the world.
Why each of us must choose
I've never understood . . .
ROBERT JAMES SMITH, "This Is a Lie" (The Cure, *Wild Mood Swings*)

Jack-Alain Léger published two books in the final year of his life, 2012. *Zanzaro Circus* appeared in January, with the following claim by the narrator on its back cover: "I swear on my honor, dear reader, that I have invented nothing; that these pages are on the spot reporting." *Zanzaro Circus* repeats the themes of so many previous books by Léger: a critique of the *société du spectacle* and of commodity fetishism, which make up a "new totalitarian order"; the massacre of Algerians in Paris on October 17, 1961; homosexuality; his dead brother; the injustices done to him by publishers and critics. Old grudges, feuds, and obsessions are resuscitated once again. But in addition to all this, and closely tied to all these familiar themes, *Zanzaro Circus* is his principal memoir of bipolar disorder, which Léger calls "a singular disease, which has little to do with ordinary depression." His mother was treated for it, with electro-shock therapy that "had no effect other than aggravating her distress"; Léger utterly rejects the value of shock therapy, comparing it to the torture that was used by the French in Algeria and claiming that it can lead to suicide.[229] The narrator's mother attempts suicide by throwing herself in front of a bus; she dies of a heart attack a few days later.[230] *Zanzaro Circus* thus suggests that the narrator—Jack-Alain Léger—inherited his bipolar disease from his mother, and, one might have guessed, would eventually follow her in suicide.

In *An Unquiet Mind*, an American memoir of bipolar disorder, Kay Redfield Jamison states that the disease "kill[s] tens of thousands of people every year" and that "many are among the most imaginative and gifted that we as a society have. . . . This quicksilver illness can both kill and create."[231] In *Touched with Fire: Manic-Depressive Illness and the Artistic Temperament,* Jamison states that "one-fifth of manic-depressive patients die by suicide." And "virtually all of the psychosis in creative individuals is manic-depressive rather than schizophrenic in nature." Another of Jamison's arguments is equally important to state here in relation to Jack-Alain Léger: that attention to mental illness in no way detracts from the complexity of a writer's creations; quite the contrary.[232]

Bipolar is, she states, "a genetic disease"; and she adds: "Strangely enough, I would choose to have it."[233] Jamison, unlike Léger, has survived the disease and even thrived as a clinical psychologist and writer. *Touched with Fire* examines the controversial hypothesis that "a destructive, often psychotic, and frequently lethal disease such as manic-depressive illness might convey certain advantages (such as heightened imaginative powers, intensified emotional responses, and increased energy)" (loc. 71). Much of the pattern that Jamison describes here sounds exactly like that of Jack-Alain Léger, with his "inflated self-esteem" and "chaotic patterns of personal and professional relationships"[234] (loc. 212).

Looking back to the authors we have read in this study, we should recall first the case of George Eliot/Mary Ann Evans. A biographer suggests that her self-doubling was not entirely healthy: "The shifting identities must be perceived as elements of internal confusion: not that she was unaware of who she was, but that unconsciously she had difficulty in identifying which self she was at any given time. . . . She had lost her moorings."[235] In a letter to Harriet Beecher Stowe, Eliot (signing as M. E. Lewes) introduced herself as someone with a "mental sickness," describing "the paralyzing despondency in which many days of my writing life have been past [*sic*]."[236] She linked her illness directly to her literary work: "I shall carry to my grave the mental diseases with which they [her novels] have contaminated me."[237] And, moving from the sublime to the ridiculous, we have Laura Albert's convenient and dubious claim of multiple personalities, which she used to defend herself in court.

I will not attempt an amateur's pseudo-clinical extrapolation from Jamison's book to Léger's life and works. My point is that hoaxing and imposture, despite their engagement with what I have been calling the way of play, are not necessarily free of danger. Looking back to *Vivre me tue* and its heavy reliance on *Moby-Dick*, and bearing in mind that Léger said Melville was "always with me,"[238] it is interesting to note what Jamison writes about Melville: that he appears to have inherited "severe mood swings" from his father; "Themes of madness, and its interlacings with visionary grandness, permeated Melville's writings in much the same way that his melancholic temperament wended its way in and around the lives of his fictional characters. . . . Melville displayed a remarkable, if occasional, vastness of spirit and grandiosity of scale."[239] The name Léger could as readily be used in those sentences. Just as there can be no full understanding of Léger without consideration of his mental illness, his name and works should be added to the scholarship on bipolar disease and the artistic temperament.

*

The last work by Jack-Alain Léger published during his lifetime—in June 2012—was a small collection of reflections called *Place de l'opéra*. It revolves around opera, "the most constraining" discipline of all, but ranges with considerable erudition through works of literature, theater, and painting. The biographical blurb on the inside back cover, no doubt printed with Léger's permission if not authored by him, is worth quoting in its entirety; it reads like both an autobiography and an obituary, and in a counterintuitive way I think it sets the stage for his suicide:

> The author, a French novelist born in 1947, was a rock critic in the 1960s, a musician in the underground scene in the early 70s, the unforgettable creator of "Chrysler Rose." Under the pseudonym Jack-Alain Léger, he has written more than thirty books, along with four others as Paul Smaïl. In 1976 he published *Monsignore*, an epic novel relating the meteoric rise of an American prelate to the highest levels of the Vatican. It sold 300,000 copies in France and was translated into twenty-three languages, with a disastrous adaptation to the cinema starring Christopher Reeve in the title role. The author became immensely rich, then squandered his fortune in six years. He is now a poor novelist, "one of the great French writers," according to Philippe Sollers, "a famous unknown" [*Un célèbre méconnu*].

This description of a life is structured by a series of balanced pairings. The "author" remains unnamed; Jack-Alain Léger is still only a pseudonym here. So identity is both established and obscured. A fortune is made and then squandered. In the end, the author is both famous and unknown. There is an almost comforting symmetry implied in this mini-novel; everything returns to some kind of enigmatic equilibrium. (Inside the book, Léger writes: "No biographical facts can ever fully account for the methods of an artist of genius.")[240]

If there is a quest for balance inside this book as well, it may come in the passage in which Léger discusses, for the last time, one of his favorite works, Cervantes's *Don Quixote*. Focusing on the fictive Morisco translator, Sid Ahmed Ben Engeli, who is the linchpin of the story (and who featured prominently in *Ali le Magnifique*), Léger celebrates the harmonious nature of Cervantes's imagination, in the context of a Spain that was about to expel the Moors.

> Cervantes can be heard, outside the text, laughing, shouting out like his hero: "I know who I am!" *¡Hombre!* A Castillian writer of genius, which is to say Spanish as well, Jewish as well, Arab as well—in a word, universal. (*Place de l'opéra*, 45)

If it is not too forced, one might see in this a small "rebalancing" if not an atonement for the Islamophobia that Léger had put into print nine years earlier.[241] But his reliance on the concept of universalism, as nice as it seems here, is of course the most *French* of all possible gestures, the antithesis of all "communitarianisms."

The trope of balance returns in a chapter on Wagner's "indefensible" anti-Semitism (73–77). (Léger presumably saw no common ground between his own avowed Islamophobia—of which he makes no mention here—and Wagner's virulent prejudice.) His argument is that the anti-Semitism cannot change the fact that Wagner is "one of the pillars of our Western culture"; we must remain able "to think ambiguity and contradiction" (74). In the end, "it remains that we love Wagner, . . . with a clear conscience and a troubled one" [*en toute bonne et toute mauvaise conscience*] (77). Both, in balance.

It is thus bitterly and sadly ironic that Léger died by the ultimate act of imbalance, suicide by defenestration.[242] In the note that he left for his guardian, he wrote: "My mother never succeeded in killing herself. I did."[243] Compared to Gary's last words, these lack any sense of whimsy. But both authors got the last word, which is one particularly literary aspect of suicide. Suicide makes you the author of your own death and allows you to choose the time, place, and method. Leiris wrote that suicide was the only way to escape death, precisely by allowing those choices.[244]

"Wild mood swings" overcame him.[245] In *Les Aurochs et les anges* he had meditated on "the recursive obsession with suicide that you rediscover with each episode of depression" and on all possible methods for killing oneself. "So you throw yourself out the window from way, way up on the ninth floor."[246] In the end, living killed him. Time will tell whether the remark attributed to Antoine Gallimard is credible: that Jack-Alain Léger would be "a great posthumous writer."[247]

Conclusion

Is there a French tradition of intercultural literary hoaxes? Certainly. Is it the same as in the United States? No. But, as the multiple trans-Atlantic comparisons in this book have shown, there are many common characteristics and intriguing contrasts. The two traditions share various methods of disguise, subterfuge, and role-playing. Many cases on both sides of the Atlantic seem to follow a top-down trajectory of appropriation and representation. Chimo put it this way: "It's you up there, me down here"; but Chimo's book itself, like so many others in both countries, bridges the gap and brings information from "down there" "up" into writing. Whether it does so authentically or falsely is of course the question. The United States may be both more divisively multicultural and more puritanical about questions of self-representation—ostensibly more devoted to the way of truth. France's powerful universalist literary tradition appears to provide cover for all manner of play, making impostures both more permissible and less rewarding. (Perhaps that is why the Paul Smaïl novels have not been followed by further intercultural impostures in France.) But hoaxing is a richly powerful function of literature and therefore impossible for some writers in both countries to resist.

The only thing that could put an end to hoaxing would be, finally, the death of the author and the triumph of *écriture*—the driverless car of literature. It was a nice idea, but it never happened. The idea and institution of the author continues to inflect the reading of literature, and as long as that is true, impostures will be both possible and rewarding. An "author" is an open invitation to a hoax.

Are intercultural literary hoaxes "good" or "bad"? I still don't know. Each case examined here has presented a unique blend of truth and play. If the trickery of the hoax needs to be justified, the writer often cites truth to justify play. But others argue, so to speak, that the play's the thing. (Even if that allusion in fact takes us back to the way of truth: Hamlet puts on a play to "catch the conscience of the King" and reveal the truth of his father's death.) Hoaxes challenge us to decipher these intricate and not entirely comfortable interminglings of morality and aesthetics, often leaving us suspended—or perhaps shuttling—between the two.

A study such as this one cannot adjudicate once and for all the question of cultural appropriation, of which intercultural literary hoaxes are a prime and time-honored example. Returning for a moment to one of the sharpest focal points in the recent debates over that question, the painting of Emmett Till in his coffin by white artist Dana Schutz: the British-born black artist and writer Hannah Black was quoted as saying, "The subject matter is not Schutz's. . . . White free speech and white creative freedom have been founded on the constraint of others, and are not natural rights." The first statement is easy to refute, in the name of cultural hybridity, open borders, and a representational ethic of flow; and against cultural separatism, even apartheid ("*chacun chez soi*"), not to mention censorship. Any artist should be allowed to paint anyone or anything. But Black's second statement cannot be summarily dismissed. The "constraint of others" that she sees underpinning white freedom of expression is comparable to all the factors of race, gender, class, and ethnicity that have been visible in this study: each hoax has sprung out of a shortfall of literacy or, to put it another way, a difference between the ability of a dominant group to produce representations and the (perceived or real) inability of a nondominant group to do so. One example makes this clear. Beur literature existed and had already produced numerous fine novels by 1997, when Jack-Alain Léger published *Vivre me tue* as Paul Smaïl; nonetheless, the hoaxer was hailed by *Paris-Match* as "finally . . . a Beur writer with talent." Such a statement was possible only because Beur literature was "constrained" in the sense that it had obviously not made an impression on mainstream French culture. Azouz Begag was constrained; Léger, in his "white creative freedom," was not; that is how the hoax arose. In that case and in numerous others, harm was done or at least perceived. But Hannah Black's proposal to suppress that freedom is of course wrong, because it cannot undo any harm: the answer to speech you don't like is more speech, not less. No right of representation is "natural," all must be fought for. And in the longer run in France, authentic Beur literature has of course won out over fakery.

Examining hoaxes has raised questions about the reading process, and one in particular has been vexing: the idea of "telling" the identity of the author. Since the beginning of this study, the claims of readers (other than Dickens) to pinpoint authorship by reading alone has constantly been undermined. But this is not, as Romain Gary thought, necessarily an exposure of all literary criticism as a fraud. A reader can tell many things by reading alone—style, tone, beauty, even truth—but not the identity of the author. Hoaxes expose the double bind in which cross-cultural readers find themselves: they want to believe "it's the work that counts," but they also—still—want to be certain about the identity and authenticity of the author. When hoaxes reveal those to be hokum, they leave readers in a very awkward position. But many impostures live on and on, after their "truth" has been exposed: they keep telling a story that people want to hear. By hoaxing authorship, these impostures only seem to reinforce the general, indestructible belief in the identity of the author.

What, then, do hoaxes tell us about the ethics of truth in the present day? A good hoax can be fun and can in fact teach us about the truth, but we have seen many times in this study that intercultural impostures can do (perceived) harm. Perhaps the lesson of impostures is of a double awareness: on the one hand, we can acknowledge certain forms of faked otherness as worthwhile, playful thought experiments. Cui bono? Readers whose minds are stretched by these identitarian brain teasers. But on the other, we must admit that sometimes people do get hurt in the process. To hoax is human; hoaxes will rise and fall, but until the end of identity itself, imposture will remain a risky business.

Notes

Preface

1. See David Leonhardt and Stuart A. Thompson, "Trump's Lies," *New York Times*, July 21, 2017, https://www.nytimes.com/interactive/2017/06/23/opinion/trumps-lies.html/, accessed November 18, 2017; Timothy Egan, "We're with Stupid," *New York Times*, November 17, 2017, https://www.nytimes.com/2017/11/17/opinion/were-with-stupid.html?_r=0/, accessed November 18, 2017; Glenn Kessler, "365 Days of Trump Claims," *Washington Post*, May 19, 2017, https://www.washingtonpost.com/news/fact-checker/wp/2017/05/19/365-days-of-trump-claims/, accessed November 18, 2017.

Introduction

1. Magritte's 1928 painting, entitled "La trahison des images," famously declared "Ceci n'est pas une pipe." He reinforced his point by reversing it, in his 1963 painting of cheese under a glass dome: "Ceci *est* un morceau de fromage" (emphasis added). See Catherine Emerson, "To Set a Thief to Catch a Thief," in Catherine Emerson and Maria Scott, eds., *Artful Deceptions: Verbal and Visual Trickery in French Culture/Les Supercheries littéraires et visuelles: la tromperie dans la culture française* (Oxford: Peter Lang, 2006), 367. See Michel Foucault, *Ceci n'est pas une pipe* (Saint Clément de Rivière: Fata Morgana, 1973). Foucault writes, "Cet énoncé est parfaitement vrai, puisqu'il est bien évident que le dessin représentant une pipe n'est pas lui-même une pipe" (18). My point is that writing makes us forget the following, attributed to writing by Foucault (by way of explaining Magritte): "je ne suis rien d'autre que les mots que vous êtes en train de lire" (29). The last thing on our minds is the following "truth": "Nulle part, il n'y a de pipe" (35).

2. Plato, *The Republic*, ed. and trans. Chris Emlyn-Jones and William Preddy (Cambridge: Harvard University Press, 2013), vol. 6, 400–401 (book 10).

3. Plato, *The Republic* (Emlyn-Jones/Preddy), vol. 5, 257 (book 3).

4. See Jacques Rancière's comments on Plato's division of labor, which Rancière calls "a distribution of the sensible." "The exclusion of the mimetician, from the Platonic point of view, goes hand in hand with the formation of a community where work is in 'its' place." Rancière, *The Politics of Aesthetics: The Distribution of the Sensible*, trans. Gabriel Rockhill (New York: Continuum, 2004), 42, 43.

5. Plato, *The Republic* (Emlyn-Jones/Preddy), vol. 5, 259 (book 3).

6. Plato, *The Republic* in *The Dialogues of Plato*, trans. Benjamin Jowett (New York: Scribner, 1901), vol. 1, 218 (book 3), emphasis added.

7. Ramona A. Naddaff, *Exiling the Poets: The Production of Censorship in Plato's "Republic"* (Chicago: University of Chicago Press, 2002), 50, 56, 69. Naddaff explains that what is left for Plato is narrative, nonmimetic poetry, in which the poet does not "lose himself or his identity," "maintaining his own psychological unity" (54). Plato effected what sounds a lot like a hostile takeover of poetry by philosophy (see Naddaff, 67).

8. Plato, *The Republic* (Emlyn-Jones/Preddy), vol. 5, 261 (book 3).

9. Plato, *The Republic* (Emlyn-Jones/Preddy), vol. 5, 267 (book 3).

10. Plato, *The Republic* (Jowett), vol. 2, 221 (book 3). The Chris Emlyn-Jones and William Preddy translation reads: "Then it would seem that if a man who is able because of his skills to become versatile and impersonate everything were to arrive in our state wishing to show off himself and his poems, we would revere him as inspired, wonderful and delightful, but we would say that we do not have such a man in our state, nor would it be right to have one. In fact we would send him away to another city . . . while we ourselves would employ a more austere and less pleasing poet and story teller on account of his usefulness, who could reproduce for us the diction of a decent man . . ." Plato, *The Republic* (Emlyn-Jones/Preddy), vol. 5, 269 (book 3).

11. For a summary of Plato's view of three removals from nature, see Rosen's treatment of Plato/Socrates's progression from the Idea of the bed, to the crafting of a bed, to a painting of a bed, which is "at the third generation from nature." Stanley Rosen, *Plato's Republic: A Study* (New Haven: Yale University Press, 2005), 367.

12. Rosen, *Plato's Republic*, 101.

13. Mary Karr, *The Art of Memoir* (New York: Harper, 2015), 9, 10, 11.

14. See Andrea Nightingale, "Mimesis: Ancient Greek Literary Theory," in *Literary Theory and Criticism: An Oxford Guide*, ed. Patricia Waugh (New York: Oxford University Press, 2006), 39.

15. Aristotle, *The "Poetics" of Aristotle*, trans. and commentary Stephen Halliwell (Chapel Hill: University of North Carolina Press, 1987), 34.

16. Aristotle, *The "Poetics,"* 40. See Halliwell's commentary, 178. Halliwell adds that Aristotle was opposing himself to Plato, "who was prepared to apply rigorous ethical and epistemological principles to all Greek art" (178).

17. Nightingale, "Mimesis," 40.

18. "Correct standards in poetry are not identical with those in politics or in any other particular art." Aristotle, *The "Poetics,"* 61.

19. Halliwell, commentary, Aristotle, *The "Poetics,"* 180.

20. *The Republic* (Jowett), 220. The Emlyn-Jones/Preddy translation reads: "the one who impersonates decent people without the mixed elements" (vol. 5, 267, book 3). In book 10, Plato winds up allowing for only two kinds of poetry in his city: "hymns to the gods and eulogies of good men." Plato, *The Republic* (Emlyn-Jones/Preddy), vol. 5, 259.

21. Youcef M. D., quoted in Alain Salles, "Duel d'écrivains polymorphes," *Le Monde*, April 12, 2002.

22. Rivka Galchen, "What Distinguishes Cultural Exchange from Cultural Appropriation?" *New York Times Book Review*, June 11, 2017, https://www.nytimes.com/2017/06/08/books/review /bookends-cultural-appropriation.html?_r=0/, accessed June 21, 2017.

23. Melissa Katsoulis, *Literary Hoaxes: An Eye-Opening History of Famous Frauds* (New York: Skyhorse, 2009), 7.

24. Jean-François Jeandillou uses the term *la part du jeu* in his *Esthétique de la mystification: tactique et stratégie littéraire* (Paris: Les Editions de Minuit, 1994), 185–212.

25. *The Republic* (Jowett), vol. 2, 433 (book 10); the Emlyn-Jones/Preddy translation reads: "imitation is a kind of game and not serious" (vol. 6, 419). I am grateful to Edwin Duval for help with the original word *paidia*, which is defined by Liddell and Scott as "child's play, sport, pastime; a game," and not to be confused with *paideia*, "teaching" or "education."

26. Ngugi wa Thiong'o, preface to *Matigari*, trans. Wangui wa Goro (Portsmouth, NH: Heinemann, 1993), viii.

27. Roland Barthes, "The Death of the Author," trans. Richard Howard (UbuWeb Papers, n.d.); "La Mort de l'auteur," PDF, https://monoskop.org/images/3/38/Barthes_Roland_1968_1984_La _mort_de_l_auteur.pdf/, accessed February 21, 2018.

28. Pierre Bayard, *Et si les oeuvres changeaient d'auteur?* (Paris: Editions de Minuit, 2010). In the second part of his book, Bayard also comments on certain hoaxes that involve what he calls a "partial" change of author, including Emile Ajar/Romain Gary and Vernon Sullivan/Boris Vian. Bayard does not consider postcolonial or Francophone examples, and in my view understates the deceptive power of hoaxes by referring to them mainly as pseudonyms. For another post-Barthesian, post-Foucaldian consideration of the author function, see Jérôme Meizoz, *Postures littéraires: mises en scène modernes de l'auteur* (Geneva: Slatkine Erudition, 2007). Meizoz does not consider imposture.

29. Kevin Young, *Bunk: The Rise of Hoaxes, Humbug, Plagiarists, Phonies, Post-Facts, and Fake News* (New York: Graywolf Press, 2017), 119. The term "truthiness" was invented by Stephen Colbert.

30. Romain Gary, *Vie et mort d'Emile Ajar* (Paris: Gallimard, 1981), 29.

31. Henry Louis Gates, Jr., "'Authenticity, or the Lesson of Little Tree," *New York Times*, November 24, 1991.

32. Philippe Hamon, quoted in Maria Scott, "Artful Deceptions: Distortions, Seductions, and Substitutions," in Emerson and Scott, *Artful Deceptions*, 31.

33. Joe Woodward, "The Literature of Lies," *Poets & Writers*, May 1, 2006, http://www.pw.org /content/literature_lies/, accessed January 24, 2017.

34. Young, *Bunk*, 209.

35. Young, *Bunk*, 221.

36. Harry G. Frankfurt, *On Bullshit*, quoted in Young, *Bunk*, 307.

37. Clover Linh Tran, "CDS Appropriates Asian Dishes, Students Say," *Oberlin Review*, November 6, 2015, https://oberlinreview.org/9055/news/cds-appropriates-asian-dishes-students-say/, accessed March 23, 2017; Randy Kennedy, "White Artist's Painting of Emmet Till at Whitney Biennial Draws Protests," *New York Times*, March 22, 2017, https://www.nytimes.com/2017/03/21/arts /design/painting-of-emmett-till-at-whitney-biennial-draws-protests.html/, accessed March 18, 2017. The painting was by Dana Schutz. Hannah Black, a British-born black artist and writer, was quoted saying: "The subject matter is not Schutz's. . . . White free speech and white creative freedom have been founded on the constraint of others, and are not natural rights. The painting must go." Jennifer Schuessler, "Editor Resigns Over an Article Defending 'Cultural Appropriation,'" *New York Times*, May 11, 2017, https://www.nytimes.com/2017/05/11/arts/editor-resigns -over-article-defending-cultural-appropriation.html?_r=0/, accessed May 17, 2017. See also Kenan Malik, "In Defense of Cultural Appropriation," *New York Times*, June 14, 2017, https://www .nytimes.com/2017/06/14/opinion/in-defense-of-cultural-appropriation.html?ref=opinion &_r=0/ accessed June 15, 2017.

38. See Rebecca Tuvel, "A Defense of Transracial Identity," *Hypatia* 32, no. 2 (Spring 2017): 263–78; Jennifer Schuessler, "A Defense of 'Transracial' Identity Roils Philosophy World," *New York Times*, May 19, 2017, https://www.nytimes.com/2017/05/19/arts/a-defense-of-transracial

-identity-roils-philosophy-world.html/, accessed June 21, 2017. The scholars' letter: https://gen dertrender.wordpress.com/alexis-shotwell-open-letter-to-hypatia/, accessed June 21, 2017.

39. Adam Shatz, "Raw Material," blog post, *LRB Blog*, March 24, 2017: https://www.lrb.co.uk /blog/2017/03/24/adam-shatz/raw-material/ Consulted June 21, 2017.

40. Achille Mbembe, *Critique de la raison nègre* (Paris: La Découverte, 2013), 15.

41. Here I have inverted a quote from Kwame Anthony Appiah, *The Ethics of Identity* (Princeton: Princeton University Press, 2005): 28. Appiah is paraphrasing John Stuart Mill's *On Liberty*, in the following manner: "the mere fact that I do something you do not want me to do does not *eo ipso* count as my harming you."

42. The *Oxford English Dictionary* acknowledges a connection between *hoax* and *hoc est corpus meum*, but finds no direct evidence of the relationship. Nevertheless, I'm investing in the connection.

43. I borrow the phrase "temporary visit" from Joe Lockard, afterword, in Mattie Griffith, *Autobiography of a Female Slave* (Jackson: University of Mississippi Press, 1998 [1856]), 404. This definition of literary imposture as a temporary visit thus distinguishes my work here from that of Sarah Burton in *Impostors: Six Kinds of Liar* (New York: Viking Press, 2000). She writes about impostors who leave their real lives, which are "often intolerable and oppressive," behind in order to "change themselves" (2). With a few notable exceptions, literary impostors limit their hoax to their writing and do not lead an alternate life. "Clark Rockefeller" would have been a perfect subject for her book, but not for mine. See the critique of Burton's book in Young, *Bunk*, 331.

44. On Perec, see Scott, "Artful Deceptions." See also the studies of imposture in the novels of Zola, Bernanos, and other French authors, in Arlette Bouloumié, ed., *L'Imposture dans la littérature* (Angers: Presses de l'Université d'Angers, 2001).

45. On the heteronym, the example of the Portuguese writer Fernando Pessoa is extraordinary: he used approximately seventy-five, preferring "heteronym" to "pseudonym."

46. The "Piltdown Man," "discovered" in 1908, was supposed to be the missing link between man and beast, and was entirely faked. See Miles Russell, *Piltdown Man: The Secret Life of Charles Dawson and the World's Greatest Archeological Hoax* (Stroud, UK: Tempus, 2003). On the Tasaday controversy, see John Nance, *The Gentle Tasaday: A Stone-Age People in the Philippine Rain Forest*, with a preface by Charles A. Lindbergh (New York: Harcourt, Brace, Jovanovich, 1975), quoted pp. x and xi. See also Robin Hemley, *Invented Eden: The Elusive, Disputed History of the Tasaday* (New York: Farrar, Strauss and Giroux, 2003).

47. Young, *Bunk*, 182.

48. JT LeRoy [Laura Albert], *Sarah* (New York: Bloomsbury, 2000), 71.

49. Mark Blaisse, "Painted Souls: The Beauty of Our Origins," preface to Jimmy Nelson, *Before They Pass Away* (Kempen, Germany: teNeues, 2013), 3.

50. Blaisse, "Painted Souls," 3.

51. Anny Wynchand, "Fictions d'Afriques: les intellectuels français et leurs visions," *Afriques imaginaires: regards réciproques et discours littéraires* (Paris: L'Harmattan, 1995), 76.

52. Susan Stewart, *Crimes of Writing: Problems in the Containment of Representation* (New York: Oxford University Press, 1991), 31, 33.

53. Rodney Needham, *Exemplars* (Berkeley: University of California Press, 1985), 84; see the annotated bibliography on Psalmanazar, 229–240. See also Richard M. Swiderski, *The False Formosan: George Psalmanazar and the Eighteenth-Century Experiment of Identity* (San Francisco: Mellen Research University Press 1991); Michael Keevak, *The Pretended Asian: George Psalmanazar's Eighteenth-Century Formosan Hoax* (Detroit: Wayne State University Press, 2004); Stewart *Crimes of Writing*, 32–57; and Tzvetan Todorov, *Les Morales de l'histoire* (Paris: Grasset, 1991), 134–41.

54. Keevak, *The Pretended Asian*, 81. See Swiderski, *The False Formosan*, 76.

55. George Psalmanazar, *An Historical and Geographical Description of Formosa: An Island Subject to the Emperor of Japan, Giving an Account of the Religion, Customs, Manners, &c., of the Inhabitants, Together with a Relation of What Happen'd to the Author in his Travels . . . : Also the History and Reasons of his Conversion to Christianity* (London: Daniel Brown et al., 1705).

56. Needham, *Exemplars*, 85.

57. Needham, *Exemplars*, 84.

58. Percy G. Adams, *Travelers and Travel Liars: 1660–1800* (Berkeley: University of California Press, 1962), 92; see Young, *Bunk*, 75.

59. Young, *Bunk*, 75.

60. Needham, *Exemplars*, 88.

61. Needham, *Exemplars*, 90.

62. Derek Freeman, "Was Margaret Mead Misled or Did She Mislead on Samoa?" *Current Anthropology* 41, no. 4 (August–September 2000): 610. This article supplements Freeman's previous books *Margaret Mead and Samoa: The Making and Unmaking of an Anthropological Myth* (Cambridge: Harvard University Press, 1983) and *The Fateful Hoaxing of Margaret Mead* (Boulder: Westview Press, 1999).

63. On the widespread influence of Mead's work, see Freeman, *The Fateful Hoaxing*, 191.

64. Margaret Mead, *Coming of Age in Samoa: A Psychological Study of Primitive Youth for Western Civilisation* (New York: W. Morrow & Co, 1932). One needn't subscribe to Freeman's claim that "a whole view of the human species was constructed out of the innocent lies of two young women" (quoted in James E. Côté, "Was *Coming of Age in Samoa* Based on a 'Fateful Hoaxing'?," *Current Anthropology* 41, no. 4 (August–September 2000): 617) in order to believe that something strange took place here. In a dissenting view, Martin Orans asserts that Mead was "more misleading in some important matters than misled" (quoted in Freeman, "Was Margaret Mead Misled?," 613). The debate between Freeman and Orans as to whether Mead was simply duped or "knew better" and deliberately misled her readers seems less important to me than one basic point: the informants, for their own reasons, provided false information, which Mead passed on to the world. Côté rejects the idea that Mead was hoaxed; see Freeman's reply, 620–22. I find Freeman's argument to be, overall, convincing.

65. Mead, quoted in Freeman, *The Fateful Hoaxing*, 183.

66. See Donald R. Wright, "Uprooting Kunta Kinte: On the Perils of Relying on Encyclopedic Informants," *History in Africa* 8 (1981): 205–17. Following in Haley's footsteps in Gambia, Wright found out that the "griot" Fofana, who had performed for Haley, was neither a real griot (*jali*) nor reliable.

67. Amadou Hampâté Bâ, *L'Etrange destin de Wangrin* (Paris: Union Générale d'Editions, 1973); *Oui, mon commandant!* (Paris: Actes Sud, 1994).

68. Quoted in Frederick Karl, *George Eliot: Voice of a Century* (New York: W. W. Norton, 1995), 269. This letter is not included in Hartley's selected letters, below.

69. Gates, "'Authenticity.'"

70. Lia Brozgal, "Hostages of Authenticity: Paul Smaïl, Azouz Begag, and the Invention of the Beur Author," *French Forum* 34, no. 2 (Spring 2009): 117.

71. Karr, *The Art of Memoir*, 83. Karr was herself fooled into endorsing a fake memoir, that of Binjamin Wilkomirski (81–82); on Karr and JT LeRoy, see note XX, below.

72. Michel Foucault, "Qu'est-ce qu'un auteur?," *Bulletin de la Société Française de Philosophie* 63, no. 3 (July–September 1969); translated as "What Is an Author," in *The Foucault Reader*, ed. Paul Rabinow (New York: Pantheon Books, 1984), 112.

73. Charles Dickens, letter to George Eliot, January 18, 1858, *The Selected Letters of Charles Dickens*, ed. Jenny Hartley (Oxford: Oxford University Press, 2012), 331–32.

74. The literary blogger Maria Popova writes, "[Dickens's letter to Eliot] is a pinnacle of praise, written with equal parts professional admiration, generosity of spirit, and the special kindness Dickens reserved for his kin." https://www.brainpickings.org/2013/11/22/charles-dickens-fan-mail -george-eliot/, accessed March 19, 2018.

75. See Alexander Welsh, *George Eliot and Blackmail* (Cambridge: Harvard University Press, 1985), 123.

76. About ten years earlier, George Henry Lewes discerned that the pseudonymous author of *Jane Eyre*—"Currer Bell" or Charlotte Brontë—was a woman, by reading alone. Lewes wrote of *Jane Eyre*: "The writer is evidently a woman . . ." George Henry Lewes, "Recent Novels, French and English," *Fraser's Magazine*, December 1847, 690, https://www.bl.uk/collection-items/review -of-jane-eyre-by-george-henry-lewes. He who had unmasked Charlotte Brontë in the 1840s became a zealous protector of his lover's own gender secret in the 50s. See Kathryn Hughes, *George Eliot: The Last Victorian* (New York: Farrar Strauss Giroux, 1998), 219. I am grateful to Margaret Homans for guidance with questions related to George Eliot.

77. Karl, *George Eliot*, 308; see also 238. George Henry Lewes, at the end of the incognito, said that the purpose had been "to get the book judged on its own merits, and not prejudged as the work of a woman, or of a particular woman." Quoted in Hughes, *George Eliot*, 220.

78. George Eliot/Mary Ann Evans, quoted in Rosemarie Bodenheimer, *The Real Life of Mary Ann Evans: George Eliot, Her Letters and Fiction* (Ithaca: Cornell University Press, 1994), 132.

79. Nancy Henry, *The Life of George Eliot: A Critical Biography* (Chichester: Wiley-Blackwell, 2012), 109; on secrecy, see 119n2. The mask that was the name George Eliot was doubled by "the Liggins imposture"—the rumor that one Joseph Liggins was the real author of George Eliot's works. Bodenheimer writes: "The truth about why this impoverished, ne'er-do-well Nuneaton clergyman was credited with the authorship of George Eliot's fiction is unknown to this day . . ." (*The Real Life of Mary Ann Evans*, 137). Welsh explains: "By doing little other than refusing to deny that he was George Eliot, [Liggins] shamelessly exploited the secret of her authorship to his own satisfaction" (*George Eliot and Blackmail*, 129–30). Of the web of deceptions that Evans deployed, Frederick Karl writes: "She has, in effect, become another person: literally taking on another identity, somewhere between male and female . . . She has become, in these respects, *fiction itself*, part of the imaginative process in which transformation is key." Karl, *George Eliot*, 235, emphasis added. Writing as George Eliot, Evans told her publishers of her delight with Dickens's appraisal; but she fiercely maintained her secrecy for two more years (267, 292). Dickens pressed the case, writing to the publisher again (268–69); the publishers, once in on the secret, worried about the fallout from Eliot's real identity and gender being revealed (326–27, 341). She never revealed her true identity in any formal way, but the truth dribbled out, and she finally stopped refuting it. Hughes, *George Eliot*, 207–20, comprises the best narrative account of Eliot's incognito and its undoing. In the scholarship that I have read on this subject, I have seen no suggestion that Dickens had access to any information hinting at the real gender of George Eliot, outside of his reading of the text.

80. See Karl, *George Eliot*, 235.

81. Paraphrase of and then quote from Dickens, letter to Blackwood, January 27, 1858, in Karl, *George Eliot*, 268.

82. George Eliot (Mary Ann Evans), "The Sad Fortunes of the Rev. Amos Barton" in *Scenes of Clerical Life* (London: Dent, 1910), 5, 9, 13, 18–19. A further hint—perhaps a wink on Eliot's part—

is visible in this passage: "[Mrs. Barton] was even trying to persuade her husband to leave off tight pantaloons, because if he would wear the ordinary gun-cases, she knew that she could make them so well that *no one would suspect the sex of the tailor*" (22, emphasis added). In our times, Dickens could have recourse to a "gender detecting" web site, http://www.hackerfactor.com/Gen derGuesser.php, based on research by linguists, which claims 60–70 percent accuracy based on a minimum three hundred–word sample. Testing the paragraph that begins "Soothing, unspeakable charm of gentle womanhood!" (18–19), the site reported that as "informal" writing (a term that is not defined by the site), the passage is 67 percent male ("verdict: Male"); as "formal" writing, the verdict was "weak Female," or 54 percent female. Dickens did better. For a feminist reading of gendered rhetoric in Eliot, covering Eliot's concern to set herself apart from "lady novelists," and amounting to an after-the-fact forensic reading of gender in her prose, see Robyn R. Warhol, *Gendered Interventions: Narrative Discourse in the Victorian Novel* (New Brunswick: Rutgers University Press, 1989), 115–33.

83. I owe my awareness of the Dickens-Eliot case to Deborah Heller, letter to the editor, *New York Times*, January 5, 1992. Gender switching as practiced by so many female writers in the nineteenth century is, of course, different from the kind of intercultural imposture that is the main object of this study. To take only the most obvious point: women like George Eliot and George Sand *needed* in some way to adopt an artificial male identity in order to get published and taken seriously. In a similar vein, Jonathan Littell *needed* to submit his manuscript to Gallimard under the name Jean Petit, to pass as French, before *Les Bienveillantes* was accepted. These are not hoaxes per se—which are never "necessary."

84. Unsigned review, *Saturday Review*, April 14, 1860, in *George Eliot: The Critical Heritage*, ed. David Carroll (New York: Barnes & Noble, 1971), 114.

85. "An 1872 law prohibiting [French] state authorities from collecting data on individuals' ethnicity or religious beliefs was reaffirmed by a 1978 law emphasizing the prohibition of the collection or exploitation of personal data revealing an individual's race, ethnicity, or political, philosophical, or religious opinions." CIA, *The World Factbook*, https://www.cia.gov/library/publica tions/the-world-factbook/fields/2122.html/, accessed February 16, 2017.

86. Françoise Vergès, "Les Troubles de mémoire: traite négrière, esclavage, et écriture de l'histoire," *Cahiers d'études africaines* 179–80 (2005): 25.

87. Maurice Samuels, *The Right to Difference: French Universalism and the Jews* (Chicago: University of Chicago Press, 2016), 4.

88. Laura Browder, *Slippery Characters: Ethnic Impersonators and American Identities* (Chapel Hill: University of North Carolina Press, 2000), 7.

89. Note that Browder is focused on impersonator autobiographies: the (false) self itself is exposed in these texts; the author is actually seeking to escape his/her ethnic position. In the French cases, this is less than clear.

Part One

1. *The Slave: or Memoirs of Archy Moore* (Boston: John H. Eastburn, 1936); the name Richard Hildreth did not appear in the book; a preface presented the work as a found manuscript. Mattie Griffith, *Autobiography of a Female Slave* (Jackson: University of Mississippi Press, 1998 [1856]); see afterword by Joe Lockard, 403. Lockard describes the work as "a temporary visit into an imagined blackness" (404), in a context where "few readers seemed to credit the narrative voice as one that belonged to a former slave" (411). Griffith freed her slaves, enabled by the proceeds from the

book and a grant from the American Anti-Slavery Society (407, 414). Lockard's essay concludes with nuanced thoughts about the ethics of representation implicit in Griffith's work, which are more complex than they might appear at first glance.

2. Joslyn T. Pine, "Note," in Harriet Jacobs, *Incidents in the Life of a Slave Girl* (Mineola, NY: Dover, 2001), vi.

3. Young, *Bunk*, 8–9.

4. Browder, *Slippery Characters*, 32.

5. Katsoulis, *Literary Hoaxes*, 87.

6. Gina Caison, "Claiming the Unclaimable: Forrest Carter, *The Education of Little Tree*, and Land Claim in the Native South," *Mississippi Quarterly: The Journal of Southern Cultures* 64: 3–4 (2011): 573–95. The story of the Forrest Carter hoax is told in a documentary film (marred by some re-created scenes), "The Reconstruction of Asa Carter" (2011, dir. Marco Ricci, 58 min.), available on Youtube: https://www.youtube.com/watch?v=5xZ_5kPli7A/, accessed February 26, 2018. The film includes appearances by writers I cite here, including Wayne Greenhaw, Dan T. Carter, and Laura Browder (on whose book, *Slippery Characters*, the film is based). The film also shows the extent to which Carter played Cherokee in real life after moving to Texas, fooling friends into thinking he "looked Cherokee." Despite the definitive unveiling of the imposture by Dan T. Carter in 1991, a feature film aimed at children was made in 1997: *The Education of Little Tree* (113 min). The credits announce that the film is "based on the novel by Forrest Carter," with no mention of Asa Carter or the hoax. In style and sentiment, the film is reminiscent of the television series *The Waltons*.

7. Forrest Carter, *The Education of Little Tree* (New York: Delacorte Press, 1976).

8. Rennard Strickland, "Sharing *Little Tree*," foreword (dated November 1985) to Forrest Carter, *The Education of Little Tree* (Albuquerque: University of New Mexico Press, 1986), vi.

9. See Dan T. Carter, "Southern History, American Fiction: The Secret Life of Southwestern Novelist Forrest Carter," in *Rewriting the South: History and Fiction*, ed. Lothar Hönnighausen and Valeria Gennaro Lerda (Tübingen: Francke, 1993), 286–304.

10. Browder, *Slippery Characters*, 132.

11. Jeff Roche, "Asa/Forrest Carter and Regional/Political Identity," in *The Southern Albatross: Race and Ethnicity in the American South*, ed. Philip D. Dillard and Randall L. Hall (Macon, GA: Mercer University Press, 1999), 235–74.

12. Dan T. Carter, "The Transformation of a Klansman," op-ed, *New York Times*, October 4, 1991, http://www.nytimes.com/1991/10/04/opinion/the-transformation-of-a-klansman.html/. Carter followed this with the scholarly essay "Southern History, American Fiction," which gives the most complete account of the affair. See also Roche, "Asa/Forrest Carter and Regional/Political Identity."

13. Mark McGurl, "Learning from Little Tree: The Political Education of the Counterculture," *Yale Journal of Criticism* 18, no. 2 (2005): 244. McGurl points out that both cases provoked "panicked rereadings" (244).

14. See Dan T. Carter, "Southern History, American Fiction," 300; and an unsigned article ("Special to The New York Times") by Wayne Greenhaw, "Is Forrest Carter Really Asa Carter? Only Josey Wales May Know for Sure," *New York Times*, August 26, 1976, 45, https://www.ny times.com/1976/08/26/archives/is-forrest-carter-really-asa-carter-only-josey-wales-may-know -for.html/, accessed March 8, 2018. Despite the questioning title, the article leaves no doubt that Forrest Carter is in fact Asa Carter, and it explains his background in racism. Interviewed for the piece, "Forrest" Carter maintains the hoax, claiming that he is not Asa Carter; he says he is "both a cowboy and an Indian and that his next book, *The Education of Little Tree*, will tell all about

his own Indian childhood." In a letter to *Publishers Weekly* (November 15, 1991, p. 8), Greenhaw identifies himself as the author of the 1976 *Times* article and complains bitterly that his unveiling of the hoax was ignored by both the *Times* subsequently (the newspaper "forgot" its own story) and Dan T. Carter.

15. Caison, "Claiming the Unclaimable," 583.

16. Quoted in Dan T. Carter, "Southern History, American Fiction," 300–301.

17. Caison, "Claiming the Unclaimable," 578. See also Peter Shaheen, "*The Education of Little Tree*: A Real True Story," in Anne Ruggles Gere (ed. and introd.), Peter Shaheen (ed. and introd.), Sarah Robbins (introd. and afterword), and Jeremy Wells (introd.), *Making American Literatures in High School and College* (Urbana, IL: National Council of Teachers of English, 2001), 82–89.

18. See Caison, "Claiming the Unclaimable," 575.

19. Browder, *Slippery Characters*, 139.

20. http://www.goodreads.com/book/show/116236.The_Education_of_Little_Tree/.

21. Eleanor Friede, quoted in Felicia R. Lee, "Best Seller Is a Fake, Professor Asserts," *New York Times*, October 4, 1991, http://www.nytimes.com/1991/10/04/us/best-seller-is-a-fake-profes sor-asserts.html/, accessed February 27, 2018, emphasis added.

22. Shaheen, "*The Education of Little Tree*," 82, 85. Uses of the words "government" (or "govmint," pp. 39, 44, 45) "politician," and "bureaucrat" in the novel clearly support a "states' rights" agenda.

23. Young, *Bunk*, 96.

24. Browder, *Slippery Characters*, 134, 135.

25. David Scott, quoted in "The Reconstruction of Asa Carter: Video Extra," youtube, http://www.youtube.com/watch?v=pU3WDXZTsL8/.

26. Dan T. Carter, "Southern History, American Fiction," 301; McGurl, "Learning from Little Tree," 251.

27. Caison, "Claiming the Unclaimable," 580.

28. Browder, *Slippery Characters*, 232–33; see also 251.

29. Danny Santiago, *Famous All Over Town* (New York: Plume-Penguin Books, 1983), 30.

30. Daniel James, letter to John Gregory Dunne, quoted in John Gregory Dunne, "The Se-cret of Danny Santiago," *New York Review of Books*, August 16, 1984, http://www.nybooks.com /articles/1984/08/16/the-secret-of-danny-santiago/, accessed March 5, 2018.

31. Arnd Bohm comments that for Browder, "the novel is a sort of clever game played for private reasons." But Bohm's own reading also remains focused on James and his motivations, claiming that the author "never abandoned the socialist principles he had learned during . . . the Depression" and that the novel is "an orthodox Marxist critique of capitalism in the U.S." Arnd Bohm, "Socialist Realism and the Success of *Famous All Over Town*," *International Fiction Re-view* 34, nos. 1 and 2 (2007), https://journals.lib.unb.ca/index.php/IFR/article/view/4232/4766/.

32. Bohm, "Socialist Realism."

33. David Quammen, "*Famous All Over Town* by Danny Santiago," *New York Times Book Re-view*, April 24, 1983, 12.

34. Eileen I. Oliver, quoted in Bohm, "Socialist Realism."

35. Quote on back cover of *Famous All Over Town* (Plume-Penguin edition).

36. Edwin McDowell, "Daniel Lewis James Is Dead at 77; Wrote about Los Angeles Barrio," *New York Times*, May 21, 1988, http://www.nytimes.com/1988/05/21/obituaries/daniel-lewis-james -is-dead-at-77-wrote-about-los-andgeles-barrio.html?pagewanted=print/, accessed March 5, 2018.

37. Dunne, "The Secret of Danny Santiago." Dunne aided James in the hoax, paving the way for publication of *Famous All Over Town* by writing "an obfuscating covering letter" to the edi-tor Carl Brandt. Dunne says he asked James for permission to expose the hoax, but he does not

say what James's response was. James's first publication as Danny Santiago, according to Dunne, dated back sixteen years. Arnd Bohm says that James emerged as Danny Santiago in 1965: Bohm, "Socialist Realism."

38. Daniel James, quoted in Edwin McDowell, "A Noted 'Hispanic' Novelist Proves to Be Someone Else," *New York Times*, July 22, 1984, http://www.nytimes.com/1984/07/22/arts/a-noted -hispanic-novelist-proves-to-be-someone-else.html/, accessed March 5, 2018, emphasis added. Dunne says that James voiced the same view to him: "I asked if he had considered the possibility of being accused of manufacturing a hoax. He shrugged and said the book itself was the only answer. If the book were good, it was good under whatever identity the author chose to use." Dunne, "The Secret of Danny Santiago."

39. See Azouz Begag, as discussed in part 3, on Jack-Alain Léger, in this book.

40. McDowell, "A Noted 'Hispanic' Novelist"; Bohm, "Socialist Realism."

41. "He is working on another book with a Mexican-American theme, also set in Los Angeles. It too will appear under the name of Danny Santiago." McDowell, "A Noted 'Hispanic' Novelist."

42. Lee Cronbach, "Chicano Humor Captured in a Warm Story," comment, August 23, 2015, Amazon.com, https://www.amazon.com/Famous-Over-Town-Danny-Santiago/dp/0452259746/ref=sr _1_1?ie=UTF8&qid=1394201257&sr=8-1&keywords=Famous+All+Over+Town/.

43. Browder, *Slippery Characters*, 269.

44. Bohm, "Socialist Realism."

45. See Eric Lott, *Love and Theft: Blackface Minstrelsy and the American Working Class* (New York: Oxford University Press, 2013), 40. Lott does not actually develop the concept of theft itself very much, preferring terms like "crude racial appropriation" and "counterfeit" (104).

46. I do not necessarily attribute this view to Browder, based on this quote. Her conclusion is: "We too often read ethnic autobiography to find out the definitive truth of a group's experience. *Famous All Over Town* not only defies our expectations but teaches us their futility" (269).

47. Anonymous, *Go Ask Alice* (New York: Simon Pulse, 2006), 18.

48. Susan Ziegler, "Queering the Drug Diary: *Go Ask Alice* and Its Victorian Genealogies," *Genre* 39 (Spring 2006): 90, 94.

49. The cover of a recently purchased edition claims "More than five millions copies sold." Anonymous, *Go Ask Alice* (New York: Simon Pulse, 2006). See Mark Oppenheimer, "Just Say 'Uh-Oh,'" *New York Times Book Review*, November 15, 1998, http://www.nytimes.com/1998/11/15 /books/just-say-uh-oh.html/.

50. Lina Goldberg, "'Curiouser and Curiouser': Fact, Fiction, and the Anonymous Author of *Go Ask Alice*," Linagoldberg.com, October 2[, no year given], http://archive.is/AlNFT/, accessed June 22, 2017. See American Library Association, "100 Most Frequently Challenged Books By Decade," 1990–1999 (*Go Ask Alice* is no. 25); and 2000–2009 (no. 18). http://www.ala.org/bbooks /frequentlychallengedbooks/top100/.

51. Ziegler, "Queering the Drug Diary," 91.

52. "Two months after [James] Frey's lies were revealed, *A Million Little Pieces* was still sitting pretty at No. 2 on the *New York Times* best-selling paperback *non*fiction list." Woodward, "The Literature of Lies."

53. David Mikkelson, writing on the rumor-correction web site Snopes.com, asks, "How is it that after more than thirty years . . . no intrepid reporter has managed to track down the identity of *Go Ask Alice*'s 'anonymous' author?" "Was *Go Ask Alice* the Real-life Diary of a Teenage Girl?," http://www.snopes.com/language/literary/askalice.asp. However, Alleen Pace Nilsen did precisely that in 1979, finding Beatrice Sparks in "the house that Alice built" in Provo, Utah; see below.

54. Alleen Pace Nilsen, "The House That Alice Built: An Interview with the Author Who Brought You *Go Ask Alice*," *School Library Journal* 26, no. 2 (October 1979): 109–12.

"The question of how much of *Go Ask Alice* was written by the real Alice and how much by Beatrice Sparks can only be conjectured. The two diaries which Alice wrote are locked away at Prentice-Hall, but even with these it would be an impossible question because as Sparks deciphered the notes from pieces of brown paper bags and other scrap paper, she says she thoughtlessly dropped these parts of the diaries into her wastebasket" (111). But there remains no proof that Alice, her diary, or her parents ever existed. Sparks, a Mormon, thus produces a story that echoes the narrative behind *The Book of Mormon*: the lost teenager's diary is comparable to the golden plates that Joseph Smith claimed to have received from the angel Moroni, then returned: both sources are unavailable for verification. (According to Nilsen, Sparks owns "a glass enclosed book cupboard that once belonged to Brigham Young." "The House That Alice Built," 110.) The Nilsen article displays a strange combination of credulity ("Sparks had once held a job in a drug abuse clinic"; "Yes, there was a real Alice") and skepticism (Sparks "was vague about the specifics"; "I was given no evidence of formal training or professional affiliation," 110). Although billed as an interview, this piece is written almost entirely in indirect speech, which severely limits its use value.

55. An email inquiry that I sent to Michelle Orr, a representative of Pearson, the successor to Prentice-Hall, produced no information about the diary. The 2006 Simon Pulse edition states in its Library of Congress cataloguing information: "Based on the diary of a fifteen-year-old drug user chronicling her struggle to escape the pull of the drug world." It also has this separate statement: "This book is a work of fiction."

56. Katsoulis, *Literary Hoaxes*, 178.

57. "Beatrice Ruby Sparks," *Salt Lake Tribune*, May 20, 2012, http://www.legacy.com/obituaries/saltlaketribune/obituary-print.aspx?n=beatrice-ruby-sparks&pid=157846946/, accessed February 14, 2018.

58. Oppenheimer states that "Linda Glovach [was] exposed as one of the 'preparers'—let's call them forgers—of *Go Ask Alice*." Oppenheimer, "Just Say 'Uh-Oh.'"

59. Goldberg, "Curiouser and Curiouser."

60. Katsoulis, *Literary Hoaxes*, 179.

61. Nilsen, "The House That Alice Built," 109.

62. Mikkelson, "Was *Go Ask Alice* the Real-life Diary . . . ?"

63. Amazon.com page for *Go Ask Alice*: https://www.amazon.com/Go-Ask-Alice/dp/1416914633/ref=sr_1_1?s=books&ie=UTF8&qid=1485788633&sr=1-1&keywords=go+ask+alice/, accessed January 30, 2017.

64. Simon & Schuster Simon Pulse edition, back cover.

65. Troy Jollimore, "How *Go Ask Alice* Became Just Say No: A Historian Argues the Late 1970's Begat the Reagan Era and Today" (review of Philip Jenkins, *Decade of Nightmares: The End of the Sixties and the Making of the Eighties* (New York: Oxford University Press, 2006)), *SFGate*: http://www.sfgate.com/books/article/How-Go-ask-Alice-became-just-say-no-A-2502562.php/. Jollimore comments: "Particularly notable is the national hysteria about drug use, as frequently exaggerated media reports regarding the dangers of various substances help transform the 'go ask Alice' openness of the '60s into the 'just say no' mantra of the '80s." The book *Go Ask Alice* contributed to that hysteria. Although Jenkins does not mention it, *Go Ask Alice* fits into his analysis of the shift from the 60s to the 70s: "Whether we are looking at drugs, sexuality, or cult activities [all included in *Go Ask Alice*], much of the cultural shift in domestic affairs involved a new series of threats (plausible or not) against children." Jenkins, *Decade of Nightmares*, 13.

66. Quoted in Nathaniel Rich, "Being JT LeRoy," *Paris Review* 178 (Fall 2006), https://www
.theparisreview.org/miscellaneous/5664/being-jt-leroy-nathaniel-rich/, accessed March 5, 2018.

67. Stephen Beachy, "Who Is the Real JT LeRoy? A Search for the True Identity of a Great Literary Hustler," *New York Magazine*, http://nymag.com/nymetro/news/people/features/14718/#/, accessed July 5, 2017.

68. Terminator [JT LeRoy], "Baby Doll," in *Close to the Bone: Memoirs of Hurt, Rage, and Desire*, ed. Laurie Stone (New York: Grove Press, 1997), 14–47.

69. Quotations in JT LeRoy, *Sarah* (New York: Dove's Diner Inc and Authors' Guild Digital Services [Kindle edition], 2013). Loc 3. Further citations to the novel cite *Sarah* (New York: Bloomsbury, 2000). The current edition of the novel has the same copyright information ("2000 by JT LeRoy"), but also has a preface, copyrighted 2016 by Billy Corgan. The preface describes the status of Laura Albert as "scribe," while attesting that "JT is real" (x).

70. A. O. Scott, "Review: *Author: The JT LeRoy Story* Renders a Literary Charlatan," *New York Times*, September 8, 2016, https://www.nytimes.com/2016/09/09/movies/author-the-jt-leroy-story
-review.html/, accessed March 5, 2018.

71. *Sarah*, 1, 2, 4.

72. *Sarah*, 105. At the moment of discovery, the narrator is symbolically castrated, with only his/her hair apparently being cut off. After that, he becomes a male "lizard," Sam (118).

73. *Sarah*, 48, 46.

74. *Sarah*, 160.

75. *Sarah*, 71.

76. Stephen Burt makes a similar point: the novel is "part a colorful exaggeration of urban coastal beliefs about Appalachia." "Sarah's Antidote: Is the JT LeRoy Scandal What You Think It Is?" *Slate*, June 27, 2007.

77. Rich, "Being JT LeRoy."

78. Quoted in Rich, "Being JT LeRoy."

79. Manohla Dargis, "The Harrowing Tales of the Deceitfulness of Hearts from a Highly Deceitful Author," *New York Times*, March 10, 2006, http://www.nytimes.com/2006/03/10/movies
/10hear.html/, accessed March 5, 2018. This review was written after the hoax was exposed.

80. Steve Almond, "The Heroic Lie: A Brief Inquiry into the Fake Memoir," *The Rumpus*, April 20, 2011, http://therumpus.net/2011/04/the-heroic-lie-a-brief-inquiry-into-the-fake-memoir/, accessed November 16, 2017.

81. Young, *Bunk*, 117. See Karr, *The Art of Memoir*.

82. Alan Feuer, "At Trial, Writer Recalls an Alter Ego That Took Over," *New York Times*, June 21, 2007; Laura Albert says in *Author* that she had never been to a truck stop until Asia Argento's filming of *The Heart Is Deceitful* in 2003.

83. "My publisher paid to use a photograph of a teenage boy who looked a lot like JT and got permission to run it as the author photo." Later, after the book became famous, she realized "I had to produce a body"—which was Savannah Knoop's. Laura Albert, quoted in Rich, "Being JT LeRoy."

84. "While I was still in foster care, I won a scholarship to go to the Eugene Lang College at The New School. I took every writing class I could get my hands on. I knew that the only way to make people care about my stories was to learn my craft. In my fiction class I was writing short stories, and they always had a male protagonist. I started writing a novel and I did that in a male voice. I told the professor I had to write in the male voice, but she wouldn't let me. I didn't finish the year. I ended up in a mental hospital." Laura Albert in interview, Meredith Moran,

"The Rumpus Interview with Laura Albert," December 19, 2016, http://therumpus.net/2016/12 /the-rumpus-interview-with-laura-albert/, accessed February 9, 2017.

85. A. O. Scott, "Review: *Author*." Savannah Knoop published a memoir of the hoax: *Girl Boy Girl: How I Became JT LeRoy* (New York: Seven Stories Press, 2008, Kindle edition). She reports that Speedie was at one point a nickname for another persona, Emily Frasier, a "Cockney Jew" (loc. 105).

86. Rich, "Being JT LeRoy." The film *The Cult of JT LeRoy* (dir. Marjorie Sturm, 2014, 92 min.) contains remarkable footage from various celebrity-studded readings, and lengthy testimonies from writers who were duped by the hoax.

87. Knoop, *Girl Boy Girl*, loc. 336. On similarities between this hoax and that of "Anthony Godby Johnson," a fake teenager with AIDS who turned out to be one Joanna Victoria Fraginals, see Young, *Bunk*, 200–201. Armistead Maupin, who was taken in by the hoax, tells the story in his novel *The Night Listener* (New York: HarperCollins, 2000).

88. *The Cult of JT LeRoy.*

89. JT LeRoy, *The Heart Is Deceitful Above All Things: Stories* (New York: Bloomsbury, 2001). The hideous, harrowing film directed by Asia Argento has the same title (2004, 97 min.). The third JT LeRoy book was also billed as autobiographical: *Harold's End* (San Francisco: Last Gasp, 2004). JT LeRoy befriended Gus Van Sant and was credited as an associate producer on his Columbine-inspired film, *Elephant* (2003).

90. Warren St. John, "Figure in JT LeRoy Case Says Partner Is Culprit," *New York Times*, February 7, 2006, http://www.nytimes.com/2006/02/07/books/07lero.html/, accessed March 5, 2018. This had been preceded by the revelation that Savannah Knoop was playing the role of JT LeRoy in public appearances, in Warren St. John, "The Unmasking of JT LeRoy: In Public, He's a She," *New York Times*, January 9, 2006, http://www.nytimes.com/2006/01/09/books/09book .html/, accessed March 5, 2018. Stephen Beachy first sugggesed that Laura Albert was JT LeRoy, in his exhaustive account, "Who Is the Real JT LeRoy?" "Every trail I followed led me to Laura," he writes. Laura Albert says in *Author* that she and Savannah Knoop were planning to hold on to the hoax, because there was "no proof," until Geoff Knoop talked to Warren St. John and con- firmed the story.

91. See Colin Moynihan, "Asia Argento and Others Are Angry About Being in JT LeRoy Documentary," *New York Times*, September 11, 2016. *Author* is a slick vehicle for Laura Albert's story and self-justifications; it includes animated and dramatized recreations of her claims about the past (including scenes from the Argento film) and about the hoax. The director/writer/ producer of *Author*, Jeff Feuerzeig, is an unabashed supporter of Laura Albert, whom he calls "a truly great and original writer" in his preface to the 2016 edition of *The Heart Is Deceitful Above All Things* (loc. 89).

92. Mary Karr, "His So-Called Life," *New York Times*, January 15, 2006, http://www.nytimes .com/2006/01/15/opinion/his-socalled-life.html/, accessed March 7, 2018.

93. See Karr, *The Art of Memoir*; the quote on objective truth is from Karr, "His So-Called Life."

94. The *Times* was duped by Laura Albert, who as JT LeRoy sold a travel piece about Euro Disneyland: JT LeRoy, "Uncle Walt, Parlez-Vous Français?," *T Magazine*, September 25, 2005, http://query.nytimes.com/gst/fullpage.html?res=9B06E1DC133EF936A1575AC0A9639C8B63/, accessed March 5, 2018. Regarding the Terry Gross interview the NPR website states, "Due to an agreement with the guest, the audio for this interview is unavailable," http://www.npr .org/2001/11/26/1133882/author-j-t-leroy/, accessed February 7, 2017. Parts of the interview can

be heard in the films *The Cult of JT LeRoy* and *Author*, including the moment where Terry Gross raises the possibility of a hoax; no reply is heard from JT LeRoy in either film.

95. Quoted in Katsoulis, *Literary Hoaxes*, 198.

96. Quoted in Rich, "Being JT LeRoy."

97. Laura Albert, "Ten Years Later, the 'Real' JT Leroy Tells All," *New York Times Style Magazine*, August 1, 2016.

98. See Kelsey Osgood, "Is JT LeRoy's Fiction Any Good?" *New Republic*, September 12, 2016, https://newrepublic.com/article/136715/jt-leroys-fiction-good/, accessed March 7, 2018.

99. I owe this observation to Shanna Jean-Baptiste.

100. Quoted in Beachy, "Who Is the Real JT LeRoy?"

101. Alan Feuer, "Jury Finds JT LeRoy Was Fraud," *New York Times*, June 23, 2007.

102. Feuer, "At Trial, Writer Recalls." That phrase is not attributed to Albert but surely was spoon-fed by her to the reporter, who later took a "road trip" with Albert, reporting on it, and questioning her veracity, in "Her Journey, All True," *New York Times*, August 23, 2007. Kevin Young does not dismiss Albert's claims of an abusive childhood: *Bunk*, 219.

103. When the Holocaust fraud published under the name Misha Levy Defonseca (*Misha: A Memoir of the Holocaust Years*, 1997) was revealed to be a hoax perpetrated by Monique de Wael, she claimed: "The story in the book is mine. It is not the actual reality—it was my reality, my way of surviving." Quoted in Katsoulis, *Literary Hoaxes*, 246.

104. Alan Feuer, "Judge Orders Author to Pay Film Company $350,000 in Legal Fees," *New York Times*, August 1, 2007. Beachy asks, "Where's the harm?" in "Who Is the Real JT LeRoy?"

105. *The Cult of JT LeRoy*.

106. The quoted words are from Dennis Cooper, in Beachy, "Who Is the Real JT LeRoy?"

107. In *The Cult of JT LeRoy*.

108. Young, *Bunk*, 97–98. See also 110: Young says that one of the harms of the hoax is that "the true stories in all senses . . . that the hoax makes use of end up not quite heard."

109. Laura Albert maintains a web site, selling books and souvenirs: www.jtleroy.com. In his preface to the current edition of *Sarah*, Billy Corgan writes: "the poseurs and half-celebrities turned and ran away when they, not Laura, were exposed as the frauds in a nasty narrative that had to play out" (x).

110. St. John, "Figure in JT LeRoy Case."

111. St. John, "The Unmasking."

112. Ira Silverberg, the literary agent for JT LeRoy, quoted in St. John, "The Unmasking."

113. Margaret B. Jones, *Love and Consequences: A Memoir of Hope and Survival* (New York: Riverhead Books, 2008), inside dust jacket.

114. Michiko Kakutani, "However Mean the Streets, Have an Exit Strategy," *New York Times*, February 26, 2008, http://www.nytimes.com/2008/02/26/books/26kaku.html/, accessed March 5, 2018.

115. Jones, *Love and Consequences*, inside dust jacket.

116. Motoko Rich, "Gang Memoir, Turning Page, Is Pure Fiction," *New York Times*, March 4, 2008. See Katsoulis, *Literary Hoaxes*, 216.

117. Motoko Rich, "Lies and Consequences: Tracking the Fallout of (Another) Literary Fraud," *New York Times*, March 5, 2008.

118. Rich, "Gang Memoir." On JT LeRoy, see also Young, *Bunk*, 190–200.

119. Ishmael Reed, letter to the editor, *New York Times Book Review*, March 8, 2015, https://www.nytimes.com/2015/03/15/books/review/letters-james-baldwin-richard-wright.html/, accessed March 5, 2018.

120. Misha Defonseca [Monique de Wael], *Misha: A Mémoire of the Holocaust Years* (Boston: Mt. Ivy Press, 1997). According to Lee and Defonseca, Defonseca told her story in French to Lee, who taped it and wrote it in English. The editor, Jane Daniel, took over the writing process and eliminated Lee from the title page. Like Beatrice Sparks, Defonseca claimed that the story had been recorded in a diary, which is no longer available (because her foster mothers in Belgium burned it after the war: *Misha*, 244). Both Lee and Defonseca are quoted in David Mehegan, "Incredible Journey: From Misha Defonseca's Flight from the Nazis to Publication of Her Memoir, Life Has Been a Battle Against the Odds," Boston.com, October 31, 2001. *Misha* may have been modeled on another Holocaust hoax, published in 1995 and exposed in 1998: Binjamin Wilkomirski (pseudonym of Bruno Dösseker), *Fragments: Memories of a Wartime Childhood*, trans. Carol Brown Janeway (New York: Schocken Books, 1996). See Doreen Carvajal, "A Holocaust Memoir in Doubt; Swiss Records Contradict a Book on Childhood Horror," *New York Times*, November 3, 1998; and unsigned article, "Publisher Drops Holocaust Book," *New York Times*, November 3, 1999. The Wilkomirski book fooled Mary Karr; see *The Art of Memoir*, 81–82.

121. Misha Defonseca, "avec la collaboration de Vera Lee, adaptation française de Marie-Thérèse Cuny," *Survivre avec les loups: de la Belgique à l'Ukraine, une enfant juive à travers l'Europe nazie, 1941–1944* (Paris: Robert Laffont, 1997). This edition includes a map spanning two pages (10–11), representing "mon périple" covering 3335 kilometers. The film by Véra Belmont is oriented toward and marketed to children: *Survivre avec les loups* (2007). The original subtitle of the film was "*d'après l'histoire vraie de Misha Defonseca*," but was changed to "*Inspiré du roman de Misha Defonseca*"; the DVD box says "d'après l'ouvrage de Misha Defonseca." The slippage is significant. See Anne Kling, "Une Histoire belge: Misha Defonseca, ou mentir avec les loups," in her book *Menteurs et affabulateurs de la Shoah* ([France]: Editions Mithra, 2013), 99.

122. "Misha Defonseca, with the collaboration of Vera Lee and Marie-Thérèse Cuny, translated from the French by Sue Rose," *Surviving with Wolves: The Most Extraordinary Story of World War II* (London: Portrait, 2006). A quote from the *Sunday Times* on the cover calls the book a memoir. To make matters more confusing, a book that examines the exposed hoax partly shares the same title: Lionel Duroy, *Survivre avec les loups: la véritable histoire de Misha Defonseca* (Paris: XO Editions, 2011).

123. In Defonseca, *Survivre avec les loups* (Laffont edition), the name Valle appears on p. 32. After the hoax was exposed, a new French edition appeared, with a significant change of classification: now it was a *novel*. Misha Defonseca, "avec la collaboration de Vera Lee, avec la collaboration de Marie-Thérèse Cuny," *Survivre avec les loups: roman. Nouvelle édition* (Paris: XO Editions, 2008). The name Valle appears in this edition on p. 22. A preface by the president of XI Editions, Bernard Fixot, explains that he was initially taken in and "*bouleversé*" by the hoax, then "*stupéfait*" to learn that the story was false. He justifies reissuing the book this way: "A l'issue de cette affaire, il reste un livre, . . . qui est donc une oeuvre de fiction. Et si on me l'avait présenté comme telle, je l'aurais publiée" (9). But the word "*roman*" appears only on the title page, nowhere on the book's cover. Another preface, by "Misha Defonseca," articulates her "Plan B" defense: this false story was her "*manière de survivre*" (9). Because the author's name is the same as the protagonist's, it would be very easy for a reader to assume that this is a true story, a memoir.

124. Sharon Sergeant, blog post on Deborah Lipstadt's blog, http://lipstadt.blogspot.com /2008/03/holocaust-hoax-co-author-tells-her-side.html/, accessed February 16, 2017.

125. Blake Estin, "Crying Wolf: Why Did It Take So Long For a Far-Fetched Holocaust Memoir to be Debunked?" *Slate.com*, February 29, 2008, http://www.slate.com/articles/arts/culture box/2008/02/crying_wolf.html#page_start/, accessed February 16, 2017.

126. Monique de Wael, quoted in Estin, "Crying Wolf."

127. "Misha Defonseca," preface to *Survivre avec les loups: roman. Nouvelle édition* (the XO Editions edition, 2008), 9.

128. Monique de Wael, "Entretien avec Monique de Wael," in Duroy, *Survivre avec les loups*, 228, 232, emphasis added; newspaper quotes, 18. The truth appears to be that her father, initially a member of the Belgian Resistance, after his arrest collaborated with the Germans (134, 227), then died in a German prison (20–21); her mother died in the gas chamber at Ravensbrück ("like the Jews," she says, 232). In this interview she tells the story of how she researched and constructed her hoax.

129. See Kling, *Menteurs et affabulateurs de la Shoah*; and Susan Rubin Suleiman, "Do Facts Matter in Holocaust Memoirs?," in her *Crises of Memory and the Second World War* (Cambridge: Harvard University Press, 2006). Both Kling and Suleiman analyze the case of Binjamin Wilkomirski, which unfolded in the late 1990s. See Kling, 11–133; Suleiman, 164–70.

130. Daniel Mendelsohn, "Stolen Suffering," *New York Times*, March 9, 2008, http://www.nytimes.com/2008/03/09/opinion/09mendelsohn.html/, accessed March 5, 2018.

131. Lott, *Love and Theft*, 106.

132. Lott, *Love and Theft*, 50.

133. Homi Bhabha, *The Location of Culture* (New York: Routledge, 1994), 112.

134. Bhabha, *The Location of Culture*, 112.

135. Jaime Hanneken, "Scandal, Choice, and the Economy of Minority Literature," *Paragraph* 34.1 (2011): 61. On the French concepts of *communautaire* and *identitaire*, see Scott Gunther, *The Elastic Closet: A History of Homosexuality in France, 1942-present* (New York: Palgrave Macmillan, 2009), table 4.4, p. 109.

136. Hanneken, "Scandal, Choice, and the Economy of Minority Literature," 50, 65n26.

137. Mark Rose, *Authors and Owners: The Invention of Copyright*, quoted in Hanneken, "Scandal, Choice, and the Economy of Minority Literature," 52.

138. Hanneken, "Scandal, Choice, and the Economy of Minority Literature," 54; he cites the example of Ishmael Beah's *A Long Way Gone*, a memoir of an African child soldier selected for the Starbucks Book Club in 2007 (53).

139. Hanneken, "Scandal, Choice, and the Economy of Minority Literature," 56.

140. Hanneken, "Scandal, Choice, and the Economy of Minority Literature," 56.

141. Christopher L. Miller, *Blank Darkness: Africanist Discourse in French* (Chicago: University of Chicago Press, 1985), 216–45.

Part Two

1. Philippe Lejeune, *Le Pacte autobiographique* (Paris: Editions du Seuil, 1975), 22–23; trans. Katherine Leary, *On Autobiography* (Minneapolis: University of Minnesota Press, 1989), 11.

2. Lejeune, *Pacte*, 27/*On Autobiography*, 15, AT. See also 23, n1/11, n8.

3. Nejiba Regaieg, "Autobiographie et mise en scène de l'écriture dans *Vivre me tue* et *Casa, la casa* de Paul Smaïl," in Habib Ben Salha, ed., *Le Roman magrébin de langue française aujourd'hui: rupture et continuité* (Tunis: Université de la Manouba, 2006), 120. As Regaieg points out, Lejeune later seemed to back away from his own theory: "Quand on sait ce que c'est écrire, l'idée même de pacte autobiographique paraît une chimère." Lejeune, "Nouveau roman et retour à l'autobiographie," 1991, quoted in Regaieg, 126.

4. Foucault, "Qu'est-ce qu'un auteur?," 73/"What Is an Author?," 101.

5. Bruce Morrissette, *The Great Rimbaud Forgery: The Affair of "La Chasse Spirituelle," with Unpublished Documents and an Anthology of Rimbaldian Pastiches* (Saint Louis: Washington Uni-

versity Studies, 1956): i, 115, 208; see 159. Morrissette summarizes the criticism that sought to certify the authenticity of the text by internal evidence, "from the *text* alone" (223).

6. See Morrissette, *The Great Rimbaud Forgery*, ii–iii.

7. The passage about the Rimbaud hoax, including these two quotations, does not appear in the print version of Foucault's lecture that I have been citing, but it is in the translation, "What Is an Author?," 188–89; and it can be found in the French version published at http://1libertaire .free.fr/MFoucault349.html/, accessed July 6, 2017.

8. Foucault, "Qu'est-ce qu'un auteur?," 83/"What Is an Author?," 107, AT, emphasis added. The original text says: "Le nom d'auteur n'est pas situé dans l'état civil des hommes, il n'est pas non plus situé dans la fiction de l'oeuvre." The published translation of the first clause as "It has no legal status" is egregiously wrong. Foucault means that the author's name, as a function, is not to be found in the office that registers births, marriages, deaths, etc. But the author's name, as Foucault points out, most certainly has legal status.

9. Foucault, "Qu'est-ce qu'un auteur?" This passage does not appear in the print version of Foucault's lecture that I have been citing, but it is in the translation, "What Is an Author?," 188–89; and it can be found at http://1libertaire.free.fr/MFoucault349.html/, accessed July 5, 2017.

10. Pierre Bayard continues the war on authorship in his *Et si les oeuvres changeaient d'auteur?* (Paris: Editions de Minuit, 2010). He refers to "l'inconvénient du nom d'auteur," which is (still) to "geler l'identité, en la restreignant à une partie d'elle-même . . . une restriction" (70).

11. Gilles Lambert, "Petit guide du faux littéraire," *Gulliver* 1–2 (1972): 12.

12. The phrase "ethnic usurpation" is from Brozgal, "Hostages of Authenticity," 116.

13. See Christopher L. Miller, "Unfinished Business: Colonialism in Sub-Saharan Africa and the Ideals of the French Revolution," *The Global Ramifications of the French Revolution*, ed. Joseph Klaits and Michael H. Haltzel (Washington, DC: Woodrow Wilson Center Press; Cambridge: Cambridge University Press, 1994), 105–126.

14. See Alec G. Hargreaves, Nikki Hitchcott, and Dominic Thomas, eds., "Textual Ownership in Francophone African Writing," special issue, *Research in African Literatures* 37, no. 1 (Spring 2006).

15. Calixthe Beyala, quoted in Koffi Anyinefa, "Scandales: littérature francophone africaine et identité," *Cahiers d'Etudes Africaines* 48, no. 191 (2008): 466. "*Plagiaire récidiviste*" is Anyinefa's phrase (464). Anyinefa also mentions the questions about the work of Camara Laye, to be considered later in this study.

16. See Farid Laroussi and Christopher L. Miller, eds., "French and Francophone: The Challenge of Expanding Horizons," special issue, *Yale French Studies* 103 (2003).

17. See Gustave Brunet, preface, Joseph-Marie Quérard, *Les Supercheries littéraires dévoilées. . .* , 2nd ed. (Paris: Paul Daffis, 1969), vol. 1, p. v.

18. See Brunet, preface, Quérard, *Les Supercheries littéraires dévoilées*, 2nd ed., vol. 1, p. v.

19. Quérard, preface to 1st ed., reproduced in 2nd ed., vol. 1, p. 2.

20. Charles Nodier, *Questions de littérature légale: du plagiat, de la supposition d'auteurs, des supercheries qui ont rapport aux livres*, ed. Jean-François Jeandillou (Geneva: Droz, 2003 [1812]). We will encounter Nodier again in the section on Mérimée, below.

21. See Jeandillou, *Esthétique de la mystification*, 56.

22. Octave Delepierre, *Supercheries littéraires: pastiches, suppositions d'auteur, dans les lettres et dans les arts* (London: N. Trübner, 1872), 32, 149.

23. Gabriel Joseph de Lavergne, vicomte de Guilleragues, *Lettres portugaises, Valentins, et autres oeuvres*, ed. Frédéric Deloffre and Jacques Rougeot (Paris: Garnier, 1962). Deloffre and Rougeot are known for changing the attribution of authorship of this work, but they were building

on 1926 work by F. C. Green, who found the original *privilège du roi* with Guilleragues's name on it; see xiii-xiv. But as they say, "les partisans de l'authenticité ne désarment pas si facilement", and many scholars received Green's revelation with "silence" (xvi). See F. C. Green, "Who Was the Author of the *Lettres portugaises?*," *Modern Language Review* 21 (1926): 159–67.

24. More recently, Myriam Cyr has claimed that "Guilleragues is not the author" of the letters: *Letters of a Portuguese Nun: Uncovering the Mystery Behind a Seventeenth-Century Forbidden Love, A Historical Mystery* (New York: Hyperion, 2006), 165. Her argument is based on perceived probabilities and "inconsistencies": "how could Guilleragues have known . . . ?" "Mariama would have been more than capable" of writing the letters (166, 169).

25. See Jeandillou, *Esthétique de la mystification*, 59–108.

26. Scott Carpenter, *Aesthetics of Fraudulence in Nineteenth-Century France* (Burlington, VT: Ashgate Publishing, 2009), 1.

27. Carpenter, *Aesthetics of Fraudulence*, 11–14. Carpenter takes the study of fraudulence inside the works themselves, rather than merely dwelling on the story of their roots in falsehood (see 4).

28. Gary, *Vie et mort*, 16.

29. Donald Rayfield, "Forgiving Forgery," *Modern Language Review* 107, no. 4 (October 2012): xxv.

30. Paul F. Moulton, "A Controversy Discarded and 'Ossian' Revealed: An Argument for a Renewed Consideration of 'The Poems of Ossian,'" *College Music Symposium* 49/50 (2009/2010): 394.

31. Adrian H. Jaffe, "Chateaubriand's Use of Ossianic Language," *Comparative Literature Studies* 5, no. 2 (June 1968): 157, 161. In more recent times, there have been efforts to rehabilitate MacPherson's Ossian; see Moulton, "A Controversy Discarded." His revisionist work seems to be based on the notion that the poems are authentic in some ways, "based on genuine, ancient Gaelic poetry" (393), even if the figure of Ossian was always a fake. Quérard labeled Ossian an "invention" of MacPherson's, but says nothing more about the case: *Les Supercheries littéraires*, 24.

32. On Diderot as plagiarist and "compiler," see Lawrence L. Bongie, "Diderot, Creator and Compiler," *Transactions of the Samuel Johnson Society of the Northwest* 15 (1984): 35; and Yzabelle Martineau, *Le Faux littéraire: plagiat littéraire, intertextualité et dialogisme* (Montreal: Editions Nota Bene, 2002), 158–60. On Raynal, see Christopher L. Miller, *The French Atlantic Triangle: Literature and Culture of the Slave Trade* (Durham: Duke University Press, 2008), 84.

33. See Reginald McGinnis, *Essai sur l'origine de la mystification* (Saint-Denis: Presses Universitaires de Vincennes, 2009), 88. *Mystifications* were "des épreuves initiatiques qu'on faisait subir à des auteurs débutants" (6); and see Julia Abramson, *Learning from Lying: Paradoxes of the Literary Mystification* (Newark: University of Delaware Press, 2005), 40.

34. Abramson, *Learning from Lying*, 37. See her chapter "Inventing Mystification" for the context of mystifications in the eighteenth century and Diderot in particular (25–48). Abramson shows how *La Religieuse* was but one among four mystifications whose basis "transpired in the social sphere as interactions among friends" before becoming literary texts (53). She analyzes Diderot's *Mystification* (1769) as a case of "failed" mystification (60–78).

35. Ora Avni, "Mystification de la lecture chez Mérimée: lira bien qui rira le dernier," *Littérature* 58 (May 1985): 35. See also Abramson, *Learning from Lying*, 38.

36. Diderot, *L'Histoire et le secret de la peinture en cire*, quoted in McGinnis, *Essai sur l'origine*, 87.

37. On Diderot's relation to mystification, see McGinnis, *Essai sur l'origine*, 87–146.

38. Denis Diderot, *La Religieuse* (Paris: Garnier-Flammarion, 1968), 51, 65, 70; *The Nun*, trans. Russell Goulbourne (Oxford: Oxford University Press, 2005), 13, 26, 30.

39. On the censoring of *La Religieuse*, see Heather Lloyd, introduction to Diderot, *La Reli-*

gieuse, ed. Heather Lloyd (London: Bristol Classical Press, 2000): xix; and Georges May, *Diderot et "La Religieuse": Etude historique et littéraire* (New Haven: Yale University Press; Paris: Presses Universitaires de France, 1954), 181. The film version made by Jacques Rivette in 1966 was banned for more than one year. Among those who protested against the censorhip was Romain Gary. See Guy Amsellem, *Romain Gary: les métamorphoses de l'identité* (Paris: Harmattan, 2008), 85.

40. Béatrice Durand, "Diderot and the Nun: Portrait of the Artist as a Transvestite," in *Men Writing the Feminine: Literature, Theory, and the Question of Genders*, ed. Thaïs E. Morgan (Albany: State University of New York Press, 1994), 90.

41. Jean-François Jeandillou, *Supercheries littéraires: la vie et l'oeuvre des auteurs supposés* (Paris: Editions Usher, 1989), 483.

42. Durand, "Diderot and the Nun," 91; Diderot, *La Religieuse/The Nun*, 39/3.

43. Durand, "Diderot and the Nun," 94.

44. Durand, "Diderot and the Nun," 104.

45. May, *Diderot*, 37–45. Mylne suggests that the marquis was in fact wise to the hoax early in the correspondence: Vivienne "Truth and Illusion in the 'Préface-Annexe' to Diderot's *La Religieuse*," *Modern Language Notes* 57, no. 3 (July 1962): 350–56. Abramson writes: "If Croismare were simply playing along, then ultimately Diderot would be the only victim of his own mystification" (*Learning from Lying*, 54)—and the hoax would still be, as I am describing it, single-use.

46. See May, *Diderot*, 160.

47. Lloyd, introduction to Diderot, *La Religieuse*, x–xi.

48. May, *Diderot*, 23, emphasis added.

49. "*Préface-annexe*," in *La Religieuse*, 210, 214/154, 158, AT. The English translation of the novel by Leonard Tancock does not include either the *préface-annexe* or the letters between Madame Madin and the Marquis de Croismare that appear at the end of the volume: *The Nun* (London: Penguin Books, 1972); this has the effect of making the hoaxing dimension of the text invisible to the reader.

50. Mylne advocates "a certain skepticism about the whole incident" and examines "factual discrepencies," none of which change the fact that a hoax took place. Just because there are "lapses of fact and taste" ("Truth and Illusion," 354), and novelistic flourishes and conceits, in the text sent to the marquis—that is to say, imperfections in the hoax—doesn't mean that a hoax did not take place. The other possibility Mylne mentions is that "Grimm and his friends, realizing that the Marquis was no longer duped by their 'nun,' sat back and chuckled as they saw Diderot still taking the affair seriously" (354). But there is no proof of that, either.

51. Mylne, "Truth and Illusion," 354.

52. Quoted in Lloyd, introduction to Diderot, *La Religieuse*, xiii.

53. May, *Diderot*, 155; Robert Darnton, *The Great Cat Massacre and Other Episodes in French Cultural History* (New York: Vintage Books, 1984), 231–52.

54. Mary Anne Brun, "Faussemblance: Errors and Artifice in Diderot's *La Religieuse*," in *Authorship, Authority: Proceedings of the Fifth Annual Graduate Conference in French, Francophone, and Comparative Literature, Columbia University, March 3–4, 1995*, ed. Vincent Desroches and Geoffrey Turnovsky (New York: Columbia University Press, 1995), 114.

55. Georges May pushed back against the idea of *La Religieuse* as a purely anticlerical novel. *Diderot*, 161–96. Part of his reasoning is linked to the hoaxing of the marquis, who was himself pious: the letter had to pass as the words and thoughts of a nun (164). The real object of Diderot's critique is forced vocations, which were opposed by many in the church itself (171).

56. Françoise Lavocat suggests that the use of the first person by Diderot (and by Misha Defonseca in *Misha: A Mémoire of the Holocaust Years*) is "l'opérateur privilégié de brouillage de la frontière entre fait et fiction." *Fait et fiction: pour une frontière* (Paris: Seuil, 2016), 38.

57. See Charles Nodier, *Questions de littérature légale*; Foucault, "Qu'est-ce qu'un auteur?"/ "What Is an Author?" Nodier, a theoretician of literary property, appears again in this episode with Mérimée.

58. See Jean-François Jeandillou, "La Supercherie littéraire en images," in Emerson and Scott, *Artful Deceptions*, 274.

59. Miller, *The French Atlantic Triangle*, 179–245.

60. See Miller, *The French Atlantic Triangle*, 190–94.

61. Robert L. A. Clark, "South of North: *Carmen* and French Nationalisms," in *East of West: Cross-Cultural Performance and the Staging of Difference*, ed. Claire Sponsler and Xiaomei Chen (New York: Palgrave, 2000), 189. Note that "Gazul" and "Guzla" are anagrams.

62. Samuel Borton, "A Note on Prosper Mérimée: Not *de Clara Gazul* But *Delécluze*," *Modern Language Notes* 75, no. 4 (April 1960): 337.

63. Avni, "Mystification," 30. Roger Picard claims that *Clara Gazul* "fooled almost everyone" but "not for long" because Mérimée revealed himself as author. See Roger Picard, *Artifices et mystifications littéraires* (Montreal: Les Editions Variétés, 1945), 203.

64. Corry Cropper, "Revolution Under the Mantilla: Mérimée's Spanish Theater," *Dalhousie French Studies* 66 (Spring 2004): 12.

65. Cropper, "Revolution Under the Mantilla," 15. According to some, *Clara Gazul* was actually very influential on French Romantic theater, paving the way for Hugo's preface to *Cromwell*. See Picard, *Artifices et mystifications*, 204.

66. Cropper, "Revolution Under the Mantilla," 18. I will not explore here what Carpenter covers in his book, how Mérimée "glides from the *practice* of hoaxes (as in *La Guzla* or *Clara Gazul*) to their representation and recreation within the work itself," such as in *Lokis* (1869). Carpenter, *Aesthetics of Fraudulence*, 36.

67. Prosper Mérimée, *La Guzla, ou choix de poésies illyriques recueillies dans la Damatie, la Bosnie, la Croatie et l'Herzegovine* (Paris: F. G. Levrault, 1827). This original edition is available for downloading from the Gallica website of the Bibliothèque Nationale de France.

68. Abramson, *Learning from Lying*, 109. The ARTFL-FRANTEXT database shows that the form *illyrique* had been used by Bossuet and, once, by Charles Nodier. Elsewhere in the book, Mérimée occasionally uses the standard French term *Illyrien* (for example, 65n3).

69. Voyslav M. Yovanovitch, *"La Guzla" de Prosper Mérimée: étude d'histoire romantique* (Paris: Hachette, 1911), 527; elsewhere in the volume is a succinct summary of sources.

70. Mérimée, "avertissement" to *La Guzla*, in Mérimée, *La Double méprise* (Paris: Calmann-Lévy, 1885), 131–33.

71. Yovanovitch, *"La Guzla" de Prosper Mérimée*, 398.

72. Mérimée, letter of January 18, 1835, to Serge Alexandrovitch Sobolevski, quoted in Jean Mallion and Pierre Salomon, preface to Prosper Mérimée, *Théâtre de Clara Gazul, romans et nouvelles* (Paris: Gallimard, Bibliothèque de la Pléiade, 1978), xv.

73. Yovanovitch, *"La Guzla" de Prosper Mérimée*, 416, 400, 402, 403.

74. Yovanovitch, *"La Guzla" de Prosper Mérimée*, 472–97.

75. See Yovanovitch, *"La Guzla" de Prosper Mérimée*, 225; Abramson, *Learning from Lying*, 104. Hugo inscribed his own copy "Par M. Première Prose," an anagram of "Prosper Mérimée."

76. Johann Wolfgang von Goethe, *Uber Kunst und Altertum*, VI, no. 2 (1828), in *Sämtliche Werke: Briefe, Tagebücher, Gespräche*, vol. 22, *Ästhetische Schriften V (1824–1832)*, ed. Dieter Borchmeyer et al. (Frankfurt: Deutscher Klassiker Verlag, 1985), 454–455, quoted in Yovanovitch, *"La Guzla" de Prosper Mérimée*, 464–65. I am grateful to Andrew Kirwin for finding the original Ger-

man text, translating it, and pointing out Goethe's interesting word choice of "*eingeschwärzten*" or "darkened" for clandestine. I would also point out another implication in his vocabulary: "*untergeschoben*" is the word used both for falsely attributed writings and for a "changeling" child.

77. Abramson, *Learning from Lying*, 105.

78. "Il s'est donné les gants de la découverte afin de paraître plus malin." Mérimée, letter to Albert Stapfer, December 11, 1828, quoted in Yovanovitch, *"La Guzla" de Prosper Mérimée*, 467. See Abramson, *Learning from Lying*, 171n58.

79. Yovanovitch, *"La Guzla" de Prosper Mérimée*, 470.

80. See Picard, *Artifices et mystifications*, 210–11.

81. Leslie O'Bell, "Pushkin's *Songs of the Western Slavs*: Ballads of Betrayal," *Russian Language Journal* 53, no. 174/176 (Winter-Spring-Fall 1999): 141; Richard Switzer, "Charles Nodier and the Introduction of Illyrian Literature into France," *Mosaic* 6, no 4 (Summer 1973): 229. On Pushkin, see Yovanovitch, *"La Guzla" de Prosper Mérimée*, 498–510.

82. (Comtesse) Matilde Colonna, *Contes de la Bosnie* (Paris: P. Lamm, 1898). See Yovanovitch, *"La Guzla" de Prosper Mérimée*, 437–44; Picard, *Artifices et mystifications*, 212.

83. Avni, "Mystification," 31.

84. Mallion and Salomon, preface to Mérimée, *Théâtre de Clara Gazul*, xv.

85. Quoted in Jennifer Wallace, "A (Hi)story of Illyria," *Greece & Rome* 45, no. 2 (October 1998): 213.

86. Wallace, "A (Hi)story of Illyria," 214.

87. For a map of the French "Illyrian Provinces" in 1812, see Matthew Gibson, *Dracula and the Eastern Question: British and French Vampire Narratives of the Nineteenth-Century Near East* (Basingstoke: Palgrave MacMillan, 2006), 35.

88. Yovanovitch, *"La Guzla" de Prosper Mérimée*, 62.

89. Wallace, "A (Hi)story of Illyria," 219.

90. Napoléon Bonaparte, *Lettre de Sa majesté impériale et royale au président du sénat*, ARTFL database, http://artflsrv02.uchicago.edu/cgi-bin/philologic/showrest_?conc.6.1.8528.0.288.fran text0513/, accessed March 1, 2017.

91. "Je voulais y introduire, y enraciner nos doctrines, notre administration, nos codes: c'était un pas de plus vers la *régénération* européenne." Napoléon Bonaparte, quoted in Emmanuel-Auguste-Dieudonné, conte de Las Cases, *Le Mémorial de Sainte-Hélène* (Paris, Gallimard, 1956–1957): 901, emphasis added. Las Cases had actually served in French Illyria, as a *maître des requêtes* (Yovanovitch, *"La Guzla" de Prosper Mérimée*, 62). On "regeneration," a term for what will later be called assimilation, see Alyssa Goldstein Sepinwall, *The Abbé Grégoire and the French Revolution: The Making of Modern Universalism* (Berkeley: University of California Press, 2005); and Samuels, *The Right to Difference*, 20.

92. Barbara Jelavich, *History of the Balkans: Eigtheenth and Nineteenth Centuries* (Cambridge: Cambridge University Press, 1983), vol. 1, 162–63, emphasis added. See also Stevan K. Pavlowitch, *A History of the Balkans 1804-1945* (London: Longman, 1999), 42–43.

93. Yovanovitch, *"La Guzla" de Prosper Mérimée*, 64.

94. Charles Nodier, *Jean Sbogar*, in *Romans* (Paris: Charpentier, 1884), 87.

95. Switzer, "Charles Nodier," 226, 227.

96. Switzer, "Charles Nodier," 229. On Nodier, see Gibson, *Dracula*, 127–36.

97. This body of work is extensively documented in Yovanovitch, *"La Guzla" de Prosper Mérimée*. See also Picard, *Artifices et mystifications*, 205; Alberto Fortis, *Voyage en Dalmatie . . .* trans. from the Italian (Berne: Chez la Société Typographique, 1778).

98. See Albert Lord, *The Singer of Tales* (Cambridge: Harvard University Press, 1960), 21.

99. See Claude Charles Fauriel, *Chants populaires de la Grèce moderne, recueillis et publiés, avec une traduction française, des éclaircissements et des notes* (Paris: Firmin Didot and Dondey-Dupré, 1824–25), 2 vols.

100. See Miller, *The French Atlantic Triangle*, 246–73.

101. See Antonia Fonyi, preface, Prosper Mérimée, *La Guzla* (Paris: Editions Kimé, 1994), 8.

102. Picard, *Artifices et mystifications*, 207.

103. See Jacob W. Gruber, "Ethnographic Salvage and the Shaping of Anthropology," *American Anthropologist* 72, no. 6 (December 1970): 1289–99. In one of Mérimée's notes, the false transcriber sniffs about one tale: "Cette ballade peut donner une idée du goût moderne. On y voit un commencement de prétention qui se mêle déjà à la simplicité des anciennes poésies illyriques" (111n1).

104. Jimmy Nelson, *Before They Pass Away* (Kempen, Germany: teNeues, 2013).

105. See Camara Laye's comments on present-day griots, *Le Maître de la parole* (Paris: Plon, 1978), 20.

106. For an interesting and engaged rhetorical reading of *La Guzla*, see Gibson, *Dracula*, 136–46. I do not follow Gibson to his conclusion that "Mérimée provides us with the only truly pro-colonial vampire narrative of the Near East in this period" (146).

107. See Carpenter's excellent reading of this passage, as an example of how "Mérimée's stories actually *represent* mystifications at the same time that they *commit* them." Carpenter, *Aesthetics of Fraudulence*, 27. On the connection between mystification and the fantastic, see Carpenter, 43, and Avni, "Mystification," 36.

108. Avni, "Mystification," 32.

109. Yovanovitch, *"La Guzla" de Prosper Mérimée*, 298.

110. My interpretation is hard to reconcile with Gibson's argument, pertaining to *La Guzla* as a whole, that "Mérimée is surreptitiously bemoaning the failure of the 'Grande [sic] Empire' to stamp its identity upon Illyria" (*Dracula*, 145). We saw that Nodier did precisely that bemoaning earlier.

111. Gibson, *Dracula*, 136. Gibson says that Nodier's "love of primitive societies was genuine" (ibid.). I think that Mérimée's was not. But see Fonyi's view: "La poésie, selon Mérimée, n'existe que dans des sociétés primitives" (preface to *La Guzla*, 13).

112. Alan Sokal, "Transgressing the Boundaries: Toward a Transformative Hermeneutics of Quantum Gravity," *Social Text* 46/47 (Spring/Summer 1996): 217–52.

113. Alan Sokal, "A Physicist Experiments with Cultural Studies," originally published in *Lingua Franca*, June 5, 1996, http://www.physics.nyu.edu/faculty/sokal/lingua_franca_v4/lingua_franca_v4.html/, accessed March 8, 2017.

114. Bruce Robbins and Andrew Ross, coeditors, for *Social Text*, in *Lingua Franca*, http://linguafranca.mirror.theinfo.org/9607/mst.html/, accessed March 8, 2017.

115. Mérimée, "avertissement" to *La Guzla*, in Mérimée, *La Double méprise*, 133.

116. Perhaps not surprisingly, the scholar who wrote 566 pages about *La Guzla* and called it "one of [Mérimée's] weakest works" (531) sees it as "more than a simple mystification," in fact the vessel of something "eternally true"—a portrait that Mérimée painted of "his ancestors" (Yovanovitch, *"La Guzla" de Prosper Mérimée*, 529).

117. Ahmadou Mapaté Diagne, *Les Trois volontés de Malic* (Paris: Larousse, 1921).

118. Lamine Senghor, *La Violation d'un pays* (Paris: Bureau d'Editions, de Diffusion, et de Publicité, 1927).

119. Mohamadou Kane, preface, Bakary Diallo, *Force-Bonté* (Dakar: Les Nouvelles Editions Africaines, 1985), vi.

120. János Riesz, "The *Tirailleur Sénégalais* Who Did Not Want to Be a 'Grand Enfant': Bakary Diallo's *Force-Bonté* (1926) Reconsidered," *Research in African Literatures* 27, no. 4 (Winter 1996): 157. See also Riesz, "'Audible Gasps From the Audience': Accusations of Plagiarism Against Several African Authors and Their Historical Context," *Yearbook of Comparative and General Literature* 43 (1995): 84–97.

121. Bernard Mouralis, quoted in Riesz, "The *Tirailleur Sénégalais*," 158; Kane, preface, xvi.

122. Kane, preface, v.

123. Kane, preface, v.

124. Jean-Richard Bloch, "avertissement," Diallo, *Force-Bonté*, 1.

125. Robert Pageard, *Littérature négro-africaine d'expression française: le mouvement littéraire contemporain dans l'Afrique noire d'expression français* (Paris: l'Ecole, 1979 [orig. 1966]), 12. See Frederic Michelman, "The Beginnings of French-African Fiction," *Research in African Literatures* 2, no. 1 (Spring 1971): 10–11. Michelman points out that there is a difference of point of view between Cousturier's own writings, which are critical of colonialism, and Diallo's panegyric (11); but that could simply mean that Cousturier faithfully channeled Diallo's views into writing. On shared authorship, see also Alec G. Hargreaves, "Testimony, Co-Authorship, and Dispossession Among Women of Maghrebi Origin in France," *Research in African Literatures* 37, no. 1 (Spring 2006): 42–54.

126. See Dorothy Blair, *African Literature in French: A History of Creative Writing in French from West and Equatorial Africa* (London: Cambridge University Press, 1976), 16–17.

127. Abiola Irele, "In Search of Camara Laye," *Research in African Literatures* 37, no. 1 (Spring 2006): 113; Alain Ricard, quoted in Irele, 114.

128. Irele, "In Search of Camara Laye," 114. Irele nonetheless makes statements about what he takes to be "Diallo's voice," which he says "comes through" (114); and he claims "we can be certain that Cousturier was not acquainted with this pidgin" (*petit nègre*) (113)—whereas the opposite is likely true (Cousturier frequented the *tirailleurs sénégalais*, and that was their lingua franca). Irele discusses Diallo as a springboard and a counterexample for his defense of Camara Laye's authorship.

129. Mireille Rosello, "Elissa Rhaïs: Scandals, Impostures, Who Owns the Story?," in Alec G. Hargreaves, Nikki Hitchcott, and Dominic Thomas, eds., "Textual Ownership in Francophone African Writing," special issue, *Research in African Literatures* 37, no. 1 (Spring 2006): 1. On Rhaïs see also Philippe Di Folco, "Rhaïs (Elissa)," in his *Les Grandes impostures littéraires: canulars, escroqueries, supercheries, et autres mystifications* (Paris: Ecriture, 2006), 217–20.

130. Patricia Sorel, *Plon: le sens de l'histoire* (Rennes: Presses Universitaires de Rennes, 2016), 94, 64–65, 107–108. The infamous anti-Semite and collaborator Robert Brasillach was published by Plon; see Sorel, *Plon*, 111. Plon also published a volume that included the famous early essay by Léopold Sédar Senghor, "Ce que l'homme noir apporte," in *L'Homme de couleur* (Paris: Plon, 1939); the volume was not anticolonial. Sorel, *Plon*, 120. Sorel unfortunately says nothing about Rhaïs.

131. Sorel, *Plon*, 285.

132. Plon press release, quoted in Rosello, "Elissa Rhaïs," 10.

133. See Rosello, "Elissa Rhaïs," 12n2. According to the Jewish Women's Archive, "Her publishers preferred to conceal her Jewish background, and, with her consent, advertised the novel as the work of a Muslim woman. . . . They hoped this deception would attract readers; novels

by a cloistered 'Oriental' woman would be sure to contain exciting insights about mysterious Algeria. Furthermore, the fact that she chose to write in the language she had learned in school was living proof of the success of the colonial enterprise. Readers were obviously unaware that Muslim women, unlike Jewish women, had as yet had no access to a French education." Sonia Assa, "Elissa Rhaïs," *Jewish Women's Archive Encyclopedia*, https://jwa.org/encyclopedia/article /rhais-elissa/, accessed April 4, 2017.

134. See Richard Watts, "'Qu'est-ce qu'un auteur indigène?' De la littérature coloniale à la littérature maghrébine," *Expressions maghrébines* 1, no. 1 (Summer 2002): 59–75. Watts places the birth of the category of the "native author" in 1920 (60). His analysis of the use of Arab or Arab-sounding pseudonyms (67), often encoding various messages, helps explain the context in which the name Elissa Rhaïs was invented. See also Watts, *Packaging Post/coloniality: The Manufacture of Literary Identity in the Francophone World* (Lanham, MD: Lexington Books, 2005), 52–65.

135. Jules Roy, quoted in Med Médiène, "Elissa Rhaïs (1882–1940): une judéité singulière," http://www.mmediene.com/article-28581537.html/, accessed July 4, 2017.

136. Elissa Rhaïs, *Le Mariage de Hanifa* (Paris: Plon, 1926), 38. See Patricia Lorcin, "Sex, Gender, and Race in the Colonial Novels of Elissa Rhaïs and Lucienne Favre," in *The Color of Liberty: Histories of Race in France*, ed. Sue Peabody and Tyler Stoval (Durham: Duke University Press, 2003), 115.

137. Paul Tabet, *Elissa Rhaïs* (Paris: Grasset, 1982). On the back cover the book is called a *récit authentique*. Judith Roumani speaks of the "enslavement" of Raoul by Elissa/Rosine. "*Elissa Rhaïs*: Enslaved Imagination in Colonial Africa," *Revue CELFAN* 2, no. 1 (1982): 12–15. Roumani may have been thinking of, but not mentioning, the word for ghostwriter in French, *nègre*, which used to mean slave. On Tabet's dubious reliability, see Emily Apter (who interviewed him), *Continental Drift: From National Characters to Virtual Subjects* (Chicago: University of Chicago Press, 1999), 259 n11.

138. Rosello, "Elissa Rhaïs," 13–14n8. Jean Pierre Allali and Guy Dugas, postface, Elissa Rhaïs, *Enfants de Palestine et autres nouvelles* (Paris: Editions Le Manuscrit, 2007), describe his role as simply that of "scribe . . . a kind of private secretary" to Elissa Rhaïs (243).

139. Elissa Rhaïs, *Saâda, la Marocaine* (Paris: Plon-Nourrit, 1919), 15; Rhaïs, *Le Mariage de Hanifa*, 30.

140. Apter, *Continental Drift*, 119.

141. Apter, *Continental Drift*, 129.

142. See Samuels, *The Right to Difference*, 77–82. Rhaïs's *Le Mariage de Hanifa* tells the story of an Arab girl who is, counterfactually, sent to a French girls' school by her eager parents. The image of French colonial education is entirely positive; the schoolmistress, with her "douce générosité de Française," tells her students: "Nous sommes toutes égales, mes chéries" (38). Hanifa gains all the advantages of French literacy but is said to be barely affected by it, thus remaining culturally intact (193). A similarly propagandistic view of French colonial education was given to Sub-Saharan Africans a few years earlier, in Diagne's *Les Trois volontés de Malic*, the first Sub-Saharan Francophone work of fiction.

143. "Raoul Dahan, dit Rhaïs" is cited in Tabet, *Elissa Rhaïs*, 8; Rhaïs is identified as "un pseudonyme d'écrivain hérité d'une tante." Tabet reproduces letters, whose authenticity is not confirmed, documenting the rise and fall of Rhaïs as a candidate for the Légion d'honneur. Two months after the ministry decided that she would receive the honor, the director of Plon wrote and revealed the "swindle": "Madame Rhaïs n'a pas écrit une ligne de toute l'oeuvre qu'elle a

signée. Elle est même illettrée, presque analphabète." A detective's report that was included with the letter reveals that Elissa Rhaïs was Jewish: "selon le mode de transmission judaïque, elle ne peut pas ne pas l'être." Quoted in Tabet, *Elissa Rhaïs,* 176, 178. Joseph Boumendil reports that he was unable to find any *demande* for the Légion d'honneur and therefore says it could not have been refused: *Elissa ou le mystère d'une écriture* (Paris: Séguier, 2008), 167. See also Jacqueline Piatier, "Le Mystère d'Elissa Rhaïs," *Le Monde,* June 4, 1982.

144. Charles Hagel, *Le Péril juif* (Algiers: Editions Nouvelles Africaines, 1934), 69–75. Hagel refers to the Jewish "race à laquelle elle a l'honneur d'appartenir" (70).

145. Rosello, citing Marie Virolle and Denise Brahimi, in "Elissa Rhaïs," 7–8.

146. Thus Denise Brahimi sees in *Les Juifs ou la Fille d'Eléazar* "[des] renseignements [qui] viennent de l'intérieur et témoignent d'une participation personnelle qui dépasse de loin les possibilités et les prétentions de l'orientalisme descriptif." Brahimi, *Femmes arabes et soeurs musulmanes* (Paris: Tierce, 1984), 187.

147. Back cover, Elissa Rhaïs, *Les Juifs ou la Fille d'Eléazar* (Paris: Archipel, 1997).

148. Paul Tabet, preface to 1997 edition of Rhaïs, *Les Juifs ou la Fille d'Eléazar,* 6. Other recent editions of Rhaïs make no mention of the pseudonym or hoax on the cover: for example, *Enfants de Palestine et autres nouvelles* (Paris: Editions Le Manuscrit, 2007).

149. See Bayard, *Et si les oeuvres.*

150. Roumani, "*Elissa Rhaïs,*" 13–14.

151. Letter quoted in Tabet, *Elissa Rhaïs,* 179.

152. See Boumendil, *Elissa,* 144–46.

153. Rosello, "Elissa Rhaïs," 4.

154. See Douglas Smith, "Raymond Queneau's 1916 Easter Rising: *On est toujours trop bon avec les femmes* as (Post-)Historical Novel," *Irish Journal of French Studies* 13 (2013): 151–73. On Camus and hard-boiled fiction, see Alice Kaplan, *Looking for the Stranger: Albert Camus and the Life of a Literary Classic* (Chicago: University of Chicago Press, 2016), 46–48.

155. On Vian's life and background, see Christopher M. Jones, *Boris Vian Transatlantic: Sources, Myths, and Dreams* (New York: Peter Lang, 1998).

156. See Boris Vian, *Chroniques de jazz,* ed. Lucien Malson (Paris: Christian Bourgois-Union Générale d'Editions, 1971); Jones, *Boris Vian Transatlantic.*

157. Vian, *Chroniques de jazz,* 61. The information about the league against racism is reported by the volume editor, Lucien Malson, 14.

158. "Repères bio-bibliographiques," in Boris Vian, *J'irai cracher sur vos tombes* (Paris: Christian Bourgois, 1973), 218; Marc Lapprand, "The Dark Side of Boris Vian," introduction to Boris Vian, *I Spit On Your Graves,* trans. Boris Vian and Milton Rosenthal (Los Angeles: TamTam Books, 1998), i. On the income from the Sullivan novels, see Jones, *Boris Vian Transatlantic,* 135.

159. Lapprand, "The Dark Side of Boris Vian," ii.

160. Vian, *J'irai cracher,* 7.

161. Rebecca Ruquist, "Paris, Race, and Universalism in the Black Atlantic: Léopold Sédar Senghor, Simone de Beauvoir, Boris Vian, and Richard Wright," dissertation, Yale University Department of French, 2003, p. 204. See also Bayard, who says that Vernon Sullivan had to be American, mostly for commercial reasons: *Et si les oeuvres,* 67.

162. Boris Vian as Vernon Sullivan, *Les Morts ont tous la même peau* (Paris: Editions Scorpion, 1947; Christian Bourgois, 1973); *Et on tuera tous les affreux* (Paris: Editions du Scorpion, 1948; Fayard, 1996); *Elle se rendent pas compte* [sic] (Paris: Editions du Scorpion, 1950; Fayard, 1996). These books are all currently in print and are widely available in French bookstores. The

covers and title pages say Boris Vian in large print at the top, followed by Vernon Sullivan in smaller letters or parentheses.

163. Boris Vian with Milton Rosenthal, but title page reads "Vernon Sullivan, with an introduction by Boris Vian," *I Shall Spit on Your Graves* (Paris: Vendôme Press, 1948). The reedition of the translation by Marc Lapprand, *I Spit on Your Graves*, corrects the Vian-Rosenthal translation in a number of instances.

164. Boris Vian, preface (printed as postface), *Les Morts ont tous la même peau*, 147, 149.

165. See Noël Arnaud, *Le Dossier de l'affaire "J'irai cracher sur vos tombes"* (Paris: Christian Bourgois, 1974), 135, 242. Raymond Queneau testified for the defense (175–76, 179–81). The court learned at a certain point that Vian was the author, and not merely the translator, of the Vernon Sullivan books; see the judgment, Arnaud, 240. For the fine, see 243; for the distinction between interdiction and seizure, see 247. The final disposition of the case dragged into 1953, when a court of appeals suppressed the fine, sentenced the defendants to fifteen days in prison, and then declared amnesty in the case (Arnaud, 252).

166. Arnaud, *Dossier*, 244–46.

167. Bayard, *Et si les oeuvres*, 66.

168. The last sentence was mistranslated by Vian and Rosenthal: "Through his torn pants seat his black-white bottom stuck out mockingly at the world" (201). *Bas-ventre* does not refer to "bottom" but to the lower *front* of the torso, including the sex organs.

169. See Arnaud, *Dossier*, 62; the coverage of the murder linked to the novel is on 48–64.

170. Arnaud, *Dossier*, 293. See Lapprand, "The Dark Side of Boris Vian," iv; "Repères bio-bibliographiques," 220; Boris Vian, *Oeuvres*, vol. 1, ed. Ursula Vian Kübler, with documentation by Nicole Bertolt (Paris: Fayard, 1999), 463. The film is *J'irai cracher sur vos tombes* (dir. Michel Gast, 100 min., 1959).

171. Jones, *Boris Vian Transatlantic*, 107.

172. J. Hoberman, blurb on back cover of translation, *I Spit on Your Graves*.

173. Allen Thiher, *Raymond Queneau* (Boston: Twayne, 1985), 9, emphasis added; 136.

174. Raymond Queneau, *On est toujours trop bon avec les femmes* (Paris: Gallimard, 1971 [1947]); trans. Barbara Wright, *We Always Treat Women Too Well* (New York: New York Review of Books Classics, 2003).

175. Jean-Yves Pouilloux, "Note sur le texte," in Raymond Queneau, *Oeuvres complètes* (Paris: Gallimard, Bibliothèque de la Pléiade, 1989), vol. 3, 1738.

176. See Thiher, *Raymond Queneau*, 69.

177. Thiher, *Raymond Queneau*, refers to the Sally Mara texts as "pseudonymous works" (109) and does not discuss them as hoaxes.

178. Pouilloux, "Note sur le texte," 1738.

179. See quotation from the weekly magazine *Inter* (May 26, 1948), in Arnaud, *Dossier*, 140.

180. See Raymond Queneau, *Romans, Oeuvres complètes* II (Paris: Gallimard, Bibliothèque de la Pléiade, 2006), 1503. In the *Oeuvres complètes de Sally Mara*, published in 1962, Presle's preface was embedded in a larger preface by Sally Mara, which "calls into question" both names. Jordan Stump, *Naming and Unnaming: On Raymond Queneau* (Lincoln: University of Nebraska Press, 1998), 138. See Queneau, *Les Oeuvres complètes de Sally Mara*, in the Pléiade volume *Romans*, 693–95.

181. Thiher, *Raymond Queneau*, 109.

182. Smith, "Raymond Queneau's 1916 Easter Rising," 157.

183. Jordan Stump, "Exercises in Wile: Raymond Queneau, the Novelist as Trickster," *Bookforum* 10 (Fall 2003): 12.

184. Thiher, *Raymond Queneau*, 53.

185. Gertie is represented as inert when the second rebel, Caffrey, is having sex with or rap-ing her (151/118). While still on top of her, his head is blown off by a British shell (155/121). Later she refers to "vos héroïques camarades qui m'ont violée" (215/169).

186. Queneau, *On est toujours trop bon*, 157/ *We Always Treat Women Too Well*, 122.

187. Stump, "Exercises in Wile," 14.

188. Valerie Caton, foreword to Raymond Queneau, *We Always Treat Women Too Well*, trans. Barbara Wright (London: John Calder, 1981), 4–5. The same translation of the novel has been reissued by New York Review Books.

189. Raymond Queneau, in *Front National*, December 1944, quoted in Caton, foreword to Queneau, *We Always Treat Women Too Well*, 3.

190. Thiher writes: "Queneau was using popular genres in order to undermine them," and he goes on to compare *On est toujours* to works of pop art and their relation to popular culture. *Raymond Queneau*, 111.

191. In addition to the 1959 film that Vian detested, *J'irai cracher sur vos tombes* (dir. Michel Gast, 104 min.), which he was viewing when he died, a second film was made using the same title: a hideous 2010 low-budget product directed by Steven R. Monroe, *I Spit on Your Grave*, "based [not on Vian but] on Meir Zarchi's motion picture 'The Day of the Woman.'" It retains only the theme of violent revenge for violence, as if the title had become a brand for that idea af-ter Vian. A film was made from the Queneau novel by Michel Boisrond, *On est toujours trop bon avec les femmes* (77 min., 1971).

192. Mongo Beti, "Choses vues au festival des arts africains de Berlin-Ouest (du 22 juin au 15 juillet 1979)," *Peuples noirs, peuples africains* 11 (1979): 58, 62.

193. Adele King, *Rereading Camara Laye* (Lincoln: University of Nebraska Press, 2002), 3.

194. Lilyan Kesteloot, *Anthologie négro-africaine* (Verviers, Belgium: Nouvelles Editions Mar-about, 1981), 468n1.

195. Claire Ducournau points out that King's work provoked negative reactions among Ameri-can critics and hardly any echoes of any kind in France: *La Fabrique des classiques africains: écrivains d'Afrique subsaharienne francophone* (Paris: CNRS Editions, 2017), 18.

196. King, *Rereading*, 46. King was unable to find any trace of Aude Joncourt in the colonial archives or elsewhere (*Rereading*, 161–62), and there is uncertainty about all aspects of her par-ticipation in the creation of *L'Enfant noir*. What King has learned about Joncourt comes from the writer Simon Njami, through his father (who knew Camara in the 1950s): that Joncourt was an anthropology student and very anticolonial; she had spent time in West Africa, where her father was a civil servant (King, 89). There is a weakness in King's work on this question: she quotes an obituary of Camara by Mamadou Traoré Ray Autra (cited below), which stated that Camara told his life story to "a young Frenchwoman." King then says "I have been told it was Aude Joncourt" (21), but does not say who told her this; so the link is murky. When King then writes that "the Frenchwoman Joncourt helped [Camara] by writing down his memories" (24) and "it is Joncourt to whom Autra refers as the Frenchwoman to whom Laye told the story of his life" (89), it is unclear how she can be certain. She then increases the uncertainty by referring to "the woman I have called Aude Joncourt," in the conclusion (169). The existence of Lefaucheux, on the other hand, is well documented. She was a *Résistante* during the war, a "firm supporter of the French Union" and member of its assembly from 1947 to 1958 (13, 92), and she helped find jobs for Camara in France; she was "the person whose interest led to French government support" for Camara's publications (22; see 90–98). Her party supported publications that would "develop mutual knowledge and understanding among peoples and races" (93).

197. King, *Rereading*, 6. On the Trojan Horse as a model of literary mystification, see Jeandillou, *Esthétique de la mystification*, 8–9.

198. See Cornélie Kunze, "L'Européen déraciné et l'Afrique guérisseuse: une relecture du roman *Le Regard du roi* de Camara Laye," in *Littérature et maladie en Afrique: image et fonction de la maladie dans la production littéraire* (Paris: Harmattan, 1994), 75–93.

199. The information in this paragraph is all from King, *Rereading*, 4–5, 45, 99, 118–19, 123–31.

200. King, *Rereading*, 3, 163–65.

201. King, *Rereading*, 162, 3; Hargreaves, Hitchcott, and Thomas, "introduction," in "Textual Ownership in Francophone African Writing," special issue, *Research in African Literatures* 37, no. 1 (Spring 2006): vii; Irele, "In Search of Camara Laye."

202. Sorel, *Plon*, 17–18, 64–65, 173, 289.

203. There are numerous comparisons that can be made between *L'Enfant noir* and *The Education of Little Tree*. Both are Bildungsromanen, written in a simple style designed to create a folkloric, pastoral atmosphere. Both traffic in filial piety, family and ethnic bonds, and occult knowledge. See *Little Tree*, 62, and Camara Laye, *L'Enfant noir* (Paris: Plon, 1953): 22; *The Dark Child*, trans. James Kirkup and Ernest Jones (New York: Farrar, Straus and Giroux, 1954): 26. Both novels use iterative verbs extensively in order to create a sense of timelessness (*Little Tree*, 147, 150, 161–62; *L'Enfant noir*, 11, 30, 51/17, 34, 51). Francis Soulié had written favorably during World War II about Belgian colonial policies in the Congo, which "encouraged maintaining the original style of life of the Negroes" (quoted in King, *Rereading*, 111).

204. Irele, "In Search of Camara Laye," 111, 114, 115.

205. Irele, "In Search of Camara Laye," 117, 116.

206. King, *Rereading*, 51–52.

207. Those reports of confessions are not, of course, of equal value, since Simon Bolivar Njami's testimony comes only indirectly, through his son, whereas Kesteloot reported directly, in writing, what she heard Camara tell her. The critic I refer to here is Kyle Wanberg, in "Translations of Identity: Eschewing Authority in Narratives about White Colonials in *Heart of Darkness* and *Le Regard du roi*," in *At the Crossroads: Readings of the Postcolonial and the Global in African Literature and Visual Art*, ed. Ghirmai Negash, Andrea Frohne, and Samuel Zadi (Trenton, NJ: Africa World Press, 2014), 78. In "Ghostwriting History: Subverting the Reception of *Le Regard du roi* and *Le Devoir de violence*," *Comparative Literature Studies* 50, no. 4 (2013): 589–617, Wanberg argues that "staking the value of a work on the identity of the author disengages one from the text and can lead to violent misreadings" (590). I would argue that ignoring questions about an author's identity does nothing to protect the work against misreadings. Resorting to a Derrida-inflected concept of "ghostwriting" that skirts around the "pure originality or identity" (590) of the author, Wanberg gives an inaccurate account of the questions of authorship that were raised by Kesteloot, King, and others. In "Départ d'un ami," Kesteloot did not write that Camara "could not have written the novel" (as Wanberg claims, 603); she said that such elements "divided the critics." Much more importantly, she had reported Camara's confession to her, in which he stated clearly that he had not written *Regard*, a fact that Wanberg ignores. His dismissal of King's work as "a passionate hunch" (603) is also inaccurate, for the same reason. Wanberg seems to want it both ways: to restore (without evidence) Camara's identity as author while simultaneously claiming that authorship itself is an obsolete Western concept. His version of Camara can be a subversive "ghostwriter" only if he is the writer of *Regard* in the first place, which few now believe. Camara Laye was not Yambo Ouologuem, an authentic author who subverted authenticity.

208. I see this as a strength, rather than the weakness that David Wilkin claims it to be, in his review of *Rereading Camara Laye*, *African Studies Review* 46, no. 3 (December 2003): 171.

209. See King, *Rereading*, 34–35. Irele argues that the two novels are linked by a single style that is "immediately recognizable in Laye's *normal habit of speech*, as I was to discover in a two-hour discussion with him only three days before his death." Irele, "Camara Laye: An Imagination Attuned to the Spiritual," *West Africa* 3272 (April 7, 1980): 618.

210. In these two paragraphs I am reproducing some of the remarks in my review of King's book, *Research in African Literatures* 28, no. 3 (Fall 2003): 125–28.

211. Kyle Wanberg calls this "the silence that has enshrouded Laye's work since the publication of King's book," an "abysmal hush." "Ghostwriting History," 603, 605.

212. Even Kenneth Harrow, who critiques King's approach and accuses her of "essentialism" based on her attributions of style to certain kinds of persons, concedes that "it does seem probable that Laye was not the author of *Regard*—alas." Review of *Rereading Camara Laye*, *Research in African Literatures* 35, no. 3 (Autumn 2004): 174.

213. I use the distinction between the specific and the singular deployed by Peter Hallward in his *Absolutely Postcolonial: Writing Between the Singular and the Specific* (Manchester: Manchester University Press, 2001).

214. Christopher L. Miller, *Theories of Africans: Francophone Literature and Anthropology in Africa* (Chicago: University of Chicago Press, 1990), 114–80.

215. King identifies them as two white Frenchwomen who "played prominent roles in the creation of *L'Enfant noir*." *Rereading*, 89.

216. "On avait l'impression que quelqu'un lui avait soufflé ça [*totem*]." Beti is invoking the image of a prompter—a "provider of missing words"—in a theater, who whispers forgotten lines to the actors. *Mongo Beti parle: testament d'un esprit rebelle. Entretiens avec Ambroise Kom* (Paris: Editions Homnisphères, 2006), 207. Although these interviews took place in 1998 and 1999, Beti had in fact flagged the word and concept of the totem in his initial review of *L'Enfant noir*, writing as "A. B.," in *Présence Africaine* 1–2 (April-July 1955): 419–20. He wrote: "Lorsqu'il parle de totem, sort, génie, il fait tout simplement pitié," and went on to say, as if to raise doubts about the authenticity of the novel: "Il n'y rien dans ce livre qu'un petit bourgeois européen n'ait déjà appris par la radio, un reportage de son quotidien habituel ou n'importe quel magazine de la chaîne 'France-Soir' " (420).

217. *Mongo Beti parle*, 141.

218. Robert Green, "*L'Enfant noir* and the Art of Auto-Archaeology," *English Studies in Africa* 27, no. 1 (1984): 61–72; Judith Cochrane, "The African Child: A Vibration of the Soul," *Ariel* 11, no. 2 (1980): 81–91; Ada Uzoamaka Azodo, "The Work in Gold as Spiritual Journey in Camara Laye's *The African Child*," *Journal of Religion in Africa* 24, no. 1 (1994): 52–61; King, *Rereading*, 70. King also compares the case of Camara to that of Rigoberta Menchú, 70.

219. Cornélie Kunze compares *Regard* to the works of Michel Leiris, and advances a theory that Leiris may have been the real author of the novel or a co-conspirator in its creation along with Camara (of which there is no evidence). The thesis is unconvincing, since it is based only on a small set of thematic similarities, all of which are explicable as the influence of Leiris's *Afrique fantôme* on the author of *Regard*, likely Soulié. See King, *Rereading*, 129. Kunze, "L'Européen déraciné et l'Afrique guérisseuse," 75–94.

220. Camara Laye, *Le Regard du roi* (Paris: Plon, 1954), 104; *The Radiance of the King*, trans. James Kirkup (New York: New York Review Books, 2001), 112. Further references to the novel and translation, respectively, will appear in parentheses.

221. "Aziana," a town that Clarence passes through, does not appear to be a real place name (*Regard*, 106; *Radiance*, 114). There is a character named Samba Baloum, and one bearing an Akan name, Akissi. And a real African language, Malinké/Bambara, appears briefly, in three numbers: "tan" for ten, "mouan" for twenty, and "tan saba" for thirty (*Regard*, 166, 167, 168/*Radiance*, 181, 182, 183). Soulié could easily have learned these numbers either from Camara or from his adopted son Kelefa Keita.

222. Jahnheinz Jahn, "Camara Laye: An Interpretation," *Black Orpheus* 6 (November 1959): 36; King, *Rereading*, 60, 61 (citing her earlier work, *The Writings of Camara Laye* [London: Heinemann, 1980]); Kenneth Harrow, "A Sufi Interpretation of *Le Regard du roi*," *Research in African Literatures* 14, no. 2 (Summer 1983): 135–64; and, published years after King's *Rereading*, David Cook, "Camara Laye's *The Radiance of the King*: An Open and Closed Reassessment," in *The Responsible Critic: Essays on African Literature in Honor of Professor Ben Obumselu*, ed. Isidore Diala (Trenton, NJ: Africa World Press, 2006), 43.

223. King, *Rereading*, 137.

224. Quoted in King, *Rereading*, 155. According to King, Robert Poulet was also the author of a review of *L'Enfant noir* that appeared in the Belgian newspaper *Rivarol*, no. 5 (November 7, 1953): 5. In condescending tones, he credits the novel with "authenticity," and—perhaps giving his own show away—represents it as a corrective to "trente ans de fallacieuse négrophilie."

225. A. B. [Mongo Beti], "Afrique noire, littérature rose," *Présence Africaine* 1–2 (April-July 1955): 143.

226. Léopold Sédar Senghor, "Laye Camara et Lamine Niang ou l'art doit être incarné," in *Liberté* I (Paris: Seuil, 1964), 173–74. The essay was first published in 1955.

227. King, *Rereading*, 30–31.

228. Claude Wauthier, *L'Afrique des Africains: inventaire de la négritude* (Paris: Seuil, 1964), 75; trans. Shirley Kay, *The Literature and Thought of Modern Africa: A Survey* (London: Pall Mall Press, 1966), 71.

229. Wole Soyinka, "From a Common Backcloth," *American Scholar* 32, no. 3 (Summer 1963): 388. Later, in his *Myth, Literature, and the African World* (Cambridge: Cambridge University Press, 1976), Soyinka moderated his view, describing *Radiance* as "too derivative," but "unquestionably African" (126).

230. Lilyan Kesteloot, *Black Writers in French: A Literary History of Negritude*, trans. Ellen Conroy Kennedy (Philadelphia: Temple University Press, 1974, first published as Les Ecrivains noir de langue française, 1963); Mohamadou Kane, *Roman africain et tradition* (Dakar: Nouvelles Editions Africaines, 1982). *Le Regard du roi* is listed in Kane's bibliography (502) but never mentioned in the text.

231. Mamadou Traoré Ray Autra, "Principales étapes de la vie de Camara Laye," *Notes africaines* 175 (July 1982): 57–58.

232. "Pour notre part une conversation avec lui sur ce sujet acheva de nous convaincre qu'il avait prêté son nom pour cautionner l'oeuvre d'un ami français." Lilyan Kesteloot, "Camara Laye ou le départ d'un ami," *Notes africaines* 175 (July 1982): 58–59.

233. Mongo Beti, interviews in *Mongo Beti parle*, 141, 207.

234. Birago Diop, *Et les yeux pour me dire: mémoires V* (Paris: Harmattan, 1989), 41. See also Jean-Claude Blachère, *Négritures: les écrivains d'Afrique noire et la langue française* (Paris: Harmattan, 1993), 168. Roger and Arlette Chemain reported rumors about Camara's authorship of *Le Regard* in "Pour une lecture politique de *Le Regard du roi* de Camara Laye," *Présence Africaine* 131 (1984): 155–68.

235. Toni Morrison, "On 'The Radiance of the King,'" *New York Review of Books*, August 9, 2001, 18–20, emphasis added. The book-introduction version has slight differences of phrasing. Toni Morrison, introduction, Camara Laye, *The Radiance of the King*, trans. James Kirkup (New York: New York Review Books, 2001), xi–xxiv.

236. See Miller, *Blank Darkness*.

237. The quotations from two critics are footnoted in the book-introduction version of Morrison's essay: Albert S. Gérard's introduction to one edition of the translation (New York: Collier/Macmillan, 1971) and Sonia Lee's book *Camara Laye* (Boston: Twayne, 1984), neither of which makes mention of the questions about the authenticity of *Le Regard*. Morrison, introduction to *The Radiance of the King*, xxi.

238. Christopher L. Miller, letter to the editor, *New York Review of Books*, August 10, 2001.

239. A. B. [Beti], "Afrique noire," 136.

240. In an interview with Camara Laye, Jacqueline Leiner caught him in a contradiction about knowing or not knowing his "totem." Camara then responded incoherently, speaking about Kafka: "Quand on affirme, par exemple, que je copie Kafka. . . . Non! Au contraire c'est peut-être Kafka qui nous copie? Kafka copie l'Afrique sans le savoir."

Another moment of incoherence came when Camara, in the same interview, pointed to the repetition of the word *seul* "at the beginning of *L'Enfant noir*" as a sign of his style; but that word does not appear even once in the entire first chapter. Jacqueline Leiner, "Interview avec Camara Laye: propos recueillis par Jacqueline Leiner," *Présence Francophone* 10 (Spring 1975): 165, 160.

241. Janis L. Pallister, review of *Rereading Camara Laye*, *French Review* 78, no. 2 (December 2004): 362.

242. Wanberg, "Ghostwriting History."

243. I borrow this riff on Barthes and Mark Twain from Hargreaves, Hitchcott, and Thomas, "introduction," in "Textual Ownership in Francophone African Writing," special issue, *Research in African Literatures* 37, no. 1 (Spring 2006): vi.

244. On the history of Gary's names, see David Bellos, *Romain Gary: A Tall Story* (London: Harvill Secker, 2010), chapter 12, "Games with Names."

245. Raphaëlle Rérolle, "Ajar alias Gary," *Le Monde*, August 28, 2003, http://www.lemonde.fr/archives/article/2003/08/27/ajar-alias-gary_331713_1819218.html?xtmc=ajar_alias_gary&xtcr=14/, accessed March 3, 2018.

246. Julia Elsky, "French and Foreign: Immigrant Authors in Occupied France," dissertation, Yale University, Department of French, 2014.

247. "*The Roots of Heaven*," screenplay by Gary (dir. John Huston, 126 min., 1958).

248. Nancy Huston, *Tombeau de Romain Gary* (Paris: Actes Sud, 1995), 18.

249. "To be blunt, part of what Gary wrote is bullshit." Bellos, *Romain Gary*, loc. 1796. Nancy Huston refers to Gary's public image as "grand-Français-couvert-de-décorations-militaires-et-littéraires." *Tombeau de Romain Gary*, 89.

250. Rérolle, "Ajar alias Gary."

251. Romain Gary, *Pour Sganarelle: recherche d'un personnage et d'un roman. Frère Océan, I* (Paris: Gallimard, 1965), 19, 23.

252. Gary, *Pour Sganarelle*, 84–85.

253. Bellos, *Romain Gary*, loc. 4831.

254. Romain Gary (Emile Ajar), *Pseudo (Paris: Mercure de France, 1976)*, 202.

255. Bellos, *Romain Gary*, loc. 4764. Huston, *Tombeau de Romain Gary*, 62. On the effects of Gary's change of identity, interpreted as a "change of author," see Bayard, *Et si les oeuvres*, 60–61.

256. Romain Gary (Emile Ajar), *Au-delà de cette limite votre ticket n'est plus valable* (Paris: Gallimard, 1975), 76; *Your Ticket Is No Longer Valid*, trans. Sophie Wilkins (New York: George Braziller, 1977), 56, AT. Bellos says that Gary wrote *Au-delà de cette limite* immediately after composing the first Ajar novel, *Gros-Câlin* (Bellos, *Romain Gary*, loc. 5516). See also Ralph Schoolcraft, *Romain Gary: The Man Who Sold His Shadow* (Philadelphia: University of Pennsylvania Press, 2002), 107–113. As Schoolcraft writes, "this duo of master and slave find their positions to be potentially reversible" (110); and "Gary wished to lead the critics into eventual ridicule by giving them what they were looking for," i.e. an image of Gary that was pathetic (111).

257. "G. B." (a critic identified by Schoolcraft as "Georges Bratschi?") in *Romain Gary*, 182, 108, and 182n25.

258. Gary, *Vie et mort*, 28.

259. Bellos, *Romain Gary*, loc. 2505.

260. Gary/Ajar, *Pseudo*, 16.

261. See Morrissette, *The Great Rimbaud Forgery*, 154: "to prove one's ability and to get revenge."

262. Gary, *Vie et mort*, 17.

263. See Myriam Anissimov, *Romain Gary, le caméléon* (Paris: Denoël, 2004), 521; and Bellos, *Romain Gary*, loc. 5359.

264. Bellos, *Romain Gary*, loc. 5359.

265. Anissimov, *Romain Gary, le caméléon*, 531; Bellos, *Romain Gary*, loc. 5359; see Paul Pavlowitch, *L'Homme que l'on croyait* (Paris: Fayard, 1981), 74. Schoolcraft points out that "*Your Ticket Is No Longer Valid* saw Rainier go into a tough neighborhood in North Paris seeking a young, disreputable character to rejuvenate his imagination" (Schoolcraft, *Romain Gary*, 112–13). But that gesture is represented differently in *Au-delà de cette limite*: the narrator goes to the Goutte d'Or neighborhood not once but repeatedly, and the narrator explicitly critiques the potentially exploitative nature of his relation with the people there, fearing that he is being "racist" and "insulting," that he and his girlfriend are there as "voyeurs" (*Au-delà de cette limite*, 152/ *Your Ticket*, 121). The narrator goes on to say: "Racism is when it doesn't count. When they don't count. When one can do anything with them, it doesn't matter what, because they are not *people like us*. Do you see? Not *our kind*" (153/121; see also 162/129). This passage of *Au-delà de cette limite* can thus be read as both a self-critique by Gary (of his own racial voyeurism) and a statement of his core beliefs. The passage confirms Gary's belief that difference itself is the foundation of racism, which is what his Madame Rosa asserts. On the other hand, the narrator is seduced by difference later in the novel, when he visits an Arab neighborhood: "Je ne sais pourquoi je me sentais si libre parmi ces visages si différents du mien" (206/165). We will see that Jack-Alain Léger used more or less the same procedure, of taking a field trip to an ethnic neighborhood in Paris, with similar results. Another point of confluence between Gary and Léger is that, in *Au-delà de cette limite*, the narrator says: "J'étais tué. Je pouvais à présent continuer à vivre"/"I had been killed. Now I could go on living" (247/200). This is close to the title of the Léger/Smaïl novel *Vivre me tue*.

266. See Pavlowitch, *L'Homme*, 22; Marion Van Renterghem, "Qui êtes-vous, Paul Pavlowitch?," *Le Monde*, February 2, 2000. See also Rérolle, "Ajar alias Gary."

267. Schoolcraft, *Romain Gary*, 101.

268. Pavlowitch was not in fact the nephew of Gary but the "cousin germain" of Pavlowitch's mother. Gary used the terms "petit cousin" and "cousin à la mode de Bretagne." *Vie et mort*, 19, 22. See also Bette H. Lustig, "Emile Ajar Demystified," *French Review* 57, no. 2 (December 1983):

203–12. Lustig lists the small group of people, including Robert Gallimard, who knew about the hoax from the beginning (209).

269. Anissimov, *Romain Gary, le caméléon*, 595, 532–33, 569; Pavlowitch, *L'Homme*, 7, 198–99.

270. Anissimov, *Romain Gary, le caméléon*, 565; Katsoulis, *Literary Hoaxes*, 313.

271. Bellos, *Romain Gary*, loc. 2333. Sales figures are jealously guarded by publishing houses, and I have not been able to confirm the status of *La Vie devant soi*.

272. The Open Syllabus Project lists *La Vie devant soi* at 64,261 in rank. See http://explorer.opensyllabusproject.org/text/10355003/, accessed April 21, 2017.

273. Anissimov, *Romain Gary, le caméléon*, 522; the *fiche* that Gary submitted for/as Ajar gave his name as "Raja (Ajar), Emile." See Bellos, *Romain Gary*, loc 5451; Pavlowitch, *L'Homme*, 85, 87.

274. See Jeandillou, *Esthétique de la mystification*, 99–101.

275. Pavlowitch, *L'Homme*, 306; Anissimov, *Romain Gary, le caméléon*, 548.

276. Jacqueline Piatier, "Goncourt: Emile Ajar en dépit du mystère," *Le Monde*, November 18, 1975.

277. Yvonne Baby, "Entretien: La Maison d'Ajar, rencontre avec l'auteur de *La Vie devant soi*," *Le Monde*, October 10, 1975, 20; reprinted as "Entretien d'Emile Ajar avec Yvonne Baby à Copenhague, le 30 septembre 1975," in Emile Ajar, *La Vie devant soi* (Paris: Librairie Jules Tallandier, 1976): the pages are numbered 1–13 but appear at the end of the volume, which is a reissue of the novel. The interview was printed in *Le Monde* on October 10, 1975, the day that the Goncourt nominations, including that of *La Vie devant soi*, were published. An advertisement for the novel was printed on 19.

For Pavlowitch's commentary on the interview, see *L'Homme*, 123.

278. Bellos, *Romain Gary*, loc. 5617.

279. Jacqueline Piatier, "La Tendresse des 'paumés,'" *Le Monde*, September 17, 1975.

280. Pavlowitch, *L'Homme*, 172–75.

281. Anissimov, *Romain Gary, le caméléon*, 559, 575.

282. It was a close call, as can be seen in John L. Hess, "Madame Rosa in Charge," *New York Times Book Review*, April 2, 1978: 15.

283. André Gattolin, "Prélude à une théorie du hoax et de son usage subversif," *Multitudes* 25 (2006): 153–54.

284. Anissimov, *Romain Gary, le caméléon*, 556. Gary, *Vie et mort*, 41; Rérolle, "Ajar alias Gary."

285. Unsigned, "Ajar refuse le Goncourt," *Le Monde*, November 11, 1975.

286. Mireille Sacotte, "L'Affaire Emile Ajar," in Romain Gary/Emile Ajar, *Légendes du Je: récits, romans*, ed. Mireille Sacotte (Paris: Gallimard, 2009), 1097. Paul Pavlowitch, speaking on *Apostrophes*, July 3, 1981.

287. Gary, *Au-delà de cette limite*, 214; *Your Ticket*, 172.

288. Bellos, *Romain Gary*, loc. 5769; Anissimov, *Romain Gary, le caméléon*, 602–3.

289. Pavlowitch, *L'Homme*, 233.

290. Bellos, *Romain Gary*, loc. 5341.

291. Gary, *Vie et mort*, 22; Gary/Ajar, *Pseudo*, 12.

292. Huston, *Tombeau de Romain Gary*, 91. A "hapax logomenon" is something said only once.

293. Bellos, *Romain Gary*, loc. 5722.

294. The last words of *Au-delà de cette limite* express this same idea of closure as self-erasure: "Je n'ai jamais vu aussi clairement en moi-même qu'en ce moment, où je ne vois plus

rien"/"Never before have I seen so clearly into myself as I do now, where I no longer see anything at all" (248/201).

295. Pierre Bayard, *Il était deux fois Romain Gary* (Paris: PUF, 1990), 113.

296. The line appears in *La Vie devant soi* (Paris: Mercure de France, 1975), 63; trans. Ralph Manheim, *The Life Before Us ("Madame Rosa")* (New York: New Directions, 1977), 38. Further references to the novel and its translation, respectively, will appear in parentheses. Bellos cites a "computerized stylistic analysis" of the last Ajar novel, *Le Roi Solomon*, performed by Vina Tirgendvadum, which apparently succeeded in identifying Gary as the probable author. Bellos points out that this was simply because Gary was no longer trying to disguise his style. Bellos, *Romain Gary*, loc. 5792. See Tirgendvadum, "Linguistic Fingerprints and Literary Fraud," *Computing in the Humanities Working Papers* A.9 (1998).

297. Jacqueline Piatier, "La Mort d'Emile Ajar," *Le Monde* July 2, 1981; see Schoolcraft, *Romain Gary*, 130; Bellos, *Romain Gary*, loc. 5700.

298. Pavlowitch, *L'Homme*, 229.

299. Bellos, *Romain Gary*, loc. 5810; Pavlowitch, *L'Homme*, 307; see Anissimov, *Romain Gary, le caméléon*, 572.

300. Mireille Sacotte, postface, in Romain Gary/Emile Ajar, *Légendes du Je*, 1402.

301. Piatier, "La Mort d'Emile Ajar."

302. Quoted in Needham, *Exemplars*, 84.

303. Lustig asks this question, in "Emil Ajar Demystified," 212.

304. Emily Apter, "What Is Yours, Ours, and Mine: Authorial Ownership and the Creative Commons," *October* 126 (Fall 2008): 112.

305. Romain Gary's suicide note, quoted in Anissimov, *Romain Gary, le caméléon*, 643.

306. Roland A. Champagne, "Ajar Emile. *La Vie devant soi*," review in *Modern Language Journal* 61, nos. 1–2 (January-February 1977): 65.

307. Nicole M. Fouletier-Smith, "Les Nord-Africains en France: réalités et représentations littéraires," *French Review* 51, no. 5 (April 1978): 687. The quote from *La Quinzaine littéraire* is by Jean-Baptiste Mauroux, quoted 689.

308. Anissimov, *Romain Gary, le caméléon*, 538. See David Bellos, "Ce que Momo veut dire: la mémoire de la Shoah dans *La Vie devant soi* de Romain Gary," *Perspectives: Revue de l'Université Hébraïque de Jérusalem* 6 (1999): 55–66.

309. Mathieu Galey, quoted in Anissimov, *Romain Gary, le caméléon*, 650.

310. Claude Michel Cluny, writing in *Le Magazine littéraire*, quoted in Pavlowitch, *L'Homme*, 141.

311. Pavlowitch, *L'Homme*, 154.

312. *Bienvenue à Marly-Gomont/The African Doctor* is presented as the true story of a Congolese family, told from the point of view of the doctor's son, although the director of the film is Julien Rambaldi.

313. David Bellos makes the comparison between Gary's *La Vie devant soi* and Eric-Emmanuel Schmitt's novel *Monsieur Ibrahim*, "a feel-good morality tale whose success proves that you can go on fooling people for a very long time." *Romain Gary*, loc. 6948, n18.

314. See Piatier, "La Tendresse des 'paumés.'"

315. Schoolcraft points out: "Momo is the diminutive of both Mohammed and Moses, prophets of their respective religions" (*Romain Gary*, 114).

316. Bellos, *Romain Gary*, loc. 5405. Jack-Alain Léger will repeat this coup: his fake underclass French was studied and put into dictionaries.

317. Anissimov, *Romain Gary, le caméléon*, 516. Gary (writing as Ajar) had to insist that publishers not correct the mistakes: "Vos correcteurs doivent scrupuleusement respecter les 'fautes' du manuscrit" (517).

318. Bellos calls this "a totally inauthentic image of a racial melting pot." *Romain Gary*, loc. 5472.

319. Romain Gary, *La Promesse de l'aube* (Paris: Gallimard, 1980 [1960]): 249. See Julia Elsky's analysis of the confluence between immigrant writers including Gary, with their roots in Polish Romanticism, and Republican "principles": "French and Foreign," 146–47.

320. Romain Gary, *Le Sens de ma vie* (Paris: Gallimard, 2014), 40. The text is that of a filmed interview done a few months before Gary's death. He also says that he is agnostic (99), but that the "meaning of [his] life" can be located in a feminine understanding of Christ: "la parole du Christ dans ce qu'elle a de féminin" (100).

321. This exact handling of the trinity of Republican values (those stated in the Declaration of the Rights of Man), with "liberty" elided, occurs in the first text of Francophone African prose fiction: *Les Trois volontés de Malic* (1920); see Miller, "Unfinished Business," 105–26.

322. Elizabeth Ezra, *The Colonial Unconscious: Race and Culture in Interwar France* (Ithaca: Cornell University Press, 2000), 101. The antiracist inclusive version of French Republicanism that is visible in *La Vie devant soi* is consistent with Gary's larger thinking. Bellos writes: "He really did think Jews and Blacks were identical, as equal (and equally deplorable) members of the human race." *Romain Gary*, loc. 1978. If Madame Rosa is comparable to Papa Mélé, it is interesting to note that Josephine Baker herself, like Madame Rosa, famously raised a rainbow tribe of orphans—but in real life. Madame Rosa is based on Gary's real mother, who is affectionately depicted in his autobiographical novel *La Promesse de l'aube*. Her love of France, which she imbued in her son, is said to be comparable only to de Gaulle's (101–2).

323. Picard, *Artifices et mystifications*, 213, quoted in Schoolcraft, *Romain Gary*, 161.

324. In the various versions and adaptations of the novel, it is interesting to see how the focus of the title toggles back and forth between Momo and Madame Rosa. *La Vie devant soi* or *The Life Before Me* (my own translation of the title) can only refer to young Momo. The first edition of the English translation by Ralph Manheim was called *Momo* (Garden City, NY: Doubleday Books, 1978), but the same translation was reprinted with the title *Madame Rosa* (New York: Berkley Publishing Group, 1979), then as *The Life Before Us ("Madame Rosa")*, with an afterword by James Laughlin (New York: New Directions, 1986). The film, featuring Simone Signoret (and likely because of her star power), was called *Madame Rosa*; then the television film of 2010 was again *La Vie devant soi*. There was also a version for theater, *La Vie devant soi*, produced in 2007, in an adaptation by Xavier Jaillard, directed by Didier Long.

325. Gérard Dupuy, in *Libération*, quoted in Schoolcraft, *Romain Gary*, 166.

326. Schoolcraft, *Romain Gary*, 170.

327. Mireille Rosello, *Declining the Stereotype: Ethnicity and Representation in French Cultures* (Hanover: University Press of New England, 1998),129.

328. Gary, quoted in Schoolcraft, *Romain Gary*, 114.

329. Romain Gary, quoted in Anissimov, *Romain Gary, le caméléon*, 636.

330. See Bellos's very helpful chapter, "Gary's Politics," in *Romain Gary*. Bellos writes: "Gary's ideals were familiar, simple, and close to those of Victor Hugo: an end to racism and discrimination of all kinds; an end to war and violence; love between men and women." Loc. 2896. Gary remained neutral and nearly silent about Algerian independence.

331. Rérolle, "Ajar alias Gary."

332. Huston compares Gary's suicide to the crucifixion of Jesus, followed by the "resurrection" implicit in his posthumous unveiling of the hoax. *Tombeau de Romain Gary*, 100.

333. Gary, *Le Sens de ma vie*, 16.

334. See Anyinefa, "Scandales"; Pierre Assouline, "L'Affaire Beyala rebondit: l'Académie Française a pris le risque de cautionner un auteur dont l'oeuvre est truffée de plagiats," *Lire* 252 (February 1997): 8–11. This article features side-by-side comparisons of passages from *Le Petit prince de Belleville* (Paris: Albin Michel, 1992) and *La Vie devant soi* as well as Paule Constant, *White Spirit* (Paris: Folio, 1992), and Alice Walker, *La Couleur pourpre* (Paris: J'ai Lu, 1987).

335. Suzanne Gauch, "Sampling Globalization in Calixthe Beyala's *Le Petit prince de Belleville*," *Research in African Literature* 41, no. 2 (Summer 2010): 208.

336. Avertissement de l'éditeur, Chimo, *Lila dit ça* (Paris: Plon, 1996), 7; "French Publisher's Note," in Chimo, *Lila Says*, trans. David Watson (London: Fourth Estate, 1996), n.p. (AT).

337. In the French edition, 41, 44, 70, 148, 170.

338. Olivier Orban, quoted in Marion Van Renterghem, "Chimo, mystérieux écrivain débutant, ou supercherie littéraire?," *Le Monde*, April 27, 1996, http://abonnes.lemonde.fr/ar chives/article/1996/04/27/chimo-mysterieux-ecrivain-debutant-ou-supercherie-litteraire_372 6844_1819218.html?xtmc=chimo_mysterieux_ecrivain_debutant&xtcr=1/, accessed March 5, 2018.

339. Raphaël Meltz, "Chimo: l'écriture sans figure," *R de réel*, vol. D (July-August 2000), http://rdereel.free.fr/volDZ1.html/, accessed April 28, 2017. It was also suggested that Chimo was code for "Christine [Orban's wife] aime Olivier" and that the husband and wife were the authors together. Van Renterghem, "Chimo."

340. "L'Enigme Chimo," *Le Point*, April 4, 1996, http://www.lepoint.fr/actualites-societe/1996 -04-27/l-enigme-chimo/920/0/103603/, accessed March 3, 2018.

341. Alec G. Hargreaves suspects that *Lila dit ça* is a "commercially-motivated hoax." *Voices From the North-African Immigrant Community in France: Immigration and Identity in Beur Fiction* (New York: Berg Publishers, 1991), 177. Chimo teases the reader with the idea of commercial exploitation by beginning the sequel, *J'ai peur*, in his lawyer's office, hearing about the millions of francs he is earning from *Lila dit ça*. Chimo, *J'ai peur* (Paris: Plon, 1997), 7.

342. The film *Lila dit ça* (dir. Ziad Doueiri, 2005, 89 min.) moderates the intense sexuality of the novel and transposes the setting to Marseilles; instead of dying after being raped, Lila moves away. No doubt due to these modifications, the film was very successful. See the analysis of the film in Sylvie Blum, "Dans le pays Chimo," in *Où en est la littérature "beur"* (Paris: Harmattan, 2012), 93–105. The film was called "startlingly erotic and surprisingly moving . . . as sweet as it is dirty" by the *Washington Post*. Michael O'Sullivan, "'Lila Says' Talks a Blue Streak," *Washington Post*, August 26, 2006, http://www.washingtonpost.com/wp-dyn/content/article/2005/08/25/AR 2005082500583.html/, accessed March 3, 2018. The *New York Times* called it "gripping," with "a hauntingly realistic aura." Caryn James, "Films Take a More Sophisticated Look at Teenage Sex," *New York Times*, July 6, 2005, http://www.nytimes.com/2005/07/06/movies/films-take-a-more -sophisticated-look-at-teenage-sex.html/, accessed March 3, 2018.

343. Van Renterghem, "Chimo."

344. Plon was sold and reorganized in the early 1960s. See Sorel, *Plon*, 281–84. Plon still maintains a strong Catholic inflection in many of its publications, and yet publishes Nedjma. See Nedjma, *L'Amande: récit intime* (Paris: Plon, 2004).

345. Azouz Begag, *Quand on est mort, c'est pour toute la vie* (Paris: Gallimard, 1994).

346. In the sequel novel by Chimo, *J'ai peur*, Lila is said to have been "vierge en plus jusqu'à son viol" (37).

347. Sylvie Blum argues that *Lila dit ça* has little new to offer except its take on feminine sexuality and language, which she associates with both the "liberation of feminine language" (a phrase by Zinaid Meeran) and male fantasy. Blum, "Dans le pays Chimo," in *Où en est la littérature "beur,"* 100.

348. On Chimo as writer, see Michel Laronde, "The Post-Colonial Writer Between Anonymity and the Institution: Inscriptions of the Author in Chimo and Paul Smaïl," in *Immigrant Narratives in Contemporary France*, ed. Susan Ireland and Patrice J. Proulx (Westport, CT: Greenwood Press, 2001), 93–103.

349. One counterexample deserves mention here: the case of Omar Ba, whose supposed memoir of a harrowing immigration to Europe, *Soif d'Europe: Témoignage d'un clandestin* (Paris: Editions du Cygne, 2008), was denounced as a fake by Senegalese writers. They could tell. Bathie Ngoye Thiam, a Senegalese writer and artist, spoke up in July 2008 after seeing Omar Ba tell his tale on television. Reviewing Ba's adventures and various aspects that strain credulity, Thiam comments, "Superman wouldn't have done better." Bathie Ngoye Thiam, "*Soif d'Europe*: l'imposture d'un immigré." *Afriqu'Echos Magazine*, July 16, 2008, http://archive.is/bS8w/, accessed March 6, 2018. Such objections, however, could only chip away at the plausibility of the story, without necessarily disproving anything. Almost a year later, the mainstream press picked up on this story and pursued it further. *Le Monde* published an investigative article in July 2009, in which the factual basis of Ba's entire narrative crumbled. Cross-examined at length and repeatedly by *Le Monde*, finally cornered, Ba retracted parts of his story; but even the remaining facts did not comport with conditions documented by the newspaper at the time. Benoît Hopquin, "Contre-enquête sur un affabulateur," *Le Monde*, July 7, 2009, and Benoît Hopquin, "Un 'imposteur' repéré par la diaspora sénégalaise," July 7, 2009, http://www.lemonde.fr/so ciete/article/2009/07/07/un-imposteur-repere-par-la-diaspora-senegalaise_1216191_3224 .html#ens_id=1216285/. Two days later *L'Humanité* denounced Ba as an "impostor" who "plays with the misfortunes of Sengalese clandestins" and his text as "stuffed with inconsistencies." Philippe Peter, "Un imposteur joue du malheur des clandestins sénégalais," *L'Humanité*, July 9, 2009, http://www.humanite.fr/node/420377/. *L'Express* confessed that it had swallowed Ba's "Dantesque" story—which he had served up in tearful interviews—in its entirety. The magazine issued an apology for its lack of "critical perspective." Anne Vidalie, "Omar m'a berner," *L'Express*, July 8, 2009; Eric Mettout, "Omar Ba nous a tous berner, ou pourquoi il faut être sceptique," *L'Express*, July 10, 2009, http://blogs.lexpress.fr/nouvelleformule/2009/07/10/djeuner_avec_ma _copine_anne//, accessed March 3, 2018. See also Ruben Andersson, "Wild Man at Europe's Gates: The Crafting of Clandestines in Spain's *Cayuco* Crisis," *Etnofoor* 22, no. 2 (2010): 31–32. Ba was named a "model citizen" by a Senegalese civic organization in 2015: http://www.leral.net /Photos-Le-Club-Model-a-honore-ses-Citoyens-modeles-de-l-annee-2015_a164342.html/.

Part Three

1. http://www.actualitte.com/societe/romancier-et-musicien-jack-alain-leger-s-est-suicide-43 926.htm/, accessed March 20, 2018.

2. Raphaëlle Leyris, "L'Ecrivain Jack-Alain Léger s'est donné la mort," *Le Monde*, July 17, 2013, http://abonnes.lemonde.fr/disparitions/article/2013/07/17/mort-de-l-ecrivain-jack-alain -leger_3449194_3382.html?xtmc=l_ecrivain_jack_alain_leger_s_est_donne_la_mort&xtcr=3/, accessed March 5, 2018. See also Philippe Matsas, "Jack-Alain Léger," *Le Monde*, July 20, 2013; Mathieu Lindon, "Jack-Alain Léger, le coeur lourd," *Libération*, July 18, 2013, http://next.libera tion.fr/culture/2013/07/18/jack-alain-leger-le-coeur-lourd_919278/, accessed March 5, 2018.

3. Jack-Alain Léger, *Autoportrait au loup* (Paris: Flammarion, 1982), 23. That sentence is immediately followed by this: "Ni vivre." The phrase "homosexuellement incorrect" was used by Léger's friend Colette Kerber, quoted in Lindon, "Jack-Alain Léger, le coeur lourd."

4. http://en.wikipedia.org/wiki/Oscar_Wilde/.

5. *Tarantula* par Bob Dylan; adapté de l'américain et suivi de "Portrait de l'artiste en pop star" par Dashiell Hedayat ([Paris]: Christian Bourgois, 1972). Various other translations and music recordings under this name can be found in the BNF catalogue.

6. Dashiell Hedayat (Jack-Alain Léger), *Le Livre des morts-vivants* (Paris: Christian Bourgois, 1972), back cover.

7. See Christophe Conte, "Jack-Alain Léger/Dashiell Hedayat (1947–2013)," *Les Inrockupti bles*, July 18, 2013, http://www.lesinrocks.com/2013/07/18/musique/jack-alain-leger-dashiell-he dayat-1947-2013-11410142/, accessed March 20, 2018. For a 1972 interview with Léger as Dashiell Hedayat, see https://www.youtube.com/watch?v=wkGFjYNiPSE/. See also http://www.ac tualitte.com/societe/romancier-et-musicien-jack-alain-leger-s-est-suicide-43926.htm/. The €500 figure is cited by Adrian Dannatt, "Jack-Alain Léger: Writer and Singer Who Worked Under Multiple Guises," *Independent*, September 30, 2013, http://www.independent.co.uk/news/obituaries /jack-alain-l-ger-writer-and-singer-who-worked-under-multiple-guises-8849484.html/.

8. Dashiell Hedayat (Jack-Alain Léger), "Chrysler Rose," *Obsolèle* ([Paris?]: Shandar, 1971).

9. Emmanuel Pierrat, quoted in David Caviglioli, "Jack-Alain Léger, l'écrivain aux cinq noms, est mort," *Le Nouvel Observateur*, July 18, 2013.

10. See Léger, *Autoportrait au loup*, 168.

11. The "lifespans" and productivity of the author/personae in question here can thus be summarized as follows, in the order of their first appearance: Melmoth (1969): 1 book, 1 album; Dashiell Hedayat (1971–75): 6 books including 2 translations, 1 album; Jack-Alain Léger (1973–2013): 26 books; Eve Saint-Roch (1988): 1 book; Paul Smaïl (1997–2001): 4 books. The total: 5 names, 38 books; 2 albums.

12. See Mathieu Lindon, "Léger, Jack-Alain et les autres," *Libération*, January 12, 2006; Leyris, "L'Ecrivain Jack-Alain Léger s'est donné la mort."

13. Email from Emmanuel Pierrat to author, July 14, 2017. For the father's writing see, for example, the column "Livres" in *Paris-Match*: no. 1010 (September 14, 1968): p. 83; no. 1012 (September 28, 1968): p. 101; no. 1121 (October 31, 1970): p. 83; no. 1220 (September 23, 1972): p. 67. The articles by the father that I have been able to find all deal with either memoirs or politics; larger, splashy literary features in *Paris-Match* were written by others.

14. In his penultimate book, *Zanzaro Circus (Paris: L'Editeur, 2012)*, Léger referred to "mon père réel, le sartrien pigiste à *Paris-Match*" (91).

15. Léger, *Autoportrait au loup*, 75, 79. The naming issues go deeper in the family history: Léger also reports that his father was "orphelin de père et que sa mère, remariée, ne portait pas le même nom que lui" (76).

16. Léger, *Autoportrait au loup*, 37.

17. Jack-Alain Léger, *Maestranza (Paris: Gallimard, 2000)*: 93.

18. Nejiba Regaieg, "Autobiographie et mise en scène de l'écriture dans *Vivre me tue* et *Casa, la casa* de Paul Smaïl," 122. Regaieg nonetheless refers to Paul Smaïl as "unfathomable" (*insond-able*) (123). For Regaieg, at this point, the real identity of the author remains ambiguous, despite the fact that Léger had revealed himself as Smaïl three years earlier.

19. Patrice Bollon, "Le peuple, ce grand oublié," *Le Magazine littéraire*, May 2012, http://www.magazine-litteraire.com/actualite/peuple-ce-grand-oublie-20-04-2012-36761/, accessed June 29,

2017. For the larger context of French writing that has attempted to "parler peuple," as a "posture" of authenticity, see Meizoz, *Postures littéraires*, 75–108. "Authenticity" is defined as "conformité de la représentation à la vie" (90).

20. "Le livre sent le vécu, et la banlieue des années 1997 y est décrite comme on ne l'a jamais fait." Walid Salem, "Jack-Alain Léger, Tartuffe se tue en plein ramadan," *Le Nouvel Observateur*, July 20, 2013, http://rue89.nouvelobs.com/rue89-culture/2013/07/20/jack-alain-leger-tartuffe -tue-plein-ramadan-244391?imprimer=1/, accessed June 29, 2017.

21. Brozgal, "Hostages of Authenticity," 125.

22. The quotation is from Léger's editor, the head of Editions Balland, Jean-Jacques Augier: "Il était amusant pour nous de retenir deux titres très voisins. C'était une façon de narguer le petit monde littéraire parisien." Quoted in Kathryn Kleppinger, "Why the *Beur* Novel? Writers and Journalists Interact to Construct a New French Voice," dissertation, New York University, 2011, p. 237. Augier also owned Salvy Editeur, which published *Ma Vie, titre provisoire* (Paris: Salvy Editeur, 1997). See Di Folco, *Les Grandes impostures*, 151. For Léger's own account of this, see Jack-Alain Léger, *Hé bien! La guerre* (Paris: Denël, 2006), 381.

23. Kleppinger, "Why the *Beur* Novel?," 235n182.

24. Jacques-Pierre Amette, "Une très allègre déprime," *Le Point* 1304 (September 13, 1997): 110; Manuel Carcassonne, "Roman: *Vivre me tue* de Paul Smaïl," *Le Point* 1311 (November 1, 1997): 91.

25. With only slight exaggeration, Cécile Guilbert wrote after his death: "pas une grande maison parisienne qui ne l'ait publié." Cécile Guilbert, "Jack-Alain Léger: l'hommage de Cécile Guilbert," *Le Figaro*, July 19, 2013, http://www.lefigaro.fr/livres/2013/07/19/03005-201307 19ARTFIG00495-jack-alain-leger-l-hommage-de-la-romanciere-cecile-guilbert.php/, accessed June 29, 2017. Léger, quoted in Lindon, "Jack-Alain Léger, le coeur lourd."

26. Françoise Verny, an editor at Gallimard, quoted in Astrid de Larminat, "La Colère du mal-aimé," *Le Figaro*, January 19, 2006. Verny is satirized in several of Léger's novels; he referred to her as "La Grosse." De Larminat writes: "On hésite à publier aujourd'hui quelqu'un qui mettra demain toute sa verve à vous insulter dans ses livres."

27. "Il s'autovirait." Emmanuel Pierrat, quoted in Lindon, "Jack-Alain Léger, le coeur lourd."

28. Yann Moix, "Jack-Alain Léger, le nain géant," *Le Figaro Livres*, July 17, 2013, http://www .lefigaro.fr/livres/2013/07/17/03005-20130717ARTFIG00423-jack-alain-leger-le-nain-geant .php/, accessed June 29, 2017. Moix is repeating Léger's own self-description in *Zanzaro Circus*: "à 13 ans, disgracieux, obèse, boudiné dans mon costume étriqué, la démarche dandinante et pesante, je suis un éléphanteau" (back cover).

29. http://www.elle.fr/Loisirs/Livres/Prix-litteraire-des-lectrices?page=3/, accessed June 29, 2017.

30. Léger, *Hé bien! la guerre*, 503.

31. His lawyer and guardian Emmanuel Pierrat said after he died: "J'aimerais bien que tout soit réuni sous un seul et même nom, Jack-Alain Léger. Que les pseudonymes soient conservés, mais qu'on puisse comprendre la cohérence de l'ensemble. Il avait conscience de laisser une oeuvre." Quoted in Caviglioli, "Jack-Alain Léger." Cécile Guilbert affirms that Léger's work, starting in 1989, possesses "l'unité et la cohérence que lui confère son caractère essentiellement musical." "Portrait de l'auteur en artistes," preface to Jack-Alain Léger, *Le Siècle des ténèbres, Le Roman, Jacob Jacobi* (Paris: Denoël, 2006), vi–vii.

32. Léger, *Autoportrait au loup*, 11.

33. Hedayat (Léger), *Le Livre des morts-vivants*, 15.

34. Léger, *Maestranza*, 92.

35. Jack-Alain Léger, *Le Siècle des ténèbres*, in *Le Siècle des ténèbres, Le Roman, Jacob Jacobi*, 32; see 134.

36. The narrator of *Jacob Jacobi* says that he was to be named after his stillborn older brother, Daniel, but came out fat and different, and was thus named for the saint's day on which he was born, Saint-Léger. This is thus one derivation of the name Léger (ironic for a fat baby and child). (But in this novel, the clerk records the baby's name as Lazare, in a further twist on the theme of resuscitation.)

37. Jack-Alain Léger, *La Gloire est le deuil éclatant du bonheur (Paris: Julliard, 1995)*, 23.

38. Léger, *Autoportrait*, 135.

39. See Annie Ernaux, *L'Autre fille* (Paris: Nil, 2011); Philippe Grimbert, *Un Secret* (Paris: B. Grasset, 2004).

40. Léger, *Ma Vie, titre provisoire*, 160.

41. Léger, *On en est là: roman (sorte de)* (Paris: Denoël, 2003), 84, 86.

42. Jack-Alain Léger, *Le Roman*, in *Le Siècle des ténèbres, Le Roman, Jacob Jacobi*, 530.

43. Léger, *Le Siècle des ténèbres*, 219.

44. Jack-Alain Léger, *Les Aurochs et les anges* (Paris: Rivages, 2007), 15.

45. Léger, *On en est là*, 84, 86, 115. Léger repeated this formula in his article "Qu'ils lisent des romans, ces crétins!," *Libération*, February 3, 2001, and in *Tartuffe fait Ramadan* (Paris: Denoël, 2003).

46. Léger, *Maestranza*, 119.

47. Léger, *Maestranza*, 130.

48. Léger, *Ma Vie, titre provisoire*, 90.

49. Léger, *Les Aurochs et les anges*, 51.

50. Léger, *Maestranza*, 36.

51. Jack-Alain Léger, *Jacob Jacobi*, in *Le Siècle des ténèbres, Le Roman, Jacob Jacobi*, 865.

52. Léger, *Maestranza*, 18.

53. Léger, *Ma Vie, titre provisoire*, 218. The critic in *Le Point* hailed this book as "vif, drôle, allègre, injuste, hérissé . . ." and told Léger, "Vous êtes sauvé littérairement." Jacques-Pierre Amette, "Une très allègre déprime," *Le Point* 1304 (September 13, 1997): 110.

54. Léger, *On en est là*, 283.

55. Baptiste Liger, "Jack-Alain Léger, écrivain maudit," *L'Express* (February 1, 2006), https://www.lexpress.fr/culture/livre/he-bien-la-guerre_810964.html/.

56. *Monsignore*, DVD, front and back covers (dir. Frank Perry, 1982, 121 min.).

57. Guilbert, "Jack-Alain Léger."

58. J. N., "Vatican Connection," *Le Monde*, October 15, 1982, http://abonnes.lemonde.fr/archives/article/1982/10/15/vatican-connection_2892470_1819218.html?xtmc=vatican_connection&xtcr=5/, accessed March 5, 2018.

59. Leyris, "L'Ecrivain Jack-Alain Léger s'est donné la mort"; Guilbert, "Jack-Alain Léger."

60. Scott Gunther, "Building a More Stately Closet: French Gay Movements Since the Early 1980's," *Journal of the History of Sexuality* 13, no. 3 (2004): 331.

61. Frédéric Martel, quoted in Gunther, "Building a More Stately Closet," 333.

62. See Gunther, "Building a More Stately Closet," 336.

63. Murray Pratt, "Authorship, Impersonation, and the Republic: Outing *Ali le magnifique*," *Essays in French Literature* 43 (July 2006): 168.

64. Guilbert, "Jack-Alain Léger."

65. Léger, *Ma Vie, titre provisoire*, 162.

66. On Mishima and Proust, see Léger, *Autoportrait au loup*, 94–106. Léger seems to have found the inspiration for his title in Yukio Mishima's autobiography, *Confessions of a Mask*, trans. Meredith Weatherby (New York: New Directions, 1958).

67. Jack-Alain Léger, *Les Souliers rouges de la duchesse* (Paris: François Bourin, 1992), 79.

68. *Apostrophes*, September 17, 1982.

69. Léger, *Ma Vie, titre provisoire*, 91. In *Maestranza*, Léger returned to this theme in a bitter and scathing critique of gay culture as seen in the Marais, where, Léger says, he is never so ashamed as on Gay Pride Day (39–45): ". . . insidieux terrorisme . . . ce narcissisme de masse, cette bonne conscience suffisante, cette volonté d'assimilation mais à ses seuls semblables . . . me font horreur" (44).

70. Because of Léger's pathologizing of homosexuality, it is somewhat inaccurate for Cécile Guilbert to assert that *Autoportrait au loup* was "traîné dans la boue" only because it was twenty years ahead of its time; ahead of "la déferlante des confessions trash qui nous ont submergés depuis." Guilbert, "Portrait de l'auteur en artistes," preface to Léger, *Le Siècle des ténèbres, Le Roman, Jacob Jacobi*, vi.

71. Léger, *Ma Vie, titre provisoire*, 93, 94.

72. Colette Kerber, quoted in Marie-Dominique Lelièvre, "Comme une plume," *Libération*, Sept. 23, 2000.

73. Preface to second edition of Jack-Alain Léger, *L'Heure du tigre* (Paris: La Table Ronde, 1990), iv.

74. Léger, *Ma Vie, titre provisoire*, 91.

75. Gunther, "Building a More Stately Closet," 331n11.

76. Christopher Robinson, "Sexuality and Textuality in Contemporary French Gay Fiction," *French Studies* 52, no. 2 (1998): 179, 185n14. It would be useful to compare *Autoportrait* to some of the works of Renaud Camus—unlike Léger, a canonical "gay" writer—even as Camus "refuses sexual definition" (Robinson, 183).

77. For a comparison and a counterexample, see Christopher Robinson's treatment of Jean Genet's "negative portrait of homosexuality," which nonetheless preserves Genet's place in the gay canon. Christopher Robinson, *Scandal in the Ink: Male and Female Homosexuality in Twentieth-Century French Literature* (London: Cassell, 1995), 67.

78. Léger, *Ma Vie, titre provisoire*, 197.

79. Léger, *On en est là*, 179. What Léger described is thus a classic example of questions examined in Bayard's *Et si les oeuvres changeaient d'auteur?*

80. Jacqueline Piatier, "Portrait de l'artiste en nègre," *Le Monde*, October 1, 1993, http://abon nes.lemonde.fr/archives/article/1993/10/01/portrait-de-l-artiste-en-negre_3942966_1819218 .html?xtmc=portrait_de_l_artiste_en_negre&xtcr=3/, accessed March 5, 2018.

81. Léger, *Jacob Jacobi*, 556–57.

82. *Nardène* apparently comes from "na' din' mouk" or "nardinamouk," Arabic for "damn the religion of your mother." See Pierre Merle, *Petit traité de l'injure* (Paris: L'Archipel, Kindle edition, 2004), loc. 1305.

83. Léger, *On en est là*, 176.

84. A term invented in 1977 by Serge Doubrovsky to describe his novel *Fils*.

85. Azouz Begag, *Le Gone du Chaâba* (Paris: Seuil, 1986), 87.

86. Paul Smaïl, *Vivre me tue* (Paris: J'ai Lu, 1997), trans. Simon Pleasance and Fronza Woods with Janine Dupont, *Smile: A Novel by Paul Smaïl* (London: Serpent's Tail, 2000). Further references, to the original and the translation in that order, will appear in parentheses. Altered translations

will be marked AT. The English translation places the disclaimer, called "author's note," at the beginning of the book, before the epigraph from Melville.

87. Lejeune, *Pacte*, 26/*On Autobiography*, 14.

88. Salles, "Duel d'écrivains polymorphes."

89. Léger, *On en est là*, 256.

90. In an article in *Libération*, September 4, 2003, "La Pègre des lettres," Léger said that Paul Smaïl was his "alter ego."

91. Christian Laborde offered "proof" that Smaïl was Léger, but the so-called proof consisted of a simple coincidence of vocabulary: Smaïl uses the term *nuit grave* to refer to a cigarette— because a cigarette *nuit gravement à la santé* (*Ali le magnifique* [Paris: Denoël, 2001], 111), and Léger used the term during a bookstore appearance presenting *Maestranza*. But as Rosello points out, this proves nothing, since slang circulates and is not, by definition, any one person's language. See Mireille Rosello, "Paul (Smaïl) et le loup: de carna comme un des Beaux-Arts," *Présence Francophone* 58 (2002): 55.

92. Bruno Tessarach, *Art nègre* (Paris: Libella, 2013), 223.

93. Kleppinger, "Why the *Beur* Novel?," 235, 244. The quotation is Kleppinger's paraphrase of what Léger told her in 2010.

94. Mireille Rosello, *Postcolonial Hospitality: The Immigrant as Guest* (Stanford: Stanford University Press, 2001), 5.

95. Azouz Begag, *L'Intégration* (Paris: Le Cavalier Bleu, 2003), 10.

96. Michel Poniatowski, *Que survive la France*, quoted in Begag, *L'Intégration*, 57.

97. Hervé Tchumkam, *State Power, Stigmatization, and Youth Resistance Culture in the French Banlieues* (Lanham, Md: Lexington Books, 2015), 12. Tchumkam explains with stark clarity how French universalism blocks awareness of and responses to what he calls "the true problem," which is that racial discrimination "on the basis of bodily traits" has produced a "post-colonial fracture" in the Republic, one that the Republic's own precepts deny (12).

98. See Alec G. Hargreaves, *Immigration and Identity in Beur Fiction: Voices from the North African Immigrant Community in France* (New York: Berg, 1997); Michel Laronde, *Autour du roman beur* (Paris: L'Harmattan, 1993).

99. Hargreaves, *Immigration and Identity*, 11.

100. Kathryn A. Kleppinger, *Branding the "Beur" Author: Minority Writing and the Media in France, 1983–2013* (Liverpool: Liverpool University Press, 2015), 6.

101. Kleppinger, "Why the *Beur* Novel?," 246.

102. Smaïl, *Vivre me tue*, 9/*Smile*, 1. The translation egregiously fails to echo Melville, opting for "You can call me Smaïl."

103. See the documentary by Yamina Benguigui, *Le Plafond de verre* (2008, 104 min.). Cited in Marie-Hélène Koffi-Tessio, "Voyageurs français sur le continent africain," dissertation, Princeton University, 2007.

104. Farid Laroussi, *Postcolonial Counterpoint: Orientalism, France, and the Maghreb* (Toronto: University of Toronto Press, 2016), 158.

105. See Kleppinger, *Branding the "Beur" Author*, 8n9.

106. The book that we are reading may or may not be the one he began with the words "Vivre me tue," then abandoned because that phrase "said everything" (139; this passage is unfortunately left out of the translation, 110).

107. The narrator as outstanding student, and ostracized for it, is another common denominator between *Vivre me tue* and *Le Gone du Chaâba* (see *Le Gone*, 90, 95).

108. "Je remercie Dieu de m'avoir fait naître citoyen d'un pays où je peux ne pas croire en lui." IMEC, Fonds Jack-Alain Léger, Folder "Réflexions sur la littérature et la critique."

109. Hélène Jaccomard, "Extremists and Moderates: French Writers and Muslims of France," in *Muslim Citizens in the West: Spaces and Agents of Inclusion and Exclusion* (Burlington, VT: Ashgate Press, 2014), 182.

110. Joseph Conrad, *The Nigger of the "Narcissus,"* Kindle loc. 414. On the homosocial aspects of maritime literature, see Miller, *The French Atlantic Triangle*, 277–81.

111. Browder, *Slippery Characters*, 241.

112. Conrad's narrator in fact addresses the importance of literature in the lives of uneducated people, in this case sailors: "The popularity of Bulwer Lytton [author of *Pelham: or The Adventures of a Gentleman*, 1828] in the forecastles of Southern-going ships is a wonderful and bizarre phenomenon. What ideas do his polished and so curiously insincere sentences awaken in the simple minds of the big children who people those dark and wandering places of the earth?" Conrad, *The Nigger of the "Narcissus,"* Kindle loc. 135.

113. See Jean-Luc Einaudi, *La Bataille de Paris: 17 octobre 1961* (Paris: Seuil, 1991), a book that is cited in *Vivre me tue*, 178/*Smile*, 144 (the translation adds an allusion to Kristallnacht).

114. At the end of that passage he says his father was a secret supporter of Algerian independence (*Maestranza*, 133).

115. A scene of hygienic inspection, involving the feet instead of the head, is found in Azouz Begag's first novel, *Le Gone du Chaâba* (97–104). In a further "coincidence," in both cases, the inspection leads to a revolt; in *Le Gone*, it is an Arab student who, insulted, revolts against the French teacher. On this passage in *Le Gone*, see Laura Reeck, *Writerly Identities in Beur Fiction and Beyond* (Lanham, Md: Lexington Books, 2011), 31. As Reeck points out in a note, the preoccupation with hygiene in postcolonial France was analyzed by Kristin Ross in *Fast Cars, Clean Bodies*.

116. Conrad, *The Nigger of the "Narcissus,"* Kindle loc. 14.

117. See also Rosello, *Declining the Stereotype*.

118. See Rosello, *Postcolonial Hospitality*.

119. Lott, *Love and Theft*, 105.

120. Jean-Luc Douin, "*Vivre me tue*, de Paul Smaïl," *Le Monde*, August 29, 1997, http://abonnes .lemonde.fr/archives/article/1997/08/29/vivre-me-tue-de-paul-smail_3773779_1819218.html ?xtmc=vivre_me_tue_de_paul_smail&xtcr=13/, accessed March 5, 2018.

121. Maati Kabbal, "Smaïl, les pépins du melon: livreur de pizza, veilleur de nuit, réceptionniste et victime du racisme ambiant: à la première personne du singulier, les troubles identitaires d'un jeune beur homosexuel." *Libération*, October 2, 1997, http://next.liberation.fr/livres/1997/10 /02/smail-les-pepins-du-melon-livreur-de-pizza-veilleur-de-nuit-receptionniste-et-victime-du -racisme-amb_218407/, accessed March 5, 2018.

122. Jack-Alain Léger, letter to Antoine de Gaudemar, undated, Fonds Jack-Alain Léger, IMEC, Dossier de Presse Paul Smaïl, JAL 26. There is no signature on the printout of the letter that Léger kept. On the narrator's sexuality, see *Vivre me tue*, 48, 54–55/*Smile*, 33, 39–40.

123. Paul Smaïl, *Casa, la casa* (Paris: Balland, 1998), 178. This novel was reprinted: *Casa, la casa* (Paris: Editions Cartouche, 2010). My references will be to the original edition.

124. See Farida Belghoul, *Georgette!* (Paris: B. Barrault, 1986); Mehdi Charef, *Le Thé au harem de Archi Ahmed* (Paris: Mercure de France, 1983).

125. Unsigned, "Le Sens d'une vie," *Le Devoir*, January 24, 1998, http://www.ledevoir.com/re cherche?expression=paul+sma%C3%AFl/.

126. Marie-Christine Luton, "Les Mots qui sauvent de la haine," *Journal du dimanche*, September 21 [1997], Fonds Jack-Alain Léger, IMEC, Dossier de Presse Paul Smaïl, JAL 26.

127. Léger, *Hé bien! la guerre*, 61.

128. F. G., "La France m'a tuer," *Elle*, October 6, 1997, 59.

129. Anne Crignon, "Smaïl nous écrit du Maroc," *Le Nouvel Observateur*, October 9–15, 1997, 138.

130. Fonds Jack-Alain Léger, IMEC, Dossier de Presse Paul Smaïl, JAL 26. This is a press clipping with no publishing information.

131. Unsigned, "Smaïl détrône Chimo," *Le Figaro*, October 3, 1997.

132. Fabrice Lanfranchi, "La Rage des mots," *L'Humanité*, November 7, 1997, http://www.humanite.fr/node/170151/.

133. Jean Tanguy, "Livres-Jeunesse," http://www.livres-jeunesse.net/Ouvrages/smail.htm/, accessed July 8, 2017.

134. Carcassonne, "Roman: *Vivre me tue* de Paul Smaïl," 91. *Vivre me tue* was on the bestseller list in *Le Point* from October 4 to November 1, 1997.

135. Fayçal Chehat, "*Vivre me tue* de Paul Smaïl," *Africultures*, December 31, 1997, http://www.africultures.com/php/index.php?nav=article&no=271&texte_recherche=paul%20sma%Efl/, accessed June 29, 2017.

136. Hélène Morin, "Le Français des banlieues selon les écrivains arabes ou beurs," *Qantara: Magazine des cultures arabe et méditerrannéenne* 16 (Winter 1997–98): 42.

137. Dominique Le Boucher, "Enigme littéraire: rien à voir . . ." *Algérie Littérature/Action* 17 (January 1998): 37, 38, 39, 44. Le Boucher compares *Vivre me tue* to Mounsi's *Noce des fous* (Paris: Stock, 1990).

138. See Jean-Pierre Goudaillier, *Comment tu tchatches! Dictionnaire du français contemporain des cités* (Paris: Maisonneuve et Larose, 1998). *Vivre me tue* is one of eight recent novels cited as sources; see *Comment tu tchatches!*, 38. The citations are under: *ahchouma* (Smaïl spells it *heichma*), *bounty, dope, frankaoui, kahlouche, roumi, sidi, tchi (keutchi)*. The two authors were Youcef M. D. in *Je rêve d'une autre vie* and Y. B. (Yahia Belhouchet) in *Allah Superstar*; see James Kilpatrick, "Paul Smaïl's *Casa, la casa*: A Critical Translation," dissertation, Rice University, 2005, 52.

139. Farida Abu-Haidar, "Voices of Change: Interlanguage in Franco-Maghrebi Texts," in *Immigrant Narratives in Contemporary France*, ed. Susan Ireland and Patrice J. Proulx (Westport, CT: Greenwood Press, 2001), 87, 86.

140. Letter from Association de Solidarité avec les Travailleurs immigrés, October 3, 1997, Fonds Jack-Alain Léger, IMEC, Correspondance H–W.

141. Letter from *Pote@Pote*, February 5, 1999, Fonds Jack-Alain Léger, IMEC, Correspondance H–W. On its web site, *Pote@Pote* states its mission to be "le porte parole de tous ceux qui vivent ou réfléchissent sur les quartiers." http://www.maisondespotes.fr/pote-a-pote-le-magazine-des-quartiers/, accessed March 20, 2018.

142. Di Folco, *Les Grandes impostures*, 153. I have not been able to confirm this.

143. Kleppinger, *Branding the "Beur" Author*, 260.

144. See Kleppinger, *Branding the "Beur" Author*, 261.

145. Letter of Jack-Alain Léger as Paul Smaïl to Prix des Lycées Professionnels du Haut Rhin, February 5, 1999, in Fonds Jack-Alain Léger, IMEC, Correspondance H–W.

146. Undated fax of Jack-Alain Léger as Paul Smaïl, Fonds Jack-Alain Léger, IMEC, Dossier de Presse Paul Smaïl, JAL 26. The fax was addressed to Marc Weitzman at *Les Inrockuptibles*.

147. Jack-Alain Léger as Paul Smaïl, undated letter, Fonds Jack-Alain Léger, IMEC: Correspondance A–G.

148. Jack-Alain Léger as Paul Smaïl, undated letter, Fonds Jack-Alain Léger, IMEC: Correspondance H–W.

149. Jack-Alain Léger as Paul Smaïl, undated letter, Fonds Jack-Alain Léger, IMEC: Correspondance H–W.

150. Fonds Jack-Alain Léger, IMEC, Dossier Calmann-Lévy.

151. Fonds Jack-Alain Léger, IMEC, Dossier Balland-Salvy.

152. Jack-Alain Léger as Paul Smaïl, undated letter to Anne Crignon, Fonds Jack-Alain Léger, IMEC, Dossier *Nouvel Observateur*.

153. See Kleppinger, *Branding the "Beur" Author*, 254, for Léger's explanation of the setup. In Kleppinger's words: "Léger wrote his answers and sent them to Morocco so that they could then be faxed back to Paris!" and "the journalist never verified her sources."

154. Crignon, "Smaïl nous écrit du Maroc," 138.

155. See Kleppinger, *Branding the "Beur" Author*, 255: "Léger told me that this strategy [of the interview by fax] achieved his goal, which was to discredit the *attachée de presse* of Balland who had already begun to spread doubt about Smaïl's authenticity."

156. *Casa, la casa*. The use of *second* (which implies second and final), as opposed to *deuxième*, suggests that this was intended to be the last Smaïl novel; but two more appeared thereafter.

157. Kleppinger, *Branding the "Beur" Author*, 237–38.

158. Cécile Rol-Tanguy, press release, November 7, 1997. Fonds Jack-Alain Léger, IMEC, Dossier Balland-Salvy. See (unsigned) "Smaïl m'a tuer," *Le Monde*, November 21, 1997.

The ungrammatical formula "*m'a tuer*" is an allusion to the sensational Omar Raddad affair of 1991. A Moroccan gardener was accused of killing a Frenchwoman, whose body was found near an ungrammatical inscription, "Omar m'a tuer." The trial revolved around the question of whether a native speaker of French like the victim could make such an error, confusing the infinitive with the past participle. The form has been repeated in many titles (a film *Omar m'a tuer*, a book *Sarko m'a tuer*, etc.).

159. "Je viens d'arriver à Paris. Pour apprendre qu'une salope écrit aux journaux que 'Smail m'a tuer.' Et que la rumeur a repris de plus belle." Jack-Alain Léger as Paul Smaïl, undated fax to Anne Crignon, Fonds Jack-Alain Léger, IMEC, Correspondance, folder *Nouvel Observateur*.

160. Jack-Alain Léger, letters to Jean-Jacques Augier, September 4 and 5, 1997, Fonds Jack-Alain Léger, IMEC, Dossier Balland-Salvy, subfolder Balland Augier.

161. Léger's correspondence makes it clear that Jean-Luc Douin was in on the secret before it was formally unveiled in 2003. On February 17, 2001, Léger wrote to Douin: "Je voulais te dire ma gratitude pour l'attention bienveillante que tu me portes et qui m'est très précieuse alors que je subis une fois encore le tabassage que me réservent les 'gens de lettres et de maison' . . . Et j'ai su tout de suite que ce livre, *Vivre me tue*, était un livre juste: quand, avant même sa parution, un de mes tous premiers lecteurs, un Beur, Ahmed B., apprenant la vérité sur l'identité de l'auteur s'est écrié: 'Quelle importance, puisque ton livre est vrai.' Et c'est, depuis, ce qui s'est reproduit chaque fois qu'un Beur, ou un Maghrébin, a su la vérité . . . Paul Smaïl continuera de vivre, et d'écrire, et de publier." Jack-Alain Léger, letter to Jean-Luc Douin, February 17, 2001, Fonds Jack-Alain Léger, IMEC, Correspondance A–G.

162. Jack-Alain Léger, letter to Jean-Jacques Augier, November 10, 1997, Fonds Jack-Alain Léger, IMEC, Dossier Balland-Salvy, subfolder Balland Augier.

163. *Vivre me tue* (dir. Jean-Pierre Sinapi, screenplay by Daniel Tonachella and Jean-Pierre

Sinapi, 86 min. DVD One Plus One, 2006). See Murray Pratt and Denis M. Provencher, "(Re) casting Sami Bouajila: An Ambiguous Model of Integration, Belonging, and Citizenship," in *Screening Integration: Recasting Maghrebi Immigration in Contemporary France,* ed. Sylvie Durmelat and Vinay Swamy (Lincoln: University of Nebraska Press, 2012), 194–210. As Pratt and Provencher point out, the film "focuses on the fraternal relations between the characters rather than the author's internal meditations on political correctness in France" (199); and there is an important shift of focus, literally, as much of the film shows Paul in Hamburg reflecting on life in Paris (199). On ticket sales, see 198.

164. Anne Crignon, "*Casa* me tue: le deuxième roman de Paul Smaïl," *Le Nouvel Observateur,* August 27-September 2, 1998, 74.

165. Hélène Le Beau, "Vivre me plaît," *Le Devoir,* [only date visible is "le samedi 23," year not shown; press clipping in IMEC]. Le Beau writes: "On l'approuve de ne pas se prêter au jeu du beur de service. . . ."

166. Isabelle Martin, "Au tournant du deuxième roman: Paul Smaïl: l'auteur n'est peut-être pas celui qu'on croit," *Le Temps,* October 3, 1998. Martin says that she is responding to rumors.

167. Léger, *Ma Vie, titre provisoire,* p. 53/*Vivre me tue,* 10. The full quote in the latter novel is, "Je ne suis pas une ressource humaine, j'ai trop sale gueule." The phrase is repeated with reference to the death of the brother in *Vivre me tue*: "Du moins, il ne serait jamais une ressource humaine" (12). In 2001 Christian Laborde found a similar coincidence (*nuit grave* for cigarette) and cited it as "proof" that Jack-Alain Léger was Paul Smaïl; quoted in Rosello, "Paul (Smaïl) et le loup," 55.

168. Ziad Elmarsafy, "'Hath Not an Arab Eyes?' Paul Smaïl and the Conformist Inferno," *SubStance* 30, no. 3, issue 96 (2001): 99n6.

169. Anonymous letter to Daniel Théron, Fonds Jack-Alain Léger, IMEC. Folder JAL 21, "Lettres de lecteurs," subfolder 4 (2000–2003). The letter is undated but postmarked "Paris 14," December 29, 2000.

170. It is hard to understand how Léger could claim that Smaïl was unmasked "against [his] will." Jean-Luc Douin, "Un homme en 'mélancolère,'" interview with Jack-Alain Léger, *Le Monde,* January 6, 2006, http://abonnes.lemonde.fr/livres/article/2006/01/05/jack-alain-leger-un -homme-en-melancolere_727495_3260.html?xtmc=un_homme_en_melancolere&xtcr=1/, accessed March 5, 2018.

171. Kleppinger, *Branding the "Beur" Author,* 238.

172. Smaïl, *Casa, la casa,* 176.

173. Paul Smaïl, *La Passion selon moi (Paris: Robert Laffont, 1999),* 51, 139.

174. Paul Smaïl, *Ali le magnifique,* 158. On this enormous novel (618 pages), which is based on the 1999–2000 case of the "train killer" Sid Ahmed Rezala, see Pratt, "Authorship, Impersonation, and the Republic," 147–74. Pratt reviews the Smaïl hoax as "ethnic drag" (150) and reads *Ali* as "both a novel by a Beur author called Paul Smaïl *and* a literary hoax perpetuated [*sic*] by a Republican, secular essayist called Jack-Alain Léger" (151). On *Ali* see also Jaccomard, "Extremists and Moderates," 186. I am not sure I agree with Jaccomard's reductive reading, in which *Ali* is simply "a warning that France's tolerance towards Beur delinquents 'is nothing less than a capitulation to fascism.'" The latter quote she takes from Pratt (150), but he is referring not to the novel, but to something much broader: Léger's view of "politically correct and communitarian attitudes" in France more generally.

175. Léger, *On en est là,* 187–88.

176. Léger, *Tartuffe fait Ramadan,* 116.

177. Douin, "Un homme en 'mélancolère.'"

178. Léger, *Hé bien! La guerre*, 58.

179. Only two of those were received before the end of 1997, in the first three months after the publication of *Vivre me tue*. I have been told by the staff at IMEC: "En ce qui concerne la correspondance, nous vous avons communiqué tout ce que nous avons trouvé dans l'appartement de Jack-Alain Léger concernant *Vivre me tue*." Email from Elisa Martos, IMEC, June 17, 2015. I am not authorized to cite the names of those who wrote to Léger/Smaïl.

180. Letters quoted here are in the Fonds Jack-Alain Léger, IMEC. Folder JAL 21, "Lettres de lecteurs, 1997–2003."

181. Jack-Alain Léger as Paul Smaïl, letter to students at Lycée Louis Armand, Mulhouse, July 2, 1999 Fonds Jack-Alain Léger, IMEC, Folder JAL 21, "Lettres de lecteurs," subfolder H-W.

182. Léger, *Tartuffe fait Ramadan*, 113. In another book Léger avows his "aversion grandissante pour le communautarisme musulman . . ." (60), which he says is a consequence of the "unworthy" French government treatment of immigrants. *Les Aurochs et les anges*, 60.

183. Léger, *Les Aurochs et les anges*, 96–97.

184. Pratt, "Authorship, Impersonation, and the Republic," 150, 151.

185. Léger, letter to Jean-Luc Douin, February 17, 2001, Fonds Jack-Alain Léger, IMEC, Correspondance A–G.

186. Once the second Paul Smaïl novel, *Casa, la casa*, was published, letter-writers began to comment on both books. In a letter to Hélène Le Beau, who had written about *Vivre me tue* in *Le Devoir* (Montreal), Léger (as Paul Smaïl) wrote, "Je continue de recevoir un flot de courrier de lecteurs qui me fait aussi chaud au coeur que votre article."

187. Léger, *Tartuffe fait Ramadan*, 115.

188. Léger, *Les Aurochs et les anges*, 12. Note that this reproduces the situation in the earlier novel *Jacob Jacobi*, in which an author's work under someone else's name is more successful than his own.

189. E. C. Riley, *Cervantes's Theory of the Novel* (Oxford: Clarendon Press,1968), 209, 205.

190. See *El Ingenioso Hidalgo Don Quixote de la Mancha, compuesto por Miguel de Cervantes Saavedra* (Madrid: Juan de la Cuesta, 1605), https://commons.wikimedia.org/wiki/File:El_inge nioso_hidalgo_don_Quijote_de_la_Mancha.jpg#/media/File:El_ingenioso_hidalgo_don_Qui jote_de_la_Mancha.jpg/. For an interesting discussion of the prologue and its narrator's pose as historian, and on the word *compuesto* in the title, see Charles D. Presberg, *Adventures in Paradox: "Don Quixote" and the Western Tradition* (University Park: Pennsylvania State University Press, 2001), 84–103.

191. Léger, *Tartuffe fait Ramadan*, 115.

192. Donald P. McCrory, *No Ordinary Man: The Life and Times of Miguel de Cervantes* (London: Peter Owen, 2005), 199, 202.

193. Unsigned, "Paul Smaïl est . . . Jack-Alain Léger," *Le Figaro*, February 2, 2009.

194. http://www.magazine-litteraire.com/actualite/peuple-ce-grand-oublie-20-04-2012-36761/.

195. Paul Smaïl makes fun of those rich people ("banlieusards de Neuilly") who think Barbès is a banlieue, in *Casa, la casa*, 43.

196. See Pratt, "Authorship, Impersonation, and the Republic," 153.

197. Najib Redouane, "Paul Smaïl, *Vivre me tue*," *Le Maghreb littéraire* 6 (1999): 139, 145. Redouane cited the use of "l'argot parisien varié" in the novel as a sign of vitality and authenticity (146).

198. Dayna Osherwitz, "Writing Home: Exile, Identity, and Textuality in Paul Smaïl's *Vivre me tue*," *Mots pluriels* 17 (April 2001): 1, 5.

199. Elmarsafy, "Hath Not an Arab Eyes?," 88.

200. Elmarsafy, "Hath Not an Arab Eyes?," 99n6.

201. Michel Laronde, "Prise de parole du roman de la post-colonialité en France: vers une sociocritique du canon littéraire," in *Beginnings in French Literature*, ed. Freeman G. Henry (Amsterdam: Rodopi, 2002), 169, 178. Laronde made a similar argument about both Chimo and Paul Smaïl in "The Post-Colonial Writer," 93–103. Laronde argues that these two authors exploit anonymity in order to "counter the [literary] Institution's classification of their work as social documentation" (100).

202. Mootacem Bellah Mhiri, "A Study in Self-Writing and Identity: The Transcultural and Transnational Poetics of Ameen Rihani and Paul Smaïl," dissertation, Pennsylvania State University, 2005, 179.

203. Kilpatrick, "Paul Smaïl's *Casa, la casa*," 316.

204. Laura Kathleen Reeck, "Unauthoring the Text," in *Literature and the Writer*, ed. Michael J. Meyer (Amsterdam: Rodopi, 2004), 51n4.

205. Reeck, *Writerly Identities*.

206. Kleppinger, *Branding the "Beur" Author*.

207. Gates, "Authenticity."

208. Touriya Fili, "Paroles déplacées et stratégies discursives," in Charles Bonn, ed., *Migrations des identités et des textes entre l'Algérie et la France, dans les littératures des deux rives* (Paris: L'Harmattan, 2004), 123, 125. Fili's paper, available on line, was originally dated 2003. See http://www.limag.com/Textes/ColLyon2003/Tome1Mars2004.pdf/.

209. "Qu'ai-je fait de plus que mon travail de romancier en écrivant *Vivre me tue*? Qu'ai-je fait de mal? D'avoir également imaginé l'auteur?" Léger, *On en est là*, 186.

210. Di Folco, *Les Grandes impostures*, 153. I have seen no confirmation of this.

211. Jaccomard, "Extremists and Moderates," 194. See Begag's memoir of this, *Un Mouton dans la baignoire* (Paris: Fayard, 2007).

212. In 1995 Begag had published a book for young readers whose title (as Begag himself points out) bears a strange remblance to *Vivre me tue*: *Quand on est mort, c'est pour toute la vie*. On Begag, see Reeck, *Writerly Identities*, chapter 1, "Culture Wars and Critical Debate Around Azouz Begag" (25–49).

213. Azouz Begag, "Of Imposture and Incompetence: Paul Smaïl's *Vivre me tue*," *Research in African Literatures* 37, no. 1 (2006): 55–71. I am indebted to Lia Brozgal's "Hostages of Authenticity," a critique of Begag's essay.

214. Léger's critiques of Islam appeared in *Tartuffe fait Ramadan* (2003) and *A contre Coran* (Paris: Editions Hors Commerce, 2004).

215. Pratt, "Authorship, Impersonation, and the Republic," 150.

216. Douin, "Un homme en 'mélancolère.'"

217. Brozgal, "Hostages of Authenticity," 5.

218. Brozgal, "Hostages of Authenticity," 9.

219. Douin, "Un homme en 'mélancolère.'"

220. In *Le Gone*: "Tu as dix-sept sur vingt. La meilleure note de la classe. Le prof a même lu ta rédaction. Il a dit qu'il la garderait comme exemple." *Le Gone du Chaâba*, 224. In *Vivre me tue*: ". . . j'avais les meilleures notes. . . . Parce que le prof de français a lu un jour à toute la classe ma rédac, en la donnant comme modèle" (24). The imitation stops short of actual plagiarism, but follows closely enough to send a message of appropriation and provocation to Begag.

221. Smaïl, *Ali le magnifique*, 501. Another allusion to Begag is found in *Casa, la casa*, 140.

See Alec G. Hargreaves's translation of this quotation, which I have altered here, in Begag, "Of Imposture and Incompetence," 19.

222. Barbara Johnson, then director of undergraduate studies in the Yale French department, made this point in a report on complaints about sexism in the Capretz method of language instruction.

223. Appiah, *The Ethics of Identity*, 28.

224. Pratt, "Authorship, Impersonation, and the Republic," 164.

225. From: http://thebrain.mcgill.ca/flash/a/a_02/a_02_p/a_02_p_vis/a_02_p_vis.html "In the first, classic example shown to the right here, two profiles facing each other delimit a space that can be seen as a goblet, and your perception can alternate between the profiles and the goblet. If you focus most of your attention on the light part of the image, you will perceive that part as the figure and automatically see the dark part as simply the background. The reverse is also true. Thus, *perceiving one figure prevents you from perceiving the other.*" Emphasis added.

226. Hanneken, "Scandal, Choice and the Economy of Minority Literature," 54. He cites the example of Ishmael Beah's *A Long Way Gone*, a memoir of an African child soldier selected for the Starbucks Book Club in 2007 (53).

227. Pratt, "Authorship, Impersonation, and the Republic," 150.

228. "God gave Noah the rainbow sign, / No more water, the fire next time!" is from a Negro spiritual and is the epigraph to James Baldwin's book.

229. Léger, *Zanzaro Circus*, 53, 56. Electroconvulsive therapy has regained respect, including as a treatment for bipolar disorder (which is what Léger claims it is contraindicated for), starting as early as 1987, in the middle of Léger's life. See http://www.nytimes.com/1987/11/22/magazine/shock-therapy-s-return-to-respectability.html/. Jamison calls electroconvulsive therapy "an excellent treatment for certain types of severe depression." Kay Redfield Jamison, *An Unquiet Mind: A Memoir of Moods and Madness* (New York: Random House, 1995), 109.

230. Léger, *Zanzaro Circus*, 168–70.

231. Jamison, *An Unquiet Mind*, 3, 5. See her remarks on the false impressions that the term "bipolar" can create (180).

232. Kay Redfield Jamison, *Touched with Fire: Manic-Depressive Illness and the Artistic Temperament* (New York: Simon & Schuster, 1993, Kindle edition), loc. 722, 1027, 1474.

233. Jamison, *An Unquiet Mind*, 188, 215.

234. Jamison, *Touched with Fire*, loc. 71, 212.

235. Karl, *George Eliot*, 380–81.

236. George Eliot (Mary Ann Lewes [Evans]), letter to Harriet Beecher Stowe, May 8, 1869, in *The George Eliot Letters*, ed. Gordon S. Haight (New Haven: Yale University Press, 1955), 5: 29.

237. Mary Ann Evans, letter of March 16, 1839, quoted in Rosemarie Bodenheimer, *The Real Life of Mary Ann Evans: George Eliot, Her Letters and Fiction* (Ithaca: Cornell University Press, 1994), 275n33.

238. Quoted in Kleppinger, "Why the *Beur* Novel?," 234.

239. Jamison, *Touched with Fire*, loc. 3521.

240. Léger, *Place de l'opéra (Paris: Editions Cartouche, 2012)*: 68.

241. Léger, *Tartuffe fait Ramadan*. Léger associated Islam (and not just radical *Islamisme*) with a dangerous *communautarisme* (64). He was opposed to both religion and racism.

242. Léger spoke frankly about his life, his multiple identities, and his bipolar disease in a television interview with Thierry Ardisson, on *Tout le monde en parle*, January 28, 2006. http://www.ina.fr/video/I09198510/interview-de-jack-alain-leger-video.html, consulted March 19, 2018.

Kleppinger reported, "Sadly, Léger's prolific publishing career has recently come to an end, as he has been diagnosed with Amyotrophic Lateral Schlerosis (Lou Gehrig's Disease)" (239).

243. "Ma mère n'a jamais réussi à se suicider. Moi, si." Quoted in Lindon, "Jack-Alain Léger, le coeur lourd."

244. Michel Leiris, *L'Age d'homme* (Paris: Gallimard, 1946), 94.

245. "Wild Mood Swings" is the title of the album by The Cure that includes the song "This Is a Lie," quoted in *Vivre me tue* and cited here as an epigraph.

246. Léger, *Les Aurochs et les anges*, 38.

247. Quoted in Guilbert, "Jack-Alain Léger."

Index

Ricard, Alain, 76, 94, 102
right to die, 114
Rimbaud, Arthur, 46–47
Robbe-Grillet, Alain, 104
Roger, Jacques-François, 68, 74
Rol-Tanguy, Cécile, 154–56, 163
roman à clé, 8
romanticism, French, 53
Rose, Joel, 33
Rose, Mark, 43
Rosello, Mireille, 77, 79, 81, 117, 140, 164–65, 224n91
Rosen, Stanley, 4
Roumain, Jacques, 3
Roumani, Judith, 80, 206n137
Rousseau, Jean-Jacques, 59; *Confessions*, 13
Ruquist, Rebecca, 82–83

Saint-Roch, Eve, 126
Salem, Walid, 128
salvage, in modern anthropology, 69
Samuels, Maurice, 19
Sand, George, 53, 189n83
Santiago, Danny. *See* James, Daniel L.
Sarah (LeRoy), 33, *34*, 36–37
Sartre, Jean-Paul, 104
scandal, 43
Schmitt, Eric-Emmanuel, *Monsieur Ibrahim*, 216n313
Schoolcraft, Ralph, 104, 117, 214n256, 214n265, 216n315
Schutz, Dana, 180, 185n37
Schwartz-Bart, André, 51
Scott, A. O., 33
Sebbar, Leïla, 140
Seberg, Jean, 104
self-determination, 59, 113, 116
self-multiplication (self-duplication), 106, 110, 112, 119
self-representation, 17, 42, 75, 179; cultural, 171; ethnic, 28, 113; rights of, 46, 75, 171
Seltzer, Margaret "Peggy," 39; *Love and Consequences: A Memoir of Hope and Survival*, 38–39
Sembene, Ousmane, 50–51
Sen, Amartya, 44, 172
Senghor, Lamine, 75
Senghor, Léopold Sédar, 99, 205n130
Sergeant, Sharon, 40
sex (sexuality, sexual content), 31–35, 56, 81–82, 88, 121, 123, 218n342, 219n347; as a weapon, 89
sexual abuse, 35, 37
sexual revolution of the 1960s and 1970s, 15
Shakespeare, William, 47, 141, 144, 174; *The Merchant of Venice*, 144, 146
Shatz, Adam, 9
Signoret, Simone, 112, *116*, 217n324
Sinatra, Nancy, 35
slang, 32–33, 38, 114, 140, 150, 158, 169, 224n91. *See also* underclass speech

slave narratives, 21–22
slave trade in French literature, 60
Smaïl, Paul. *See* Léger, Jack-Alain
Smith, Joseph, 193n54
Smith, Robert James, 175
Snopes.com, 192n53
social mobility, 38
Sokal, Alan, 10, 72–73
Soulié, Francis, 92, 98–101, 136, 210n203, 212n221
Soyinka, Wole, 100, 212n229
Sparks, Beatrice, 31–32, 192n53, 193n54. *See also Go Ask Alice*
Spivak, Gayatri, 42
St. John, Warren, 35
states'-rights agenda, in *Little Tree*, 24, 191n22
Stendhal, 53
stereotypes, 117, 145–46, 164
street slang, 38, 88, 114, 139
Strickland, Rennard, 22
Stump, Jordan, 89
style (stylistic evidence), 32, 35, 60, 96
Styron, William, 16
subaltern speech, 3, 15, 42–43, 59, 79
suicide: of Gary, 111–12, 118–19, 147, 178, 218n332; of Léger, 125, 132, 147, 175, 177–78
Sullivan, Vernon. *See* Vian, Boris
supercherie (Fr. hoax), 53
supervised literature, 76, 94, 102

Tabet, Paul, 78–81, 206n143
Tabet, Raoul, 78–80
Tasaday, 12, 34
Tchumkam, Hervé, 140, 224n97
Tessarech, Bruno, 139
Théâtre de Clara Gazul (Mérimée), 61–62, 64–65, 202n63, 202n65
Thiam, Bathie Ngoye, 219n349
Thiher, Allen, 209n190
Till, Emmett, 180
totalitarianism, 105, 131
totem, 96–97, 211n216, 213n240
transgenderism, 38
translation, fake, 82, 87–88
transracialism, 9
transubstantiation, 10
Traoré, Mamadou (pseud. Ray Autra), 100, 209n196
Trump, Donald, ix–x, 8
truth, 4–5, 36, 130–31, 167, 181; crisis of, 9; and play, 7, 10–11; totalitarian, 105
truth lies, and lying, 161–62
truthiness, 7, 185n29

underclass speech, 147. *See also* slang
universalism, French, 1, 19, 48–49, 70, 115, 124, 128, 141, 145, 178, 224n97. *See also* French Republic, and its values

Printed and bound by CPI Group (UK) Ltd, Croydon, CR0 4YY

09/06/2025

14685681-0002